QUEERING THE COUNTRYSIDE

INTERSECTIONS: TRANSDISCIPLINARY PERSPECTIVES
ON GENDERS AND SEXUALITIES
General Editors: Michael Kimmel and Suzanna Walters

Queering the Countryside

New Frontiers in Rural Queer Studies

Edited by

Mary L. Gray, Colin R. Johnson, *and* Brian J. Gilley

NEW YORK UNIVERSITY PRESS

New York & London

NEW YORK UNIVERSITY PRESS
New York and London
www.nyupress.org

References to Internet websites (URLs) were accurate at the time of writing. Neither the author nor New York University Press is responsible for URLs that may have expired or changed since the manuscript was prepared.

ISBN: 978-1-4798-3077-0 (hardback)
ISBN: 978-1-4798-8058-4 (paperback)

For Library of Congress Cataloging-in-Publication data, please contact the Library of Congress.

New York University Press books are printed on acid-free paper, and their binding materials are chosen for strength and durability. We strive to use environmentally responsible suppliers and materials to the greatest extent possible in publishing our books.

Manufactured in the United States of America

10 9 8 7 6 5 4 3 2 1

Also available as an ebook

CONTENTS

ACKNOWLEDGMENTS

The co-editors would like to thank the original workshop participants for their engagement and the final contributors to this volume for their patience and willingness to offer the gems of their exemplary scholarship to this collection. We would also like to thank the indefatigable Andrea Alarcón, Kaeleigh Herstad, Rebecca Hoffman, and Jason Qualls, our research assistants, for their editorial and management prowess. We would not have a volume to contribute to this growing field of inquiry if Andrea, Kaeleigh, Rebecca, and Jason had not kept our paperwork in order. Lastly, we would like to thank our families and friends for their encouragement and unwavering support through all stages of this publication.

Introduction

COLIN R. JOHNSON, BRIAN J. GILLEY, AND MARY L. GRAY

In the year 2020, the United States of America will commemorate an important anniversary: its first century as a demographically urban nation. By then, more than 80 percent of Americans will live either in cities with populations of at least fifty thousand or in what the U.S. Census Bureau refers to as "urban clusters"—groups of slightly smaller, effectively interrelated municipalities, which most people call "suburbs." Clearly, American modernity and the American metropolis go hand-in-hand.

Yet, as profoundly normal as some form of urban existence has come to be for the vast majority of Americans, urban space itself is oddly atypical of the U.S. national landscape. Including Alaska, statistically urbanized areas account for a mere 2.62 percent of the United States' total land area. Remove Alaska from the equation and that number increases slightly, but only to 3.12 percent. This means that in the United States, almost 97 percent of territory—some 3,443,773 square miles in total—remains nonurbanized, or "rural," in character. It should probably come as little surprise, then, that the *idea* of rurality continues to figure prominently in the collective ethos of American society, and indeed the ethos of many urbanized societies around the world, not just as a name we give to sparsely populated regions, but to something that is imagined to be a distinctive way life complete with its own traditions, institutions, and worldviews.

Not that our persistent investment in an idea of rurality actually requires all that much explaining, especially today when it arguably does more conceptual work than it ever has before. In fact, and as literary critic Raymond Williams noted decades ago, rurality has long served as a kind of constitutive outside to urban life precisely because its overwhelming vastness accommodates an absolutely dizzying array of fantasies and associations, including the popular conceit that rural life is, by definition, unchanging.[1] Or, if not entirely unchanging, then rural life is at least thought by many to be significantly *slower* than life in cities, a characteristic that is itself rife with disparate connotations ranging from stupidity (in people) to welcome relief (on weekends). Slowness can also suggest prudence or stubborn recalcitrance, and people who identify as "rural," or who have been identified in that way, surely exhibit both tendencies, not unlike the population at large. For example, where the natural environment is concerned, people who make their living as farmers understand far better than most where food comes from, and at what cost. As a result, they tend to be much more attuned to the astounding complexity and fragility of the global food supply than people who have simply come to expect that the shelves of their local supermarket will be fully stocked every time they stop to grab something for dinner on the way home from the office. But many farmers also deeply resent organized efforts to "save" the natural environment, or "protect" it—so much so, in fact, that the American Farm Bureau Federation and the U.S. Environmental Protection Agency have essentially become sworn enemies. This is a deep irony, if ever there was one, particularly given the fact that farmers and the rural communities they tend to live in arguably have more to lose than anyone in the environment's gradual destruction. But this apparent contradiction is also a perfectly predictable consequence of capitalism's capacity to erase the history of labor from commodities, even as it transforms everything, including "unspoiled nature," into one.

Of course, when people talk about "rural" life today, they are not just referring to farming; they are often also referring to things like religiosity, which is typically thought to inform the worldviews of rural and small-town Americans to a much greater extent than it does the lives of city-dwellers. What is more, in the United States, where "rural" religiosity is almost uniformly thought of as being Christian in character, it is usually imagined to be of a distinctly puritanical, fire-and-brimstone, "old-timey," Southern Baptist variety, not that touchy-feely, "New Age" Jew-nitarian stuff one encounters in more permissive urban churches and reformed synagogues. There is some truth in this, certainly. But there is also a lot of untruth, at least historically speaking. In addition the fact that Roger Williams, who founded the American Baptist Church, was actually branded a heretic by the Puritans of the

Massachusetts Bay Colony and run off into the woods, or the fact that American Unitarianism is almost as old the United States itself, it is also important to remember that Pentecostalism, and various other forms of antiliberal theology that have flowed from the American fundamentalist movement, are decidedly modern innovations dating back to the early *twentieth* century, a period rife with potential for would-be evangelists precisely because it was so uncertain at that point what the future of organized religion would be in the United States.

To be sure, knowing this does not change the fact that urbanization and secularization do seem to have something very important to do with each other as long-term processes of social and cultural transformation. But it does suggest that we need to think twice before acceding to the all-too-familiar notion that a particular kind of religiosity is the inevitable consequence of rural life. Nor, for that matter, are ignorance, racism, or membership in the Republican Party, although these are also attributes that are routinely hinted at when left-leaning political commentators puzzle themselves silly over the behavior of "rural voters," including their much commented-upon tendency to vote against their own economic interests, narrowly understood.

We also need to think twice before acceding to the notion that rural life necessarily involves isolation from broader national and international trends. In fact, rural America has been quite radically transformed since 1920, particularly through the rise of new communication, information, and transportation technologies, and often in ways that accord remarkably well with the predictions of Karl Marx and others who made prescient note early on of capitalism's tendency to "annihilate space" by tethering local economies together into national and international markets. In addition to an unparalleled expansion of the national transportation infrastructure in the years since World War II, the United States has witnessed one communications revolution after another, especially over the past century—revolutions that have effectively knit the nation-state together into a complex web of strong and weak ties. As a result, it has in some respects become difficult to differentiate between rural American life and American life in general.

This does not mean that that rural America is going away, however. In fact, since 1920, the number of people who live in statistically rural areas has slowly increased from just over 51 million to just under 60 million, a figure roughly comparable to the total population of many European nations including Italy, France, and United Kingdom. What is more, as of 2000, the *vast* majority of these people—about 46 million of them, or roughly 16 percent of the United States' total population—live in areas with population densities of 999 people per square mile or fewer—areas that are so sparsely settled that the U.S. Census Bureau officially classifies those who live in them as people who are "not in a place" at all.

As students of culture, we are always a little wary of statistics. We are also suspicious of the kinds of classificatory terms that seem to arise whenever they are put to use. For example, in the preceding paragraphs we talk about "Americans," "U.S. territory," and "nations" as if the meanings of such terms were self-evident and uncontested when nothing could be farther from the truth. Nevertheless, and as conscious as we are of the inherently exclusionary logic that subtends such a vocabulary, we find statistics to be useful here because they help to illustrate the peculiar position that rural space has come to occupy in the context of twenty-first-century American culture.

Put simply, "rural America" is strange. Some might even go so far as to say it is queer. At the very least it is complicated, and at times downright confounding, at least for a concept that is as supposedly commonsensical and familiar as the idea of rurality is often imagined to be. It is simultaneously everywhere in general and nowhere in particular. It is ever-present and yet a thing of the past. It is at once archetypically American and atypical of America. It even shrinks (as a *percentage* of the overall population) as it expands (in real population numbers).[2] Rural America is strange as well in the sense that it has come to represent many qualities that a lot of the people who live there (wherever "there" is) simply do not possess, including whiteness, deeply rooted American nativity, and, most importantly for our purposes here, heterosexuality.[3] Indeed, for all that the term "rural" *does* connote in the context of twenty-first-century American culture, one thing that it is almost never used to signify is gender or sexual diversity. On the contrary, when most people talk about "rural and small-town values," they are referring at least in part to a culture of sexual conservatism that is generally assumed to be intolerant of gender and sexual diversity at best, if not overtly sexist and homophobic.

Given everything we have just said about the capaciousness and mal-leability of the term "rural"—its astonishing capacity to accommodate and reflexively corroborate demonstrably amorphous and even patently ahistorical presumptions about the character of nonmetropolitan life—the reader will probably not be surprised to learn that the editors of this volume actively resist the automatic yoking together of rurality and pretty much anything, including overt homophobia. But in truth, the perception that "rural" Americans are increasingly arrayed against LGBT Americans is not without some basis in fact. Indeed, over the past several decades especially, rural Americans have arguably done more than their fair share to block various efforts to advance the civil rights, and even the basic human rights, of LGBT people in the United States. What is more, they have often claimed to take these actions *in defense of rural America* and the way of life it supposedly represents, as if to suggest that same-sex desire and gender nonconformity are themselves respon-sible somehow for the myriad problems that many nonmetropolitan communities have been dealing with since the farm crisis of the Reagan Era—problems that include job loss, persistent outmigration, eroding tax bases, school consolidation, crumbling infrastructure, and, most re-cently, a surge in methamphetamine use among rural young people that is so extreme that meth addiction has almost certainly eclipsed crack cocaine addiction as the United States' most significant drug problem.[4]

And yet, for all this—for all the finger-pointing, fiery invective, and viciously discriminatory ballot initiatives to have come out of nonmet-ropolitan communities in recent years—we have also seen how impor-tant rural America can be in the movement to expand equality for LGBT people. Just consider the fact that Vermont, America's most rural state, was also the first state to legalize gay marriage by legislative action in 2009. Three years later, Maine, which ranks third on that list, became the first state to approve marriage equality by popular referendum. Consider as well that in January 2013, Vicco, Kentucky, population 335, became the smallest municipality to pass an ordinance banning discrimina-tion based on sexual orientation and gender identity.[5] In California, by contrast, where nearly 90 percent of residents live in statistically urban areas, making it the fourth most urban state in the United States, it took a decision by the U.S. Supreme Court to restore marriage rights to same-sex couples after voters elected to ban the practice of same-sex marriage by constitutional amendment in 2008. Similarly, in Florida, America's fifth most urban state, lesbians and gay men were not only barred from marrying by constitutional amendment until 2015 when the matter was decided on the national level by the U.S. Supreme Court; they were effectively forbidden to adopt otherwise unwanted children, a policy that was so blatantly mean-spirited that not even states like Wyoming and Alabama (both of which are predominantly rural *and* notoriously conservative) had it.

To be sure, there are big differences between states like Florida or California and states such as Kentucky or Vermont. Most obviously, Florida and California are unusually large, both in terms of their population and their geographical size.[6] Vermont and Kentucky, on the other hand, are unusually small. Florida and California are also extremely diverse in the sense that both states contain densely populated coastal areas that abut more sparsely populated, agriculturally productive inland regions. As such, their social, economic, and political landscapes arguably more closely resemble the social, economic, and political landscape of the nation as a whole than they do the landscape of smaller, more socially, economically, and politically uniform states like Kentucky or Vermont. Still, the fact remains that when future historians sit down to write the story of lesbians' and gay men's fitful struggle to overcome what some have already characterized as the last and most important barrier to full social and political enfranchisement, they are necessarily going to have to contend with what we might choose to describe as the city's limits within the landscape of early twenty-first-century American politics. For while it is undoubtedly true that "city air makes one free" in certain respects, it clearly does not make one a rights-bearing citizen, particularly in the context of a nation that cleaves as tenaciously as the United States does to centuries-old regional antagonisms and various other sorts of unfinished business with roots stretching back in time to the founding of the Republic, and even deeper in some cases.

To be clear, the significant point here is not just that predominantly rural regions or states can be unexpectedly supportive of gender and sexual minorities; nor is it even that predominantly urban states can be surprisingly hostile to them, although both of these statements have turned out to be true in the American case. The point is that the spatial politics of gender and sexuality are enormously complicated—far more complicated, certainly, than they are often imagined to be. As recent events have clearly shown, they are also profoundly consequential to pretty much everyone's everyday life. This obviously includes lesbians, gay men, bisexuals, transgender individuals, and any number of other queer folks whose access to resources and protections now literally depends in many cases on where they stand. But it also includes the unprecedented number of straight people who increasingly feel obliged to take a position on the "question" of gender and sexual diversity's proper place in American culture, either by affirming their faith in the durability of social and cultural pluralism or by affirming their faith in a wrathful and, we are told, decidedly angry god—and this regardless of where they live.

Today more than ever, space matters where the politics of gender and sexuality in the United States are concerned, not because it is so powerfully determinative, but because its effects are so wildly unpredictable. Recent developments in the ongoing struggle for LGBT rights suggest this. The American public's eager embrace of films like *Brokeback Mountain* suggests this. Even geospatially sensitive queer social and sexual networking platforms suggest this. Just try it. The next time you find yourself in the "middle of nowhere," take a moment to fire up an app like Grindr. Turns out, we really are everywhere. What is more, queers really do want everything, just as the old Queer Nation slogan used to assert. They want friends. They want lovers. Some of them want to get out more; others want to stay in. Some of them are looking for their one and only, others for a third or a fourth. Some are really into muscular arms. Others are much more deeply invested in their Second Amendment right to keep and bear them. All of which is not to say that located-ness no longer matters. Rather, it is to suggest that we can no longer presume to know in advance what located-ness will mean. And in fact, we probably never could.

It is really here—at the place where familiar spatial categories cease to explain Americans' experiences of gender and sexual difference and instead begin to raise new questions about those experiences—that *Queering the Countryside* aims to intercede. To be sure, many of the essays that comprise this volume do depend for their analytic coherence upon the notion that the concept of rurality continues to mean something in the context of contemporary American culture. Quite a few of them also shed new light on the experiences of LGBT Americans who reside in undeniably nonmetropolitan locales. But this volume was not conceived as an effort to plug a hole in the existing scholarly literature dealing with LGBT life in the United States. Nor do we intend to spend much time proffering hectoring correctives to queer studies, a field that all three of the editors of this volume have critiqued at various points in the past for its widely acknowledged tendency to turn a blind eye toward the rural and nonmetropolitan. Instead, our primary goal is to explore the conceptual space that begins to open up once we acknowledge that "rural America" is neither a monolith nor an apparition.

If *Queering the Countryside* demonstrates anything, it is that "rural" is first and foremost a name we give to an astoundingly complex assemblage of people, places, and positionalities. In this respect, "rural" is not entirely unlike "queer" itself, a term that surely carries with it both a troubled and troubling past, but one that was actively reclaimed by LGBT activists and scholars beginning in the 1990s precisely because it is indeterminate and unstable, as well as because, frankly, it had often been used as a term of derision, one that was meant to shame gender and sexual nonconformers in much the same way that terms like "hayseed," "redneck," and "hick" have been used to shame uncouth nonmetropolitans. Of course, recognizing that rurality shares certainly family resemblances with queerness does not necessarily clarify what "rural America" is; in fact, it may further complicate matters. And this can be frustrating in much the same way that theorizing "queerness" can sometimes be frustrating. After all, one does eventually begin to feel the need to find something definite to hold on to, with space as much as sex—some understanding of what constitutes the "rural" that can help one begin to decide what one should be looking at, or to whom, and where, exactly. Nevertheless, we believe that it is the very conceptual instability that the phrase "rural America" neatly covers over that makes it so interesting, and so rife with untapped possibility.

It is worth noting, of course, that we are not the first scholars to sense this possibility. In fact, this volume might be seen as a direct response to repeated calls issued by a number of scholars over the past ten or fifteen years for paying increased attention to nonmetropolitan America generally, particularly in the context queer studies, a field that has indeed tended to focus more often than not on urban life. But we also hope that this volume will help to move the current debate beyond a sustained critique of "metronormativity," a term theorist J. Jack Halberstam coined nearly a decade ago to describe the tendency of LGBT culture, including LGBT scholarship, to valorize the conspicuous urbanity of queer life in the United States and elsewhere, and even to presume it.[7]

At some point, critique does begin to harden into dogmatic orthodoxy. And when that happens, people understandably begin to feel less challenged and transformed than chastened and policed by incessant reminders of all they take for granted. This does not mean that such reminders should necessarily cease or give way simply because some people decide that they are "over it." But such critiques do eventually need to give rise to something more than endlessly reiterated variations on themselves. So, for example, it is understandable if some queer studies scholars who were initially moved to self-reflectivity by early critiques of rampant metronormativity within the field, and within queer culture generally speaking, have started to push back somewhat by asking what it is, precisely, that their metro-chauvinism has supposedly forestalled them from seeing, or understanding, about the predicament of queer life, or its potential. Equally understandable are encouraging, but we think perhaps premature, pronouncements that the field of queer studies has itself borne witness to a "rural turn" in recent years that is already well on its way toward being played out. "Don't we already *know* that there are lesbians, gay men, trans folks and other queers in rural areas?" one occasionally hears someone ask these days. "Haven't we always?"

Our initial response to such questions is "No, not really." At best, much early work in the field of LGBT studies, and later queer studies, left the possibility open for subsequent investigation; at worst, it dispensed with concern for nonmetropolitan history and culture altogether. But as we have already noted, all that is water under the proverbial bridge so far as we are concerned. Far more disturbing than the glib dismissiveness of such questions, from our perspective, is their astounding reductionism. After all, is that really what LGBT and queer studies have been? What they are? A now three-decades' long mission to explore queer new worlds, to seek out new lesbians and gays, to boldly go where we (apparently) have always been aware that we were before anyway? Perhaps on some level. Certainly no one can deny the genuine thrill of discovering evidence of subversion where one had previously assumed strict compliance, or even mere perversion where one previously assumed banal "normalcy." Still, we can think of no serious scholars of LGBT life in either the country or the city who have ever contented themselves by proving that same-sex sexual behavior and gender nonconformity happens, or happened, or that such behavior has often led to a sense of difference or distinctiveness that some come to think of as a sexual identity.

Nevertheless, let us assume for the sake of argument that we *do* already know this one thing about rural queer life: that it exists, and most likely has existed in some form another for a long time. Are we therefore done? In other words, is that all we really need to know, or even *care* to know, about what is happening, or what has happened, in ninety-seven out of each one hundred square miles of territory that comprise the United States? Is that all we care to know about what has happened in the rest of the world, the vast majority of which is also "rural" in a similar sense? We think not. We think not because this is precisely the sort of instrumental shorthand that has tended to reduce "rural America" to little more than a belated location populated by a dwindling number of people whose primary relevance to the study of American culture are the contributions they made a century ago or, worse still, their seemingly inevitable fated-ness to eventually become, in the words of historian John L. Shover, America's "last minority."[8] But we also think not because we know that there are numerous genuinely vexing conceptual problems related to gender and sexuality that the idea of the rural can help us begin to work through.

Take the meaning of "conservatism"—generally, but especially in terms of the role that conservatism supposedly does or does not play in LGBT and queer life in the United States. *Traditionally*, gender and sexual nonconformers of all varieties have tended to be imagined as radical actors within the landscape of American social and political life—and not just by social and political conservatives. *Traditionally*, many gender and sexual nonconformers have tended to imagine themselves radical actors. As Jasbir Puar has noted, however, and Karl Marx before her, vanguardism has a strange tendency to switch polarities. Thus, what was radical yesterday—say, the demand for marriage equality in a society that measures enfranchisement in terms of perceived legitimacy and access to institutions like marriage—can easily come to represent collusion with the status quo today. This in turn creates spaces for new modes of critique, modes that are often subtended by an impulse to resist interpolation into the highly charged national/globalized discourse of identity politics. Are such shifts and reversals necessarily evidence that queer politicking always operates at what is properly understood as the *leading edge* of political engagement, however? Or are there ways in which the moving of the bar might actually be thought of as a queer form of conservatism—one that involves a lot of bargaining and the acceptance of half-measures, while also seeking to maintain what might be characterized as a tradition of antisexist, antihomophobic dissent in the face of normativity, including ascendant forms of homonormativity?

As we noted above, Americans have shown few signs that they are ready to abandon the term "rural" as an ostensibly meaningful descriptor for particular places, certain kinds of people, and entire ways of life. In fact, there is a strong indication that the idea is actually taking on new life in the twenty-first century. That is, at least in the United States, what the term "rural" names today is something more than sparsely populated territory. Rather, what it names is a world view, and a decidedly conservative one at that. We are not saying that all people who identify with "rurality" are conservative; nor are we saying that all conservatives are automatically appreciative of "rurality." But we are saying that the term "rural" seems to imply certain things these days, not the least important of which is a stubbornly persistent attachment to highly traditional views regarding gender and sexuality and, by extension, an aggressive, sometimes even murderous, antipathy toward gender and sexual difference. Those who identify themselves and are identified by outsiders as rural are raised with certain orientations toward outsiders, locals, social responsibility, community responsibility, and "how to behave." The various manifestations of socialization are endless and influenced by social class, religion, and race. The political expression of rural socialization can range from the fundamentalist Christian or the libertarian all the way to the far left of progressive communal living on the coasts.

Unfortunately, the history of nonmetropolitan spaces as locales of intolerance combined with a reluctance for rapid change have fashioned the rural as inherently backward and hostile. Yet, the supposed sharp borders between where overt hostility ends and moves to tolerance and eventually into celebration are less clear when thinking through the subject positions upon which the rural is constituted. As one heads out to the country, the institutional frameworks positioning subjects become more vague, more customary, more local, and more difficult to discern without insider knowledge. What it means to be rural is mired in power-laden signs, by which individuals are included, excluded, surveilled, and dominated within and by the social field. Therefore, the dominant discourse about the ideal types or the "common sense" of rurality are challenged by rural queers, not by inventing a new form of queerness, but rather by using existing signs from the social field in distinct and novel ways as a critique of limitations on conservatism and rurality.[9]

The Two Imaginaries and a Rural "Impasse"

The editors of this volume and the scholars who contributed essays to it are attempting to think through a fundamental problem in queer scholarship: the tendency to generate imaginary spaces on the two distinct poles of freedom and intolerance. Traditionally, these poles have been between the small town and the urban. In her landmark essay, "Get Thee to a Big City," Kath Weston tells us: "The gay imaginary is not just a dream of a freedom to be gay that requires an urban location, but a symbolic space that configures gayness itself by elaborating an opposition between urban and rural life."[10] The structure of thinking Weston reveals—an urban versus rural dichotomy—is written throughout the history of queer studies as well as through the popular and activist queer imagination. This structure, despite being inadequate for describing queer rural lives, masks the ways in which the imaginary of urban gay emancipation and the imaginary of a heteropatriarchal rural life co-construct one another. We are not denying there is a core of realities to the imaginary, yet the conflation of everyday life with the phantasmal produces and imposes particular subjectivities that gloss over individual and collective constructions of queer selfhoods. Co-constructed imaginaries allow each pole of geographically queer distance to "otherly" reify one another. In this descriptive locality, every story of homophobic violence in Middle America, such as that of Brandon Teena and Matthew Shepard, gives urban America a location for antiqueer violence. In turn, the carefully constructed media activist image of urban gay sexual freedom and emancipation politics gives those living in carefully negotiated rural contexts an unattainable guidepost for their own subjectivity. Metro- and rural normativity become dependent on one another to signal a form of modern sexual achievement—or a distinct, notable lack of it. Modern urban sexual achievement becomes an azimuth of queer visibility upon which the homophobia clinometric slides increasingly toward the rural. Metrosexuality knows who and what it is based on: its temporal, social, and geographic distance from the heteronormative. Through this construction, what the rural imagines about itself and the ways it is imagined discursively proffer the erosion of visibility and tolerance as one heads north, east, south, or west from the metropole.

Recent work on the queer urban-rural dichotomy focuses on the constructedness of a "metronormavity" and its hegemonic encompassing of queer subjectivity. As Halberstam tells us, "the metronormative story of migration from 'country' to 'town' is a spatial narrative within which the subject moves to a place of tolerance after enduring life in a place of suspicion, persecution, and secrecy."[11] The movement from persecution to tolerance is sketched on the life trajectory of rural queers through ideas of coming out and their eventual emancipation through relocation to urban spaces. The temporality of the narrative is given spatial capital by providing the discursive platform for geographic metronormative hegemony. Spatial metronormativity is skillfully harnessed in both popular and academic understandings of queer lives outside the city. Scott Herring cautions us to see metronormativity not as only existing in this or any other particular moment of modernity, but instead "to see any particular instance of metronormativity as a historically conditioned social field whose components try desperately to exceed and even more desperately to naturalize this historical specificity."[12] Naturalizations come in the form of typological renderings of the metronormative, which are the most easily identifiable because they are the most visible. Typologies of metronormativity produced by specific historic moments seen as sociopolitical positives—Stonewall, ACT UP New York—normalize an urbane sexual/gender expression. The naturalization of rural heteronormativity finds its footing in the equally negative experiences of violence, intolerance, and right-wing political discourse. The rural queer lacks visibility not only because of local hostility, but also because the absence of visibility is required as a structural component of metronormativity. Metronormativity itself becomes part of the epistemological apparatus distancing rural queers from what Karen Tongson refers to as the "enlightened liberal subject [who has emerged] from out of the darkness."[13]

Drawing on queer rurality to challenge metronormativity has been and continues to be useful for critiquing particular forms of queer spatial hegemony, and the contributors to this volume make good use of this strategy. Yet, what if we move from, or at least amend, a spatially defined dichotomy to a more affective mediated space, such as Lauren Berlant's notion of "attachment"? For Berlant attachments are relations to "compromised conditions of possibility," which are inevitably fantasies of perfect life circumstances.[14] These perfect life circumstances circulate in the form of fantasies about a "good life," which is not sustainable in present sociopolitical conditions. Yet, these fantasies of the good life become "a cluster of promises we want someone or something to make to us and make possible for us."[15] For Berlant these promises exist in contrast to the conditions that wear on people daily and create a need to adjust to encounters with the realities that challenge fantasy. These encounters generate "impasses," which are opportunities for melancholy over the poor fit between reality and fantasy. Simultaneously, impasses are also crises of the ordinary, which provide opportunities for "developing skills for adjusting to newly proliferating pressures to scramble for modes of living on."[16] Choosing to optimistically attach oneself, and one's desire, to fantasy rather than recognizing the destructive conditions of attachments reproduces the conditions of hegemonic normativity. Fantasmal optimism masks "a bad life that wears out the subject who nonetheless, and at the same time, finds their conditions of possibility within it." Thinking through impasses would potentially push "queer rurality" in the realm of "bad attachments."[17] Berlant's point, relative to our discussion, is that it is elitist and reproductively hegemonic to dismiss bad attachments simply because they are bad by normative standards, particularly given the fact that bad attachments are often the best attachments that many people can afford.

The sentiment of urban enlightened and sexually free subjects creates an impasse that effectively tells rural LGBTQ-identifying people that they cannot be happily queer right where they are and should expect hostility—and in fact deserve it—if they do stay in their communities. This attitude toward rural queers produces sets of knowledge that ignore the dialectical relationship between queer desires within the spaces in which they occur and the ways they "mutually shape one another."[18] The social, economic, and political positioning of rural queers forces a kind of synthesis between desire and secrecy. The synthesis, which may be momentary, marks geographic spaces in hostile environments, but also discursively claims ideological space. This process of mutual shaping, however, is often seen as lacking agency. The synthesis of desire and secrecy purposefully lacks a visibility out of fear or absence of sociopolitical voice and is thus unintelligible to nonrural queers. We also have to consider whether the lack of visibility necessitating the dialectic is less a reflection of the absence of urban-defined agency and more a complex set of negotiations required to synthesize sexual desire with connection to place. In this way, many rural queers struggle with reconciling their deep connection to or pride in their hometowns with the popular representation of their communities as backward, ignorant, and unlivable— not just for queer folks, but for anyone with taste or class. They feel they are not supposed to see their communities as viable places to live, and they are told that they need to choose between being queerly out of place in the country or moving to a big city to find legitimate visibility.

We are also being careful not to gloss over the heterogeneity of urban queer landscapes framed by socioeconomics and race. These landscapes are also the sociopolitical victims of metronormativity. As Jasbir K. Puar writes, "propping up urban scapes as optimal for the proliferation of homonationalisms both effaces the varied topography of cities and functions as a displacement of urban queer bashing in favor of fetishistic renderings of violence encountered in small towns and rural areas."[19] The negative experiences of the urban queer of color are just now finding their way into the literature and being theoretically considered as an aspect of broader configurations of queer subjectivity. The "effacement" of the race, gender, and sexual "topography" of the urban queer subject continues to undermine the variegated landscape of the urban, and the historic retrofitting of the queer into urban space benefits from a reconsideration of outsider social openings. The rural queer bears a much greater resemblance to urban queer subcultures than either equates to "global gay models" of metronormativity.[20] Both the contours of the rural queer and heterogenous scapes of sexuality, gender, and trans-identification require insider knowledge of power differentials, cultural hybridity, and a visibility attuned to local history and the realities of social life as it is lived "on the ground," wherever that ground may be.

Queer as Country

The political registers of a gay activism and a queer theory position rurality as a marginal subjective space. But like many organizing categories, this one was mobilized selectively and often took the form of a conspicuous preoccupation with *urban* sexual subcultures. This emphasis on the urban was partly a consequence of the serendipity of politics, but it was also a product of the circumstances under which sex and sexuality were brought into the orbit of scholarly scrutiny in the first place. Of course, even if one or more of these things were true—even if the story of queer life in the United States up until now were prohibitively difficult or impossible to write in retrospect—we would still need a variant of queer studies that focused on rural and nonmetropolitan space. After all, and regardless of whether or not there was such a thing as queer rural life in the past, the fact is that there is most definitely such a thing as rural queer life in the United States today. It may not be ideal. It may not even be a form of life that most queers would elect for themselves at the beginning of the twenty-first century given the choice. But that does not mean it does not exist.

It most certainly does exist: just look online. While it is undoubtedly true that the Internet has made the world a smaller place by transmitting cultural knowledge from point A to point B virtually instantaneously, and while it is certainly possible, as Dennis Altman and others have suggested, that this instantaneous transmission of cultural knowledge has had the effect of homogenizing lesbian and gay culture on a global scale, the Internet has also revealed the world to be a much larger and more complicated place than many of us previously thought that it was. For instance, a cursory glance at most lesbian and gay social networking sites reveals just how geographically far flung the modern queer "community" actually is. Of course, users of these sites do not typically spend a lot of time explaining *why* they live where they live. And even when they do, they are seldom free from ambivalence or conflict about their own provincial circumstances. But being ambivalent or conflicted is something different from being irrelevant, or unimportant; and it is certainly something entirely different from not being at all. If there is one pretense of lesbian and gay historiography that we believe rural queer studies has the potential to unsettle, it is the notion that lesbian and gay identity can (or should) be conceived as homogenous across time and space. For example, it is fairly common for skeptics to concede that same-sex sexuality behavior and gender nonconformity have nonmetropolitan histories while simultaneously insisting that modern gay identity is in fact a product of the social aggregation that occurred in American cities as a consequence of twentieth-century urbanization. This sort of compromise position is certainly a welcome relief from the wildly generalized overstatements about the sheer improbability of rural queer life that passed for empirical knowledge of it during the early years of the field's formation. But even this compromise assumes a great deal. For one thing, it assumes that identity formation is the proper measure of history. For another, it assumes that gender and sexual identities are formed only one way—through the recognition of similarity in others, of sameness. But is it really an awareness of our *similarity* to one another that has defined queer experience in the United States? What about the experience of being *different*? Surely that is not an experience that simply goes away when one passes through the city gates. And if it is not something that simply goes away—if difference is as constitutive of queer experience as similarity—then why would we not have something important to learn from studying rural queer lives even, or perhaps especially, if those lives are marked by forms of difficulty, discrimination, and isolation that are relatively unknown in urban contexts? And even if they weren't unknown, when has popularity or the relative desirability of a subject or circumstance ever determined whether or not we would bring our critical attention to bear on it? As we hope that the reader will discover, the essays that comprise this volume entertain and wrestle thoughtfully with all of these important questions, and then some.

Queering the Countryside: A First Step

Many of the essays included in this volume were first presented as working papers at a conference held on the campus of Indiana University Bloomington in November of 2010. The scholars who authored them range widely in terms of both their disciplinary affiliations and professional rank. That diversity is intentional and important: intentional because we wanted to make sure that readers would have the opportunity to hear from both scholars whom they already know and trust and scholars whom they will undoubtedly come to know and learn to trust in the years ahead; important because we wanted to make clear that, like so many of the most transformative fields of inquiry that have emerged over the past several decades, the project of rural queer studies must be conceived of as an emphatically interdisciplinary one from the outset.

We have organized this volume into four sections. Each section emphasizes one perspective on rural queer studies that we believe needs highlighting in order to demonstrate persuasively that this emerging area of inquiry is the viable, intellectually vibrant subfield that we already know it to be.

To date, many scholars have simply assumed that relevant evidence would be scarce or that familiar archives have nothing important to say about queer life in rural and nonmetropolitan contexts. One of our primary goals is to dispel these myths straight away by front-loading the volume with a multidisciplinary selection of essays authored by new and emerging scholars whose work demonstrates in no uncertain terms what the next wave of rural queer studies scholarship is likely to look like, as well as what it has to offer. While the essays in Part I, "New Archives, New Epistemologies," are topically and methodologically diverse, each one is significant in a scholarly sense either because it engages a new or relatively unknown archive of source materials or because it revisits more familiar source materials, but from a decidedly innovative rural queer studies perspective.

Like so many aspects of American life, the history of rural life in the United States has been powerfully shaped by race and class. The essays contained in the second part of the volume, "The Rural Turn: Considering Cartographies of Race and Class," seek to foreground this fact. They also seek to demonstrate what new forms of critical leverage might be gained on the discourses of race and class by approaching them from the vantage point of rural queer studies. Some of the essays accomplish these tasks by way of the particular case studies they investigate; others do so by advancing new conceptual frameworks for thinking about race and/or class in relation to gender and sexuality. But all of the essays share the common goal of demonstrating how race and class can and should take center stage in our consideration of queer life beyond the city gates.

If we have learned anything from two decades' worth of spatially-minded queer studies scholarship, it is that "urban" and "rural" are dynamic terms rather than static ones. Indeed, they are terms that have always existed in dialectical relation to one another even during those periods when urban culture was receiving the lion's share of scholarly attention. Because one of the aims of this volume is to build connections between the emerging field of rural queer studies and the predominantly urbanist queer studies scholarship that has preceded it, the essays contained in Part III turn a critical eye toward the concept of rurality itself *even* as they demonstrate its undeniable importance to the future of gender and sexuality studies. Some of the essays included in "Back and Forth: Rural Queer Life in Circulation and Transition" do this by emphasizing the transit of bodies and discourses across the real or imagined boundaries that appear to separate rural and urban space; other essays interrogate the gendered and sexual implications of the urban/rural binary itself.

Finally, the essays in the volume's last part, "Bodies of Evidence: Methodologies and Their Discontents," take up the question of methodology, albeit from numerous perspectives and always in relation to topics or case studies that merit careful critical attention on their own terms. It is worth noting that we have intentionally deferred addressing methodology until the end of the volume because we sincerely believe that this collection has the potential to be field-defining. As such, our goal was not to assemble a volume that presents itself as the last word on rural queer studies but rather to assemble one that has the potential to function as a catalyst by suggesting exciting new possibilities and novel approaches to the study of queer life in the United States and beyond. Put somewhat differently, we wanted to conclude with essays that we think will help readers begin to imagine their own fruitful new beginnings in this vibrant and still largely unexplored domain of scholarly inquiry. Regardless of their differences, however, what all of the essays that comprise this volume share in common is a clear sense that there remains something exceedingly important to be said about the role that rural and nonmetropolitan spaces play in shaping gender and sexuality in the United States and beyond. Having scrutinized the work that follows relatively closely over the course of assembling this volume, we are certainly convinced on this point. We hope that you will be as well.

It is difficult to say in any definitive sense how large a percentage of the general population a group needs to be in order for its members' experiences and perspectives to matter in the broader scheme of things. But speaking as scholars of American culture we can say this: our understanding of American life will be grossly distorted unless we allow those individuals' experiences and perspectives at the margins to inform and shape ongoing debates, especially scholarly ones. Indeed, if we have learned anything over the past three decades, it is that scholars ignore the margins at their peril. They also do a great disservice to the complexity of human experience when they habitually separate forms of marginality that actually overlap in the context of at least some people's everyday lives. As an emerging field of inquiry, rural queer studies is obviously in no position to make claims of comprehensiveness where attentiveness to the experience of life live at the margin is concerned. But as we hope the reader will agree, it does have a great deal to contribute to that work—work that should be of the utmost importance to all of us regardless of where we are located.

NOTES

1 See generally, Williams, *The Country and the City.*

2 In this last respect at least, then, and probably in quite a few others, "rural America" is a lot like "white America"—which may explain why the two are so easily thought of as being synonymous, even though they are not, as anyone who has lived anywhere besides the Northeast or Midwest can attest.

3 Coleman, "A Camera in the Garden of Eden."

4 Reding, *Methland.*

5 Barry, "Sewers, Curfews, and a Ban on Gay Bias."

6 Mason, *Oklahomo.*

7 Halberstam, *In a Queer Time and Place.*

8 Shover, *First Majority–Last Minority.*

9 Gramsci, *Prison Notebooks,* 330–1.

10 Weston, *Families We Choose,* 274.

11 Halberstam, *In a Queer Time and Place,* 36–7.

12 Herring, *Another Country,* 17.

13 Tongson, *Relocations,* 152.

14 Berlant, *Cruel Optimism,* 24.

15 Ibid., 23.
16 Ibid., 8.
17 Ibid., 27.
18 Howard, *Men Like That*, xiv.
19 Puar, *Terrorist Assemblages*, 70.
20 Leung, *Undercurrents*, 15.

PART I

New Archives, New Epistemologies

1

Out Back Home

An Exploration of LGBT Identities and Community in Rural Nova Scotia, Canada

KELLY BAKER

For some of us you can take the homo out of the country but
you can't take the country out of the homo, and like a flock
of geese in fall we eventually find our way back home.
—"A Rural Point of View," *Wayves Magazine*, Halifax,
December 2008

This essay explores the identities and experiences of community
among lesbians, gays, and transgendered people living in rural Nova
Scotia, Eastern Canada. Based on fourteen interviews and participant
observation, I consider how sexual identity is spatially constructed outside of the urban center, and uncover some of the ways in which rural
LGBT identities and communities are experienced. Because academic
and popular representations of rural areas often portray them as "backward" or "traditional"—and thus heterosexual—I look at participants'
reasons for living outside the city. How do rural settings influence the
ways rural LGBT individuals identify? Do those who decide to stay
in, or return to, their rural hometowns feel integrated within their
communities? Do they experience a sense of commonality with other
people in their area? Is community actively sought? In examining such
questions, I challenge the prevalent assumption that LGBT communities are inherently urban. I also circumvent the widespread depictions
of rural areas as being ultimately homophobic and hostile to LGBT
difference. Lastly, I highlight the ways rural nonheterosexuality works
to challenge dominant notions of sexual identity, community, and rural
space.

Rural Nova Scotia as a Case Study

As Nova Scotian historian Robin Metcalfe points out, Halifax has had a prominent history of gay and lesbian community organizing and activism in Canada.[1] But as a small city located in the Maritime provinces, Halifax's LGBT community has had to struggle to get its particular issues raised and its voice heard within the wider LGBT movement.[2] These issues have been even more difficult for LGBT communities in rural areas. Indeed, many of the problems faced by rural LGBT people are similar to the problems those in cities faced almost two decades prior; many rural LGBT communities are still relatively isolated and are struggling to establish networks and create spaces within which LGBT people feel safe.[3] And unlike many other Canadian provinces, Nova Scotia also continues to have a high percentage of rural dwellers: with a rural population of nearly 75 percent, Nova Scotia has the third highest rural population in the country.[4]

The socioeconomic status of rural Nova Scotia appears below the national, as well as provincial, urban average in a number of areas. The education level of rural Nova Scotians, for instance, is substantially lower than that of urban residents;[5] at the same time, unemployment rates in rural Nova Scotia are substantially higher than the national average for rural areas.[6] Incomes in Nova Scotia are also lower than the national average, and the gap between urban and rural incomes is larger than in any other province.[7] Fisheries and agriculture, two prominent industries for the region, have both experienced a sharp decline in recent years; while the number of people employed in fisheries has been decreasing, farm debt has, for the past thirteen years, been greater than farm receipts—and this gap is widening. And while total wages and salaries in the mining, oil, and gas industries have been increasing, the number of people employed in these industries has decreased. In recent years, however, multiple research initiatives have taken place to help bolster the development of healthy, sustainable communities throughout rural Nova Scotia. The Coastal Communities Network (CCN), along with the Rural Communities Impacting Policy project (RCIP), has been active in helping to "promot[e] the survival and enhancement" of the province's rural communities.[8] Official reports borne from such initiatives have lauded such Nova Scotian communities as having a strong sense of community spirit and community values, as well as a deep appreciation for those who work to strengthen them.[9]

During the summer of 2008, however, tensions emerged among a number of northern Nova Scotian counties when the mayor of Truro started what some have called a "rural trend" of refusing to raise the pride flag during Nova Scotia's gay pride week celebrations. Despite the fact that same-sex marriages have been legally recognized in Nova Scotia since September 24, 2004, the mayor, citing his religious convictions, stated that "God says 'I'm not in favor [of gay pride]' . . . and I have to look at it and say, I guess I'm not either."[10] Both Pictou and Cumberland counties followed, implementing policies that would prevent nongovernment flags from being flown on municipal poles. While the mayor's position may have confirmed for many the stereotyped beliefs surrounding small-town backwardness and oppressiveness, this incident, which received national attention, allowed the issues and experiences of rural LGBT Nova Scotians to gain visibility and recognition throughout Canada. It illuminated the fact that Nova Scotia contains a number of rural LGBT communities that are actively promoting acceptance and equality within their wider rural communities.

* * *

During the summer of 2008, I conducted fourteen interviews with individuals ranging from twenty-one to seventy-one years old. Of these, eight self-identified as lesbians, five self-identified as gay males, and one self-identified as transsexual. My sample was primarily within a working- and middle-class range. While seven of my participants were born and raised in rural Nova Scotia, two grew up in Halifax County and moved to rural Nova Scotia as young adults. Two others grew up in other provinces (rural Prince Edward Island and suburban Quebec), and the remaining three grew up in other countries (England, the United States, and the Netherlands).

Reflecting the fact that many communities throughout rural Nova Scotia are predominately white,[11] thirteen of my informants were white, while one was native. As Kennedy and Davis note, race and class have a crucial impact on individuals' perceptions and experiences of LGBT community.[12] Similarly, Creed and Ching explain that rural identity inflects, and is inflected by, other dimensions such as race, class, and gender.[13] Containing only one non-white participant, my sample does not represent those rural LGBT individuals whose experiences and sexual identifications are inflected by nondominant racial and ethnic identities.

Since LGBT people in rural Nova Scotia are, to a certain extent, invisible and scattered, my method of recruitment was snowball sampling, which involved eliciting the assistance of my initial research participants and their acquaintances in order to build up my sample group. As Kennedy and Davis point out, this technique is often used among hidden populations, who are difficult for researchers to access.[14] This method proved particularly useful, as it allowed me to examine the interconnections and experiences of community that exist, on varying levels, among individuals dispersed throughout the province. Because my sample was small, it cannot be considered representative of rural LGBT people in Nova Scotia. However, anthropological studies based on individual cases routinely rely more heavily upon depth than breadth.[15] Often utilizing a variety of methods such as in-depth interviews, group interviews, and participant observation, anthropologists consider sample extensiveness to be less applicable to qualitative research; rather, sample size is considered adequate when repetitiveness in data occurs.[16]

My research was also multi-sited. While eight of my participants resided along various parts of the South Shore, six resided in more northern parts of Nova Scotia. Multi-sited research methods have emerged in response to both "empirical changes in the world" as well as new understandings of "the field."[17] Indeed, Green argues that "the field" must be understood not as something that is "effected once and for all" but as "an emerging process . . . made of social encounters."[18] As such, strategies of following various connections, associations, and relationships are at the "very heart" of multi-sited research.[19] Such methods therefore allowed me to investigate the social encounters which constituted rural Nova Scotia as "the field." Witnessing and engaging the various interconnections and networks among my participants, who are geographically dispersed, yet socially connected, was essential to my understanding of identity and community among LGBT individuals scattered throughout rural Nova Scotia.

Locating LGBT People in Rural Space

The notion of space has become a useful lens through which to understand identity and community, as well as relations of power and oppression.[20] No longer seen as a backdrop or container for social relations, space is deemed crucial to the constitution and reproduction of social relations and identities.[21] The queering[22] of both public and private spaces is therefore understood as being crucial to the historical formation of early gay politics and collective identities.[23] Indeed, throughout the twentieth century, gay spaces such as bars, clubs, and cruising grounds created the possibility for collective consciousness, struggle, and activity.[24] The establishment of gay spaces, such as parades, cafes, centres, and neighborhoods, made it possible for political consciousness and movements for public recognition to emerge. They provided safety, visibility, and a sense of commonality,[25] eventually leading to a grassroots liberation movement and becoming the essential means of combating homophobia and maintaining a sense of collectivity.[26]

Work on LGBT identities and space has, however, been criticized for neglecting the important distinction between urban and rural space.[27] As Creed and Ching point out, work on space and identity "unquestionably posits an urbanized subject" without considering the vital role of its opposition—the rural or rustic.[28] This "cultural hierarchy" has overshadowed the significance of rural-based identities and has devalued, and sometimes erased, rural space.[29] For anthropologist Kath Weston, this hierarchy has also falsely located all LGBT people within the city and has overlooked their presence outside of it.[30]

Certainly, the social and economic conditions within many North American cities after World War II provided a space within which gay identity, collectivity, and politics could emerge.[31] The city, with its anonymity and heterogeneity, as well as its population size and density, has been theorized as a beacon of tolerance and the ideal arena for sexual outsiders.[32] The city may well have played this role historically, but in representations of urban and rural spaces, the latter is portrayed as inherently backward and oppressive,[33] with tales of isolation, prejudice, and physical violence being used to characterize the experiences of the LGBT people who live there.[34] Rural areas are often posited as "closets" and are deemed antithetical to the constitution of gay subjectivity.[35] Much writing about the lives of gay people has not only overlooked their presence outside of the city, but also discounted the significance of rural space in the construction and experience of LGBT identities.

Rural areas in Western countries face particular challenges with regard to global capitalism, and these challenges have influenced the mobility patterns and decisions taking place in these areas.[36] Rural areas of Canadian Maritime provinces have experienced particular migration patterns, with rural out-migration both a local and an international concern.[37] The social constructivist approach to rurality "emphasizes symbols and signs people imagine"[38]—that is, how people construct rural places and themselves as rural. It has been argued that this construction of rurality is integral to "the unique character of Canadian society" and "closely linked to natural resource extraction, modes of production, remoteness, rurality and the North."[39] The current social transformations that are occurring in rural Canada are informed by the processes of global capitalism and neoliberal policies. Rural Canada has also shown resilience through historical waves of industry, communities, and cultural traditions.[40] Rurality has been historically associated with strong social attachments,[41] characterized in part by a need to place people, as well as strong attachment to family and place.[42] Traditional ideals of masculinity and femininity also persist in rural areas,[43] which include occupational, gendered, and sexual identities.

Recent inquiry into the lives of rural LGBT people, albeit sparse, has, however, revealed a significant number of rural same-sex couples[44] and has uncovered large numbers of LGBT-identified individuals who live in small towns and enjoy doing so.[45] Many rural gays and lesbians have developed support networks that "facilitate . . . the creation of spatially disparate but strongly interwoven communities."[46] Developments in global communication technologies have bolstered this process, and phone lines, Internet, and satellite television have offered alternative ways in which rural LGBT people can locate, experience, and participate in various forms of community.[47]

This was certainly the case for the participants in my study. None of my participants spoke of having experienced any physical violence, and fewer than half (five) spoke of having directly experienced verbal homophobia while living in rural Nova Scotia. Of those five who did experience verbal homophobia in their rural towns, two also reported having experienced homophobia (and to higher degrees) while living in the city. Of the remaining three who had experienced verbal homophobia, one had never lived in a city, while two had not been out until living in rural Nova Scotia. For participants, homophobia was not directly linked to rural space; rarely experienced, verbal homophobia manifested in both urban and rural areas.

All my interviewees experienced varying degrees—in some cases, surprisingly high degrees—of acceptance in their rural towns. For instance, Bonnie, who grew up in Prince Edward Island but came out in rural Nova Scotia, stated, "I live in . . . a very rural area. And everybody knows that I'm a lesbian. . . . And never once have I felt a homophobic neighbor. . . . It's been amazing actually. You'd think it would be different but, it's never been. . . . I've never felt any rejection. And so, that's kinda cool. Yeah." Gordon, who grew up in the Netherlands and also came out in rural Nova Scotia, echoed Bonnie's experience: "The town . . . has been very supportive in that we never experienced any backlash from the public. On the contrary, it has been a comfortable and indeed rewarding existence. When we married, people went out of their way to congratulate us!"

Experiences were surprisingly similar for those who moved to rural Nova Scotia after growing up and coming out elsewhere. While Wilson noted that "unknown outsiders are never welcomed in small towns,"[48] participants appeared to have had little trouble breaking through their "outsider" status. For instance, Manny, who grew up and came out in Dartmouth, said, "Compared to a lot of other places I've seen, yeah, here's good. . . . Sometimes you just get surprised by people." This was echoed by Betty, who grew up and came out near Halifax: "I feel like I'm a part of the community. . . . I'm sure 50 percent of the community knows who I am and they seem to like me and to have accepted me for what I am. It's not a problem. . . . I fit right in here, no problem at all." For Manny and Betty, relocating to rural Nova Scotia from their more urban hometowns was not made difficult by their nonheterosexuality; albeit "surprised," they felt as though they fit in and were accepted without trouble.

Experiences were also similar for those who continue to live in their rural hometowns. For instance, Donna, who grew up, came out, and continues to live in Yarmouth, observed:

"This [coming out] was a long time ago, twenty years ago, and people were very upset at first, and very, very quickly people were just fine with it. I was very surprised. . . . [My parents] were and are very fundamentalist Christian, and I was kind of shocked by how easily they kind of adapted. . . . But everybody was very accepting, and it's been wonderful."

Charlotte, who was born and raised and came out in a rural area, had a similar experience:

[When I came out] it was less difficult than I imagined it would be. You build up a certain thing in your mind of what you think things are going to be like . . . and you're young. . . . Back when you're so impressionable, back when you're trying to fit in, it's very difficult. . . . Going up into my twenties and thirties and forties I'm like 'to hell with 'em, I don't care' kinda thing. . . . At this point in my life, I'm just going to live my life. I'm too old to do otherwise. . . . Life is too short."

For Charlotte, the fear and anxiety she experienced while coming out was tied not to rural or urban space, but to her age. Because she came out in her early twenties, a time when she felt "impressionable" and was "trying to fit in," her own fears and anxieties made coming out more difficult. However, as she got older, and was "out" to all of her friends and family, she stopped "car[ing] what Joe Blow here down the street thinks" and was able to just live her life. She believes that when one is young, "you think you have something to lose, but you really don't. Because your parents love you unconditionally."

Indeed, the highest degrees of verbal homophobia were cited by some of my youngest participants—Randy and Kat, both twenty-three. Both came out in high school and were close friends throughout their junior and senior high school years. Though both had positive experiences coming out to family, both had very negative experiences of coming out and being gay in school. With regard to his family, Randy stated: "They've always really known; they knew I was going to be gay . . . so it was easy for me. They already knew, so it was just a matter of me admitting it." At school, however, Randy had a more negative experience: "It's like you have to hide it at all times. If you don't, then, it's not going to be good. So you try to hide it as much as possible. And you know what's coming, you know immediately what's coming, and it's like constant shit." Kat spoke of a similar high school experience: "I didn't understand like, when everyone [classmates] realized I was gay, why was it all 'oh she's gay, let's make fun of her.' ... It was horrible. ... It's like the next day all of a sudden you wake up . . . and everybody you know, and everybody you don't even know, is calling you gay."

For both participants, their high school peers and classmates were the primary source of homophobia and hostility. Upon leaving high school, people's attitudes appeared to have changed dramatically. Randy explained:

> "Since like, high school . . . it's been a lot better. Like, a lot more people have accepted it, like, when working . . . and whatnot, nobody ever says anything, like I've never had anyone since I left high school call me a fag or anything. . . . It just finally goes away and you're like 'fuuuck I can just breathe now.' But things are comfortable now I find."

Participants' experiences therefore contradicted prominent understandings of rural space; often perceived as backward, traditional, and homophobic, rural areas provided my participants with varying levels of tolerance and acceptance. For those who did recount experiences of homophobia, it was associated with peers and classmates at school. Older participants, who came out after high school, cited little to no homophobia, while younger participants—those in their early twenties—noted its absence after high school.

Accessing LGBT Identities and Communities in Rural Space

Isolation, Weston points out, is often conceived as the "customary starting point" in claiming or constructing an LGBT identity.[49] The sense of being "different" or "the only one" is often prevalent in one's discovery of his or her LGBT sexuality.[50] Isolation can be especially salient for those LGBT people living in rural areas. One's discovery of gayness, or what Weston calls "the gay imaginary," is often dependent upon access to print, television, and other media.[51] This often requires, especially for those who came out prior to the Internet Age, access to certain resources such as libraries, bookstores, and movie theaters—many of which are located in urban centers.[52] For those who came out during the Internet Age, the Internet was a primary means by which LGBT identities were constructed. The Internet has become a significant vehicle through which individuals—especially those who are relatively isolated—can come out, be politically active, find community, and establish LGBT identities.[53] It allows LGBT youth and adults alike to expand their local LGBT worlds and feel included within imagined LGBT communities beyond their hometown.[54]

When asked about the importance of the Internet, James, twenty-two, noted, "I wanted to know about safe sex, about the [gay] lifestyle, I wanted to fit into something. I wanted something that was me, and I found it online. I connected with people, and it made me feel normal." This was echoed by Dot, a sixty-two-year-old transsexual woman, who stated: "The Internet was probably my savior." Lacking a substantial face-to-face community, many participants utilized the Internet to construct and experience their own sexual identities and forms of belonging.[55] The Internet also helped participants break through rural isolation and access a community that is often linked to urban space.

As Valentine and Skelton point out, finding "the scene" or community is important insofar as it not only facilitates the construction of self-identities, but also offers one a space within which others can provide validation.[56] For many LGBT individuals, the LGBT community represents the first space of belonging; it offers them a chance to exist outside of the heteronormative world within which they often feel marginalized.[57] The search for community, however, often necessitates a symbolic and sometimes physical journey through space.[58] "Like" others, Weston notes, immediately become spatially located—not only is there "someone like me," but that someone is "out there somewhere."[59] For those born and raised in rural areas, that initial "somewhere" is usually thought to be a city.[60]

At some point, many of my rural-born participants ventured to the city in search of LGBT community. They saw the anonymity, size, and heterogeneity of cities as promising a general acceptance of "difference" not found in rural areas. Accordingly, Weston notes that the combination within cities of physical proximity and social distance, or, indifference, has been theorized as a politics of tolerance; differences are by default generally accepted, or at the very least, tolerated.[61] As Gray points out, cities themselves are built on the "aggregation . . . of differentiated interests."[62] Charlotte, fifty-eight, associated the city with a general acceptance of "difference" or eccentricity:

> "You gotta understand . . . in a small community, when you find out you are different, you think you are the only one. . . . I mean, Halifax is a city, so actually you can go up and see somebody dressed very eccentrically or differently, or whatever, it's the norm. You come down here, and if you see something that's different, it's like, everybody looks. . . . Here, everybody over the years, after being a small town all your life, you get to know everybody. . . . Yeah, if you were in the city you'd go and do your own thing, and nobody stops to take the time to give a darn one way or the other. But here, you have to be careful."

For Charlotte, the anonymity and "big population" of the city were linked to the increased acceptance of overall diversity, in direct contrast to her small community, where everyone quickly got to know everyone else. Because of their close social proximity in a small community, those who were different had to be careful not to overtly assert their difference, whereas those in the city were free to "go and do [their] own thing."

For many born-and-raised rural participants, the city—Halifax— therefore offered a symbolic, and in some instances, real, space for forming community. As Charlotte also noted:

> "It wasn't until I was older that we went into the city; we used to go to some of the dances up there. That's how I really got into it, finding out . . . when the conferences were and going to the dances and stuff like that. Meeting so many [lesbians], and just feeling like I was home. I just felt, the very first time I went, I just felt 'I'm home, this is where I'm supposed to be.'"

Similarly, Betty, age fifty, said, "I had to go into Halifax to try to find my own kind. . . . I thought, 'Yup, that's where I need to start.'" This was also the case for James, twenty-three, who "thought [the city] was infested with gay people. . . . A gaytopia." For these participants, the city, and Halifax in particular, served as a symbolic homeland—an anchor for the LGBT community.

Limitations of Urban LGBT Community

"In relationship to an urban homeland," Weston writes, "individuals constructed themselves as 'gay people': sexual subjects in search of others like themselves."[63] Many journeys into this homeland, however, do not result in the discovery of the "Promised Land." Rather, some find the urban community to be "insular and exclusionary."[64] At the same time, the community is also divided by gender, ethnicity, age, and class.[65] Access to and inclusion within the urban LGBT community is therefore dependent on factors outside of claiming LGBT identities.[66] The search for community thus extends far beyond simply entering the space of the city.

For instance, after moving to Halifax at eighteen and finding his way into the community, twenty-three-year-old James said that "[the gay community] met my ideals for a while; I did a lot of partying. Education made me see it differently, though. It's really subdivided—I had to identify with a type [of gay person] and live with it." For James, simply claiming a gay identity and being in the space of urban gay clubs did not grant him immediate inclusion into the community. Because the community was "subdivided," he had to negotiate his own identity—as a particular type of gay person—so that he could feel as though he fit in.

For some participants, disappointment or dissatisfaction with the urban community was framed as a contrast between urban and rural space. Charlotte, fifty-eight, spent only two years living in Halifax. However, she traveled between her small town and Halifax, attending many dances and conferences. As previously noted, Charlotte, upon first visiting the city, felt like she was "home"; however, as a "little ol' small-town girl," Charlotte found that she did not necessarily fit in with the urban lesbian-feminist community:

"Umm the city, I found, like I didn't really meet up to their standards. I wasn't as informed and I didn't know the lingo, the correct way to be, or talk or whatever. I was just me, little ol' small-town girl, farmer's daughter. . . . I wasn't able to . . . I fit in but I was very quiet, because so many of them talked, and their food and their lifestyle was so different than what I was used to. You know, meat and potatoes, I didn't know about garlics and you know, the dishes, and you know, it just overwhelmed me . . . that kind of lifestyle, and culture, and cuisine, I felt like a little country bumpkin, you know [laughs]. . . . I felt a little intimidated."

For Charlotte, entrance into the urban lesbian-feminist community involved an entirely new urban lifestyle. As a "country bumpkin" and a "farmer's daughter," she did not have the knowledge and language associated with 1970s lesbian feminism; nor was she acquainted with urban culture and cuisine. For Charlotte, acceptance into Halifax's lesbian-feminist community was not only dependent upon a being in the right space and having the right identity; it necessitated a certain amount of "cultural capital"[67]—that is, a certain kind of knowledge, a certain vocabulary, and a certain type of taste. Although she identified as a lesbian, because she was born and raised on a farm, Charlotte lacked the necessary prerequisites for being included into the urban lesbian-feminist community and felt as though she "didn't really meet up to their standards."

The urban LGBT community was also seen by some, especially gay men, as a space of particular danger. As Valentine and Skelton point out, urban LGBT communities present gendered vulnerabilities to lesbians and gay men.[68] Gay male spaces, for instance, can be extremely sexualized and can present many risks with regard to drug abuse and unsafe sexual practices.[69] As Manny pointed out: "Yeah, here [in my small town] I'd say is . . . a little more safer, yeah. By a long shot. . . . In the city, like, I know the younger you are the more pedophiles cling to you. . . . You've got your pedophiles, your gay bashers. . . . It's just ridiculous. But here seems a lot less." This notion of urban danger was also cited by Chris:

"Gay communities are more settled in rural places. You have a partner, you're settled, you live a basic life as opposed to parties, sex, and drugs. . . . The [urban] gay community is very promiscuous, with sex parties . . . [and] it's spreading to rural areas. . . . Young gay men move to Halifax and get caught up in it, have sex with three guys in one day. . . . With subcultures, people lose that 'we're part of a larger community.' . . . It's self-destructive."

For Manny and Chris, the city posed a number of dangers, such as "pedophiles," "gay bashers," and hypersexualized and drug-infested subcultures—dangers they did not consider to be inherent to rural areas. The dense population and increased number of gays, while on the one hand promoting acceptance and community, could, on the other hand, create particular urban dangers, especially for gay men.

Rural Identity, Acceptance, and Community Interdependence

As both Williams and Scott note, tensions between rural and urban life rose in the modern era of industrial capitalism, when the city became associated with progress and modernity.[70] Cast as "folksy" and "irrational,"[71] rural areas were perceived and often experienced as being bound by tradition, while cities were associated with linear progress and deemed "the brain of the whole society."[72] The deeply rooted opposition between urban and rural space therefore became highly significant in the construction of identity. Manifested in everyday "mundane cultural activities," such as music, food, and recreation, it helped to generate personal and social identification.[73]

Wilson points out that rural places are often "riddled with insider/outsider social structures,"[74] with the key to survival being social conformity and community interdependence.[75] In his book exploring the lives of LGBT people in rural Canada, Michael Riordon similarly observes that many rural LGBT people find that they are judged primarily by their farming abilities, their community involvement, and their roles as good neighbors.[76] Indeed, social involvement and community participation are strongly embraced within rural communities and are the primary means by which respect and reciprocity are achieved.[77] Certainly, while rural areas do contain varying levels of homophobia, the power of small-town loyalty and familial ties should not be overlooked.[78] In places built upon solidarity, familiarity, and belonging, and where familiar locals are valued above any other identity claim, such ties work to transform the "stranger" into someone who is both recognizable and familiar.[79]

This is especially true for those who were born and raised, and continue to live, in their rural hometowns. For instance, discussing her experiences of coming out, Donna said:

> "People just kept treating me like me . . . I think that was the ticket. . . . They just said, 'You know, it's somebody who we've known forever, and she is who she is. She's not hurting anybody, so what the hey.' So people were just, in fact, if anything . . . it seemed like people were going out of their way to be really nice to me. . . . I totally attribute it to small communities where people know each other. And I have been a part of this community forever, I mean, I grew up here, I helped people out, like . . . as a teenager, I'd always go and help somebody paint their house and I'd go buy groceries for the old lady down the road, you know, that was the community, you'd just help people out. And so it wasn't like 'Oh yeah, I knew her, she grew up down the road,' it was 'Oh yeah, she's been in my house, you know.' And I was totally, totally accepted."

For Donna, because she had been an active member of the rural community throughout her entire life, she was "totally accepted." Moreover, people even went out of their way to make her feel accepted.

Although Janis did not move to rural Nova Scotia until she was in her twenties, she attributes her hard work and community involvement as granting her respect and acceptance within the rural community. As she observed:

> "People in the country are more capable of accepting us. They are more dependent on us, and they're more aware of that. . . . My involvement has protected me . . . helping people, repairing things. My neighbor was a well-respected member of the community, a very solid neighbor. . . . In the country you're protected by certain things. . . . Hard work is respected, and they saw that I was working hard, and was working good with people."

For Janis, the community interdependency that characterizes rural areas renders rural folk more capable of accepting difference. Her involvement within the community, via hard work, helping people, and repairing things, helped her earn respect and acceptance. The fact that her neighbor was "solid" and a well-respected member of the community also helped her achieve acceptance; this helped protect her, as well as integrate her into the rest of the community.

Contesting the Closet Model

Within the "closet model" of sexual identity,[80] LGBT subjectivity initially lies dormant, "awaiting only the right set of circumstances to emerge."[81] Such circumstances have often been situated within an urban location;[82] establishing a core lesbian or gay identity has often coincided with the construction of urban subcultures and has involved an integration "into the dense social networks of an exclusive outsider world."[83] As such, "the rural" has often been conceptualized as a closet for "authentic" urban sexual identities.[84] LGBT identities that exist in rural areas are often portrayed as and thought to be "out of place."[85]

Halberstam points out, however, that not all LGBT people leave home to become LGBT. Thus, we must consider the possibilities that "the condition of 'staying put'" may offer in terms of producing alternative or complex LGBT subjectivities.[86] Indeed, the politics of visibility that underlie modern, authentic LGBT identities, are, as Gray observes, "tailor-made" for urban space.[87] The familial reliance, local power dynamics, class relations, and cultural marginalization inherent to rural areas renders them ill-suited for such politics.[88] Rural sexual communities must therefore be understood as a "complex interactive model of space, embodiment, locality, and desire."[89] Rural LGBT people may not position sexuality as the "definitive characteristic of self."[90] Rather, as Gray argues, they may enact a "politics of rural recognition," which privileges one's credentials as "just another local" and denounces claims of difference.[91] Rather than simply being "out and proud," they may express their nonheterosexuality within and through the norms of their communities.

For instance, Chris, who teaches high school in the same town in which he grew up, stated: "Ninety-nine percent of my students have been supportive. . . . I mean, [their families] knew me since they were born. It [being gay] doesn't make me different." For Chris, the fact that his students and their families have known him all his life has earned him support and acceptance. Being gay does not set him apart from the community. "I don't let that aspect define me," he said. Chris's claims to sameness, inherent within Gray's "politics of rural recognition,"[92] undermine the privileging of sexual difference as a defining element of the self in much urban LGBT identity politics. In a similar vein, Betty pointed out: "They seem to like me and to have accepted me for what I am, it's not a problem. But I'm not out there 'I'm lesbian,' I'm just me. I'm just, you know . . . you probably wouldn't even know [that I was a lesbian] if I was in a crowd, you know how you can tell sometimes." For Betty, sexuality is not the definitive aspect of her identity, and she makes no effort to make her sexuality blatantly obvious. Rather, as she said, "I'm just me." While most of the rural community is aware of and has accepted her sexuality, she does not feel the need to be overt or blatant about it. Bonnie also echoed these feelings:

"I was never one to be, you know, rash and overt about my orientation. . . . So you know, I didn't push the envelope. . . . Everybody knows that I'm a lesbian. . . . I don't shy away from being who I am but I am also not overt about my being queer. It's within a context of neighborliness and friendships and just kind of sharing, you know, going to community events at the local hall, and you know, being a part of the community."

Although Bonnie is not in the closet and does not shy away from being herself, she neither overly displays nor announces her sexual difference. Rather, the importance for her sense of self lies in the rural values of "neighborliness," "friendships," and "community events." Thus, Bonnie values her sexuality without building her life around it; she approaches it as an identity thread, rather than a core identity.[93] Such an approach, Halberstam points out, does not necessarily signify the closet.[94] Rather, for some rural LGBT people, the spatial construction and experience of LGBT identities in nonurban contexts may defy or complicate dominant conceptions of the closet model.[95] LGBT identities may be negotiated so as not to undermine other elements of one's identity. Rural locality shapes Bonnie's sense of her own sexual identity; framed within a socio-spatial context of rurality, Bonnie's self-described lesbian/queer identity emerges through a rural sense of being "another local," which is entwined with rural values such as neighborliness and community, where difference carries limited value and familiarity is prized.

Certainly, identity politics operationalize identity as a "crucial ground of experience, a course of social knowledge, and a basis for activism"; they rely on collective identification as a mode of political empowerment.[96] So while the current goals and achievements of the gay movement revolve around acceptance and assimilation, they also include the right to be different and to be legitimated based upon that difference.[97] Visibility politics draw upon this assertion and champion the "out-ness" and visibility of this difference as instrumental in achieving such legitimation and liberation. Rural subjectivities, however, are inherently incompatible with such visibility claims. While the internal makeup of cities, or what urban sociologist Georg Simmel referred to as "the conditions of metropolitan life,"[98] revolve around the conglomeration of large numbers of people with diverse interests and perspectives, rural areas, in contrast, are governed by sameness and familiarity and are organized around an appreciation for solidarity, which is expressed through blending in.[99] Rooted particularly in family connections, familiarity and belonging are central to the structures of rural life. While much urban LGBT visibility politics, at their very tamest, center on the different-but-equal paradigm, rural LGBT visibility politics involve a delicate balance of nonheterosexuality and localness, putting forth a logic of different-but-similar.

At the same time, however, some participants pointed out the perceived problem of rural LGBT invisibility. Drawing upon dominant notions of sexual identity and community, where sexuality is perceived as constituting selfhood, many cited the importance of visibility in achieving acceptance for LGBT communities—especially those in rural areas. For instance, Dot asked: "How can we improve things in rural districts? Visibility. If we're not seen, we can't be appreciated. . . . How we're seen is how we grow." This idea was echoed by Gordon, who said that "one major problem is that not all members of our community are willing to 'come out' of their proverbial closets and give assistance. This is true of [his town] as well as any other community in this province and elsewhere. Numbers do matter."

Similarly, Betty pointed out, "It's quite amazing how many [gay people] there are [in my town]. . . . But it's kind of unfortunate. . . . I think people are still kind of afraid [to come out]. Not me, but they are." Similarly, Manny, who said, "I find here that they are very low-key, like, it's like they don't want a lot of people to find out. . . . Why? I don't know." For these participants, acceptance can be achieved only through visibility and being "out" about one's sexuality; in their minds, LGBT identities should not be maneuvered around or negotiated. While they know a number of LGBT individuals within their communities who are afraid of potential rejection and are thus closeted, such fear, they believe, is not warranted. Rather, it is the responsibility of such closeted individuals to be out and visible and help raise awareness of LGBT issues within their communities.

Conclusion

My research has drawn attention to, and attempted to fill, some of the gaps that currently exist within the literature regarding rural LGBT identities and experience. Since preliminary work on this topic has focused on rural contexts in the United States,[100] it is important to address this gap as it exists in the Canadian context, and examine how rural LGBT individuals approach and negotiate their sexual identities, as well as establish and maintain a sense of community, in a province whose rural population remains at nearly 75 percent. In the context of Nova Scotia, the rural/urban binary played a pivotal role in shaping participants' identities and experiences. A rural or "small town" life appealed to urban- and rural-born LGBT people alike. Often perceived as backward and homophobic, rural areas, for the participants of this study, were a source of varying levels of acceptance, as well as community, both rural and LGBT.

At the same time, the isolation of rural life required, in some cases, additional effort to find or access LGBT community. For some, this involved physically going to the city. Regardless, for my participants, a sense of LGBT community provided a sense of collectivity, reassurance, and acceptance. Accessed through books, Internet, and, eventually, face-to-face contact, a sense of LGBT community helped both urban and rural participants, especially those from older generations, to break through isolation. For some participants, LGBT community was assumed to be inherently urban; some did travel to the city to find their "own kind." However, for others, LGBT community was experienced most intensely within the rural setting. Having spent varying amounts of time in the city, many rural participants did not actually feel part of the imagined urban community; experienced as exclusionary, insular, and in some cases, dangerous, the urban LGBT community was not always the "homeland" it was promised to be. Class and cultural differences between urban and rural LGBT people overshadowed the sharing of a truly common LGBT identity.

There was, however, evidence of pressures to conform. Some participants noted the closeted nature of many rural LGBT individuals, while others appeared to negotiate their nonheterosexuality or their difference as a way to foster inclusion within the rural community. At the same time, it is important to acknowledge that the construction and experience of LGBT identities takes a different shape in rural space and can work to complicate dominant models—such as the closet model—of sexual identity and community. Indeed, highly informed by notions of rural interdependency and reciprocity, some participants challenged the closet model, as well as a conception of identity in which sexuality is seen as being fundamentally characteristic of one's self.

Increased media attention is also being paid to LGBT issues. Thus, the changing perceptions of rural heterosexuals ought to be examined. For instance, many participants spoke of the significance of public policy like gay marriage in "humanizing" LGBT people, especially those in small towns. As Bonnie explained: "Within the conservative general population of the rural area . . . the fact that legislation has it now that same-sex couples can marry . . . we're normalizing those relationships. . . . The more we kind of normalize it, the more community and society is going to accept it."

With the development of technology, the lines between urban and rural space are also being increasingly blurred. Indeed, conceptions of "the rural" have shifted dramatically; no longer conceived of as "separate" and "self-contained,"[101] rural and urban spaces are increasingly overlapping.[102] For instance, Nova Scotia has taken extra steps to bolster the development of sustainable rural communities and connect rural and urban space. The Broadband for Rural Nova Scotia initiative, for example, which was completed at the end of 2009, delivered high-speed Internet access to all Nova Scotians, making Nova Scotia one "of the most connected jurisdictions in North America."[103] A bulwark of urbanization,[104] the Internet will provide all rural Nova Scotians with access to various services that were previously unavailable to them.

As a result, Nova Scotia's urban and rural LGBT communities are also becoming increasingly blurred. Available at many locations throughout rural Nova Scotia, *Wayves*, a Halifax-based LGBT newspaper, has recently become available online.[105] Atlantic Canada's source of both rural and urban LGBT-related news and activities, *Wayves* has taken great strides to bridge urban-rural gaps, including hosting a series of LGBT town hall meetings, geared at "discuss[ing] Atlantic Canada's emerging rural rainbow communities, the joys and problems of country living, and how LGBT media can best report and further celebrate [rural LGBT people's] lives."[106] Vehicles of globalization such as television, print media, and the Internet have thus changed the face of rural life and are offering unique opportunities to reexamine the relationship among LGBT identities, community, and urban and rural spaces.

NOTES

1 Metcalfe and Bruhm, eds., *Queer Looking, Queer Acting*.

2 Ibid.

3 Warner, *Fear of a Queer Planet*, 308.

4 *Rural Report: Demographics*, Rural Communities Impacting Policy Report, October 2003, http://www.ruralnovascotia.ca/RCIP/Demographics/Demographics. htm#PopulationOfCountyByAge.

5 According to the 2001 census, 11% of rural Nova Scotians had less than a grade nine education, compared to only 4% of urban Nova Scotians. In rural Nova Scotia (including Cape Breton County), 41% did not have a high school diploma, compared to only 25% in Halifax Regional Municipality. Ibid., 8.

6 While the Canadian average is 7.7%, rural regions in Nova Scotia experience a much higher unemployment rate. For example, the unemployment rates range from 7.8% in the Annapolis Valley to 17.0% in Cape Breton. Ibid., 37, 21.

7 While residents of Halifax's earnings are on par with the Canadian average, incomes in the rest of Nova Scotia fall below it. Guysborough County's average employment income, for example, is only 53% of the Canadian average. Ibid., 16.

8 Ibid.

9 Ibid., 30.

10 CBC News, "Truro in Gay Flag Flap," August 3, 2007, http://www. cbc.ca/ canada/ nova-scotia/ story/2007/08/03/truro-gay.html.

11 African-Canadians make up 2.2% of the total population, First Nations make up 1.9%, and other visible minorities (Chinese, South Asian, Black, Filipino, Latin American, Southeast Asian, Arab, West Asian, Korean, Japanese) make up 3.8%. *Rural Report: Demographics*, 8.

12 Kennedy and Davis, *Boots of Leather, Slippers of Gold*, 16.

13 Creed and Ching, *Knowing Your Place*, 22.

14 Kennedy and Davis, *Boots of Leather, Slippers of Gold*, 15.

15 Sobal, "Sample Extensiveness in Qualitative Nutrition Education Research," 185.

16 Ibid.

17 Marcus, "Ethnography in/of the World System," 97; Green, "Disrupting the Field," 413.

18 Green, "Disrupting the Field," 413.

19 Marcus, "Ethnography in/of the World System," 97.

20 Brown, *Closet Space*; Retter, Bouthillette, and Ingram, *Queers in Space*, 32.

21 Valentine, "Queer Bodies and the Production of Space," 146.

22 I use the acronym "LGBT" for lesbian, gay, bisexual, and transgendered to refer to participants as a whole. I distinguish this from "queer," which I use to refer to academic usages of the term as part of Queer Theory, or in cases where participants self-identify as such.

23 Retter, Bouthillette, and Ingram, *Queers in Space*, 3; Valentine, "Queer Bodies and the Production of Space."

24 D'Emilio, "Gay Politics and Community in San Francisco since World War II," 456–473; Valentine, "Queer Bodies and the Production of Space."

25 Valentine, "Queer Bodies and the Production of Space."

26 Valentine, "Queer Bodies and the Production of Space."

27 Creed and Ching, *Knowing Your Place*, 7.

28 Ibid.

29 Ibid.

30 Weston, "Get Thee to a Big City," 41.

31 D'Emilio, "Gay Politics and Community," 458.

32 Bell and Valentine, "Queer Country," 114; Weston, "Get Thee to a Big City," 40; Phillips, Shuttleton, and Watt, eds., *De-Centering Sexualities*, 129.

33 Bell and Valentine, "Queer Country," 115; Little and Leyshon, "Embodied Rural Geographies," 269.

34 Smith and Mancoske, eds., *Rural Gays and Lesbians*, 4–6; Bell and Valentine, "Queer Country," 116–17.

35 Weston, "Lesbian/Gay Studies in the House of Anthropology," 339–67; Halberstam, "The Brandon Teena Archive," 159–69.

36 Hanson, *The Maritimer Way?*

37 Brown and Schafft, *Rural People & Communities in the 21st Century*.

38 Ibid., 5.

39 Parkins and Reed, Introduction, 5.

40 Ibid.

41 Williams, *The Country and the City*.

42 Young, "Maritime Gothic Sensibility."

43 Leach, "Producing Globalization"; Valentine, "Queer Bodies and the Production of Space," 146.

44 Bell, "Farm Boys and Wild Men," 547–61; Weston, "Get Thee to a Big City."

45 Wilson, "Getting Your Kicks on Route 66!," 214.

46 Bell and Valentine, "Queer Country," 116.

47 Riordon, *Out Our Way*; Bell and Valentine, "Queer Country"; Wakeford, "New Technologies and 'Cyber-Queer' Research," 115–44.

48 Wilson, "Getting Your Kicks," 208.

49 Weston, "Get Thee to a Big City," 34; Wilson, "Getting Your Kicks."

50 Ibid.

51 Weston, "Get Thee to a Big City," 36; Riordon, *Out Our Way*; Bell and Valentine, "Queer Country"; Gray, *Out in the Country*.

52 Weston, "Get Thee to a Big City," 36–37.

53 Wakeford, "New Technologies and 'Cyber-Queer' Research," 123; Gray, *Out in the Country*.

54 Gray, *Out in the Country*, 15.

55 Ibid., 128.

56 Valentine and Skelton, "Finding Oneself, Losing Oneself," 854.

57 Ibid., 855.

58 Weston, "Get Thee to a Big City"; Halberstam, *In a Queer Time and Place*; Tonkiss, *Space, the City and Social Theory*.

59 Weston, "Get Thee to a Big City," 39.

60 Weston, "Get Thee to a Big City"; Halberstam, "Brandon Teena Archive"; Halberstam, *In a Queer Time and Place*; Valentine, "Queer Bodies and the Production of Space"; Gray, *Out in the Country*.

61 Weston, "Get Thee to a Big City," 23.

62 Gray, *Out in the Country*, 38.

63 Weston, "Get Thee to a Big City," 49.

64 Valentine and Skelton, "Finding Oneself, Losing Oneself," 861.

65 Weston, "Get Thee to a Big City," 49.

66 Valentine and Skelton, "Finding Oneself, Losing Oneself," 861; Weston, "Get Thee to a Big City."

67 Bourdieu, "Cultural Reproduction and Social Reproduction," 71–112.

68 Valentine and Skelton, "Finding Oneself, Losing Oneself," 857.

69 Ibid.

70 Williams, *The Country and the City*; Scott, *Seeing like a State*.

71 Tonkiss, *Space, the City and Social Theory*, 14–15.

72 Scott, *Seeing like a State*, 112.

73 Creed and Ching, *Knowing Your Place*, 197, 3.

74 Wilson, "Getting Your Kicks," 208.

75 Wilson, "Getting Your Kicks"; Smith and Mancoske, *Rural Gays and Lesbians*, 17.

76 Riordon, *Out Our Way*, 47.

77 Smith and Mancoske, *Rural Gays and Lesbians*, 17; Wilson, "Getting Your Kicks," 208; McCarthy, "Poppies in a Wheat Field," 75–94.

78 Wilson, "Getting Your Kicks," 214.

79 Gray, *Out in the Country*, 31, 38–39.

80 Halberstam, "The Brandon Teena Archive," 163.

81 Ibid.

82 Halberstam, "The Brandon Teena Archive"; Weston, "Get Thee to a Big City"; Phillips, Shuttleton, and Watt, *De-Centering Sexualities*.

83 Seidman, *Beyond the Closet*, 11.

84 Bell and Valentine, "Queer Country"; Wilson, "Getting Your Kicks"; Halberstam, "Brandon Teena Archive," 163.

85 Gray, *Out in the Country*, 167.

86 Ibid.

87 Ibid., 30.

88 Ibid.

89 Halberstam, *In a Queer Time and Place*, 45.

90 Wilson, "Getting Your Kicks," 210.

91 Gray, *Out in the Country*, 37.

92 Ibid.

93 Seidman, *Beyond the Closet*, 89.

94 Halberstam, "The Brandon Teena Archive," 163.

95 Ibid., 89; Wilson, "Getting Your Kicks."

96 Halperin and Traub, eds., *Gay Shame*, 25.

97 Ibid., 3.

98 Simmel, *The Sociology of Georg Simmel*, 410.

99 Gray, *Out in the Country*, 38.

100 For example, Gray, *Out in the Country*.

101 Weston, "Get Thee to a Big City," 41; Halberstam, *In a Queer Time and Place*, 30.

102 Creed and Ching, *Knowing Your Place*, 2; Weston, "Get Thee to a Big City," 41–42.

103 Government of Nova Scotia, "Economic and Rural Development: Broadband for Rural Nova Scotia," 2009, http://www.gov.ns.ca/econ/broadband/updates/.

104 Lohr, "The Internet as an Influence on Urbanization."

105 *Wayves Magazine*, 2009, www.wayves.ca.

106 Ibid.

2

Horatio Alger's Queer Frontier

GEOFFREY W. BATEMAN

Introduction: Alger's Unnatural Familiarity with Boys

On December 8, 1864, the First Unitarian Church of Brewster, Massachusetts, ordained Horatio Alger, Jr., as its new minister. For the next fifteen months, he enthusiastically dedicated himself to his new position and gained the respect of his congregation.[1] But this good fortune came to an abrupt halt in the spring of the following year. Responding to rumors that Alger had sexually molested two boys, aged thirteen and fifteen, the church declined to renew his contract. On March 19, 1866, the committee charged with investigating Alger concluded that he had practiced "deeds . . . too revolting to relate." Admitting he had been "imprudent" with the boys, Alger quickly left town and returned to his parents' home in South Natick, Massachusetts. In their final report, the committee concluded that Alger was guilty of "gross immorality and a most heinous crime, a crime of no less magnitude than the abominable and revolting crime of unnatural familiarity with *boys*."[2]

Ironically, this scandal transformed Alger into a reasonably successful writer of juvenile fiction. Forced from the ministry, he recast his transgressive interest in young men into a more palatable form of avuncular mentoring, becoming one of our nation's most popular literary "boy workers," a term that describes the role that adult men played as they intervened in boys' lives throughout the nineteenth and twentieth centuries.[3] For the next forty years, Alger drew upon his didactic charm and wrote over a hundred novels for boys, many of which were set in New York City or in small eastern towns. These texts imagine a homoerotic public sphere of white manhood in which destitute—and often "queer"—young men attain middle-class respectability through the intimate mentoring of older men, as in *Ragged Dick*, the 1867 novel in which this erotic sensibility first appeared.[4] Looking back on his career in 1896, Alger wrote that his juvenile fiction allowed him to "exert a powerful and salutary influence" on young men and helped his "boy readers grow into a worthy and noble manhood." "A boy's heart," Alger observed, "opens to the man who understands him."[5]

In 1874, Alger published *Julius: Or, the Street Boy Out West*, relocating his sentimental interest in his young heroes' respectability to the rural spaces of the North American frontier. This regional shift represents an equally important shift in Alger's thinking about same-sex relations, for *Julius* and Alger's subsequent western novels—including titles like *Joe's Luck* and the four novels that comprised his *Pacific* series—imagine an alternative history of sexuality that privileges rural Wisconsin farms and the mining camps of the California gold rush as homoerotic sites of reform for the juvenile delinquent. This problem increasingly plagued nineteenth-century reformers and shaped a new understanding of a young person's teenage years: adolescence. In 1904, G. Stanley Hall popularized this new phase of life when he published his encyclopedic study on the topic, reflecting a shift in American and European attitudes that industrialization had fostered over the course of the previous century.[6]

In this essay, I read Alger's frontier fantasy as a particular historical manifestation of queering the countryside at the very moment in which the rural frontier was seen to be closing, revealing a distinctly western location from which to rethink sexuality and its history.[7] What I describe as Alger's queer frontier uses its distance from the urban landscape to recuperate his young protagonists' adolescent deviance through the homoerotic interest of other men—both middle-aged boy workers and older youth—who mentor these boys into middle-class manhood. This rural eroticism arrests the teleology of the history of sexuality itself, for it imagines a sexual subjectivity of robust, masculine same-sex desire within the frontier, which is distinct from the emerging discourse of sexual pathologies, whether in the form of inversion, homosexuality, or even sexuality itself.[8] Rather, these texts promote an alternative to the very regime of sexuality that ties erotic and affective practices to a discrete and describable identity. But Alger's representation of same-sex desire also involves an impulse toward racial sameness, achieving legitimacy at the expense of another western sojourner, the racialized figure of the Chinaman onto whom Alger's young white men displace the burden of queerness as they achieve respectability.

In its preservation of erotic and sexual subjectivities that are no longer visible in our culture or have been forgotten, repressed, or never understood, Alger's texts manifest what Bruce Burgett describes as a "queer history of sexuality," one that involves focusing not on the histories (or prehistories) of identity formation, but rather on imagining ourselves as "archeologists attentive to less familiar ways of talking about the relations among bodies, politics, and pleasure."[9] In its own historical orientation, Alger's mining-camp fiction from the 1880s and early 1890s looks back more than thirty years to provide a solution to the emerging ills of urbanization, circulating a nostalgic pleasure for the past as a way to animate a sexual subjectivity of the present. As he pivots away from the punitive discourse of sexual pathology, he continues to "feel backward" for a representation of same-sex desire untainted by degeneracy. As Heather Love notes, such a move constitutes a "potential resistance . . . to the touch of the contemporary queer historian," which might help us "understand queerness as an absence of or an aversion to sex."[10] For Alger, this backward feeling embraces adolescence, circulating an erotic subjectivity that preserves an intensity of same-sex desire but locates it squarely within the robust manliness of the frontier.

In this way, Alger's personal indiscretions and his participation in the literary discourse of adolescence raise important questions for the study of the history of sexuality, queer literary production, and the rural location of such inquiry, for it affords us the opportunity to rethink the emergence of homosexuality as *the* sexual subjectivity of the mid- to late-nineteenth century worth our attention and places this queering of homosexuality's history within the nonurban spaces of the North American West. By recuperating the depraved adolescent through the generous mentoring of his narrative gaze, Alger's texts circulate a kind of intimacy at odds with sexual deviance and use the rural spaces of his western imagination to make this erotic interest suitable to the nation.

Farming Street Boys Out West

When Alger published *Julius: Or, the Street Boy Out West* in 1874, he transplanted *Ragged Dick*'s successful "rags-to-respectability" formula from its urban roots and promoted the rural virtues of an agricultural apprenticeship for his boy heroes.[11] In this novel, Alger describes how the Children's Aid Society, a relief organization that Charles Loring Brace founded in 1853 to address what he described as the threat of the "dangerous classes," places Julius, a former vagabond, with a family in Brookeville, Wisconsin, hoping that hard work and self-restraint will reform him into a respectable man.[12] As Alger writes, "In his new surroundings, my young hero parts with the bad habits contracted in his vagabond life, and, inspired by a worthy ambition, labors to acquire a good education, and to qualify himself for a respectable position in society."[13] Exemplifying the mission of the Children's Aid Society, Alger's novel imagines this agricultural space as purifying and domesticating Julius's unruliness. Coupled with the loving tutelage of his foster-father, it awakens him to the "pleasures of property,"[14] channeling his youthful delinquency into an erotic economy that cultivates the rural landscape of the North American frontier.

In this way, *Julius* exemplifies popular nineteenth-century notions about the western frontier within the U.S. social imaginary, even as it endows this space with its own rural eroticism. As Frederick Jackson Turner famously proclaimed, the frontier "furnish[ed] the forces dominating American character," which was highly individualistic, agriculturally based, strongly drawn, and essential to democracy.[15] Yet Alger's work queers this pioneering process, situating same-sex desire squarely within the ever-moving line of the frontier, even as it paradoxically valorizes the yeoman farmer as a sentimental and heterosexual icon of work, family, and middle-class respectability. In this way, *Julius* emphasizes the West's power to lend respectability to the restless energies of male adolescence and cure its pathology, imagining the region as an ideal one within which to develop a young man's manhood. As Julius explains, Wisconsin will heal him, and as he tells a friend in the city, "I'm goin' West for my health,"[16] where a vigorous life of pastoral labor will help him "grow up respectable."[17] Healthy and respectable, the western farm also represents economic opportunity, for as one of his benefactors says to Julius when he arrives in Brookeline, "You'll have a better chance in the West than you would in New York."[18] Linking the democratic potential of the frontier to the opening of the youth's latent manhood, he concludes, "His Western life will make a man out of him."[19]

Julius achieves this manhood through the intimate attention that his foster-father pays him, a familiarity that Alger naturalizes through the discourse of family and farming and that stands in sharp contrast to his own "unnatural" inclinations. Still, Julius's transition becomes possible only to the extent that he opens his heart up to this older man and becomes physically available to the novel's narrative gaze. Taking great care to update the reader on Julius's growing body, the narrator reveals his own erotic interest in Julius's physical and moral transformations. In New York, Julius "was meager and rather undersized. Want and privation had checked his growth," but since his relocation, "he had lived generously, enjoyed the pure air, and a sufficiency of out-of-door exercise, and these combined had wrought a surprising change in his appearance. He had grown three inches in height; his form had expanded; the pale, unhealthy hue of his cheek had given place to a healthy bloom, and his strength had considerably increased. This change was very gratifying to Julius."[20] It apparently gratifies the narrator, as well, for he remarks that Julius has "strengthened his muscles, and developed his figure," and "would now be regarded as quite a good-looking boy."[21] As Michael Moon argues, "sexual attractiveness is the one characteristic Alger's heroes all have in common," his narrators being "fierce discriminators of good looks in boys."[22] Rousing the narrator's admiration, Julius's attractiveness also earns him the respect of his new family, and his good looks reflect that he is and always has been fundamentally good. Throughout his fiction, Alger makes clear that despite the occasional cosmetic blemish, his boy heroes engender homoerotic sympathy by virtue of their inherent goodness. How a boy looks means a great deal in all of Alger's fiction, but in the context of his first western novel, Julius's robust physical health springs from an essential internal quality with which the degeneracy of urban life has unnaturally interfered. For Alger, the rural West serves as a potent catalyst for the reclamation of virtuous white manhood from the degenerating influence of the city streets. Like the idealized landscape so common to the representations of the West as a region, Julius's body is a wonder unto itself, worthy of awe and admiration, embodying a robust frontier homoeroticism that eschews the potential deviancy of same-sex desire.

Enacting Turner's vision of the pioneer farmer's role in developing the West and through it, the nation, Mr. Taylor disciplines Julius's unruly adolescence through agricultural labor. As he tells Julius when he first meets him, "I'm going to make a Western farmer out of you," disclosing the path Julius will take as he develops the moral sympathy necessary for becoming a suitable citizen.[23] Under Mr. Taylor's tutelage, Julius prospers, marries, and ultimately becomes a proponent of the intimate attachments that make his success possible. When a group of boys in New York City assemble to hear Julius testify about his experience, he says, "I was induced by Mr. O'Connor to go West. There I found kind friends and a good home. . . . Now I carry on a large farm for my benefactor, and . . . I hope in time to become rich. I tell you boys, it will pay you to leave the city streets and go out West. . . . If you want to prosper, and grow up respectable, I advise you to come out as soon as you get the chance."[24] As this speech suggests, *Julius* circulates the same-sex desire of boy work to refuse its scandalous implication. Farming on the frontier thus serves to reclaim adolescence, and this rural space allows Julius to overcome the threat that the perils of adolescence poses to his personhood and the nation, but does so through the narrative intimacies of age-differentiated homoerotic desire that nurture his embodiment of citizenship as a yeoman farmer.

Economies of Adolescent Desire in the California Gold Rush

In subsequent western novels, Alger moves away from farming as the means to rehabilitate the delinquent nineteenth-century American adolescent and adopts California as the redemptive space for such work. Within the homoerotic economy of the rural West, Alger's man-boy love becomes something other than a degenerate sexuality, even as this reclamation of same-sex desire serves imperialistic ends. In these tales, his heroes' adolescent appetites initially threaten the social order through their lack of self-restraint and restlessness. As one of his boy heroes, Dean Dunham, says as he travels West, "I am ashamed of my appetite, but I can't help it." Another character concurs, saying, "Young folks is mostly hungry."[25] In his mining-camp fiction, Alger transforms this adolescent hunger and the bodies that feel it into a rare and valuable commodity in the transitory, homoerotic economy of the California gold rush.

Starting with the serialization of *Joe's Luck* in 1878 and continuing through his 1892 novel, *Digging for Gold*, Alger patterns a series of novels around the plot of disenfranchised youth who face economic hardship in their eastern villages. In response, they head west, hoping to strike it rich in California. Once there, Alger's boy heroes colonize and domesticate the queer spaces of this frontier to attain white middle-class manhood. Young adventurers like Joe Mason, Tom Nelson, Ben Stanton, and Grant Colburn do so by resisting the immoral temptations of these lawless places, cultivating self-restraint, and securing financial independence. Their diligence pay off, for they not only unearth extremely valuable nuggets of gold, but also make savvy investments in San Francisco real estate based on the advice of the older men who take an affectionate interest in them. Having mastered the frontier and made their fortunes, they return to the East as respectable men, able to rescue their downtrodden families from financial ruin with the wealth they extract from California.

In many ways, this transformation continues the pattern Alger established in *Ragged Dick*, but these western novels engage queerly with the rural spaces of California's natural landscapes. Within this context, the desire of other men transforms Alger's boy heroes into rare commodities: like the gold they seek, these young boys play a central role in the economy of rural eroticism that grounds Alger's ideal America. Alger's narrative nostalgia for the lost homoerotic cultures of the gold rush, in which, as he writes, "friendships ripened fast,"[26] only intensifies the desire that circulates between adult men and the adolescent boys even as he distances this erotic economy from the emerging specter of pathological inversion or homosexuality. Deferring the discourse of sexuality, Alger's novels balance the lush possibilities of masculine romance, mentoring, and partnership for white men against the dangerous terror of implicit homosexuality, effeminacy, and racial degeneracy. For Alger, this tension results in recuperating same-sex desire by desexualizing man-boy love and contrasting the robust health of young white men with the racialized degeneracy of the figure of the Chinaman.

Alger introduces his readers to this world in *Joe's Luck*, in which he repeatedly emphasizes the strange atmosphere of California mining camps. This world differs so markedly from that of the East that it prompts one character to proclaim, "It's a queer country"[27]—an observation that reflects the crisis of representation that Susan Johnson argues the gold rush presented to many middle-class easterners, as if invoking the word "California" would somehow tarnish the speaker's virtue.[28] For example, when Tom Thatcher tells his mother about his plans to go to California and reclaim his father's reputation and fortune, she says, "It seems very strange."[29] Despite her fears, Tom, like all of Alger's western heroes, embraces this region's strangeness and defies the social norms that would keep him at home as a subservient factory worker or farm hand. In *The Young Explorer*, when Ben Stanton refuses to work for low wages, the town's deacon tells him, "Boys don't have much judgment." Ben's dismissal of such commonsense advice marks him as a "cur'us boy," one whose actions others view as "very queer." Even Ben's uncle, who sympathizes with him, is shocked to learn of his plans. When Ben says he wants to go west to mine for gold, his uncle "gasp[s]," "Gracious sakes! Want to go to California! . . . What put that idea into your head?"[30] A sign of disrepute, California conjures up a chain of negative associations that reflect the region's depravity, and Ben's insistence on seeking his fortune in the mining camps only intensifies the connection between his disruptive adolescent desires and the frontier.

Despite California's strange illegibility, its lawlessness provides these young men a context within which to claim their emerging manhood as they resist its many temptations. Concerned about the camp's rampant disregard for the rule of law, Mr. Dewey observes in *Ben's Nugget* that "it is strange how this wild and lonely life effects [sic] the character."[31] Having barely escaped being lynched by a group of angry miners, Dewey questions the impact the camp's freedoms have on respectable citizenship and expresses the moral apprehension many white middle-class Americans felt about California during the gold rush.[32] Yet Alger's characters "prefer the freedom of the mining camp," for despite the "strange life [they] are leading," it is "free, and independent, and healthful."[33] When Tom Nelson travels from San Francisco to the mines, he thinks, "Here I am my own man, and don't need to run at anybody's bidding," prompting the narrator to conclude, "His wanderings had inspired self-reliance."[34] Confronting the strange lawlessness of these frontier spaces, Alger's young men thus cultivate the qualities that the boy workers of the nineteenth century so tirelessly promoted as necessary for their wards if they were to achieve respectable manhood.

Yet Alger paradoxically tempers this path to manly self-reliance by cultivating this respectability within the rural landscape of the homoerotic frontier. Figuring California as an untrammeled paradise opens up spaces for Alger's boys to nurture their affection for the older men who guide them on their journey through adolescence, the empty beauty of this paradise purifying their desire for each other. Even as Ben enjoys his fanciful daydream of solitary exploration, "he was glad, however, to have the company of Jake Bradley. . . . Had he started alone, [his chances of success] would have been much smaller, and certainly he would have found it exceedingly lonesome."[35] As self-reliant as Ben must be in order to become a man, he counters the isolating independence this journey requires by relying on the affectionate interest of other men. For Alger, manhood becomes legible not only by testing itself against the physical and ideological challenge that the western landscape poses to his imperialist impulses, but also by affirming the intimacy that unites two men as they overcome these challenges together.

Alger uses this colonial romance with the natural landscape of California to imagine a respectable form of same-sex desire that originates in the frontier's rural eroticism. He accounts for these relationships as a product of a particular historical moment, and his western novels present a different kind of history of sexual subjectivity, even as he revises it according to his own desires. As the narrator of *Joe's Luck* explains, the California gold rush fostered especially close relations between men: "In the early history of California friendships ripened fast. There was more confidence between man and man, and I am assured that even now . . . the people are bound together by more friendly ties and exhibit less of cold caution than in the East."[36] The discourse of friendship runs throughout all of Alger's novels and forming such friendships is essential for the boy hero's success in navigating the social world he is attempting to ascend. But in his re-imaging of the California gold rush, Alger endows such friendship with particular and even peculiar western qualities. Less cautious, friendlier, and more tightly bound, Californians are more amenable to Alger's homoerotic social imaginary than those who live in New York City, and their relationships are somehow more natural and authentic than those of the degenerating spaces of civilization.

Alger intensifies the erotic qualities of these distinctly western friendships by situating his colonial fantasies of manifest destiny within the biblical account of creation. Even though many writers have gendered the landscapes of the American West in terms of feminine purity, Alger

transforms virginity into a representational strategy in which rural homoeroticism can flourish.[37] When Joe and Joshua set out together for
the mining camp, Joshua becomes anxious at the idea of being so far
away from San Francisco, "out . . . in the wilderness." He feels like he
and Joe are the "only human critters in the world," which prompts Joe to
compare their situation with that of Adam and Eve's:

> "So we can fancy how Adam felt when he was set down in Paradise," said
> Joe.
> "I guess he felt kinder lonely."
> "Probably he did, till Eve came. He had Eve and I have you for
> company."
> "I guess Eve wasn't quite like me," said Joshua with a grin.
> He was lying at full length on the greensward, looking awkward and
> ungainly enough, but his countenance, homely as it was, looked honest
> and trustworthy, and Joe preferred his company to that of many pos-
> sessed of more outward polish. He could not help smiling at Mr. Bick-
> ford's remark.
> "Probably Eve was not as robust as you are," he replied. "I doubt if she
> was as tall either."[38]

In this affectionate exchange, Alger rewrites Genesis as a story of
gender-bending homoeroticism. Joe is Alger's new American Adam, a
"self-reliant and self-propelling" figure who constituted one of the dominant social imaginaries in nineteenth-century U.S. culture.[39] Yet, like
Ben's affection for Jake, Joe's preference for Joshua's awkward honesty
and his robust physique not only tempers Alger's celebration of his self-
reliance, but also recasts Eve as a robust young man in the Garden of
Eden. As the newly coupled colonizers bask in this Californian paradise,
Joe and Joshua are able to lay claim to it, Alger suggests, by virtue of
their homoerotic partnership. Their awkward honesty, robust strength,
and tender affection unite them and allow them to tame the wilderness, extracting both mineral wealth and respectable manhood from it.
For Alger, such affection moves his boy heroes through the frontier and
into adulthood; it harnesses potentially disruptive desire to their drive to
master the frontier, allowing them to secure their manhood in partnership with each other.

Just as Alger rewrites the story of Adam and Eve into a romance of same-sex affection, he reimagines older men's desires for their younger friends, legitimizing them as a form of filial love that seeks to protect the boys, restrain their adolescent appetites, and discipline them into respectability. In many of these novels, these couples must momentarily part, and when they do, the boy's absence further increases his desirability and value in the eyes of his older friend. For example, when John Miles temporarily leaves the mines, he misses Tom intensely. "That's a good boy, Tom," he thinks. "I wish he were here with me to-night. Why didn't I urge him to come with me? . . . I don't know what gives me such an interest in that boy, but I'd sooner do him a good turn than any man I know."[40] Here, John's inexplicable desire highlights the intense physical longing these men feel for their boys, for in the erotic economy of the mining camps the boy's value as a commodity exceeds that of gold. As Alger writes in *Ben's Nugget*, when Ben receives a number of friendly overtures to share claims with the miners he meets, "A boy was a rarity in California at that time—at any rate, in the mining districts. . . . The sight of [Ben's] fresh young face and boyish figure recalled to many miners the sons whom they had left behind them, and helped to make more vivid the picture of home which their imaginations often conjured up, and they would have liked to have Ben join their company."[41] Like the filial love that many mentors feel for their boys, these miners nostalgically see Ben as the embodiment of their past domestic lives. Yet as with John's desire for Tom, Ben's "fresh young face" and "boyish figure" suggest an erotic undercurrent to the miners' attention to and objectification of his physical body, even if he also represents the sons they left far behind in the East. Unable to possess him, they idealize the figure of the boy, feminizing him into a diminutive object of their melancholic longing.

But such feminization does not last, for as these intimacies mature, so do the boys. Once they accept the attention of their older men, they begin to play a much more active and equitable role in these relationships. At the very point when they strike it rich, the older man recognizes that they "have worked together, and been mutual helpers."[42] Dividing their new-found wealth equally between them reflects the boy's burgeoning manhood and refigures the nature of their relationship, signifying the near completion of his journey through the frontier.

Having used the California gold rush to recuperate adolescence, Alger invites his young readers to imagine their manhood by harnessing their appetites in the mining camps and embodying a valuable commodity in the homoerotic economy of frontier desire. Refigured as an object of desire, they can thus transform into an independent, respectable man.

The Figure of Alger's Chinaman: Not an American Man

Despite the richness of Alger's rural homoeroticism and the role it plays in reforming male adolescence in the later nineteenth century, his queer frontier more sinisterly displaces the degeneracy of a racialized sexuality onto the non-white, feminized male subject who temporarily inhabits Alger's frontier. In their adventures in California, Alger's adolescent heroes encounter other queer subjects who manifest themselves most visibly as racialized and feminized Chinese immigrant laborers. In one of Alger's intended comic interludes in *The Young Miner*, he introduces his readers to Ah Sin and Ah Jim, a pair of Chinese miners who live together in an isolated cabin and work a claim far removed from the other, mostly white camps. Their duplicitous natures, effeminacy, and the "deviant heterosexuality" of their "bachelor sexuality" contrast markedly with Tom's emerging white, middle-class manhood, showing Alger's readers what kind of men they should not become.[43]

When he introduces these characters, Alger marks their deficient manhood through their heavily accented speech. When Ah Sin watches the villain Bill Crane steal gold dust from Tom's friend and companion John Miles, he murmurs, "'Melican man very smart." As Alger explains, "My readers are probably aware that our Mongolian visitors find a difficulty in pronouncing the letter *r*, and invariably replace it by *l*."[44] Basing his characterization on racialized linguistic stereotypes, Alger uses their accents and transitory status, as well as tropes of inscrutability and effeminacy, to distinguish between and evaluate alternative codes of masculinity on the frontier, closely linking figures like Ah Sin and Ah Jim to racial degeneracy and sexual depravity. Later when Bill confronts the pair and asks them why they "don't pronounce [their] English better," they respond, "Because Chinamen not 'Melican men."[45]

In Alger's queer frontier, characters like Ah Sin and Ah Jim are pointedly not fit for American manhood, and as Karen Leong argues, depictions of the Chinese in the exclusion debates of the 1870s positioned the "Chinese male as immoral, uncivilized, and fundamentally unfit for American citizenship."[46] Despite the fact that Chinese men very much constitute a form of queer domesticity within the mining camps, Alger also reinforces a sense of their "filthy and diseased 'race,'" illustrating a larger view that Chinese interlopers were ultimately "contrary to respectable domesticity and capable of undermining American morality and family life."[47] In this way, the problem of pronunciation reflects an anxious need to define white, middle-class American manhood against a foreign body that threatens the stability of American gender regulations. Yet this anxiety grows out of the overdetermined illegibility of these foreign bodies, both in terms of language and gender.

For example, in *Ben's Nugget*, when Ki Sing, a Chinese servant to the young hero and his friends, is forced to tell a pair of white thieves who his "Melican" master is, he says, "Dickee Dawee." "The name," Alger continues, "seemed still more odd as the Chinaman pronounced it," which prompts one of the thieves to say, "Well, he's got a queer name, that's all I can say."[48] Like Ah Sin's and Ah Jim's, Ki Sing's queer speech renders the familiar strange and incomprehensible. Unlike the generative strangeness of California's cultural geography, these characters' faces and braids, their partnerships, and the seemingly comic effect of their accents signify their status as "deceptive interlopers." Such "effeminate, deviant men, unable to perform normative masculinity" contrast sharply to the white middle-class miners, who, despite their equally temporary status, feel entitled to enforce their culture of manhood on these Chinese immigrants.[49]

Most obviously, Ah Sin's name connotes immorality within the Christian cosmology of sentimental fiction. These heathens, as they are consistently referred to, exist outside the world of pious morality, and their inscrutable physical appearance reflects the distrust and even disgust that the narrator feels for them. Ah Sin's "face was smooth and bland, and wore an expression of childlike innocence which was well calculated to deceive. Ah Sin possessed the usual craft of his countrymen, and understood very well how to advance his worldly fortunes."[50] Infantilizing Ah Sin, Alger deploys the discourse of primitivism to tarnish the Chinese with a duplicitous immorality that manifests itself as racial difference. Full of "natural cunning," Ah Sin and Ah Jim easily trick another white man out of his gold. As Alger writes, "Bret Harte has not told us whether the heathen Chinese has a conscience; but if he has, neither Ah Sin nor Ah Jim experienced any inconvenience from its possession."[51] Embodying what Gary Scharnhorst terms "the stereotype of the 'inscrutable Oriental,'"[52] even sympathetic characters like Ki Sing appear unable or unwilling to reflect their internal feelings openly in their faces. Thus, Alger's Chinese characters remain mysteriously unreadable to the white men who struggle to consolidate their own masculine authority in these frontier spaces.

In a world where appearances are meant to convey the inner worth of men, the deceptive inscrutability and violence of Alger's Chinese immigrants threaten to foil the system of moral transparency that Alger's rags-to-respectability stories depend upon. They also thwart Alger's vision of a robust California populated by physically fit, hard-working young white men of the American republic. Alger's ambivalent hostility thus reveals a racialized homoeroticism—a homoraciality based on an attraction to sameness that is both racial and sexual. This homoraciality privileges the erotics of white manhood organized around the differential of age at the expense of racialized male subjects who bear the brunt of sexualized degeneracy and whose agency is limited within Alger's queer frontier.

Alger inscribes this logic onto the bodies of the Chinese men most visibly by feminizing their role within the camps. Grousing about Ki Sing's unwillingness to betray his master, one antagonist complains, "Why didn't he speak up like a man and tell me what I wanted to hear?"[53] In the confrontation that ensues, the narrator tells us, "of course, the Chinaman counted for nothing."[54] Even Ki Sing's boy companion perceives him in this way, arguing that "he wouldn't be much in a scrimmage. Them Chinamen are half women, accordin' to my reckonin'. They look like it and speak like it."[55] The speech of Ki Sing as a half-woman stands in for his "willingness to do 'feminine' work," signifying his "unnatural" role and placing him "outside the gendered divisions of labor that reinforced masculine citizenship in American society."[56] Together, his incomprehensible speech and gender codes disqualify him and other Chinese men, no matter how virtuous or loyal they may be, from embodying a legitimate form of manhood in Alger's frontier imaginary. Nor can they enter into romantic partnership with white men, for as Dewey says when Ben and Jake find him convalescing in a mountain cabin, attended only by his Chinese servant, "I was sighing for the sight of one of my own color, who would understand my wants better than that poor fellow, faithful as he is."[57] Unable to sigh for Ki Sing, Dewey's languishing desire for whiteness reveals that Ki Sing's less than ideal status as an object of white men's desire results from his racialized feminization.

It is perhaps Ki Sing's braid, though, that elicits the most violent response from his fellow miners. Although Ki Sing sees it as an "ornament of honor and male pride,"[58] for the Irish miner, Patrick O'Reilly, it marks Ki Sing's racial and sexual degeneracy. "Ain't he a beauty," he sneers, "jist wid his long pigtail hangin' down his back like a monkey's tail?"[59] For O'Reilly, the braid is a phallic symbol of Ki Sing's exotic animalistic masculinity, but one that flaunts U.S. gender conventions. This tension prompts O'Reilly to attack the Chinese servant, whom Dewey then takes under his protection, but in a way that further compromises his status in the camp. "Ki Sing followed him to his tent," Alger writes, "as a child follows a guardian."[60] Infantalizing Ki Sing, Alger presents us with a different kind of minor—not an adolescent boy who needs the guidance of an older man, but a childish primitive who can never embody manhood within this frontier setting.

What Ki Sing can be, though, is a sort of houseboy, for in the sequel to this novel, Ki Sing rescues Dewey from an accident and nurses him back to health. When Ben and Bradley discover the two in a mountain cabin in *Ben's Nugget* and decide to work the claim together, forming an industrious same-sex household, it is Ki Sing who "was cook and general servant to the party." Performing "his duty in a very satisfactory manner—better than either Ben or Bradley could have done," Ki Sing "left his white employers free to work at the more congenial occupation of searching for gold."[61] Even as Ki Sing's domestic labor allows the other men to work their claim, his presence threatens to undermine the respectability of the homoerotic domesticity that the three white men enjoy. As Nayan Shah observes, "Chinese 'houseboys' represented a gender inversion of household service that made questionable their intentions, their care, and their manliness."[62] With his "childlike and bland" smile representing his role as the ethnic angel of the house, Ki Sing thus taints the nonreproductive eros of their arrangement with his racialized, infantilized body.[63]

What these sections of Alger's novels suggest is that respectable manhood is available only to white adolescents as they journey through the California frontier and into adulthood. Yet this process depends upon encountering the deviant interloper to stabilize and normalize its own trajectory. Without the presence of figures like Ah Sin, Ah Jim, and Ki Sing, Tom's and Ben's honesty, transparency, and desire for sameness would not resonate as clearly as it does with the larger project of consolidating middle-class respectability. In Alger's frontier imaginary, becoming a man thus requires the white adolescent to read his body against the "inscrutable Oriental," projecting his own fantasy of feminization onto the figure of the Chinaman. He must distance whiteness from racial impurity while also strengthening it by protecting the effeminate, racial other. In this way, Alger's mining-camp fiction reflects the discourse from within the city of San Francisco at this time. As Shah argues, "Public health rhetoric about the contagion of Chinatown bachelor society provided white middle-class female missionaries and white male labor leaders the necessary foil against which they could elaborate the vision and norms for nuclear-family domestic life and a sanitary social order."[64]

A scene from *Ben's Nugget* best illustrates this complex interplay. On their return trip to San Francisco, Dewey, Jake, Ben, and Ki Sing lodge in the Golden Gulch Hotel, but the proprietor bridles at having Ki Sing sit and eat with his white patrons and "remonstrate[s]": "You don't mean to say you want that heathen to sit down at the table with you." Dewey defends Ki Sing, explaining, "Ki Sing is a friend of mine, though he is acting as my servant, and I want him to have equal privileges."[65] Yet in this scene, equality is not exactly equal. Dewey voices sympathy for Ki Sing and defends him, but at the precise moment that he sympathizes with Ki Sing, he emphasizes Ki Sing's service and dependence, buttressing Dewey's own independent manhood. At the same time, Dewey's defense also marks the white men as suspect, for they are guilty by association. The proprietor returns, very upset: "Strangers," he says, "I reckoned there was something wrong with you when you let that yaller heathen sit down with you. Now I know it. You ain't square respectable men."[66] Paradoxically, as their servant, Ki Sing provides the white men with the material support to help them mentor Ben into adulthood, but at the same time, his presence endangers their own claim to respectability by tainting their white homoeroticism with his queer, racialized body.

Conclusion

As much as Alger's western fiction privileges homoracial and homo-erotic desire in his protagonists' journey, his narratives ultimately require that the adolescent hero forego the manly pleasures of the mining camp and return to his family. His western life may make him a man, but this newly achieved manhood becomes legible only in the East. For example, when Tom Nelson returns to save his family's home from the wicked Squire Hudson, he uses his newfound wealth to claim authority. No longer a child, "his voice ha[s] a manly ring" when he successfully outbids Squire Hudson for his father's property.[67] In a chapter tellingly titled "Manhood," Tom's transformation from adolescent boy to property-owning man is complete. Even though his western adventures underwrite this transformation, it occurs only when he is no longer in California. Although Tom must escape the challenging economic conditions of his eastern home to romance his manhood in the rural West, Alger suggests that these adventurous interludes come to an end in service to his boys' re-immersion into the histories they sought to break with in the first place if they are to count in the social order.

In spite of the heteronormative insistence that these young men must leave California's homoerotic frontier, the endings comprise such a brief moment in the actual narrative, it is tempting to resist the closure they work so hard to create, in part because the texts themselves flirt with other possibilities. Certainly, a number of Alger's heroes end up married and living in the East, but just as many do not. These unmarried heroes return to the West and remain bachelors, continuing to circulate Alger's fantasy of an all-male social world within the West, even as the frontier's material reality shifted with increasing white settlement in the latter part of the nineteenth century. Keeping this queer sensibility alive within places like Denver and San Francisco, these men insinuate their desires for sameness and whiteness into the regional future of these western cities.

The significance of Alger's queer frontier, then, is how it illustrates the assumptions about same-sex desire in a period in which "intense, passionate relationships between two similar [same-sex] souls thrived in addition to . . . and alongside marriage."[68] But Alger's novels take the ubiquity of men's passionate desires for each other and suggest an alternative to the categorical possibilities of sexual identity that were coalescing around these late-nineteenth century writers. In his western fiction, Alger normalizes such desire through an eager embrace of the middle-class values of self-restraint, pluck, and independence that he believed ought to ground the United States as it expanded and continued to industrialize.

In this way, Alger's novels work hard to imagine a nonpathological form of male intimacy located within the North American frontier. But in purging these desires of their degeneracy, Alger's queer project perpetuates an equally haunting dehumanizing of the racialized sexual subjectivities of Chinese manhood. Distinguishing between an orientation toward the same and a dismissal of difference, his novels thus reveal the representational price alternative sexual subjectivities often pay for belonging to the modern U.S. nation state. The recuperation of one kind of disruptive desire is possible only at the expense of demonizing and excluding other marginal desires and bodies. The rural eroticism of the queer frontier may serve to actualize young white men, but it ultimately must be shed and displaced onto the bodies of those men who cannot comprise the nation.

NOTES

1 Scharnhorst with Bales, *The Lost Life of Horatio Alger, Jr.*, 15–38, 43–65.

2 Brewster Standing Committee to Charles Lowe, March 19, 1866, Andover-Harvard Theological Library, Harvard Divinity School, Cambridge, MA, quoted in Scharnhorst with Bales, *The Lost Life of Horatio Alger, Jr.*, 66–67. Italics in original.

3 Kidd, *Making American Boys*, 1–22. See also Rotundo, *American Manhood*, and Bederman, *Manliness and Civilization*, 1–44 and 77–120.

4 As one young gentleman tells Dick, "You're a queer boy," marking his antisocial bent and framing it in terms of his vagrant life and the pleasure he takes in flaunting social convention. His subsequent domestic romance with Henry Fosdick connects the rehabilitation of the depraved male adolescent and the erotic imaginary of middle-class respectability. Alger, *Ragged Dick and Struggling Upward*, 30. See Zuckerman, "The Nursery Tales of Horatio Alger," 191–209; Moon, "The Gentle Boy from the Dangerous Classes," 87–110; and Hedler, *Public Sentiments*, 82–109.

5 Alger, "Writing Stories for Boys—IV," 37.

6 See Hall, *Adolescence*; Demos and Demos, "Adolescence in a Historical Perspective," 632–38; Kett, *Rites of Passage*; Moran, *Teaching Sex*, 1–22; Kidd, *Making American Boys*; and Baxter, *The Modern Age*, 1–43.

7 See Turner, "The Significance of the Frontier in American History." For urban histories of homosexuality, see Chauncey, *Gay New York*; Katz, *Love Stories*; and Boyd,

Wide Open Town. For studies that attend to the rural histories of same-sex desire, see Howard, *Men Like That*, and Boag, *Same-Sex Affairs*. For a critique of the urban bias in queer studies, see Tongson, "The Light that Never Goes Out." See also Weston, "Get Thee to a Big City," and Johnson, "Camp Life."

8 See Herring, *Queering the Underworld*, for an analysis of early-twentieth century writers who somewhat similarly refuse to identify within such sexual systems.

9 Burgett, "Between Speculation and Population," 122, 146.

10 Love, *Feeling Backward*, 39–40.

11 Zuckerman, "The Nursery Tales of Horatio Alger," 198.

12 See Brace, *The Best Method of Disposing of Our Pauper and Vagrant Children*; Brace, *The Dangerous Classes of New York and Twenty Years' Work among Them*; The Children's Aid Society, *The Crusade for Children*; and O'Connor, *Orphan Trains*.

13 Alger, *Strive and Succeed*, xiii.

14 Alger, *Ragged Dick*, 105. See also Hendler, *Public Sentiments*, 101–9.

15 Turner, "The Significance of the Frontier in American History," 3.

16 Alger, *Julius*, 1.

17 Ibid.

18 Ibid., 25.

19 Ibid., 31.

20 Ibid., 78.

21 Ibid., 135.

22 Moon, "The Gentle Boy from the Dangerous Classes," 94.

23 Alger, *Julius*, 58.

24 Ibid., 146.

25 Alger, *Dean Dunham*, 193.

26 Alger, *Joe's Luck*, 130.

27 Ibid., 97.

28 See Johnson, *Roaring Camp*, 99–183.

29 Alger, *Tom Thatcher's Fortune*, 104.

30 Alger, *The Young Explorer*, 20, 21, 84, 15–16.

31 Alger, *Ben's Nugget*, 156–57.

32 See Johnson, *Roaring Camp*, 99–183; Roberts, *American Alchemy*; and McLean, "Opposition to the California Gold Rush" 87–94.

33 Alger, *The Young Miner*, 220, 258.

34 Alger, *The Young Explorer*, 122, 185.

35 Ibid., 121.

36 Alger, *Joe's Luck*, 130.

37 See Smith, *Virgin Land*.

38 Alger, *Joe's Luck*, 137–38.

39 Lewis, *The American Adam*, 5.

40 Alger, *The Young Miner*, 61.

41 Alger, *Ben's Nugget*, 115–16.

42 Alger, *The Young Miner*, 270.

43 Ting, "Bachelor Society," 277.

44 Alger, *The Young Miner*, 66.

45 Ibid., *The Young Miner*, 76.

46 Leong, "A Distinct and Antagonistic Race," 132. See also Wong, "Cultural Defenders and Brokers," 7; and Bederman, *Manliness and Civilization*, 29.

47 Shah, *Contagious Divides*, 2, 77.

48 Alger, *Ben's Nugget*, 39.

49 Sears, "All that Glitters," 395. For a discussion of the "sojourner mentality" within nineteenth-century Chinese immigrant communities, see Tsai, *The Chinese Experience in America*, 34–35.

50 Alger, *The Young Miner*, 65.

51 Ibid., 72–73.

52 Scharnhorst, "Ways that Are Dark," 394.

53 Alger, *Ben's Nugget*, 46.

54 Ibid., 79.

55 Ibid., 97.

56 Leong, "A Distinct and Antagonistic Race," 144.

57 Alger, *Ben's Nugget*, 18.

58 Scharnhorst, "Ways that Are Dark," 381.

59 Alger, *The Young Explorer*, 207.

60 Ibid., 223.

61 Alger, *Ben's Nugget*, 25.

62 Shah, *Contagious Divides*, 89.

63 Alger, *The Young Explorer*, 248.

64 Shah, *Contagious Divides*, 12.

65 Alger, *Ben's Nugget*, 118.

66 Ibid., 121.

67 Alger, *The Young Miner*, 268.

68 Rupp, *A Desired Past*, 43.

3

Sherwood Anderson's "Shadowy Figure"

Rural Masculinity in the Modernizing Midwest

ANDY OLER

Sherwood Anderson's 1920 novel *Poor White* queers the countryside—
but not by attending to LGBT sexualities, nor by developing rural queer
identities.[1] In this novel, rural people and spaces resist normative definition. They disrupt nostalgic views of the country and participate in
an ambiguous, contradictory modernity. Protagonist Hugh McVey, for
instance, does not fit the common stereotypes of rural masculinity, and
his social eccentricities give him "the reputation of being queer."[2] In *Poor
White*, Hugh wanders through the Midwest, lands in the small Ohio town
of Bidwell, rises as an inventor, marries Clara Butterworth, and eventually
loses his job. Hugh's early life is split between his poor white father and
Sarah Shepard, the railroad station agent's puritanical wife, two influences
that evoke historical conflicts between Upland Southerners and migrant
Yankees.[3] Despite Hugh's reputation for queerness, then, Anderson constructs him as a prototypical Midwesterner in a manner that reflects the
region's cultural and economic history. Grappling with this mixture of
dreaminess and drive, which complicates his ability to form meaningful social relationships, Hugh seeks recourse through mobility, work,
and (usually halting) interactions with women. Using terms both individual (iterations of self-made and corporate masculinity) and communal
(migration, urbanization, mechanization), *Poor White* demonstrates its
attention to Midwestern cultural geography. Anderson clarifies this interest when the novel shifts emphasis, combining Hugh's story with rising
tensions in Bidwell between the town's rural agrarian and urban industrial
economies. In this combination, the novel suggests how regional, masculine, and modern identities have developed alongside, and been disrupted
by, each other and the period's socioeconomic changes.

Focusing on Hugh, other characters, and the town itself, this essay claims that *Poor White* queers the structures of normative rural masculinity. In this novel's version of the modernizing Midwest, nostalgic visions of rural masculinity—the self-made farmer or merchant artisan in a community-building and offspring-producing marriage relationship—prove insufficient. This becomes clear early in the novel when Hugh leaves his hometown of Mudcat Landing: "'Well, I'm going away, I'm going away to be a man among men,' [Hugh] said to himself over and over. The saying became a kind of refrain and he said it unconsciously. As he repeated the words his heart beat high in anticipation of the future he thought lay before him" (22). In this passage, Hugh plans to join an ill-defined abstraction: an unnamed and un-located, but presumably successful, group of men. Hugh assumes both his own future success and that it will occur in relation to other men. Along with the group's abstraction and non-location, Hugh's excitement and unconscious repetition suggest that Anderson universalizes and idealizes a definition of masculinity that relies on homosocial competition, mobility, and future productivity.[4] Conversely, Hugh's universalized expectations of manhood also challenge their normalization. Building on Eve Sedgwick's claim that challenges to normativity must happen within "an entire cultural network of normative definitions,"[5] I argue that the novel's sexual and socioeconomic normativities also reveal their instabilities, which create alternate possibilities for characters and the town alike.

Above all, Hugh's alternate possibility consists of the shadowy figure of a group of men—successful, future, and elsewhere. Throughout the novel Anderson both invests in that ideal and creates a space in which it does not have to exist. By merging masculinized economic expectations with an abstracted space of production and then returning the novel's action to the localized setting of a small town, Anderson suggests the existence and potential viability of queer rural spaces for those characters and communities who—independent of sexual orientation—seek usable alternatives to the teleologies of a modernizing rurality.[6] But while Anderson sees promise in Bidwell's version of a flexible, accommodating rural modernity, he also indicates the challenges of modern rural masculinity. For example, evoking the abstraction of the imagined group of men, Hugh melds ruralized and urbanized abstractions to invent a mechanized cabbage transplanter, a concrete representation of modern rurality. Ultimately, however, he cannot balance the town's socioeconomic ambiguities and conflicting cultural expectations, and he withdraws from the promising space he helped create.

Reincorporated Rural Modernity

Hugh's search for a queer rural space begins almost immediately after his departure from Mudcat Landing. Upon arriving in an Iowa town, Hugh walks out of town to a hill overlooking the Mississippi River. There, thoughts about his boyhood demonstrate the tensions within *Poor White*'s modern rurality.

> The long summer Sunday afternoons had been delightful times for Hugh, so delightful that he finally gave them up, fearing they might lead him to take up again his old sleepy way of life. Now as he sat in the darkness above the same river he had gazed on through the long Sunday afternoons, a spasm of something like loneliness swept over him. For the first time he thought about leaving the river country and going into a new land with a keen feeling of regret. (27)

Scenes such as Hugh's retreat from town and subsequent nostalgia for the "delightful times" of his youth lead many critics to complain that Anderson's writing is overly sentimental and nostalgic.[7] While the rural space enables Hugh's nostalgia, however, that same space and Hugh's existence in it are simultaneously modern. This passage emphasizes the inconsistency and complication of Hugh's feelings, which affect his experience and use of space. For example, alongside his excitement for the travel, he also regrets leaving his home country. And despite his desire for the company of successful men, he removes himself from town into the darkness and loneliness of the countryside. Thus, while *Poor White* acknowledges nostalgic modes, it juxtaposes them with more modern ways of experiencing the countryside. In that inconsistency, Hugh and the novel both define and disrupt the normalized aspects of rural modernity and masculinity.

Hugh's and Bidwell's rural modernity resist the dominant narrative of urban-industrial modernity, which economically devalues and culturally subordinates rural people and places.[8] Alan Trachtenberg has called

these socioeconomic changes and the accompanying cultural narrative "incorporation," which he defines as "the emergence of a changed,
more tightly structured society with new hierarchies of control, and
also changed conceptions of that society, of America itself."[9] Focusing
on urbanization, industrialization, and the rise of corporate capitalism, Trachtenberg explains the centralization of control and power in
American society. Although he notes that "the process [of incorpora-
tion] proceeded by contradiction and conflict,"[10] he tracks the ways
that individuals, communities, and the state were expected to become
more efficient and consolidated. In *Poor White*, Anderson explores this
tighter structure of economic and cultural hierarchies. He starts with
communal changes to Bidwell and the Midwest, naturalizing turn-of-
the-century socioeconomic changes by describing them as derived from
"a vast energy [that] seemed to come out of the breast of earth and infect
the people" (128). Furthermore, the novel's engagement with incorporation filters down to the individual level in the way that Hugh and other
characters negotiate communal change and social expectations.

Hugh's negotiation of these broad changes can be seen in the way he
responds to the region's "vast energy" (128) with a "queer determined
light [shining] in his small gray eyes" (17) but also counters that energy
with a tendency to "weariness and loneliness" (37). Hugh's response indicates how *Poor White* represents the relationship between individual
and communal in rural Midwestern communities, and it suggests how
Anderson invests in the shift away from definitions of masculinity
predicated on economic self-determination. While masculinity studies
scholars have emphasized this shift's relationship to growing urban centers, Trachtenberg's focus on the process of incorporation indicates how
industrial manufacturing entered farming communities, confronting
rural people with newly hierarchized forms of management and economic competition.[11] Hugh McVey, Anderson's version of a composite
Midwesterner, demonstrates how the incorporation narrative affects and
may be challenged by an individual male operating within the framework of modern rurality. For example, Hugh's cabbage transplanter is
inspired by rural needs and produced in a rural setting. However, capitalist speculators finance the machine, and Anderson undermines the
pastoral setting by representing the moment of invention in a quavering
modernist style in which the twilight makes Hugh appear terrifying to

a family of farmworkers. Engaging narratives of rural masculinity and industrial modernity, Anderson suggests that rural spaces, people, and products participate equally in a broad-based, shifting network of economic influences and social formations.[12]

Through a character who bridges the nostalgic self-made man and the incorporated company man, *Poor White* resists teleologies ranging from incorporation to common conceptions of literary temporality. Raymond Williams, for one, argues that a long tradition of British and Classical literature represents the country nostalgically and the city as a space of futurity. The present, then, can only be "experienced as a tension" between them.[13] Williams relegates rural spaces to a nostalgic framework of representation, which pairs easily with widespread critical acceptance of Anderson's affection for ruralized spaces, people, and values. The combination suggests that Anderson might have been expected to accept Van Wyck Brooks's 1918 charge that American authors should recover a "usable past" as a way to cope with modernity.[14] As seen in *Poor White*, however, Anderson's representation of the countryside is not entirely nostalgic, but is entwined with Hugh's inventiveness and, more generally, its potential as an active socioeconomic force. Benjamin Spencer notes that "as late as 1939 [Anderson] could declare that he did not know what a 'usable past' is, and that his concern was rather to live intensely in the present."[15] Anderson's refusal to acknowledge the historical basis of Brooks's usable past suggests a similar resistance to the nostalgia that Williams indicates is usually used to represent the country.

Rather, this novel entwines rurality with what Williams would call the future-oriented industrial economy, articulating the temporal middle ground within Williams's theory. In *Poor White*, that middle ground diminishes Brooks's historical depth and emphasizes a network of multiple discourses interacting with each other in the present. These range from the gender and economic expectations of Hugh's desire to be "a man among men" to the affective experiences suggested by representing the countryside as a dark and lonely place. Anderson, then, suggests that Midwestern rural modernity necessarily develops a *usable present*, combining the novel's present-oriented temporality with Brooks's interest in usability. But Anderson does not eliminate the past from this novel, which includes examples of self-made men as well as nostalgically represented rural community and land use. *Poor White's* usable present queers the countryside by *re*incorporating elements of the past alongside capitalist desires for growth and increased wealth. In particular, it is a challenge to define Hugh's character exclusively—as rural or urban, nostalgic or modern, independent or corporate—and this suggests that the novel retains a nostalgic vision of independent rural masculinity while also investigating the possibilities of a modernized corporate version.

Conditional Usability

Poor White suggests that modern rurality and rural masculinity resist the nostalgia of Brooks's "usable past" as well as the teleologies of urban industrial incorporation. Hugh McVey and Bidwell reincorporate ruralized identities, spaces, and products into American and Midwestern modernity, which requires them to negotiate a broad range of experiential and socioeconomic discourses. In this formulation, individuals and communities necessarily must be highly and immediately reactive, lest they be pushed aside by any among a variety of forces. Characters attempt to achieve a usable present by balancing a variety of social, economic, and gender expectations. That they must do so in a region undergoing a messy and contradictory process of modernization demonstrates the multiple contingencies at work in this novel as well as the resulting challenges to Bidwell, Hugh, and *Poor White*'s other male characters.

In Bidwell, the local economy provides the key structures of social organization. Men's strength in a largely homosocial workplace, then, extends to an enhanced position in the community at large.[16] The novel's representative example of this new rural economy is the capitalist speculation of Steve Hunter and his (male) investors:

> Steve took no chances. He engaged Ed Hall to go at night and replace the plants that did not live. "It's fair enough," he explained to Ed. "A hundred things can cause the plants to die, but if they die it'll be blamed on the machine. What will become of the town if we don't believe in the thing we're going to manufacture here?" (126–27)

Hunter's fraudulent promotion of the cabbage-setting machine results from his stated desire to make the town "believe in" the cabbage-setter and suggests that Anderson entrusts communal well-being to Bidwell's male industrialists. At this point in the novel, the life of the town is presented as primarily economic in nature and tied to incorporation's inherent organizational growth; here, Hunter attempts to create the conditions necessary for that growth.

In this instance, men stereotypically access the town's socioeconomic hierarchy via quantifiable notions of economic success. But Anderson also indicates the limits of economic achievement as a descriptor of usable masculine identities. Specifically, in *Poor White*, masculinity seems to rest on the ability to participate broadly across social groups, balancing many groups' demands alongside enduring expectations of quantifiable professional success. Steve Hunter's command to replace dying cabbage plants indicates an attempt to satisfy both "skeptical farmers" and "town enthusiasts" (126) about the machine's performance. The machine's failure is immaterial to Hunter, however, as he is more concerned about the machine's reception than its successful performance. This decision may be read as Hunter's creating his own usable present by engaging the various forces and demands at work on him to fashion the conditions for his and his business's positive growth. Notably, Hunter's actions designate a shift away from figures such as Wainsworth the harnessmaker, a "vastly independent" "tradesman of the old school" (51), who is more concerned about quality craftsmanship than widespread acceptance.

Hunter promotes modernization and economic growth as a means to improve his socioeconomic position in Bidwell, an action largely in keeping with arguments made by masculinity studies theorists that the construction of modern masculinity is based on homosocial competition. Historian George Chauncey suggests that men in the early twentieth century did not define themselves solely by attempting to obtain power over women, but rather expressed masculine anxiety by concerning themselves with their "relative virility compared to other men's."[17] *Poor White* includes a literal application of Chauncey's argument, in terms of competition for women seen via various attempts to court Clara Butterworth, but it is secondary to the novel's metaphorical treatment of the concept of competition for socioeconomic place in a changing economy. Women's entrance into the factory system is absent from this competition, eliding the workplace experiences of Midwestern women and potentially losing a great deal of attendant social complexity. But in terms of masculine experience, Chauncey's theory of competitive virility neatly matches Hunter's behavior throughout the novel. Hunter's argument regarding the complex possibilities for the cabbage plants' death suggests a concern for advancing his position relative to other men, which he attempts to do by eliminating organic instability and taking control over every element of the machine's production and reception. His attempt reveals two key concerns for this essay: first, that Anderson does not present a unified theory of the land's place in rural modernity, and second, that this novel tracks a transitional moment of gender definition. In this period, gendered conceptions of labor were unstable, particularly in terms of masculinity, which transitioned from a "self-made" ideal into other forms. Self-made manhood valued control—especially self-control—and developed within the context of relative autonomy in the workplace. Along with the growth of centralized industrial capitalism, however, that control became less attainable for most men.

Hunter attempts to eliminate the land's effects on the cabbage plants, an ethically suspect attempt to control his community of investors by controlling environmental factors. In this situation, even the soil becomes embroiled in the corporate economy: rather than a relationship in which the land and its tenders are mutually constitutive, Anderson suggests a more fragmentary approach to modernity in rural settings. Prior to the cabbage plants' replacement, Hugh brought concerns to Hunter that the machine was "too heavy to be handled by one team . . . would not work when the soil was either too wet or too dry, . . . [and] worked perfectly in both wet and dry sand but would do nothing in clay" (121). While rural people and products are essential to *Poor White's* conception of modern rurality, this is not the modernized version of a pastoral idyll. Instead, rural production relies upon industrial production, but the land is occasionally at odds with the factory.

Anderson queers the countryside by merging the socioeconomic structures and normative gender identities of a smaller, ruralized community with the new ones developed in the process of industrial urbanization. Bidwell residents therefore experience modern social and identity fragmentation, which can be seen in the farmworkers' terror and in Clara's disappointment in returning to the country. As a result, Anderson depicts a still-rural community that also corresponds to characteristic descriptions of modernity. The difference between Bidwell and standard definitions of modernity, of course, stems from its comparatively rural location and economic structure. The very representation of this community may then be seen as an act of modernist fragmentation, upending urban-oriented definitions of modernity and removing a single assumed narrative in favor of plurality. The result is that such ruralized Midwestern representations become central to literary modernism, with locations such as Bidwell providing authors and audiences both a counterpoint and a growth point. Anderson represents Bidwell, in particular, as an exemplar of this kind of rural modernity, as the people "rush[ing] pell-mell into a new age" (128) are the ruralized residents of farms and small towns across the Midwest.

I argue that one of *Poor White*'s key projects is to explore how the "pell-mell" chaos of the region's changing socioeconomic structures affects male characters' abilities to construct workable modern identities across gender, racial, and geographic lines. In his responses to the novel's other characters, the Bidwell community, and the broader socioeconomic changes at hand, Hugh McVey becomes Anderson's prime example of an individual male's attempt to construct a usable rural masculinity. He attempts to ameliorate perceived faults in his personality and gender identity, for instance, by turning to "the study of mathematical problems . . . to relieve his loneliness and to cure his inclination to dreams" (55). Furthermore, Hugh's measured, solitary study of mechanics indicates how he negotiates Bidwell's "rush . . . into a new age" of manufacturing. Anderson suggests that the key challenge and strategy for many Midwesterners was to attempt to balance competing discourses and incorporate elements of each of them into a usable, present-oriented identity that was reactive and synthetic. Here, a key problem for Hugh is that his rational reaction, rather than providing balanced usability, places him on a path to the incorporated identity definitions common to narratives of modernity. Indeed, from Hugh and his father to Hunter and Wainsworth, Anderson's strategy for representing the difficulty of this historical moment can be seen in the stories of *Poor White*'s men: while an individual white male can take action to improve his class standing, economic success in this environment presents a danger of conflating personal and communal benefits, which makes him more likely to fail at attaining a usable identity.

Contingency, Mobility, Balance

Throughout *Poor White*, the economic and affective transitions exemplified by a character such as McVey are tied to his travels throughout the Midwest. The novel emphasizes mobility and changeability as means to a usable masculine identity, suggesting that, for men, creating and manipulating a usable present in the modernizing Midwest requires not only balance and flexibility but also a willingness to change perspective. For Hugh, changing perspective means, variously, his migration from Mudcat Landing to Bidwell, his career shift from telegraph operator to inventor, and his tendency to wander when puzzled. For Bidwell, the major spatial and socioeconomic shifts are due to the effects of incorporation on both the community and its individuals. For the novel, "Hugh's first inventive effort stirred the town of Bidwell deeply" (70), creating slippage between individual and community by constructing both Hugh and Bidwell as inclined toward attempts at a usable rural present. But despite Hugh's willingness to revise his social and spatial position, Anderson ultimately writes him as failing to sustain a usable present. Hugh's successes are always contingent, which suggests that the attempt to create and sustain a personal usable present remains challenging even in a regional environment that is conducive to it.

Throughout the novel, Hugh's personal challenges are frequently mental obstacles of some sort—related to work, relationships, or his past. His response to those challenges is to wander, changing his position by walking the roads and countryside in an attempt to better comprehend and react to his situation. The following passage, in which Hugh attempts to think through the difficulties in his marriage to Clara, suggests how the spatial experience of rural modernity affects and is informed by modern gender experiences:

> For hours he walked blindly, but it did not occur to him that as he waited, hating the waiting, Clara also waited; that for her also it was a time of trial and uncertainty. To him it seemed her course was simple and easy. She was a white pure thing—waiting—for what? for courage to come in to him in order that an assault be made upon her whiteness and purity.
>
> That was the only answer to the question Hugh could find within himself. The destruction of what was white and pure was a necessary thing in

life. It was a thing men must do in order that life go on. As for women, they must be white and pure—and wait. (316)

Despite the novel's marginalization of women, Hugh's and Clara's gender experiences posit a fundamental similarity between masculine and feminine experiences of modernity. However, while similarities in their concurrent "waiting," and their "trial[s] and uncertaint[ies]," may be read as an interest in improving equality between the sexes, it does not seem to enhance relationships between individuals of different genders. In this passage, the reason that misunderstandings remain between people having otherwise equal experiences appears to be that Hugh is operating with outmoded gender role expectations. He assumes that Clara is a figure of purity rather than the educated woman and participant in modernity that she is presented to be.

That Hugh walks to assist his thinking while Clara sits at home underlines certain conflicts between them: namely, while they have similar modern relational anxieties and temporal experiences, their differences in gender role experiences and expectations affect their relationships to hierarchies of capital and power. Hugh's attempts to comprehend the difficulties of his relationship therefore focus on balancing the various influences on his conception of his personal identity and his prescribed social role. Anderson signals the act of balancing by showing Hugh walking, which indicates Hugh's attempt to change his position and his relationship to those discourses—in other words, using mobility to revise the spatial component of his experience. However, Anderson undercuts Hugh's potential success first when he indicates Hugh's blindness in the endeavor. Each step seems ill-fated as Hugh attempts to create a usable present for himself. Though Anderson spatializes Hugh's experience to provide him the ability to balance multiple discourses, Hugh remains blind to the ways in which those discourses interact, suggesting that the attempt will end in failure. Anderson also undercuts Hugh's potential success through his hatred of the experience of waiting for the courage to approach Clara. That hatred constitutes an affective exclusion of normatively and nostalgically defined gender roles such as courageous masculinity and submissive femininity and signifies Hugh's inability to balance the gender and socioeconomic discourses in which he participates.

Notably, Hugh's mobility does not follow the incorporation narrative's developmental teleology. Rather, his blind walking, his travels throughout the Midwest, and his choice to settle in Bidwell suggest a more circuitous route reincorporating rural elements—from working on farms to settling in "Pickleville" (59) to farm labor inspiring his invention—alongside the urbanizing manufacturing economy.[18] Hugh walks to stimulate his thoughts, but his walking usually fails to generate any sustained thought and instead results in a formless musing. Another passage in which Hugh "left his shop and went for a walk" (352) demonstrates how Hugh's economic rise limits his and the novel's resistance to incorporation. While wandering, Hugh reflects on his life from the time "when he was striving to come out of the filth, the flies, the poverty, the fishy smells, the shadowy dreams of his life by the river" to his inability to negotiate "a problem that could not be solved in wood and steel" (352). Here, Anderson taps into the Horatio Alger myth of a young man made good through hard work, assisted by a successful man's altruistic act to remove him from the slums.

Drawn into the world of modern industry by stationmaster Shepard and his wife, Sarah, Hugh is largely separated from his father and the filthy, shadowy culture of his birth, eventually working up—in his unconscious, dreaming way—to a more lucrative and powerful economic position. Anderson does not end Hugh's story on this Alger-style economic up-note, however, as this passage indicates his engagement with another prevalent literary narrative of the late nineteenth century—the fall of the great man, of the character whose ethical or moral failings cause him to fall from a successful socioeconomic position, as seen in W. D. Howells's *The Rise of Silas Lapham* (1885), Booth Tarkington's *The Magnificent Ambersons* (1918), and Theodore Dreiser's *Trilogy of Desire* (1912–1947).[19] But unlike the characters in these novels, Hugh does not fall prey to greed or overextension; rather, he gets caught up in a modern corporate economy that has asked him to approach his work differently.

In *Poor White*, Hugh's inventions are inspired by local farmworkers, not by profit-oriented machinations of the corporate economy, and Hugh struggles when he is forced off of his chosen developmental track. Hugh's dreaminess has merged with the Shepards' work ethic to create a working style that synthesizes many elements of his background and current environment. Early in *Poor White*, Steve Hunter capitalizes on Hugh's inventive talents, but at this point has asked him to shift his work into reverse engineering in an attempt to get around an Iowa inventor's patent on a hay-loader. However, because Anderson has positioned Hugh as a successful inventor by constructing Hugh's creativity as a synthesis of the many discourses at work on him, Hugh's talents are unsuited to Hunter's profit motive. Hugh believes that "he had lived but little in the life of the imagination, had been afraid to live that life, had been warned and re-warned against living it" (352), suggesting that he is so limited in regard to abstraction that he is unable to be productive in his new economic position.[20] If Hugh's imaginative productivity is predicated on his ability to balance influences, however, then Anderson might be seen in this passage as actually criticizing Hugh for passively accepting the task. As Anderson's prototype of modern Midwestern masculinity, Hugh must reincorporate rural influences and inspirations into his work; accepting a profit-oriented reverse engineering task means that he loses part of the synthesis that originally enabled his success.

Hugh's apparent passivity and modified economic position demonstrate the tensions within Anderson's representation of normalized masculine economic roles. As Hugh wanders, while "he should have been making new parts for the hay-loading apparatus," his thoughts turn toward "the shadowy figure of the unknown inventor in the state of Iowa, who had been brother to himself, who had worked on the same problems and had come to the same conclusions" (352–53). Describing the Iowa inventor as "shadowy" recalls Hugh's birth culture and the "wavering uncertain light" of the cabbage field (81), and it also emphasizes the tension within the Iowa man's position as both brother and competitor to Hugh. As his rurality-inspired brother, the Iowa man evokes Hugh's greatest personal and professional successes—seeing some problem in the life or work of people around him and addressing that issue, thereby tapping into the communal life in which he desires to take part. As a competitor, however, the Iowa man's invention of the hay-loading machine suggests that he has beaten Hugh and, according to Chauncey's argument about masculine competition, positioned himself as more masculine and capable. But, along with Hugh's changed position, their parallel problems of comprehension—Hugh's inability to clearly envision the Iowa man just as, earlier, the farmworkers in the cabbage field could not comprehend Hugh's appearance—suggest that perhaps we should not read their relationship as being solely competitive. In this way, Anderson seems to be critiquing the boundaries of masculinity even as he reinscribes their effects on the individual.

In the above passage and throughout the novel, Hugh's mobility might easily be explained using a pattern of American masculinity that Michael Kimmel contends was prevalent from the nineteenth century forward: "American men try to *control themselves*; they project their fears onto *others*; and when feeling too pressured, they attempt an *escape*."[21] For Kimmel, flight is a normative response to masculine anxiety, enacted in response to failures of self-control or of economic self-improvement. But Hugh's consideration of the men of his past does not demonstrate an attachment to normatively defined imitative or competitive masculinity. Rather, when "thinking of the Iowa man, Hugh began to think of other men. He thought of his father and of himself" (352). Hugh's thoughts about masculinity skip among himself, his father, the station master, and the Iowa inventor. Kimmel's idea of escape inadequately explains this mental parallel to Hugh's physical wandering.

Rather, Hugh's directionlessness seems designed to help him find a queer space—that is, to negotiate the novel's complex, "shadowy" network of thoughts and emotions. According to George Chauncey, "many middle-class writers" used "light and shadow . . . to characterize the different class worlds and moral orders coexisting in the city."[22] Anderson draws on images of queer urban sexuality to indicate the moment's complexity and suggest the multiple ideas and identities available to Hugh. In *Poor White*'s rural setting, shadows are variously associated with the passage of rural time, the factory economy, and individual thought processes. Therefore, when "the shadows of the trees lengthened" (196), when "in the corners of the old building shadows lurked and distorted thoughts began to come into his head" (97), or when Hugh contemplates "the shadowy figure of the unknown inventor" (352–3), *Poor White*'s shadows do not signal queer sexualities. Instead, they suggest possible gender identities and uses of space exceeding what is available in Bidwell's brightly lit thoroughfares. Despite his attempt to negotiate his emotions, Hugh appears unprepared to balance the various historical influences and present demands on him: "Hugh tried to think of himself and his own life. For a time that seemed a simple and easy way out of the new and intricate task he had set for his mind. His own life was a matter of history. He knew about himself" (353). Hugh nominally resists normative definitions of masculinity, but he cannot engage in the balanced incorporation of multiple discourses that Anderson suggests is a condition of usable, modern rural masculinity. His literal and figurative mobility instead devolve into a meandering, anti-teleological quandary and result in his retreat to a simple solution predicated on personal history.

Shadowy Figures, Rural Ambiguities

At the end of *Poor White*, Hugh returns home to Clara, and they stand outside amidst the sounds of farm and factory. This passage has received a good deal of critical attention, much of it addressing the novel's moral and narratological ambiguities. Irving Howe, for example, finds the novel's ending "most unsatisfactory" because of Anderson's "curious aversion to dramatic conflict."[23] Robert Morss Lovett also criticizes the ending but places fewer moral and structural demands on the novel: "*Poor White* does not end—it merely stops [but] . . . no ending is better than a false one, and perhaps any emphasis would be misplaced in Mr. Anderson's cosmos—or chaos."[24] This essay intervenes in the shadowy middle ground between Howe's criticisms and Lovett's sense of the novel's universality (benevolent or malignant, depending on "cosmos—or chaos"). I read the novel's ending as shadowy, indeterminate in how it resists reduction to a single defining element of masculine, economic, or spatial experience. Moreover, I contend that the ending's ambiguity, and the reason Howe points out a lack of conflict between the characters, is due to the intensified importance of Bidwell as a modern rural space that juxtaposes the urban futurity of a factory whistle with the gently nostalgic "sounds of farm animals stirring" (363).

That indeterminacy demands the reincorporation of a wider range of concerns, which suggests the methods and challenges of Anderson's and Hugh's attempts to create a usable present in and with the novel. Leo Marx notes the challenges of balancing multiple influences—in other words, of creating a usable present—by reframing critical discussion of literary shortcomings in political terms: "the inability of our writers to create a surrogate for the ideal of the middle landscape can hardly be accounted artistic failure."[25] In the phrase "middle landscape," Marx refers to a Jeffersonian ideal of mechanically improved agrarianism, "a happy balance of art and nature."[26] He suggests that nineteenth- and twentieth-century American writers have failed to update that ideal but attributes their failure to the displacement to the literary realm of what is primarily a sociopolitical problem. Building on Marx's point, I accept Anderson's failure in creating a usable present, but resist the attribution of utopian ideals to *Poor White*. Rather, I argue that the novel's ambiguity—its shadowy-ness—is a solution in itself, albeit imperfect, an attempt to create a usable present that does not rely exclusively on one temporal, spatial, or generic element. Anderson's engagement with modern rural masculinity thus requires reincorporating nostalgic, ruralized values alongside the future-oriented visions of economic modernization, of rural spaces and production alongside urban factory towns.

As a result, Anderson's greatest success in imagining a usable present lies not with Hugh McVey, Clara Butterworth, or modernized gender roles, but in Bidwell's potential to accommodate queer spaces. Throughout the novel, Anderson provides broad sociocultural descriptions of Bidwell that would not be out of place in sociological studies of the period, and the novel's broad strokes undeniably contribute to a generic confusion typifying widespread anxiety about the social experience of modernity.[27] Anderson fancied his novel to be a sociological document anticipating the documentary turn of Depression-era social fiction, and he claimed in a 1934 letter that *Poor White* was "'a kind of classic' illustrating 'the destructive influence of present-day uncontrolled industrialism.'"[28] Attaching a high level of social importance to his novel, Anderson theorizes the artist's relationship to society as revelatory and even prophetic; the Great Depression seems only to have emboldened his self-fulfilling claims on the novel's descriptive and predictive powers. Coupled with Anderson's description of *Poor White* in his introduction to the 1925 Modern Library edition, in which "the town was really the hero of the book,"[29] we begin to see a theory of ruralized geographic and social spaces as intimately incorporated into modern conceptions of socioeconomic order. In *Poor White*, the connection between characters and the land is not simply a preordained harnessing and directing of the land's power by those characters; nor is it a Marxist abstraction of the fall of capitalism. Rather, reading the town as the novel's main character suggests that it has a potentially unpredictable narrative arc much as any other character. It also indicates that Anderson's use of geography and collectivity is spatially oriented but not ultimately fixed to an outcome generated by the area's past.

Uncertainty permeates *Poor White*, at least partly because of the constant adaptations of Bidwell's manufacturing economy. For a time, Hugh's inventions energize Bidwell, its socioeconomic shifts allow the community to develop a usable present, and Hugh achieves his desire to become "a man among men." Still, his masculine ideals retain their shadowy ambiguity, and eventually Hugh is marginalized within his community and from the company of men. Although Hugh finds a balance between Upland Southerner and migrant Yankee, and between ruralized inspiration and urbanized manufacturing, he becomes a byproduct of the system for which he served as both catalyst and most visible success. Hugh's exclusion joins other byproducts of a usable rural present, including the labor shift from farm to factory, the demise of characters with residual identity definitions such as harness-maker Joe Wainsworth, and the challenges posed by shifting gender roles. While Anderson presents an optimistic reading of the possibilities for rural spaces, *Poor White* also demonstrates the profound instability of a usable rural present for individuals as well as communities. In queering the countryside, then, this novel explores the costs and opportunities of doing so. It offers the normative and declines it, both for people and for places. As a result, *Poor White* proposes that we read the countryside itself as a "shadowy figure," one that includes all the chaos of modern industrial America alongside elements of a nostalgic agrarianism.

NOTES

1 *Poor White*'s main representative of LGBT sexualities is Kate Chanceller, Clara Butterworth's college friend and love interest, whose sexuality (and socialism) is relegated to urban Columbus, Ohio. She disappears from the narrative prior to Clara's college graduation.

2 Anderson, *Poor White* (1993), 54. Further references to this edition of *Poor White* will be in the form of in-text parenthetical citations.

3 During U.S. westward expansion in the eighteenth and nineteenth centuries, the two major groups settling the Old Northwest came from northeastern and southern states. Many scholars have addressed the sociopolitical and economic conflicts that developed out of this combination of "Yankee" and "Upland Southerner," including Power, *Planting Corn Belt Culture*; Adams, *The Transformation of Rural Life*; Etcheson, *The Emerging Midwest*; Wilson, *Yankees in Michigan*; and Gray, *The Yankee West*. Scholars who have explored similar issues of intra-American cultural conflict between

"Puritan" and "Pioneer" include Brooks, *Van Wyck Brooks, the Early Years*, and Hegeman, *Patterns for America*.

4 For further reading on definitions of and challenges to normative masculinity in this period, see Chauncey, *Gay New York*; Kimmel, *Manhood in America*; Bederman, *Manliness and Civilization*; and Rotundo, *American Manhood*. For the concept of "male homosocial desire," I am drawing on Sedgwick, *Between Men*.

5 Sedgwick, *Epistemology of the Closet*, 11.

6 Halberstam, *In a Queer Time and Place*, explores "queer spaces" within "metronormativity," the standardized narrative of individuals' urban migration.

7 Discussion of Anderson's sentimentality and nostalgia for rural and small-town life is widespread among literary critics, ranging from Fiedler, *Love and Death in the American Novel*, to more recent scholarship such as Hegeman, *Patterns for America*; Clymer, "Modeling, Diagramming, and Early Twentieth-Century Histories of Invention and Entrepreneurship"; Farland, "Modernist Versions of Pastoral"; Gelfant, "A Novel of Becoming"; and Hogue, "From Mulberries to Machines." For a counterargument, see Van Doren, *Contemporary American Novelists, 1900–1920*.

8 Recent work in literary studies explores modernism and modernity in ruralized U.S. settings, challenging long-held assumptions of urbanity as the default location for scholarly definitions of modernism and modernity. See Herring, *Another Country*; Comentale, "'The Possibilities of Hard-Won Land,'"; and Farland, "Modernist Versions of Pastoral." For urban-oriented definitions of modernism and modernity, see Parrington, *Main Currents in American Thought*; Giddens, *The Consequences of Modernity*; and Berman, *All That Is Solid Melts into Air*. Berman calls rural-to-urban migration the "archetypal move . . . for young people" in modern society (18).

9 Trachtenberg, *The Incorporation of America*, 3–4.

10 Ibid., 7.

11 For urban-oriented discussions of the diminishing importance of economic self-determination, see Chauncey, *Gay New York*, and Kimmel, *Manhood in America*. A notable, rural-focused exception to the scholarship on masculinity at the turn of the century can be found in Ownby, *Subduing Satan*.

12 Examples of twentieth-century historical narratives in which American rural and urban economies develop in relation to each other can be found in Cronon, *Nature's Metropolis*, and Hamilton, *Trucking Country*.

13 Williams, *The Country and the City*, 297.

14 See "On Creating a Usable Past" in Brooks and Sprague, *Van Wyck Brooks, the Early Years*, 219–26.

15 Spencer, "Sherwood Anderson," 4.

16 *Poor White* problematically marginalizes its female characters, evoking common historical and representational concerns about the treatment of rural women. See Casey, *A New Heartland*; Murphy, "Journeywoman Milliner"; Neth, *Preserving the Family Farm*; Holt, *Linoleum, Better Babies, and the Modern Farm Woman, 1890–1930*; Hampsten, *Read This Only to Yourself*; Fink, *Agrarian Women*; and Adams, *The Transformation of Rural Life*.

17 Chauncey, *Gay New York*, 80.

18 "Pickleville," an area outside of Bidwell where a cucumber factory formerly stood, likely is patterned after "Sauerkrautville," a nickname for Anderson's hometown of Clyde, Ohio, according to Rideout, *Sherwood Anderson*, 1:135. These, alongside Ohio towns Celeryville, Wheat Ridge, Wheatville, and Farmersville, indicate a kind of local pride in rural production.

19 This trope falls in line with a broader concern in literary realism over the effects of increasing wealth on individuals and the moral challenges of a changing socioeconomic order, which has been explored in Kaplan, *The Social Construction of American Realism*; Martin, *Harvests of Change*; and Berthoff, *The Ferment of Realism*.

20 According to Tichi, *Shifting Gears*, Anderson's writing is nostalgic and broadly anti-technology. While I agree that Anderson underscores the losses and the hardships that coincide with Bidwell's new-built factories, he also notably details the excitement of the time alongside benefits to a variety of individuals.

21 Kimmel, *Manhood in America*, 9; emphasis in original.

22 Chauncey, *Gay New York*, 44.

23 Howe, *Sherwood Anderson*, 82.

24 Lovett, "Mr. Sherwood Anderson's America," 37.

25 Marx, *The Machine in the Garden*, 364–65.

26 Ibid., 226.

27 See Berman, *All That Is Solid Melts into Air*. In considering generic confusions, James Agee and Walker Evans famously walk the line between documentary and fiction in *Let Us Now Praise Famous Men* (1941). Furthermore, a sociological study of a small Midwestern city that shares several narrative and descriptive characteristics with *Poor White* can be found in Lynd and Lynd, *Middletown*.

28 Quoted in Rideout, *Sherwood Anderson*, 2:193.

29 Anderson, *Poor White* (1926), vi.

4

A Classroom in the Barnyard

Reproducing Heterosexuality in Interwar American 4-H

GABRIEL N. ROSENBERG

In June of 1934, Oliver Edwin Baker, a senior economist at the United States Department of Agriculture (USDA), told 4-H leaders that the nation faced a dire crisis of reproduction. Less than two years before, the eminent economic geographer offered similar warnings to the American Association of Geographers in his presidential address: "A nation must protect and preserve the children. . . . If conditions become unfavorable to the reproduction of the race, the first objective of national policy . . . should be to restore the favorable conditions."[1] Speaking to the adult chaperones of hundreds of rural youth who had traveled to Washington, D.C., for the National 4-H Camp, Baker emphasized the role of 4-H members in preventing this crisis of "reproduction" by starting their own healthy farm families. In 1934, nearly one million youth enrolled in the voluntary 4-H clubs organized by the USDA. Recognizing the popularity of the program, Baker told the assembled leaders that they could help "restor[e] . . . the family as the fundamental institution of society." Baker believed 4-H kept rural youth on farms to rear another generation of Americans in the moral, fertile embrace of the countryside. Throughout the 1930s, Baker peppered 4-H with speeches, pamphlets, and essays about his vision of an agrarian America reinvigorated by the reproductive labor of rural youth.[2]

This essay examines the effort of the American state to govern rural bodies, family life, and "heterosexual relations" in the countryside through a diffuse and sprawling network of 4-H clubs. These clubs originated in turn-of-the-century efforts to make American agriculture more rational, profitable, and efficient. Apostles of scientific agriculture targeted rural youth through clubs, contests, and home demonstrations, promising to improve participants' four Hs: head, heart, hands, and health. Youth-oriented methods enrolled local volunteers, bypassed critics, and provided a nonthreatening image for technocratic expertise. On the strength of this system of agricultural extension, Congress created a permanent appropriation for the USDA's Cooperative Extension Service (CES) in 1914. By the 1920s, 4-H clubs circulated the USDA's preferred technical methods and created robust alliances of technocratic expertise, private capital, and local voluntary labor throughout the United States.

Although the early 4-H program was narrowly concerned with the technical details of commercially profitable agriculture, its purview soon came to encompass the bodies and psychologies of its youthful charges. The focus of 4-H broadened from the efficient production of commodities, to the cultivation of reliable agricultural laborers, and, finally, to the stabilization of cultural norms of gender, race, and sexuality. By the 1930s, 4-H health programs pushed rural youth to produce healthy bodies capable of laboring and reproducing for the nation and positioned technocratic authority at the center of rural family life and social reproduction. 4-H material asserted that the economic and biological union between a revenue-producing male "farmer" and a nurturing "farmer's wife" constituted both the ideal and normal form of organization for rural life. In rural communities, popular media, and on the floor of Congress, the USDA and advocates of club work advertised the virtues of federal planning by using images of wholesome, white 4-H'ers conducting gender-appropriate labor on family farms.[3]

What, then, should we make of O. E. Baker's striking vision for 4-H as a reproductive prosthesis for a barren nation? Although Baker rehearsed clichés of nostalgic agrarianism, his vision of fecund 4-H'ers populating the future sheds light on the broader ambitions of the New Deal state. Historians note the profound transformation of American governance during the interwar period, which was marked by expanded social welfare spending, taxation, and economic regulatory capacity, but they often limit their analyses to the federal state's formal abilities to demand and force compliance from its regulatory objects. However, this period also witnessed a fundamental rearrangement of the American state's relationship to the body, which proceeded through the state's efforts to define the boundaries of normal sexuality, families, and reproduction. Historian Margot Canaday forcefully argues that the early twentieth-century federal government observed and policed sexual identities in military, immigration, and welfare institutions and laid the foundation for pervasive institutional heteronormativity after World War II.[4] This delimiting of homosexuality in the organs of the state accompanied federal efforts to promote heterosexuality and pronatalism.[5] As an ideology celebrating procreation and healthy reproduction, pronatalism held that the personal and collective management of life was a paramount objective of the American state, and, thus, ample justification for Baker's reproductive prosthesis.

Baker's speech, and the history of interwar 4-H, confirms Canaday's suggestion that historians of the state and historians of sexuality would benefit from an extended dialogue. Just as historians of the state must pay closer attention to how sexuality has constrained, rerouted, and produced state power, historians of sexuality must also consider how statist technocracy shaped modern sexual identities. But such a call for complementarity begs a thornier question: *Where* is the state and *where* is sexuality in this historical inquiry? Scholars of American political development, the American West, and environmental history document that, despite their alleged geographical marginality, nonmetropolitan spaces have been central to the story of American state-building through rural focused agencies like the Departments of Agriculture and the Interior, water-resource and massive infrastructure projects, and the federally overseen genocide of indigenous populations.[6] Historian William Novak contends that a "bottom-up" history of a sprawling state at the "peripheries" of the American polity is essential to understanding the putatively democratic governance America now exports.[7] Novak suggests that the history of global neoliberal governance runs through the American hinterlands. As Michel Foucault and his interlocutors demonstrate, such governance depends on the biopolitical management of life, often through the "self regulating capacities of subjects" and heuristics of "normal" families, bodies, and sexuality.[8] If historians know something about state-building and political economy outside cities, they still know little about the American state's efforts to produce and regulate sexuality in the countryside.

The difficulty in locating a biopolitical state in nonmetropolitan American has only been intensified by disciplinary silence around histories of rural sexuality. However, as this volume demonstrates, recent scholarship questions the division between urban sexualities and an enveloping field of normal heterosexuality by showing, for example, how queer life thrived outside of cities. My own complementary strategy is to question the stability and permanence of rural heterosexuality. I argue that the history of heterosexuality is linked to the biopolitical ambitions of the American state in these seemingly peripheral and remote spaces. The contemporary circulation of the "family farm" as an aspirational ideal foregrounds how such ambitions have permanently shaped understandings of sexual normalcy in both town and country. Given the term's lack of cultural salience prior to the 1930s, its promiscuous deployment by contemporary food activists, among others, signals the internalization of the USDA's pronatalist and eugenic ideal. Heterosexuality's *national* articulation and normalization were inseparable from the particular logistics of governing life, love, and desire in the countryside.

The history of 4-H illustrates that larger process. In the 1920s, 4-H clubs created relationships among state authorities, medical professionals, and rural bodies through health programs that popularized federal authority in rural America through the image of wholesome and attractive country youth. In the following decade, club organizers parlayed that reputation into pronatalist schemes to pair and mate "perfect specimens." Club experts attempted to train rural youth for marriage and "heterosexual relations," to contrive rural heterosexual romance, and to educate rural youth about the sexual nature and function of their bodies. This effort circulated and ultimately normalized heterosexuality as a foundation of an idealized rural life. On 4-H's family farm, the hand of the state groomed young rural people for their sexual potential, just as 4-H boys groomed their prized sows. 4-H's commitment to breeding the best met the biopolitical logistical challenges posed by the emergence of positive eugenics and pronatalism in interwar America.

Building Biopolitical Capacity in the Countryside

Early twentieth-century American culture abounded with intertwined nostalgic agrarianism and narratives of rural decline. On the one hand, nostalgic agrarianism held that country living was intrinsically superior to urban living. The narrative of rural decline, on the other hand, took nostalgic agrarianism's mythical rural past as the counterpoint to a debased and deteriorating rural present. Very real rural poverty existed, but rural progressives lacquered that truth with generous applications of moralism and class condescension, frequently eliding the economic and racial inequalities that drove rural suffering. This tendency was especially apparent in elite discussions of rural health. Agricultural progressives tended to ignore the role of resource disparity in discussions of rural health and focused almost exclusively on the role that ignorance played in generating rural squalor and blight. Reformers announced that rural people needed to obey medical professionals and public health authorities.

By the 1920s, the 4-H network joined this cause and parlayed access to rural youth into health improvement programs in rural communities. These programs featured local health examinations, sustained health education, and county and statewide health contests, creating new connections between medical professionals, extension officials, and rural people. Gertrude Warren, a senior girls' club specialist at the USDA, urged county extension and home economics agents to concentrate on health promotion work in 4-H. "In conferences, talks in public, and in publicity articles, emphasize ways in which the health of club members is being looked after through club works," Warren wrote in a manual on girls' club work in 1925. 4-H promoted good health by "tak[ing] farm girls out of the field [and] into the home," teaching them how "to keep health score cards," and enrolling them in "health club contests."[9] In 4-H health contests, doctors and nurses examined club members at county and state fairs, judged them according to a standardized score card, deducted points for defects, and, ultimately, selected a winning boy and girl as perfect "specimens."[10] By 1925, building on existing rural enthusiasm for similar "beauty" contests for babies, women, and livestock, health contests had already emerged as one the most highly publicized components of the entire 4-H program, receiving constant plaudits in newspapers for producing the "perfect boy and girl," as a headline in the *Washington Post* put it.[11]

Iowa 4-H offered one of the earliest templates for a comprehensive health program built around competitive health contests. In 1921, extension officials devised the idea of a state-wide 4-H health contest to promote better health practices and bring publicity to the extension service's rural health initiatives. County 4-H health champions assembled in Des Moines and received examinations from doctors affiliated with the Polk County Medical Association, which also provided a standard score card for the contest's use. In its inaugural year, boys and girls from half of Iowa's counties vied for the health state championship. In 1922, seven Iowa counties used the standard score card and formal medical examinations to determine which 4-H'ers should be submitted to the state competition. By 1930, ninety-two counties reported doing so, examining over 4,400 Iowa girls in the process.[12]

The effectiveness of Iowa's 4-H health program hinged on the score card—a device that permitted both medical professionals and club members to scrutinize bodies and quantify their copious "defects." The Iowa score card was composed of over seventy particular metrics, covering categories as diverse as the flushness of the lips, the symmetry of "sex characteristics," the shape and position of ears, and the quality of posture. Score cards covered health dimensions influenced by habit and behavior, but also evaluated "birth marks," flat feet, an "abnormally shape[d]" skull, and the "general impressions" of physical attractiveness.[13] Contests recognized both winners and members who had improved their scores over the course of successive examinations. This ensured that all participants, even those who were initially infirm or sickly, had motivation to have "some defects corrected [and] bring up her standing for next year."[14] Examinations enabled medical authorities to quantify both the defects and potentials of 4-H bodies, and they generated valuable bodily knowledge that could be mustered into personal or cooperative health activities executed over the course of months. The overwhelming majority of participants in 4-H health programs were female (often as high as 90 percent). Examinations made female bodies the subject of intense and invasive scrutiny, usually by male medical professionals.

Examinations provided an entrée for intensive "follow-up" work on the part of girls, agents, and medical professionals. In Webster County, for example, girls received two examinations over the course of the year. The first examination identified "any bodily defect" and prescribed improved "healthy habits." When girls were "scored down" for poor posture and skin, a local doctor lectured them about "physiology and hygiene." Based on the doctor's recommendations, the girls scored themselves at home for twelve consecutive weeks and then received a second examination to chart progress.[15] After using a similar "follow-up" system, an agent in Hancock County lauded the results. Thanks to health talks from medical professionals, club girls "looked much better than they did last spring."[16] With adequate follow-up work by medical experts and extension agents, rural youth would execute their own private plans for personal health improvement.

Given Iowa's results, similar 4-H health programs appeared in other states. Within a year, the Iowa program had inspired identical health competitions for club members at major livestock expositions in Sioux City and Chicago. The latter competition was rebranded as the National 4-H Health Competition in 1922.[17] An American Medical Association survey in 1931 reported that 40 percent of all responding medical associations cooperated with 4-H to conduct medical examinations that qualified members for the national competition.[18] By 1930, more than 100,000 U.S. youth were annually enrolled in 4-H health projects and examinations.[19]

Distressed by the paucity of boys in 4-H health programs, USDA specialists devised a health curriculum suitable for boys' agricultural clubs. As home economics specialists, the women who led girls' clubs had often studied human anatomy and health. But most county agents and male leaders lacked any training in *human* physiology and health, explained Miriam Birdseye, a USDA nutrition specialist.[20] Birdseye encouraged male agricultural agents to use their knowledge of animal and plant biology and recommended that, when speaking to boys in the context of a dairy or livestock club, club leaders and agricultural agents "us[e] a well-developed club boy, and show how these points parallel the points used in stock judging. . . . Mention parallels between the food-habits score card used by club members and good practices in feeding the kind of livestock raised by the club."[21] Birdseye suggested that club agents organize a course for club boys to show them that they were subject to "the same laws that govern the growth and development of other living creatures" and should accept their personal "responsibility" for "the improvement of the race."[22] At a 1929 extension conference, Birdseye demonstrated her methods to an audience of agricultural agents. Birdseye presented a fine calf and "pointed out its many signs of good health." Then, "as the calf was led away, its place was taken by three boys, 10, 12, and 14 years of age, dressed in track pants, with legs, feet, and torso bare." Birdseye scrutinized the boys' physiques in parallel fashion. Though the boys were preselected to display only peak fitness, they demonstrated the "different types of build and coloring" found among white adolescents.[23]

The equation of healthy rural youth with well-bred livestock fit seamlessly into the broader popular celebrations of 4-H health champions as the "healthy specimens" of a wholesome, gender-appropriate middle-class white rural lifestyle.[24] 4-H health competitions, more than any other aspect of the 4-H program, received coverage in local, regional, and even national newspapers, including the *New York Times*, the *Washington Post*, the *Los Angeles Times*, and the *Chicago Daily Tribune*.[25] Newspaper accounts frequently referred to the youth as attractive and fit and provided photographic evidence with the articles. An account of the 1928 National 4-H Health Competition, for example, lauded champion Thelma Svarstad of South Dakota for her "blond, clear skinned" appearance, while the *Times* of Alden, Iowa, celebrated Tennessee's Marguerite Martin as the "ideal of perfect health."[26] These media accounts also emphasized that this attractiveness was a natural outcome of a wholesome, gendered rural lifestyle. For boys, this meant a robust physique gained from helping out on the farm, playing on athletic teams, or hiking in the woods. For girls, it meant no makeup, helping mother in the kitchen, and getting beauty sleep. Florence Smock of Florida, the 1929 National 4-H Health Champion, "use[d] no rouge nor lipstick but ha[d] rosy cheeks" and, despite going on a "few dates," was always in bed by nine o'clock. Harold Deatline, the champion on the "masculine side," had "broad shoulders and [was] strong muscled because of 'plenty of good, hard work' on his father's farm." Deatline sternly reported that he did not "care for dancing or 'gadding about.' For recreation he [went] hunting and fishing sometimes."[27]

Newspapers focused on winners, but ignored the "defective" contest losers and the tens of thousands of non-white 4-H'ers systematically excluded from competing. Throughout the South, African American extension services prioritized rural health programs. Nearly 20 percent of all 4-H'ers in the South were African American, and they also regularly received lessons on hygiene and health from black county agents. In places like Arizona, the extension service considered health promotion an important component of work with "Mexican" and "Indian" girls.

And, yet, the National 4-H Congress permitted only white 4-H'ers to compete.[28] Nor did media accounts rhapsodize about "perfect" non-white bodies. Media descriptions conflated whiteness and attractiveness when lauding the pristine skin and hair of winners. The publicity associated with 4-H health competitions circulated the ideal 4-H body as white and, simultaneously, suggested that state experts, in cooperation with a well-ordered farm home, could produce this perfected white body.

Even as club work created relationships among rural Americans and medical professionals, it also advertised directly to rural America the benefits provided by extension services. By circulating the image of perfected white youth, 4-H could convince rural America that county agents could be trusted with the most sensitive of activities. And by producing healthy rural youth, the extension service promised to protect them from the physically degrading elements of farm life and to shelter them from the sexual depravity of the city. As the 1920s came to a close and the countryside sank deeper into economic depression, club organizers recognized that 4-H's reputation for producing wholesome, healthy youth could be used to bolster the nation's reproductive future.

From Farm Bodies to Farm Populations: Pronatalism in 1930s 4-H

The tumult of the Great Depression and the ensuing expansion of federal visibility in rural America reshaped how federal authorities conceptualized rural youth. USDA demographers reported that the national birthrate was dropping precipitously, buttressed only by a high rural birthrate. Given that reality, the USDA believed farms had a crucial new role to play in the future: rural-reared people had always been the nation's best, but now they would once again be the nation's most plentiful. New Deal employment and conservation programs could capture youthful passion and energy, but the source of discontent for many youth was as much emotional as it was economic. As Gertrude Warren explained, foreign youth movements exploited the violent, unpredictable behavior of youth driven by disintegrating home life and eroding opportunities for marriage. Over the 1930s, 4-H organizers focused on how they could train rural youth for healthy, wholesome marriages and "heterosexual relations"—training that required 4-H members to culti-vate pleasing selves and 4-H leaders to cultivate wholesome club spaces conducive to heterosexual romance. By the end of the decade, 4-H edu-cated its members about family, sex, and marriage, transforming clubs into sexual education classrooms.

Because of a declining birthrate, the extension service assumed the responsibility of maintaining both the rural birth rate and a supply of rural youth reared in wholesome farm families. USDA rural sociolo-gist Robert Foster told the 1931 National 4-H Camp that the institution of the family ensured "the reproduction of the race" and was "the best means of securing a satisfactory social control of reproduction." Family life, however, was threatened by recent events. The urban divorce rate was "too high." Nevertheless, "most problems of marriage and family life [were] remediable thru education and training" that 4-H could provide to rural youth.[29] Reflecting on the "general decline in the birth rate," Gertrude Warren agreed that early family education and training were vital.[30] Warren urged extension workers to use club work to fortify the "important institution" of the rural home. Only with a healthy home life and strong family relationships would rural youth be able to resist the temptations of city living. CES Chief Clarence Smith noted that the demographic trends meant a monumental "responsibility" was "thus placed on the farm family," as well as "on the 4-H clubs" and the various institutions dedicated to strengthening the farm family.[31]

4-H could help rural youth meet this "responsibility" by directing inchoate sexual impulses towards a managed heterosexuality. Club ex-perts presented the "human mating season" of adolescence as a cluster of impulses that were exclusively opposite-sex oriented and procreative.[32] Gertrude Warren called it an "instinctive desire," while agricultural economist Eugene Merritt pointed out that "all creatures . . . feel a drive or urge to . . . seek someone of the opposite sex . . . and establish a new home or nest."[33] Ensuring that this nascent urge resulted in healthy reproductive outcomes required careful attention on the part of club leaders and organizers. Dr. Hedley Dimock, a prominent educational theorist, told the 1935 National 4-H Congress that mixed-sex activities in 4-H clubs performed the vital service of socializing healthy "hetero-sexual relations." Homosociality "tragically" ensured sexual maturation would take place only "in a vacuum" that left boys too aggressive and girls unprepared to restrain them. Rampant promiscuity might ensue. Under the watchful eye of the county agent or local volunteer at a 4-H picnic, dance, or meeting, rural youth could be escorted into productive heterosexuality.[34]

4-H camp emerged as an important arena for heterosexual socialization. Away from parents and surrounded by new friends, in settings that emphasized leisure and socialization, 4-H youth had ample opportunities for flings and romances. One camper reported that the Minnesota 4-H Conservation Camp educated attendees about ecology and heterosexual romance by integrating courtship into nearly all of the camp's ceremonies and rituals. Camp organizers paired boys and girls and had them "march" as "partners from the assembly to the banquet," and for a candle-lighting ceremony at the headwaters of the Mississippi, camp organizers directed each boy to invite a girl to accompany him. "Emphasis again was placed on companionship," explained the camper.[35] Into the early 1940s, Arizona 4-H'ers joked about romantic camp dalliances in the pages of a publication titled the *News*.[36] "Who's the handsome guy, Charlotte? Couldn't be E.M., could it?" wrote Dorothy Ingle and Tommy Patterson from Cochise County about a budding couple. "Ruth C., can you tell us where tall, dark, and handsome is this year? We hope you haven't been too lonesome!!!" mused Nadene Bishop of Maricopa County, referring to Ruth C.'s past camp romance.[37] References like these confirmed that relationships often blossomed at camp, frequently with the encouragement of camp organizers.

Organizers strived to make other components of 4-H programs as amenable to heterosexual romance. Gertrude Warren approvingly reported that a number of state extension services were organizing mixed-sex events that could offer the "opportunity for [club girls] to meet fine, manly young men."[38] By 1936, many states attempted to comply with these recommendations. Elda Jane Barker, a home demonstration agent from Allegheny, New York, described a joint event her girls club held with a livestock club. It began with "meat-cutting" and "canning" demonstrations. Then the girls prepared a banquet for the boys, after which all attendees "adjourned to the Wee Blue Inn for a dancing party." G. W. Litton, an agricultural agent in Tazewell County, Virginia, described how he had ensnared local youth with "the '3 p's' . . . pretty, personality, and parties. Young people are interested in things that pertain to

themselves and to the opposite sex."[39] Litton's comments indicated that
4-H could serve rural youth both by providing them with opportunities
to meet prospective romantic partners and by helping them to develop
personalities and bodies pleasing to the opposite sex.

Club material asserted that cultivating a pleasing self was hard work,
but was necessary for long-term heterosexual fulfillment. West Virginia
State girls' club agent Hallie Hughes, for example, described this labor
of "self management" at the 1931 National 4-H Camp: "The individual
self must be studied, analyzed and trained. . . . Self management must be
practiced."[40] At the same camp, Robert Foster linked self-cultivation to
the ability to attract a mate and to long-term marital success. Foster suggested that good social graces and the maintenance of "personal appearance" allowed couples to amicably share domestic space. Because 4-H
could help rural youth develop self-control and a pleasing personality, it
was similarly well situated to foster these healthy family relationships.[41]

Foster's approach laid a conceptual foundation for much of the "family work" done by 4-H clubs over the course of the 1930s. Gertrude Warren praised Foster's efforts, noting that at the National Camp and local
club meetings, club members "discuss[ed] qualifications for successful
home partnerships" and became aware of "the desirable qualifications
to look for in choosing a mate." Such conversations had also "helped"
club boys shed onerous "habits," strengthen self-mastery, and attract
suitable mates.[42] Over the 1930s, USDA and CES experts advised club
leaders and members on the best routes to develop happy family relationships.[43] At the same time, 4-H literature focused on teaching boys
and girls alike how to cultivate a self that would be pleasing to the opposite sex. The January 1938 edition of the *National 4-H Club News*, for
example, listed for the benefit of its readers "the most frequent failings of
boys and girls," itemized according to "What Boys Dislike in Girls" and
"What Girls Dislike in Boys."[44]

As important as personal appearance and a pleasant personality might
be for attracting the opposite sex, 4-H literature also stressed that a girl's
long-term marital prospects depended upon her fitness as a mother
and wife. Club literature advanced the proposition that performance of
gendered "domestic" labor was intrinsically linked to a successful marriage and successful heterosexuality. Female club members scored and
recorded their "mothering" skills in projects that used younger siblings

and the children of neighbors as surrogates for their future children. By 1940, many states had integrated childcare projects into girls' club programs. Alabama 4-H provided extensive information on childcare and nurturing in "Senior Girls' Club" literature.[45] Similarly, "little mothers" Catherine Barnes and Betty Freeman applied their club lessons to the care of their nephews and nieces, winning national attention and accolades in the process. Barnes, a sixteen-year-old from Florida, "mothered 20-months old nephew Bryant for two weeks last summer while his parents took a much needed vacation."[46]

For 4-H girls, fit motherhood meant robust physical health. Although there was little programmatic uniformity from state to state, some 4-H clubs used their health entrée with rural girls to launch broader discussions of maternal health that warned against sexual promiscuity. Iowa 4-H stressed that girls needed to care for themselves with future motherhood in mind. Dr. R. E. Parry, a physician in Scranton, Iowa, who addressed the 1936 Iowa 4-H Girls State Convention, announced that 4-H health examinations were ideal for "getting acquainted with the future mothers of our community." Young mothers, Parry complained, were too "modest" about their bodies and thus hesitated to seek prenatal advice and care. 4-H examinations broke the ice and allowed doctors to "educate the future mothers" and provide a "moral influence." Parry assured his audience that he "put the fear of God in their heads in regard to sex and venereal diseases" and told "them of the actual results of stepping over the moral lines of intimacy between sexes."[47] By 1939, the Iowa extension staff made sure to include material on "Mental Hygiene for the Adolescent" and "Venereal Disease Information" to all 4-H leaders for use in clubs.[48] By the outbreak of World War II, the American Social Hygiene Society encouraged its affiliates to show films about the threats of venereal diseases in 4-H clubs. Other clubs arranged to have their members' blood tested for syphilis and gonorrhea.[49]

Discussions of motherhood in health and home economics clubs provided a context to discuss "sex education" and venereal diseases for 4-H girls, but the situation for 4-H boys was more complicated. A study of sex education among 7,500 Wisconsin high school boys from 1939 found that 7 percent received their "sex education" from 4-H clubs, suggesting that at least some discussion of sexual reproduction in boys' 4-H clubs was common.[50] Many discussions of human health were likely to involve some mention of reproduction and, depending on the perspective of the club leader, potentially social hygiene. Although 10 percent of the total 600,000 4-H boys were enrolled in health projects by 1940, some health information was provided through models of nonhuman biology in agricultural projects, which managed to educate boys about human reproduction. One popular graphic, developed by Birdseye and circulated in club publications in the 1930s and 1940s, depicted varying types of "quality" in corn and boys. For corn, the graphic displayed the spectrum from "the nubbin" on the far right— corn fit only for feed—to a "perfect" ear on the left whose kernels could be used as "seed" for another generation of corn. With this visual grammar transposed to the boys below the corn, the graphic formed an enthymeme endorsing eugenic restrictions. By implication, the boy corresponding to the nubbin—defective and unhealthy—was unfit to reproduce, while the robust youth below the perfect ear provided the seed for the future.[51]

Invocations of nonhuman biology in the context of human health did not necessarily constitute "sex education," but the labor involved in livestock breeding projects communicated sexual knowledge. 4-H literature was reticent about the animal sex act, but animal husbandry manuals provided boys with more explicit details. A superlative breeding project required a boy to select animals to be bred on the basis of registered lineage and desirable heredity traits. In cooperation with an experienced breeder, boys monitored a female animal's reproductive cycles, kept undesirable mates away, and, eventually, had her "serviced" by the male animal when she was in heat.[52] Such practices provided boys with a ready heuristic for human bodies in the form of livestock. Other breeding manuals explicitly connected the practical experience of animal breeding to human sexuality. New Jersey farmer, 4-H organizer, and geneticist Dr. James E. Russell argued in *Heredity in Dairy Cattle* that there was very little difference between human and bovine reproduction. "As long as marriages are fancy free," Russell explained, "the outcome will be a human population comparable to our mixed cattle—scrubs, grades, and pure-breds as they come."[53] Harry Cook, another manual author, warned that the disregard of the "applied science" of breeding and "the importance of race improvement" was akin to "a biological joy ride with a high cliff at the next turn." Cook urged that government should sterilize the "feeble-minded," create extensive "tabulated pedigree[s]," and restrict marriage licenses on the basis of "genetic compatibility."[54]

4-H, Popular Eugenics, and the Everyday Biopolitical State

Russell's and Cook's eugenic appeals were hardly exceptional for their moment in American history. By the 1930s, the belief that expert breeding could perfect human bodies contributed to the enactment of sterilization laws in dozens of states. Despite extensive criticism of this assumption from geneticists and biologists beginning in the 1910s, such eugenic measures enjoyed sustained popularity, and eugenic sterilizations continued in many states late into the twentieth century. Daniel Kevles argues that critics of human eugenics forced a turn toward eugenics advocacy in the 1930s that eschewed sterilizations and other coercive measures in favor of the voluntary use of contraceptives and policies to encourage the fittest to breed more prolifically.[55] "Reform" or "positive" eugenics still lauded able bodies produced by heteronormative white families and thus depended on established pronatalist celebrations of white middle-class rurality.[56] The novelty of positive eugenics lay in the belief that governing agents had the capacity not only to cull obviously defective bodies through a brutal and clumsy exercise of state-power, but also to engage in the more sophisticated task of guiding fit bodies and psychologies into fruitful procreation.

Discussions of the history of eugenics too often linger on debates about the legal right and scientific feasibility of managed reproduction, but the history of 4-H directs our attention to the *everyday biopolitical logistics* implicit in eugenic regulation. Early twentieth-century Americans argued about whether the government should engage in eugenic regulation, just as geneticists and biologists quarreled about the mechanisms of human inheritance, heredity, and genetics. But what accounted for the belief that government possessed the practical capacity to execute eugenic regulation? Why did some Americans believe that the state could inspect particular bodies, ascertain their reproductive potential, and intervene accordingly?

In mental institutions, prisons, courts, Indian schools, and border stations that acted on the bodies of criminals, mental patients, immigrants, and wards of the state, these questions entailed less of a logistical challenge. With "feeble-minded," defective, and unfit persons relegated to the boundaries of the nation and society's margins, the physical control and social abjection of them lubricated the practice of negative eugenics. In the great interior of the American social body, where state actors might be remote and the targets of eugenic regulation capable of evasion, the logistical problem was more daunting and only heightened by the emergence of reform eugenics. The targets of positive eugenics were not localized in state institutions; they were distributed throughout the state's territory and unlikely to fall under its gaze in asylums, courts, or migratory way stations.

4-H health programs provided a partial solution to this biopolitical logistical quandary. Health programs brought the bodies of 4-H'ers into voluntary, everyday contact with state and medical authorities and allowed those authorities to generate knowledge about the fitness and reproductive potential of the bodies of rural youth. Celebrations of the "perfect specimens" of club work advertised the wisdom, trustworthiness, and capacity of 4-H, medical authorities, the CES, and the USDA. Not only did 4-H assemble cultural norms about the desirability of able, white bodies; it also taught rural Americans that governing actors had the capacity to assess and manage those bodies. 4-H solved the logistical quandary and boldly announced itself as the solution. As American culture turned more noticeably to pronatalism in the 1930s, this reputation positioned 4-H as an ideal mechanism for positive eugenics. 4-H educated rural boys and girls about the sexual possibilities of their bodies and provided wholesome romantic opportunities, all in an effort to socialize healthy heterosexual relations and reseed the nation with fertile 4-H families.

4-H's promise to actualize the countryside's procreative potential through expertly managed heterosexuality placed the state at the center of rural family life and social reproduction. A representative 1937 issue of the *Rotarian* celebrated the ability of the "local 4-H leader" to "be a combined sage, confessor, counsellor, and friend" who offered wise advice on "not only club work, but also how to act when out on a date . . . what is the best age to get married . . . should a young married couple live with relatives."[57] In such moments, rural heterosexuality cohered as a set of innate sexual impulses safely managed by 4-H. Far from a natural, preordained outcome, rural heterosexuality required the state's assistance. 4-H's famous motto swore "to make the best better." In this case, the best bodies of rural America needed the state's guiding hand to reach productive heterosexuality. For an American state so biopolitically invested, such an arrangement was all for the better.

NOTES

1 Baker, "Rural-Urban Migration and the National Welfare," 92.

2 Baker, "The Outlook for Rural Youth," 1935, National Archives-College Park, 4-H Series, Record Group 33 (NACP1), Box 6, "4-H Club Studies, Volume 3," 27.

3 Rosenberg, *The 4-H Harvest*.

4 Canaday, *The Straight State*.

5 See Lovett, *Conceiving the Future*.

6 For some studies of rural-oriented statecraft in conversation with APD, see Fine-gold and Skocpol, *State and Party in America's New Deal*; Sanders, *The Roots of Reform*; and Carpenter, *The Forging of Bureaucratic Autonomy*. For the state in environmental and American western histories, see Worster, *Rivers of Empire*; White, *"It's Your Misfortune and None of My Own"*; Phillips, *This Land, This Nation*; and Gregg, *Managing the Mountains*.

7 Novak, "The Myth of the 'Weak' American State," 752–72.

8 Miller and Rose, *Governing the Present*, 26. For Foucault's major writings on biopolitics, see *The History of Sexuality, Volume 1: An Introduction*; *Security, Territory, Population*; and *The Birth of Biopolitics*.

9 Warren, "Some Suggestions on Methods of Work with Club Girls," 1925, NACP1, Box 1, "Principles and Policies Governing 4-H Club Work," 3.

10 "Decide Healthiest Juniors: Physical Specimens from Crawford and Story Counties" (Iowa), *4-H Club News* 5 (August 28, 1924): 1.

11 "The Perfect Boy and Girl," *Washington Post*, February 8, 1925, SM3.

12 Barker, "History of 4-H Club Work in Iowa,*1930 Annual Report, 4-H Series*, RS 16/1/1, Iowa State University Parks Library, Special Collections, Ames (ISU), 6; "Counties Conducting County Wide Health Contests: 1927," *1927 Annual Report, 4-H Series*.

13 "Iowa Health Score Card," *1924 Annual Report, 4-H Series*, ISU.

14 "Excerpts from County Agent Reports," *1927 Annual Report, 4-H Series*, ISU; "Health, A Definite Part of Club Program," *1928 Annual Report, 4-H Series*, ISU.

15 "From Field Agent's Annual Report–1930," *1930 Annual Report, 4-H Series*, ISU.

16 "Interesting Results of the Health Work Is [sic] Reported from All Counties," *1927 Annual Report, 4-H Series*, ISU.

17 See "General and Historical Information about the National 4-H Club Congress," 1950, National Archives-College Park,4-H Service Committee Files, Record Group 33 (NACP2), Box 1, "[Unmarked Folder]," 1.

18 W. W. Bauer, "Contesting for Better Health," NACP2, Box 1, "1933 Club Congress Folder," 3.

19 For health club enrollments see the statistical compilations found at NACP1, Box 16a, "Statistics."

20 Miriam Birdseye, "Grow Finer Club Members," 1929, NACP1, Box 1, "Principles and Policies Governing 4-H Club Work," 2.

21 Miriam Birdseye, "Suggested Plans for Growth in Connection with Boys' and Girls' Clubs," 1926, NACP1, Box 1, "Principles and Policies Governing 4-H Club Work," 6.

22 Ibid.

23 Birdseye, "Grow Finer Club Members," 3–5.

24 "Pick Healthy Specimens of Boys and Girls," *Oelwein Daily Register*, December 3, 1924, 1A.

25 For examples, see "The Perfect Boy and Girl," *Washington Post*, February 8, 1925, SM3; "Huskiest Farm Boy Is a Kentucky Lad," *New York Times*, December 1, 1926, 16; "Dakota Girl, 17, Wins National Health Contest," *Chicago Daily Tribune*, December 5, 1928, 14; "South Dakota Girl, Michigan Boy Chosen Nation's Healthiest in Chicago Contest," *New York Times*, December 5, 1928, 4; "Healthiest Boy and Girl Picked," *Los Angeles Times*, December 5, 1928, 1.

26 "So. Dakota Girl Gets 99 Rating in Health Tests," *Waterloo Evening Courier*, December 5, 1928, 9; "America's Healthiest Girl," *Alden Times*, May 24, 1924, 2.

27 "Floridian Is Healthiest Girl in U.S.," *Mason City Globe-Gazette*, December 4, 1929, 5.

28 For exclusion of non-white 4-H'ers from national events, see Carmen V. Harris, "States' Rights, Federal Bureaucrats, and Segregated 4-H Camps in the United States, 1927–1969," and Rosenberg, *The 4-H Harvest*, 172–81.

29 Robert Foster, "Social Relations and Family Life," 1931, NACP1, Box 32, "National 4-H Club Camp, June 17–23, 1931," 10.

30 Gertrude Warren, "The Social and Economic Problems of Farm Youth," 1931, NACP1, Box 1b, "[Gertrude Warren Folder]," 25.

31 C. B. Smith, "Our Enlarging Extension Objectives and What of Extension?," 1938, NACP1, Box 1b, "CB Smith Folder," 10–11.

32 Robert A. Polson, "Views of an Extension Sociologist on the Rural Youth Problem," 1934, NACP1, Box 34, "National 4-H Club Camp, June 14–20, 1934," 8.

33 Eugene Merritt, "The Farm Young People: A Memorandum to Accompany the Land Grant-Rural Youths' Committee Report," 1936, NACP1, Box 6, "4-H Club Studies, Volume III," 5; Gertrude Warren, "Meeting the Needs of Older Rural Girls," 1933, NACP1, Box 1b, "[Gertrude Warren Folder]," 5.

34 Hedley S. Dimock, untitled talk, in *Proceedings of the 1934 National 4-H Club Congress* (Chicago: National Committee on Boys and Girls Work, 1935), 9–10.

35 Charles Peterson, "County 4-H Club Representative Meet Gives Resume Conservation," *Brainerd Daily*, October 14, 1935, 3.

36 See *Reports of the University of Arizona Agricultural Extension Service, 1921–1963*, AZ305, University of Arizona Library Special Collection, 1939, 1941–1942.

37 *4-H Roundup News*, in "Club Specialist Report, 1941," UA, 10–11.

38 Warren, "Meeting the Needs of Older Rural Girls," 5.

39 C. B. Smith, "Older Rural Youth: Some Successful Solutions of their Problems by County Extension Workers," 1936, NACP1, Box 6, "4-H Club Studies, Volume III," 5, 8.

40 Hallie Hughes, "Self Management," 1931, NACP1, Box 33, "National 4-H Club Camp, June 17–23," 1.

41 Foster, "Social Relations and Family Life," 10.

42 Gertrude Warren, "Development of Happy Family Relationships through 4-H Club Work," [1937?], NACP1, Box 1b, "[Gertrude Warren Folder]," 1.

43 Robert G. Foster, "The Place of Marriage and Family Relationships in the 4-H Club Program," 1933, NACP2, Box 1, "1933 Club Congress"; Ruth Durrenburger, "Contributions of 4-H Club Work to Good Family Living with Suggestions for Increasing These Contributions," 1938, NACP1, Box 9a, "National 4-H Fellowship Program"; Lydia Lynde, "How 4-H Club Members Help to Plan Family Life," 1938, NACP1, Box 34, "National 4-H Club Camp, June 16–22, 1938."

44 "This Will Start a Discussion," *National 4-H Club News* 16 (January 1938): 4.

45 "Senior Girls' 4-H Handbook," April 1947, Auburn University Special Collections, Alabama Cooperative Extension Service Files, Box 336, 80. See also Lydia Lynde, "How 4-H Club Members Help to Plan Family Life," NACP1, Box 38, "National 4-H Club Camp, June 16–22, 1938."

46 Genevieve K. Tippett, "Little Mothers," *National 4-H Club News* 18 (January 1940): 8.

47 R. E. Parry, "What Is the Future for the Doctor and 4-H Girl?," *1936 Annual Report, 4-H Series*, ISU.

48 *1939 Annual Report, 4-H series*, ISU, 4.

49 "Sex Delinquency among Girls," *Journal of Social Hygiene* 28 (November 1943): 496; "The Program in Action in the States and Communities," *Journal of Social Hygiene* 28 (May 1942): 294; Elena Bonilla, "Action on the Home Front," *Journal of Social Hygiene* 30 (April 1944): 205–6.

50 "Wisconsin Boys and Sex Education," *Journal of Social Hygiene* 25 (April 1939).

51 See inset, "Food Nutrition and Health Unit I," 1941, NACP1, Box 3a, "State 4-H Publications (Primarily Subject-matter)."

52 See Waters and King, *Animal Husbandry*; Whitney, *The Basis of Breeding*; Russell, *Heredity in Dairy Cattle*; and Ensminger, *Beef Cattle Husbandry*.

53 Russell, *Heredity in Dairy Cattle*, 133.

54 Cook, *Like Breeds Like*, 283, 374–75.

55 Kevles, *In the Name of Eugenics*.

56 See Kline, *Building a Better Race* and Lovett, *Conceiving the Future*.

57 McDermott, "Rebirth of the Barefoot Boy and Girl," 26.

PART II

The Rural Turn

Considering Cartographies of Race and Class

5

The Waiting Arms of Gold Street

Manuel Muñoz's Faith Healer of Olive Avenue *and the Problem of the Scaffold Imaginary*

MARY PAT BRADY

"What does it mean," Sara Ahmed asks, "for sexuality to be lived as orientated?"[1] In addition to this perceptive question, it is useful to ask whether queer sexual "orientation" has entailed an unspoken metronormativity, and, if so, what happens to being "out" or being "orientated" when that metronormativity is dislodged? Ahmed's question—with its skillful invocation of spatialized embodiment—converges with Colin Johnson's and Mary Gray's questions: "Are there ways in which a 'rural turn' in queer studies might help to improve or augment our understanding of how race and class operate as discourses, experiences, and embodied practices? Alternatively, does increased attention to space and place in queer studies interrupt, damage or detract from the efforts of scholars in queer studies examining the centrality of race and class?"[2] Taken together, all of these questions ask us to consider how and whether space and place matter to living queer and writing queer desire. Of course, it is easy to say, "Yes, they matter," but in what follows I pause before that "yes" to discuss how this easy answer might well be troubled by two concepts: the seriality of time and of scale. I subsequently turn to a discussion of Manuel Muñoz's wondrous collection, *The Faith Healter of Olive Avenue* (2007), because it offers us a vision of living queerly without a reliance on metronormativity; it is not that the collection embraces a rural turn, but rather in illustrating what it means to live densely, it suggests a way to think outside of scale and straightforward time.[3]

The Seriality of Scale

When Gray and Johnson ask us to consider what happens when we add "place" to race and class, we have to tangle with the mischief caused by the seriality of categories (race, class, gender, sexuality, *place*), with the implied hierarchy of systemic structures, and with the ongoing deferral of meaning entailed in categorical dynamics. Their questions also astutely suggest that the settled sense that "we know what we mean" by highly defined processes such as race, gender, and class, and their intersections could well be unsettled by the introduction of space to the list.[4] Social scientists' tendency to use an additive narrative to describe social structures (such as race and class) has been meliorated, to a certain extent, through the invocation of intersectionality. Intersectionality is, of course, the terminology famously proposed in 1989 by Kimberlé Crenshaw to name the ways in which processes of racialization and gendering engage and constitute one another. Intersectionality has since become the name used to suggest the "relationships among multiple dimensions and modalities of social relations and subject formations."[5] In this sense, intersectionality, which attempts to engage these social processes through their mutually constitutive dynamics, undoes the indexing that such an additive naming or "horizontal seriality" seems only to register.[6] But the set of concerns in Johnson's and Gray's queries suggest that intersectionality cannot adequately accommodate a depth of differential engagements or processes if place is left out of the logic. This inadequacy would not be surprising to scholars who have worried that the categorical imperatives invoked by race, class, gender, and sexuality enact an ongoing process of normalization and homogenization that is ultimately at odds with a politics seeking to undo the repressions these categories inevitably name.

Sandy Soto argues that too often the use of intersectionality relies upon "what can only be a fantasy of a normative center inhabited by homogenous, static, racially pure, stagnant, uninteresting, and simple sovereign subjects."[7] She suggests that intersectionality as a shorthand ill serves, because it "ends up stabilizing (not to mention rendering equivalent) the discursive and material concepts brought into a single view, making it difficult not only to question their apparentness in the first place but to apprehend the dynamic transformations of power relations and epistemologies."[8] Soto finds the term "intersectionality" "too rigid and exacting." As a spatial term, it can flatten into stasis: "It seems to me that race, sexuality, and gender are much too complex, unsettled, porous (and I do mean to be wordy here), mutually constitutive, unpredictable, incommensurable, and dynamic, certainly too spatially and temporally contingent, *ever* (even if only for an instant) to travel independently of one another."[9] The spatial flattening invoked by intersectionality reinstantiates, Soto suggests, a monological index of the real.

While Soto's concern about the monological modality of categories is useful, her suggestion that in spatializing relationships by describing them as intersectional (and hence somehow discrete), we settle or sediment them unfortunately implies a concept of the spatial as opaque and undymanic, as setting and background rather than, as Doreen Massey famously writes, "as social relations stretched out."[10] Nevertheless, Soto's concern about the assumption that *processes* are reduced to discrete *categories* also points to the unspoken mischief-maker of temporality. Often "intersectionality" is invoked despite a temporal aporia; race, class, gender are usually identified in serial fashion, as an iteration, such that the gaps between them—categorically, spatially, temporally—are structured and reinforced by a linear temporality, a sense of both the recursive quality of our understanding of them and the rhetoric of progress undergirding modernity's engagement with difference. In this sense, simply adding a spatial category such as "rural" or "urban" to the mix further bedevils the problem. Put differently, intersectionality invokes the copula, for example, race and sexuality, but refuses that copula at the same time, since the categories are named iteratively. This makes it difficult to think about simultaneity both because of a categorical imperative to fold the meaning of the terms and processes into a discrete historical accounting of their morphology and because of a dominant discourse of development ever slogging its way toward normativity.[11] Inherent to the narrative practice of naming discretely is an adjacency that orders into sequences and iterations what we hope to understand simultaneously and in a temporally variegated fashion. In other words, in narrating their production, the categories get reified; the unmade gap between them becomes impossible. Thus, adding "rural" to the sequence, adding another dimension to the intersection, happens in serial fashion as an iteration. The serial structure thereby threatens to flatten our under-

standing rather than deepening it. Further making this problem difficult is that each of these categories has its own temporal scaffold, which
also reinforces a notion of developmental time. (For example, race has
historically, and continues to be to some extent, structured via the oscil-
lation between the primitive and the civilized; sexuality has tended to be
organized through a heterosexual reproductive mandate.)

And temporality, of course, is part of the technology that distin-
guishes "rural" from "urban." The "rural" is often temporally naturalized (not unlike reproductive time). What constitutes the rural is a sense
of being apart from the whoosh of progress that fills time so that the
rural gets marked by either the absence of time or the slowness of time,
by its anachronicity, its status as stuck in time, its backwardness, or its
engagement with mythical, seasonal reproduction, which is often read
nostalgically as outside of capitalist time. In that sense, the rural and the
racialized especially partake in the valuation economy of time.

The processes of stratification and flattening and disaggregating
that theories of intersectionality attempt to interrupt can too easily slip
past what a focus on the intersections themselves seeks to arrest. The
struggle to name the temporalities of these categories, to hail them as
mutually constitutive, and thereby to un-name them as categories and
rename them as processes necessarily encounters the elegant temporal ruse of modernity. As Walter Benjamin notes, "The concept of the
historical progress of mankind cannot be sundered from the concept
of its progression through a homogeneous, empty time."[12] This homogeneous, empty time vacuums up the variegated temporalities at work
in all of these sociohistorical-discursive processes that come to appear
as solidified, discrete, and given categories. The collapsing of processes
into categories—units of analysis—masks the temporalities these processes engage and perpetuate. As categories of modernity, the temporal
structures for race, class, gender, sexuality, and the rural, are unevenly
placed in flat-space relation, erasing their temporal contradictions and
altercations. Taking time into account allows us then to see how spatial
practices that racialize bodies and temporal narratives that render the
rural fallow and obsolescent share a particular repertoire of technologies
engaged with but hidden in time. A series of Manichean dyads (rich and
poor, black and white, rural and urban) seemingly stand tautly opposed,
their binary structure tempered and tautened by the Western frame of

time. Theories of intersectionality seek to countermand the impossibility of narrating simultaneity and highlight the ways in which processes are transformed into categories; unfortunately, the term itself limits its own ability to undo the serialization and linearity its very expression requires.

It may be because of this complexity that a number of queer theorists, most notably J. Jack Halberstam and Elizabeth Freeman, have engaged in striking discussions of temporality.[13] They argue that time is far more varied and dynamic than we typically imagine. Indeed, they suggest that the heterosexual family structure with all its capitalist allure depends upon a kind of temporal logic that tends to override other temporal forms. In opposition to a heteronormative timing of things, Halberstam posits queered time out of joint with sexual reproduction and particularly family instantiation. Queer time rubs family time awry. Freeman further observes that queer time necessarily combats the very linearity that troubles theories of intersectionality and structured inequalities. She argues, for example, that the production of kin relationships is one of the crucial ways in which we are taught to understand the temporal in linear terms. As she notes, "Family time, as it emerged, moved a formerly religious ritual time into women's domain, replaced sacred time with the secular rhythms of capital, feminized the temporalities considered to be outside of the linear, serial, and end-directed time of history, and demanded and depended on visual technologies that required increasingly less physical effort from their users."[14] Queer time, in contrast, "emerged from within, alongside, and beyond this heterosexually gendered double-time of stasis and progress, intimacy and genealogy."[15] What Freeman's work suggests, at the very least, is that co-constitutive processes such as racialization and gendering are deeply invested in multiple temporalities. To undo their repressive effects, a queer engagement must run afoul of linear time.

The Scaffold Imaginary

Ahmed's turn to the phenomenal is in keeping with Gray's and Johnson's interest in the spatial—orientation implies movement and relation, a there and where to the processes of being that racializing mechanisms, for example, try to delimit. But for the "rural turn" in queer studies to do more than simply stretch the horizon of seriality or iterability that I have been describing here as a problem,[16] it must take into account not only that what we call categories (race, gender) are actually *processes* and that these processes are made real, in part, through their spatialization. Rather, it must also take into account the ways in which the spatial imaginary of queer studies may be troubled by a vertical metric. In other words, the "rural turn" and the very concept of the rural, like all scalar and aggregate forms, are imbedded within the vertical hierarch of a dangerous "scaffold imaginary."[17]

"Urban" and "rural" are nested forms within a hierarchal spatial imaginary; they are aggregating terms used as explanations and as resources and as procedures to wipe out specificity and evacuate difference. The rural is the outside of the urban, but it is also an unspoken marker of the sorts of scales governing the movement of capital. These terms are also often used to define ideas of agency and resistance. As such, to call something "rural," is to immediately invoke a scalar and hierarchical relationship in which the rural is distinct from the power, resources, and movement of the urban. So the "rural turn" inevitably invokes a fixed verticality just as it resonates with a linear temporality. It also allows us to more fully understand the metronormative impulse of queer studies and why the politics of visibility cleave so intensely to urbanization.

It is not just that the rural is on a lower rung on the scaffold, but that LGBT studies, as Gray explains,

> works from an assumption that visibility and political dissent operate the same way across space and time and are readily available and universally valued no matter where one might live. Cities are imagined to draw out and bind together the nameless throngs of same-sex desiring and gender-variant people to build visibility and political power. This particular history of gay and lesbian visibility positions the city's capacities to make space for queer difference and consolidate capital as necessary precursors to modern lesbian and gay identity formation.[18]

The scaffold imaginary and the rural's apparent inadequacy thereby delimit gay identities. The rural cannot sustain what Gray astutely notes as implicit to the counterpublics Nancy Fraser and Michael Warner imagine—that is the "conspicuous though never accounted for, critical mass and urban buttressing."[19] Put bluntly, the scalar imaginary of queer studies scales out the possibility of lives lived aside from the urban.

By introducing place, Johnson and Gray provide an opening for a new set of discussions heretofore hindered by the submerged spatial imaginary. But even as they have given us that opening, I would like to unhinge my argument from the "rural" writ generalized because "rural" carries with it a scalar force, the trace of an impossibility; the rural is a product of the scaffold imaginary that consigns the rural and local to the small, disconnected, and impinged, where agency is made void. Bathed in a nostalgic small-town "main street Americana" vision, the rural, in neoliberal culture, is conflated with the left behind. The force of this imaginary presses down on inhabitants of "the rural," who, so the scaffold imaginary purports, everywhere meditate on departures and exits, always feeling magnetized by the urban. This approach is not the only one possible, however. To step out of the scaffold imaginary and linear time is to shift to thinking flatly instead of vertically and to shift the focus to networks of relationships and the obstructions and flows between people and events and the sites of their coming together as well as the shifting languages, the discursive and imaginary registers, that envision and contain these relationships. It enables a density to thinking that resists the emptying out of particularity produced by processes of rationalization or abstraction.

Writing without Scaffolds

Manuel Muñoz's *The Faith Healer of Olive Avenue*[20] is difficult to get a handle on. Rich, suggestive, delicate, and searing, the collection at first glance might appear to be only a portrait of closeted Chicano lives in rural California. Set in the area between Bakersfield and Fresno known as the "Valley," Muñoz's second collection of stories is an eloquent portrait of a place where "deep green water rushed icy from the tops of the Sierra Nevada" (19), with "roads so skinny they don't need painted lines" (3), and with "orange groves nestled on the brink of the foothills" (28) whose "deep green leaves hide meth labs" (28); this is a place where a "treacherous" highway will take you past "empty cotton fields," where "a dust devil swirled lazily, meandering" (136) over to "a miraculous horizon—the sheer blue line of the ocean meeting its own impossible expanse" (101). The stories walk us in and around gay desires and the struggles to articulate these desires amidst all the protocols attempting to maintain heterosexual masculinity at all costs.

On one hand, the text begs a reading that focuses on the controlling power of the closet. Story after story might be described as illustrating life in the closet: the belated experience of homoerotic desire; the discovery after tragedy of a son's gay affair; a character's sorrow over the toll his refusal of gender norms exacted; another character's smoldering alienation after confusing erotic encounters. The melancholy tone of so many of the stories might easily be attributed to the myriad ways that queer desire is not simply not articulated, but is disarticulated, closeted. Eve Sedgwick's proclamation that "The closet is the defining structure of gay oppression this century" seems to simmer through the collection.[21] This understanding of the closet's role in *Faith Healer* seems perfectly reasonable. Such an easy conclusion would then lend itself to conflating the closet with the rural, thereby reducing the stories to a gnarled portrait of the intersections of Chicano and queer identities as closeted in California and thus missing the collection's dramatic rejection of a vertical orientation.

Faith Healer does not pay attention to categories such as gay or straight. It does not offer a set of narratives that we might expect—bold Chicano coming of age accounts that proclaim a liberated gay identity. Such triumphant coming out stories are not offered here, nor are the narrative energies focused on a nostalgic fondness for "small town America" or an iconic and neighborly (Mexican) Main Street. These constructions seem unimportant to a writer who, in rejecting the scaffold imaginary, knows that such coming out stories frequently include the drum beat to rise above and get out—a theme that leaves the closet and the rural in the dustbin of power.[22] Put differently, rather than dig a moat around one aspect of living or of identity, such as sexuality, the collection urges us to think more densely, more intricately about the network of relations that engage these constructs.

Faith Healer begins this effort of thinking densely with a warning: "People knew that road, that intersection, how often it happens" (1). This opening sentence of the first story in the collection, "Lindo y Querido," refers to a highway intersection where accidents frequently occur. But it is also an apt sentence to open a story and a collection deeply engaged with the contours of public knowledge, open secrets, things known, particularly intersections of various kinds, but not said. Similarly, it is a touching way to annotate the frequency with which boundaries are broken, while also emphasizing a kind of communal vulnerability. The open secret is of course a desire that refuses the constraints of heteronormativity. But as the story unfolds, we learn that the *other* open secret entails a woman's tenuous relationship to legal status in the United States. Continually sounding this connection (this set of shared vulnerabilities between immigration status and sexuality), the collection repeatedly traces circuits of prohibition and constraint.

This intersection is a dangerous one; the story follows the death of a young man, Isidro, killed in a motorcycle accident at that intersection. As his mother empties his room, she comes across love letters to her son, written in a language she doesn't know; she easily recognizes, however, that they are love letters and that they have been signed by Carlos, the other young man killed in the accident. At this intersection of loss and revelation, Isidro's mother, Connie, tries to collate her new knowledge of her son with her old knowledge of her estranged husband. Muñoz gives us a portrait here of isolation and loneliness—not a nostalgic and stereotypical image of a supportive and mutually engaged community, but rather of one that knows things but does not speak them. The narrative will not let us forget that intersection—it repeats the formulation two more times over the course of the story—the second time as Connie remembers a sexual encounter with Isidro's father: "Everyone knows that road, that intersection." The story folds this memory into the fierce evocation of Connie's sense of pride, which, the narrator, in telling us of Connie's delicately forged immigration papers, dryly notes, "can be an enormous crushing weight" (2).

Connie destroys the love letters: "She rips the letters angrily, just as she did her husband's magazines all those years ago. She would not be alone in this house as she is, with the pile of letter scraps on the mattress, scraps she will wet in the sink and squish tightly into the garbage"(21). Just as she had destroyed her husband's porn after he had abandoned her and their young son Isidro, she makes the letters go away because they are documents and papers that attest to some knowledge she does not want to assimilate. The letters are signs of an illicit desire and a signal of a son's unspoken experiences. They also painfully remind her of her own letters sent to parents "who shipped her off to a husband when she was very young" (5)—letters that went unanswered. This mesh of paper, from forged citizenship documents purchased for $1,500, to returned letters, to porn, to love notes from one dead young man to another now dead young man serve as screens for her memories and for her navigation of an increasingly isolated existence. Working recursively, the narrative suggests that Isidro's father may well have been gay, but more importantly, we ultimately see Connie now grieving the loss of her son, the loss of his love letters, the loss of even a possibility of connection to Carlos's mother—and she comes to be haunted by her son's accident as it fills her dreams:

> She will dream of her son hugging Carlos as the motorcycle speeds faster: This was love. At each of the intersections, she is there watching as Isidro hugs Carlos, feeling with her son as Carlos takes in a deep breath, the boys waiting for clearance, Carlos's back widening. (22–23)

In her loss, she begins to love her son as who she now understands him to have been. At the close of "Lindo y Querido," the deadly intersection signals not danger but interconnection. And it is this interconnection that *Faith Healer* repeatedly asks us to consider. The stories mold events not in terms of individual actors but within the sites of their coming together—a coming together that is not just of bodies and (heroic) actions, but of disparate memories, shifting economies, and representational struggles.

To step outside of the scaffold imaginary means, at the very least, to look closely at these interconnections and the sites of their coming together (and, thus, to step away from reductive comparisons). *Faith Healer* amplifies the ways sites stretch to include multiple temporalities and breathing, shifting materialities. The stories locate events and experiences but do so with a sense that these locales are constitutive of the events. Such an understanding of place eschews panoramic visions, or as one character says, "Sometimes I imagine Gold Street as a living being, an entity with arms waiting" (105). In this sense, the stories suggest that not only are lives braided with other lives, but they are woven in and through a particular place. It further suggests that one must look really, really closely at a place, its peoples, the events that are their coming together. Just as crucial to the stories' coherence as character descriptions are, the accounts of the Valley entail understanding it in terms of its "liveness," its interactivity; "[when] night came, the temperature would plummet, the open Valley Sky snatching away all the heat" (128). "The Valley" is not iterable, duplicatable, abstractable, or rationalizable. Similarly, to give place texture is also to show that the characters invent themselves and their experiences through spatial transformation. So their comments on the areas around them are not mere asides, but rather engagements with the place as a way to understand themselves.

The text allows us to understand that to follow a character's story, it is also important that we learn about a town's "expanding, eating up the farmland, the field lizards still confused as they scampered around in the dust" (126). Changing economies swirl through the stories as they trace the transformations of development, often cynically:

> On this side of town there has not been much construction in a long time. Over on the North side, the town is stretching its way toward Fresno, swallowing up farmland sold by farmers who claimed that the soil was too acidic. But that's a lie. The peaches, the nectarines, were growing just fine. Then one foggy day in January, I drove past the Northern fringe of town and saw acres and acres of fruit trees pulled up, the trunks and branches gathered in piles. January, there were no leaves, no buds, just the bare dead trees, and as soon as the sun came to stay and the county waved air quality restrictions for a few days, the farmers were allowed to burn their tree piles. That's greed for you: now there are beautiful, beautiful houses up there. (151)

The movement of capital is registered here as a changing relationship to the nearby. This kind of engagement with the Valley bespeaks a sense of relationship with a place, an acknowledgement of place as enmeshed in sociality, and not simply a notch on a vertical hierarchy where real living happens elsewhere. Individuals, the stories teach us, are not outside of places; they are not apart from the "dense materialities that compose sites," nor are they the "transcendental author of those sites."[23] You cannot distinguish the actor from the stage.

Such a sense of people and place as interanimating does not give much room to a social imaginary that isolates individual actors with he-

roic coming out accounts. Instead, *Faith Healer* highlights a set of inter-
meshed relations far more in sync with Mary Gray's argument in *Out in
the Country*. There Gray persuasively shows how the politics of visibility
that have emerged as a product of the contemporary gay rights movements depend for their political utility on urban living. Visibility and
the closet therefore are inadequate metaphors for approaching an understanding of nonurban queer cultures. As she argues, "At the moment,
queer desires and embodiments are popularly and politically tethered
to prescriptions of exacting kinds of LBGT visibility. These politics and
practices, however, fail to recognize the price rural LGBT-identifying
youth pay for this 'claustrophilia.'"[24] Understanding queer cultures beyond urban locales entails both refusing the normalizing mechanisms of
queer visibility and assembling such a sensibility via other mechanisms
and technologies. She suggests that the queer youth she studied "constantly reworked boundaries" without queer visibility as the normative
or utopian end marker. In rejecting the universality of visibility politics,
Gray shifts the focus "away from the private world of individual negotiations of the closet" so that we learn how queer identities can be understood as "collective labor" and as "work shared among many rather
than the play of any one individual." That "many" includes place and the
complex of relationships among people.

Three stories in *Faith Healer* in particular illustrate Gray's concept of
collaborative labor by suggesting that what characters move toward is
not a named identity but rather a sense of living and working together,
collaboratively pursuing fulfillment or survival. The stories show that
such mutuality entails a carefully wrought series of negotiations in which
many characters labor together to find room for each other's approaches
to living, carefully acknowledging, in keeping with the collection's interest in empathy, how bodies in motion and working materialities have an
impact on each other.

In "Bring, Brang, Brung" the narrative follows Martín as he moves
home to the Valley as a single father whose lover has recently died of a
stroke. Martín must wrestle with his grief, which came "like a ghost at
the foot of the bed, just as he was sleeping" (30). He must also wrestle
with the financial demands of raising his young son, Adán, on his own,
despite his rejection of the hometown to which he has returned, despite
his sense that "the Valley was a mess of lack, of descending into dust,

of utter failure, and he had learned that long, long ago" (28). But what Martín finds in the Valley is not isolation or rejection because of his queer desires but a complex network of people. The very people whom he had once rejected now find room and ways to make him and his son welcome and finally convince him to display a photo of himself and his lost lover, Adrian. What Martín finds, ironically, is not lack, although people are poor, but engagement and the realization that he is a part of a mesh of connected people who collectively build a collaborative sense of themselves.

Similarly, in "Tell Him about Brother John," the narrator accedes to his father's request to visit with a downcast neighbor called Brother John. What unfolds in the conversation is a blisteringly sad story of queer love gone awry. The unnamed, queer narrator hears Brother John's story with grudging ambivalence and refuses to give Brother John any empathetic recognition at all. Nevertheless, the narrator finds, to his surprise, that his own father wishes to acknowledge his son's queer life, not by naming it, but by encouraging his friendship with Brother John. The father wants to build a collaborative sort of solidarity. And finally, in "Ida y Vuelta," Roberto recounts how his ex-lover's parents slowly accepted his relationship with their son. Their acceptance moves between the parents' own troubled marital relationship and Roberto's generous willingness to help them with business matters. It is a kind of bargain that Roberto does not regret, because he inhabits a network of relations that acknowledge shared vulnerabilities.

In each of these stories *Faith Healer* helps us to see this complex mesh of relations particularly as it tracks its subjects coming to terms with this interrelatedness and with their own movement within a relational mesh. The form of the collection also highlights the collaborative labor of building identity and writing densely. Rather than emphasizing the agency of individual actors, the collection repeatedly weaves the lives of various characters into and out of the stories. The same place names appear across the different stories. Minor characters in one story become the narrators of other stories. Lives and events and places overlap and fold together. This interbraiding also further undercuts the possibility of abstracting the Valley into the scale of the rural. It emphasizes instead a specificity that in its unfolding challenges the way scalar structures empty out difference and political possibilities.

Temporal Girders

To fully understand the collaborative work of identity, it is useful to disentangle identity from linear time. And just as the collection rejects the scaffold imaginary, it similarly rejects that imaginary's dependence on linear time. The problem is that linear time is, like the rural, an abstraction. We live in jagged, cut temporalities overlayed and decollaged upon each other. And yet, the momentous explanatory power of linearity swamps the language of time. Linear time works in concert with a scaffold imaginary, delimiting worlds into the past and the present, giving the global and the abstract the swoosh of movement, power, action—and draining what is not global of its vibrancy. To resist the power geometry of such a temporal/scaffold imaginary entails a refusal of the claims to aggregated accuracy. It refuses the seeming efficiencies of abstractions that crush temporalities into one seamless line.

Faith Healer suggests that we do not live and breathe in a straightforward temporal clime. Instead, it argues that every experience depends not just on memories, but on the intrusiveness of other peoples' memories and on the vibrancy of what seems past but is not. For that reason, no one person is immune to the temporalities of another. Instead, as the stories suggest, empathy, understanding, and a sense of being in place depend on concatenated memories, on sudden linkages and burst obstructions.

Repeatedly, the stories hold a character in sharp light, focusing intently on the way a long-held memory inflects the present and, on occasion, enables one to begin understanding another person. For example, at the end of "Bring, Brang, Brung" Martín, having reluctantly cared for his ailing son all day, finds himself flooded with a memory: "He thought, for the first time in years, of his father, and in the quiet of the apartment, Martín let himself inch toward understanding him" (46). A ruptured present allows Martín to shift toward, if not compassion, then a recognition of the emotions that might have pushed his own father to abandon a young Martín. Similarly, a bully-father suffused with pain after his son's suicide in "When You Come into Your Kingdom" shifts temporal planes repeatedly until he begins to "see how his son saw, and he knows what it is to be him and prove incapable of resisting his own body, how his hands and feet could move forward as if on their own" (103). As in so many moments in the collection, the verb tenses shift from phrase to phrase and within phrases (from present to past: see/saw; from present to future subjunctive: knows/could move), illustrating the instability of time. Jagged time, cracks between a linear movement from past to present, enable the possibility of empathy.

One of the ways linear time structures the scaffold imaginary is by holding temporal movement to a single direction, forming nostalgia. Nostalgia finds the rural quaint, discarded, left apart, and crushed. Characters in *Faith Healer* often rail against nostalgia, seeing it as damaging, as an intrusive attitude that freezes memories, tweaks time so that one feels "fooled and hypnotized by" it (105). Nostalgia, in other words, prevents temporal movements that enable empathy, because it is "the will of memory to rectify everything" (93), and nostalgia serves as an obstruction, gathering power if one allows it (15).

Memories shape the present so that the present tense is never quite a linear marker from past to future, but is always embedded in becomings and endings and enfoldings of the experiences of not just one person but of everyone coming in contact with each other. No time is its own; the present is a product of collective memories, of everyone else's times; this moment does not exist in isolation. It is in thinking backward and around and through time that characters reconstruct family ties both present and dissolved; but they do not think backward as if to trace direct connections. Rather they find themselves inhabiting seemingly prior moments fluctuating within a present temporal bouquet.

The larger form of the stories themselves also reflects this interbraiding of temporalities. The stories never trace a linear series of actions or events. The narratives dwell on minor moments, microscopic observations. Although one must read sequentially page by page, the stories disrupt a linear or straightforward plot by repeatedly spinning in different directions so that a readers' understanding is enlarged not just by the explanation of a prior event but also by the combustion of memories and realizations within a particular interaction. Thus, a character will begin to describe a series of actions, but before the actions can be fully explained, the character offers an associative memory that leads to another memory, which then pulses forward again or sideways into the realm of could have/should have. This formal density creates a kind of discombobulated time for the reader and, most importantly, shows that people live in a mesh of temporal relations and collaborations.

Conclusion

The Faith Healer of Olive Avenue answers Sara Ahmed's question through illustration. Instead of a definitive answer to "What does it mean for sexuality to be lived as orientated?" *Faith Healer* suggests that orientation is the condition of knowing and engaging with the mesh of relations, events, and sites in which people find themselves—but always with a sideways orientation, flat not vertical. In other words, to think about living queer is not to create an algorithm that fits every place queer people find themselves. Rather than seek out ways to buttress and add density to formulaic descriptions, *Faith Healer* calls for a radical shift away from the scaffold imaginary and linear time, away from iterative and abstracting naming practices or categorical solutions. It dismisses a liberal call for queer visibility as an end in itself. It asks instead that people listen to and walk with each other in a place that matters.

NOTES

1 Ahmed, *Queer Phenomenology*, 1.

2 These are some of the questions Johnson and Gray formulated in their call for papers for the 2010 conference "Out in the Country," hosted by Indiana University.

3 Muñoz, *The Faith Healer of Oliver Avenue*. For a wonderful and succinct introduction to Muñoz, see Yvonne Yarbro Bejaranno's "Introduction" to "Bring, Brang, Brung" in Paul Lauter, ed., *The Heath Anthology of American Literature*, 7th ed. (Boston: Cengage Publishing, 2013), 4123–25.

4 In my monograph I argue that practices of racialization and engendering are realized in part through their spatialization. Brady, *Extinct Lands, Temporal Geographies*. I expand on the critique of scale in Mary Pat Brady, "Metaphors to Love By: Toward a Chicana Aesthetics in *Their Dogs Came with Them*," in *Rebozos de Palabras: An Helena María Viramontes Critical Reader*, ed. Gabriella Gutiérrez y Muhs (Tucson: University of Arizona Press, 2013), 167–91.

5 McCall, "The Complexity of Intersectionality," 1771. To say that the literature on "intersectionality" is vast is to make an understatement. For the purposes of brevity, I will cite only a few of the relevant essays in addition to McCall's: Schueller, "Analogy and (White) Feminist Theory"; Hancock, "When Multiplication Doesn't Equal Quick Addition"; Davis, "Intersectionality as Buzzword."

6 Schueller, "Analogy," 70.

7 Soto, *Reading Chican@ Like a Queer*, 3.

8 Ibid., 6.

9 Ibid.

10 Massey, *Space, Place, and Gender*, 2.

11 Escobar, *Encountering Development.*

12 See Benjamin, "Theses on the Philosophy of History," 253.

13 Halberstam, *In a Queer Time and Place.* Freeman, *Time Binds.*

14 Freeman, 40.

15 Freeman, 23.

16 A number of scholars have shown how processes of racialization, for example, depend upon processes of spatialization. From restrictive covenants, to legalized segregation, to access to a range of facilities, to the production of spatial imaginaries via racial norms, the production of race has depended upon its spatial management. See, for example, Pulido, *Environmentalism and Economic Justice*; Abel, *Signs of the Times*; Gilmore, *Golden Gulag*; and Woods, *Development Arrested.*

17 Sallie Marston, John Paul Jones III, and Keith Woodward, have offered an extraordinary series of essays on the problem of thinking with scale; similarly, they have offered wonderful examples of how to think past scale. See Marston, Jones, and Woodward, "Human Geography without Scale"; Woodward, Jones, and Marston, "Of Eagles and Flies"; Jones, Woodward, and Marston, "Situating Flatness"; and Woodward, Jones, and Marston, "The Politics of Autonomous Space."

18 Gray, *Out in the Country*, 7.

19 Ibid., 94.

20 All pages references to *The Faith Healer* will appear in parentheses directly in the text.

21 Sedgwick, *Epistemology of the Closet*, 72.

22 Romero, "When Something Goes Queer."

23 See Woodward, Jones, and Marston, "Of Eagles and Flies," 273.

24 Gray, *Out in the Country*, 169.

6

Snorting the Powder of Life

Transgender Migration in the Land in Oz

LUCAS CRAWFORD

In 1904, L. Frank Baum published *The Marvelous Land of Oz*, the first sequel to *The Wonderful Wizard of Oz*, an "erotically antisocial queer utopia."[1] While the original text of the series (and its film) are enshrined in the halls of queer camp archives—"with Judy Garland as the star, its exaggerated characters of good and evil, and its Technicolor wonderland of vibrant colors and outlandish costumes, the film displays a queer sensibility"[2]—its sequel has not enjoyed the same queer reputation. Nonetheless, *The Marvelous Land of Oz* comprises a compelling tale of transgender and mobility, one that replaces Kansas-loving Dorothy with gender-crossing and soon-to-be rural-expat Tip. Indeed, there is a sense in which drawing out a transgender economy of Oz is *too* intuitive: if missing a brain, heart, courage, or Kansas are permitted, who would pay any mind to nonvital organs, particularly those as small as genitals, especially in a land where reproduction happens through magic and relationships are built upon "anti-reproductive intimacy?"[3] The text can be construed as a trans utopia: characters are made of "queer assortment[s]"[4] of things; body-modified bugs that "cannot be classed with ordinary insects"[5] are praised for their refutation of taxonomy; transformations can be effected with the "Powder of Life" or with "DR. NIKIDIK'S CELEBRATED WISHING PILLS."[6] It is no surprise, then, that critics have lauded Oz's general attitude towards strange bodies and transformation. Pugh, for instance, identifies a feminist overtone to the relationships enacted in Oz: people connect via "predominantly feminine community" rather than set out on "the individualist question of a lone male."[7] Remembering that the Tin Woodman accepts Jack Pumpkinhead by saying, "'You are certainly unusual, and therefore worthy to become a member of our select society,'"[8] it is difficult to argue with Alison Lurie's statement that "in the world of Oz, acceptance of minority rights is taken for granted."[9]

Argue we must, however, as the recognition of "minority rights" in this text comes at the precise cost of shutting down the possibilities of "becoming-minor"[10] in relation to the state and to this piece of literature's own possibly radical impulses—of, shutting down, in other words, "the deterritorialization of language, the connection of the individual to a political immediacy, and the collective assemblage of enunciation,"[11] as Deleuze and Guattari characterize minor literature. *The Marvelous Land of Oz* tempers the transgender-sympathetic qualities named above by figuring its mutually constitutive urbanization and upward mobility not just as happy endings but also as precisely the "transitions" through which gender change becomes possible. Protagonist Tip's journey is in many ways familiar: he is a young boy living in the country with a much-despised witch named Mombi, from whom he escapes one day and heads to Emerald City. On the way, he gathers up a motley crew of other odd personages and loners, who constitute his masculine community. Back and forth they go between the city and the country, comprising what Pugh calls (in reference to *The Wizard of Oz*) "an erotically antisocial queer utopia [that] challenges the libidinal economy of heteronormative reproduction."[12] But, a final Hollywood-caliber plot intervenes in this "queer utopia" (spoiler alert): Tip used to be a girl, and, to girlhood he shall return, as he/she/ze is revealed to be heir to the throne of the city. While this would indeed constitute a happy ending in most neoliberal accounts of the importance of state-sanctioned forms of LGBT citizenship, Deleuze and Guattari remind us that "the power of minorities is not measured by their capacity to enter and make themselves felt within the majority system";[13] rather it is measured by their capacity to bring the power of "multiplicities" against the totalizing, singular, and "denumerable" coherence of the state.[14] On one hand, then, the text illustrates a vital definition of rural and nomadic transgender: here, changing bodies are a matter of magic, uncertainty, imperceptibility, adventure, and unnatural affiliations. But, on the other, the protagonist once again heeds the imperative to "get thee to a big city"[15] and takes up a gender-restoring transformation—transitions undertaken to fulfill customs of inheritance and wealth. It is precisely the success of this transgender migration narrative that falsely ties together and tames the inchoate becomings of Tip and his queerly assembled crew.

The text is instructive to our present situation for several reasons, then, the first being its uncanny foreshadowing of today's neoliberal LGBT sensibilities, which we see in matters such as the depoliticizing of pride festivals or pro-imprisonment LGBT policing committees.[16] In this sense, the text asks us to remember that narratives of transgender or queer urban migration are often (but not always) propped up by troubling and intertwined narratives of rurality and poverty; the "community" and "minority rights" that approving critics find in the Land of Oz are reliant, then, on concepts of identity and citizenship that overestimate the importance of institutions and happy urban endings. This essay's sense of "queering" the countryside therefore entails two operations: bringing transgender analytics to bear on "queer" thinking (recognizing that the two have never been neatly separate) and taking neoliberal LGBT life as a starting point (that requires questioning) rather than as the endpoint of queer work. The second avenue of the essay is therefore to show how Baum's text unwittingly offers a number of escape routes from normalizing dynamics, including its makeover of the cultural image of the transgender child (another kind of "minor"). The text's most obvious and vital legacy, however, is the question with which this essay ends: at a time when rural trans people in so many ways seem to magically disappear, what if transgender were reconsidered as a matter of magic? Magic—pushed to the geographic edges of the city, configured as regressive and backwards, and reliant on the belief that affects traverse across bodies—gives us a model for becoming rural. By "becoming rural," I do not mean an exodus from cities, but rather, the possibility that trans/rural literatures could become part of the queer imaginaries of more people in more places, whatever the population.

Not that Kind of Queer King

It is because, not in spite, of this text's specifically fantastical, historically removed, and utopic world that it is relevant: the tale can function as a very specific fantasy of intersecting modes of mobility (gender, class, geographical). Following Žižek's arguments that "fantasy constitutes our desire, provides its co-ordinates"[17] and that "the radical intersubjectivity of fantasy" means that fantasy is "really about [our] attempts to form an identity,"[18] I argue that this text's fantasy of gender change teaches us how to desire a particular form of urban citizenship as the natural ending to rural trans upbringing. In a world of "minority rights" and "feminine community" that appears to support a utopian freedom for bodies, this text "simultaneously *closes the actual span of choices* (fantasy renders and sustains the structure of the forced choice, it tells us how we are to choose if we are to maintain the freedom of choice)."[19] This lesson about desire is played out through the juxtaposition of Tip with another would-be city-dweller, the "audaci[ous]" and "discontent[ed]"[20] young woman Jinjur, whose transgressions are disciplined while Tip's are rewarded; Jinjur's wrong choice (leading an army of girls in rebellion against the men of the city) is positioned as a threat to the democratic value of choice. This predicament feels close to a neoliberal orthodoxy: one does activist work that maintains the control of the state (marriage, hate crime law, military participation) in order to guarantee one's freedom—granted *by* the state.[21]

The context of Tip's gender change illustrates all too literally the stakes of misreading what Aren Aizura calls "the imaginary community of (trans)sexual citizenship"[22] as natural and given. Tip's migration narrative, like one of Aizura's case studies, is "a narrative of (trans)sexual citizenship that figures transgression as a necessary but momentary lapse on the way to a proper embodied belonging, a proper home and full social inclusion."[23] Tip's tremendously happy ending—the book's final chapter is entitled "The Riches of Content"[24]—is problematic, and not only for its seemingly conservative reinstallment of the protagonist's "original" gender. Following Aizura's definition, Tip's rural and transing youth is a necessary lapse on his way to a "real" gender, to a home he never knew he had, and to both social inclusion and a seat (a throne!) atop the social hierarchy of the biggest city in the land. As a representation of trans life, clearly this migration tale is not "accurate" nor could/ should it be. More importantly, its crass equations of ownership and urbanism with a restoration of birth gender cast light on what it means, today, to couch queer and trans rights claims in the language of citizenship and nations—to equate justice or happiness with a gendered and geographical "home" in one's body, house, and nation and to see citizenship as a triad upheld by "the public fiction that recognition of queerness or gender variance is gained under the aegis of universal entitlement, rather than because 'difference' has remade itself as non-transgressive or non-threatening."[25]

The figuring of the rich city and poor country in Baum's text reflects the exclusion of rural locales from the imaginary vision of the nation—a representative move that, Mary L. Gray argues, figures small towns as "inadequacies in need of urban outreach instead of a bellwether for the nationwide dismantlement of public services,"[26] thereby maintaining the illusion that all is well in the metropolis. The migration narrative of *The Marvelous Land of Oz* is one Tip begins simply enough, with a disobedient act towards an oppressive parent figure and with a disdain for home. Upon playing a practical joke on his guardian Mombi (trying to frighten her with a pumpkinhead man he had built for the purpose), Tip runs away from home to escape his punishment. This punishment was, precisely, to remain in the country forever: as Mombi threatens while preparing the potion, "'It will change or transform you into a marble statue. . . . I'm going to plant a flower garden, next Spring, and I'll put you in the middle of it, for an ornament.'"[27] Deciding with a clever pun that becoming a literal fixture in a garden is not for him—he exclaims, "'It's a hard thing, to be a marble statue'"[28]—Tip beckons the pumpkinhead (now brought to life by Mombi) and leaves behinds his life of "carry[ing] wood from the forest . . . work[ing] in the corn-fields, hoeing and husking . . . [feeding] the pigs and milk[ing]."[29] At first, the twosome's destination is indeterminate: "'Where to?' asked Jack. 'You'll know as soon as I do,' answered Tip . . . 'All we've got to do now is to tramp.'"[30] A mere page and several minutes of narrative time later, the destination is spontaneously decided: Emerald City, at "the center of the Land of Oz, and the biggest town in all the country."[31] Like many a rural trans person, Tip can say, "'never been there, myself, but I've heard all about its history.'"[32] The ubiquity of urban representation carries over to Baum's fantasyland. Early on, readers get a sense of the mobility implied by a move from the country to the city. In the country, Tip lives a nonfamilial life, friendless, amused only by the "love of mischief"[33] that leads him to the road in the first place. In Emerald City, by contrast, "sparkling green gems ornamented the fronts of the beautiful houses and the towers and turrets were all faced with emeralds. Even the green marble pavement glittered with precious stones, and it was indeed a grand and marvelous sight."[34] It is clear from the outset that the move from the country to the city is meant to be a move from relative poverty to wealth.

As many rural expats who face poverty in the grand metropolis could confirm, however, this urban aura of abundance may well be a matter of performative posturing. Scott Herring suggests that inasmuch as the rural and urban divide is "as much phantasmatic as it is factual,"[35] metronormativities can be found anywhere: "sometimes you don't need a flight to the city to fashion-police in the sticks."[36] True enough, although in *The Marvelous Land of Oz* the first instance of explicitly bodily disciplining occurs right at the gates of the city, where the guard insists that all who enter don green spectacles. The pumpkinhead—"knowing nothing of wealth and beauty"[37]—is surprised at this mandatory accessorizing: "'But why need I wear spectacles?' asked Jack. 'It's the fashion here,' said the Soldier, 'and they will keep you from being blinded by the glitter and glare of the gorgeous Emerald City.'"[38] Those who read the original book in Baum's series will remember that rather than riches and the glow of emeralds, these green spectacles are actually the relic of an earlier monarch, the Wizard of Oz; as he tells Dorothy, "as the country was so green and beautiful, I would call it the Emerald City, and to make the name fit better I put green spectacles on all the people, so that everything they saw was green."[39] Here in the second volume, the gatekeeper of the city literally institutes the way in which the space will be seen, creating *with* the glasses the very reason *for* the glasses. The hyper-able body politic of the city requires a prosthetic: not rose- but green-colored glasses—a figure, in this twisted reading, of both unbridled positive "outlooks" on the city and also a flattening out of texture through a studied and disingenuous *colorblindness*.

This is a narrative that rings too true for queer and trans people who live without the naïve comfort that cities are primarily, exclusively, or unambiguously liberating for non-normative people. As may well be the case for all but the richest city-migrants, the magnetic glow of Emerald City is revealed to be an illusion sustained by the visual culture instituted by the prosthetic prohibition against any "off-color" perspectives entering the city. Despite the open secret that the city is not the bastion of green it appears to be, the ownership of the city remains the text's definitive plot point, thereby bearing out Jay Prosser's suggestion about the desire for the gendered/geographical home: "recognizing its fictionality only fuels its mythic lure."[40] This sustained quest for illusory "homes" as both national and gendered citizens comes, in Aizura's estimation, at the cost of "requiring radical difference to recreate itself as domesticated"[41]—a description that could well describe Tip's city-sanctioned gender restoration.

Baum's text juxtaposes Tip's eventual "coming home" with another process of gendered domestication: an opposing group of young girls who threaten to overtake the city. Early in his trek to Emerald City, Tip comes upon a young woman named Jinjur, whose face "wore an expression of discontent coupled to a shade of defiance or audacity,"[42] and who intended to overthrow the king of Emerald City (the Scarecrow) on behalf of her "Army of Revolt"—a group of young women who "intend to conquer the City and run the government to suit ourselves."[43] Why, in their "jaunty and becoming"[44] uniforms, "laughing and talking together as gaily as if they had gathered for a picnic instead of a war,"[45] would these girls want to take over the city? Jinjur explains the army's reasoning to Tip:

> "Because the Emerald City has been ruled by men long enough, for one reason," said the girl. "Moreover, the city glitters with beautiful gems, which might far better be used for rings, bracelets and necklaces; and there is enough money in the King's treasury to buy every girl in our Army a dozen new gowns.[46]

From there on, the main matter of the text is Tip's growing gang of "queer" friends working to defend the Scarecrow's reign from this army of girls. What began as a parent-defying wandering trek very quickly, then, turns into a sex-segregated battle royale for rights to the city. (Tip, Jack Pumpkinhead, an animated Saw-Horse, a "Thoroughly Educated" bug, a "Gump" made out of various furniture and a stag's head, the Tin Woodman, and the Scarecrow are all coded as male.) Despite the city gatekeeper's warning to the girls—"'Go home to your mothers, my good girls, and milk the cows and bake the bread,'"[47]—the girls overtake the city with knitting needles, their weapons of choice, and put the men of the city to work at household chores. When this pack of "bros" eventually overthrows the girls once again, the mutually implicated class politics and gender politics of the text come to the fore. Upon hearing that she will soon be overthrown, Jinjur cries: "'To think . . . that after having ruled as Queen, and lived in a palace, I must go back to scrubbing floors and churning butter again! It is too horrible to think of! I will never consent!'"[48] However, all the young women are "sent home to their Mothers."[49] While Tip's choice to run away is rewarded with a kingdom, Jinjur reaps no such prize for her disruption of the gendered rule of the city. Exile from the city not only means the disbandment of the girl army, but also means a laboring life at home with Mother—a reinstallment of gender order that successfully re-domesticates the young woman subject while rewarding the young *boy* (for the moment) for his correlative disobedient journey to the city. This seems like a strange parable for a story that Baum imagines as having a female audience; as he writes in his preface, "I promised one little girl . . . that when a thousand little girls had written me a thousand letters . . . I would write the book."

Perhaps as a guard against such interpretations, the text ends with a transgender deus ex machina—that is, with a final triumphing of (un) transing femaleness, a "sex change" posing as a restoration. After defending the land from this reversal of gender roles, Tip, ironically, finds himself plunged into the haziness of just such a swap. When Tip becomes a girl once again, the equation of metro with money suggested by the aesthetic of the city is writ large on the transgender body. In the country, that is, Tip's laboring life made him "as strong and rugged as a boy may be,"[50] and after hir magical transition, hir appearance literally embodies the décor of the city: "Her eyes sparkled as two diamonds and her lips were tinted like a tourmaline. All adown her back floated tresses of ruddy gold, with a slender jeweled circlet confining them at the brow. Her robes of silken gauze floated around her like a cloud, and dainty satin slippers shod her feet."[51] To become a proper urban ruler—to take one's proper place in the family line—in this case demands not only a return to an "original" gender (a proper gender for a gendered property) but also an alchemic transition of class, a bedecking of the body that warrants far more description than the changed "sex." This transformation from rags to riches is accepted as part of Tip's (now, Princess Ozma's) urbanizing Bildungsroman, though Glinda the Good (the Witch who bids Mombi to return Tip to femalehood) emphasizes several times that this is a restoration, not a transformation. Tip's initial response sounds like a confirmation that becoming a girl would be a fate worse than being exiled from the city as the crew is earlier in the text.

> "Oh, let Jinjur be the Queen!" exclaimed Tip, ready to cry. "I want to stay a boy, and travel with the Scarecrow and the Tin Woodman, and the Woggle-Bug, and Jack—Yes! And my friend the Saw-Horse—and the Gump! I don't want to be a girl!"[52]

It is easy to read Tip's clinging to gender privilege (at even the expense of the class privilege he stands to gain) as a sign of just how good it is to be a boy. However, his protest could also be read as an affirmation of the intimacies of his crew and also a reluctance to "grow up" into a proper figure of state power. That this reluctance to accede to the throne is couched as a reluctance to re-gender himself, however, leaves readers with the unavoidable equation of the restoration of "original" gender with birthright and mobility/nobility. As a final blow to the ethic of gender mobility enacted by the text's other more interesting aspects, the "restored" Princess Ozma ends the text with a final lesson. The Tin Woodman and the Scarecrow are debating who among them is the richer (for their brains or their hearts, or, like the Scarecrow himself, for being stuffed with money) and the "little Queen" weighs in with her final word: "'You are both rich, my friends,' said Ozma, gently; 'and your riches are the only riches worth having—the riches of content!'"[53] Spoken with all the self-assuredness of those who have enough wealth to feel that money is entirely unimportant, Ozma insists on these "riches of content," while Jinjur, we may recall, was first introduced as young girl wearing an "expression of discontent."[54] In a sense, the affective lesson given to girl readers is rather totalizing: be "content" with what you have, help your mother with your chores, and remember, you still won't grow up to be a princess. Some "boy" will. Not surprisingly, readers are also led to believe that girls who choose to be content with their lot will be all the happier for it. When the Army is disbanded and sent home,

> At once the men of the Emerald City cast off their aprons. And it is said that the women were so tired of eating of their husbands' cooking that they all hailed the conquest of Jinjur with joy. . . . Harmony was immediately restored in every family.[55]

In this denouement, the assemblages, wayward children, magical bodies, and unnatural affiliations are tied up with the tight binds of familial divisions of labor in the home. It is better—even for women—to cook up dinner rather than revolution and to keep their knitting needles where they belong. Being "discontent[ed]" and "audacious," girl readers learn, will only disrupt order, which will inevitably be restored. Has this parable loosened its grip over the more than hundred years since Baum's story, during which time Tip's changing gender became all the more possible, the green color of Emerald City's glasses has taken on a new meaning in light of groups like the Human Rights Campaign, queer rural youth largely remain without "steady incomes or concrete plans (not to mention local options) for schooling beyond high school,"[56] and gender transition for rural trans people remains a matter of distance, be it financial, epistemological, affective, or just the prospect of depending on a parent to drive you those four long hours to the nearest endocrinologist? If *this* is an example, in Baum's words, of a "modernized fairy tale, in which the wonderment and joy are retained and the heart-aches and nightmares left out,"[57] let's be grateful that he didn't write horror stories.

Transgender Minors

Invested in conventions of inheritance though it is, *The Marvelous Land of Oz* remakes family dynamics; it constitutes, in Pugh's words, a world of "anti-reproductive intimacy"[58] that undoes the tenets of what Edelman calls "reproductive futurism."[59] But Baum himself conceived of his Oz series as a kid-friendly fairy tale, one that "gladly dispenses with all disagreeable incident."[60] To him, this new positive tone comprises a new Americanized[61] genre of "wonder tale," one "in which the stereotyped genie, dwarf and fairy are eliminated, together with all the horrible and blood-curdling incident devised by their [European] authors to point a fearsome moral to each tale."[62] If there is one conventional kiddie-lit moral left out of the text, however, it is the forceful imperative to listen to one's parents and guardians at all costs. Tip's whole adventure is premised on the moment he decides to run away. In this narrative, the truculent kid is *right*; the joke he plays on his guardian ends up being a ticket out of town; his decision to run away is the best one he makes. This disobedient premise, along with the bodies, affiliations, and interrelationality characteristic of Tip's trips, challenge the inter-twined upward-mobility narratives of class-urbanism-maturity traced out above. For Tip, "growing up" is achieved the moment he agrees to stay and live in the city forever. If this rings even somewhat true for some rural trans and queer kids (as it certainly does in the small village from which I wrote this essay), disrupting representations of "youth" is indeed a way to question why "growing up" seems sometimes to mean "growing out of" the country.

In 2010, the long-running Canadian television show *Degrassi* intro-duced a transgender character, a young "FTM" (though the plot and the character's presentation suggest some less determinate mode of trans-gender).[63] Though there have been many critiques and questions about this character, the fantasy of lonely rural transgender youth is used to defend and prop up the show's choices. As one blogger sees it, this char-acter is "ground-breaking . . . for the sake of the trans kids watching, maybe stuck in the middle of nowhere in a rural town, wondering if anyone else has ever felt like they feel." Who benefits from this emo-tional narrative of the rural queer or transgender child, always in need of some televised simulacra of urban practices of the body and of relation-ships? As a very specific *fantasy* of televised urban outreach, the show might tell us more about how some urbanites might like to represent themselves to themselves, rather than about what rural trans kids might be, become, want, or need. To repeat Žižek, there is a "radical intersub-jectivity of fantasy" such that "what the fantasy . . . is really about is [our] attempt to form an identity . . . that would satisfy [others]"[64] and thus make *us* the object of their desire.

In Edelman's view, evocations of the child entail a troubling muta-tion of *figure*. They set out to nullify the possibility that "the Child . . . might find an enjoyment that would nullify the figural value, itself im-posed by adult desire, of the Child as unmarked by the adult's adulter-ating implication in desire itself."[65] It would be an error, in an essay on the transgender of Oz, not to take up Edelman's suggestion in light of representations of transgender children, where figurative speech takes on a strange life—one that helps evince the always already tragic *image* of the transgender child. For instance, in a *20/20* special entitled *My Secret Self*, hosted by fervent trans-chaser Barbara Walters, a worried mother describes the first time she "knew" her child was transgender.

It was "the day she came up to me . . . [and] said, 'Mommy, when's the good fairy gonna come with her magic wand and change, you know, my genitalia?'" The specifically *tragic* note of the spectacle is produced through the supposed juxtaposition of a life problem as grave as transgender with the "empty, innocent, pur[e]"[66] language from the mouth of a babe. The juxtaposition delivers us the *image* of the child not only as "a coordinate set of *have-nots*"[67] (here, not having language to grasp the gravity of the situation) but also as the bearer of an innocence we wish to preserve. Its emotional mobilization of narrative also forgets Kincaid's point about the power of stories: that "a child's memory is developed not simply from data but from learning a canonical narrative; we know that what we are and have been comes to us from narrative forms that take on so much authority they start looking like nature."[68] The poignant but only implied answer to the child's question is, of course, the adult knowledge that no "good fairy" *will* come; the child's narrative of magic figures—without explanation—*is tragic*. Rarely do we see such an explicit instance of Edelman's contention that "the Child, in the historical epoch of our current epistemological regime, is the figure for this compulsory investment in the misrecognition of figure."[69]

In contrast, Baum's text restores the child from "figure" to agent (albeit in a fantasy world), one who engages in relational gender-making and *makes* relationships rather than merely fits into or threatens a preexisting family form. (It also, undeniably, suggests that leaving the old country house is where one's life begins.) The family of this text is transspecies, inter-generational, and comprised of "*unnatural participation*"[70] rather than genetics or law. The relationship configured as most familial in this text occurs between Tip and Jack Pumpkinhead. The latter, though he is many feet taller than the young Tip, happily calls Tip—who built him—"Father," even though it was Mombi who brought him to life. This "child" was conceived as a ruse, as an object of familial disobedience, and as a product of imagination; Jack figures, therefore, as an effect of Tip's discontented energy made manifest. Though the relationship between them is often reigned in under the sign of family—"'You must be my creator my parent my father! . . . Then I owe you obedience . . . and you owe me—support!'"[71] cries Jack—a remainder of this queer parenthood persists: Tip laughs at the idea that he is a father and interjects, "'or your inventor'"[72] with a laugh. Moreover, a sense of the unsettling quality of the relationship is also marked: "the boy, small and rather delicate in appearance seemed somewhat embarrassed at being called 'father' by the tall, awkward, pumpkinheaded man," but in order to avoid "another long and tedious explanation," Tip represses the discomfort by "chang[ing] the subject . . . abruptly."[73]

Despite the text's ambivalence towards this queer "family" dynamic, Tip's crew is made up of anomalies: each of the pack (the Scarecrow, the Cowardly Lion, the Tin Woodman, the Woggle-Bug, Jack Pumpkinhead, the Gump, and the Saw-Horse) is literally one of a kind, or "anomalous."[74] Their various refutations of taxonomic logic do not stop them from engaging in the assemblage-building practice of limb-swapping; for instance, when the animated Saw-Horse loses a leg and can no longer carry the stiff-jointed Pumpkin, the solution is a matter-of-fact one of cross-body prosthesis: as the Woggle-Bug asks, "'If the Pumpkinhead is to ride, why not use one of his legs to make a leg for the horse that carries him? I judge that both are made of wood.'"[75] With little hesitation that solution is enacted—a reassignment of limbs that fulfills the pack's imperative to move, with an understated disregard for the sovereignty of the individual. With these prosthetic assemblages traversing the boundaries of bodies, this is not, as Pugh suggests, "community";[76] if anything, it is "inoperative community,"[77] in which "the relation (the community) is, if it *is*, nothing other than what it undoes."[78] This "community," rather than shore up "the absolute-subject of metaphysics" must "*cut into* this subject,"[79] an appropriate trope for Oz and even trans narrative. Of course, the group often strives to cohere: prior to one escape from the city, the Scarecrow even commands the others to "'fetch a clothesline . . . and tie us all together.'"[80] But even this image of a forced integrity is imagined only as a way to coordinate their failure. Witness the Scarecrow's caveat: "'Then if one falls off we will all fall off.'"[81] To be sure, readers get only the humblest hint at the kind of becoming and "unnatural participation" that Deleuze and Guattari associate with the packs, affects, and multiplicities that challenge state- and family-based organizations of bodies. But in even that small peek, we can see that despite Tip's eventual capitulation to urban "original" gender adulthood, there remains a core of transing materiality in this text that challenges borders—a challenge that is urgent in light of the increasing frequency with which emotional evocations of transgender youth institutionalize and tame the potential—even the magic—of being a weirdo hick kid who knows that the interpellations of mainstream representations aren't eliciting your response.

The Magic of Contact

Thus far, this essay has drawn out a seemingly irreconcilable impasse of Oz's urbanizing mobility narrative and its less frequent moments of transing the emotional conventions of trans youth and family. Beyond this impasse, *The Marvelous Land of Oz* offers a more indeterminate question that we might recognize: What if, one morning, when you awoke from gender-troubled dreams, you found yourself transformed in your bed into a fabulous transing body? To optimistically appropriate the "principle of magic" that Freud derides in *Totem and Taboo*, what is at stake in "mistaking an ideal connection for a real one"[82]—or, moreover, challenging the division between ideal and real? By casting aside genetic narratives ("I didn't just wake up one morning and decide I was gay!"), could magic be an imaginative base from which to theorize bodily transformation? Deleuze and Guattari claim, in drawing out what they call a "politics of sorcery,"[83] that "sorcerers have always held the anomalous position, at the edge of the fields or woods. They haunt the fringes. They are at the borderline of the village, or *between* villages."[84] In this view, could there be something about the idea of transgender magic that is—if not rural "proper"—then *ruralizing* or becoming-rural?[85]

The resonance of these questions is heightened in Oz, where everything is—in relation to the "real" world—already magical: talking animals, glowing monochromatic landscapes, animated metal and wood being assembled into sentient beings, and so on. But "magic" as a trope still looms large in this already magical world, as if to mark the outside or the limit case of this text's own fantastical spaces. As a trope in Baum's text, magic is located on the fringes of both the city and of morality. Mombi, for instance, lives not in Oz but in a fringe village, where her "curious magic often frightened her neighbors."[86] (So too does Glinda live outside of Emerald City, as did the predeceased wicked witches.) The text's morality of magic is pulled strictly towards one of two poles: it is "Wicked" or it is "Good"; it is the domain both of young boys and queer crews in need of help but also of those who seek specifically to turn young wanderers into marble statues; it appears as a rural technology of evil and as an urbanizing force that helps would-be heirs find their footing to the throne. This spatial morality of magic hits its apex with the young Jinjur, whose royal undoing is generated by her own transgression of the text's implied spatial placement of magic forces. Jinjur brings witchy Mombi to Emerald City to help keep Tip's crew from regaining the throne for the Scarecrow. The crew's eventual triumph over Jinjur is grounded on one small detail: after storming the kingdom for Mombi (in order to demand that she tell them where to find the true heiress Ozma), they eventually give up and leave. As a witch who deals especially in transformations—a mode of magic Glinda specifically dismisses as "unscrupulous"[87]—Mombi hides herself during their search by turning into a rose. The entire plot turns here: the Tin Woodman, resigned to leaving the city without Mombi, picks this rose, pins it to his chest, and leaves. (After more transformations and chases outside of the city, Mombi is soon caught and made to declare Tip the rightful heir.) Through a chance encounter with not just any object but with a feigned flower—a "fake" "nature"—the figure of "bad" magic is carried out of the city because the transformation was *too* realistic. Only under the strict supervision of Glinda is an act of magic carried out in the city (Mombi "restoring" Tip's gender), and readers will recall that what appears to be urban magic in *The Wonderful Wizard of Oz*—the Wizard's stunning transformations into a woman, a beast, and an enormous head—are revealed to be mere illusions, sleights of hand masterminded by a now-disappeared fake wizard (from Omaha).

While this relegation of magic to the rural fringes in *Oz* itself suggests the text's rejection of (what it configures as) rural ways of knowing, there is something else at stake in this equation of dishonest and outmoded magic with land beyond the metropolis. That a shifting theory of knowledge is at stake in representations of magic is evident even in small moments of Baum's text. For instance, when Mombi animates the pumpkinhead—the text's *first* magical act—she asks, "staring at him intently," "'What do you know?'"[88] But when Adorno and Horkheimer begin *Dialectic of Enlightenment* by suggesting that the Enlightenment may be defined through its opposition to magic—it was "the disenchantment of the world; the dissolution of myths and the substitution of knowledge for fancy"[89]—the point is made clearer: the rural/urban divide in Oz is just as much a matter of competing theories of knowledge as anything else, ones that are irrevocably tied up in problematic economies of temporality and in fetishizing "modern" knowledge while rejecting outmoded or "backwards" thinking. Scott Herring's nuanced rereading of "Southern backwardness" makes this point in reference to Michael Meads's *Alabama Souvenirs*. In Herring's estimation, "Southern backwardness" is represented as

> committed to ideals of uncritical rusticity. Such cultural lack also ties to a temporal "backwardness," most prominently expressed in the caricature of the U.S. South as a frozen region outdated by supposedly more progressive spaces across the nation. . . . Such southern "backwardness" also links to temporal norms that structure queer metronormativity in the form of trendy fashions or being in the know.[90]

Herring suggests that, in order to reactivate the anti-urban critical potential of this "backward" stereotype, Meads employs "anachronistic stylistics"[91] in his choreographed "portraits" of Alabama men. That is, Meads's aesthetic—particularly the classical tone it produces via citations of Pater, Caravaggio, and others—"undermine[s] any sense of continuity or cross-identification"[92] from queer urbanites, "refuses to allow queer urbanites to find yet another version of their historical selves through his photography."[93] Meads uses aesthetic "backwardness"—anachronism—to bring the disruption of queer ruralities into the "traditional archives of Western gay male art that naturalize queer urbanism."[94] Likewise, magic is often figured as precisely this same kind of backwardness in relation to time and space. For instance, Freud, again, assigns magic to a particular place on his three-step linear narrative of progressing knowledge: magic turns into religion, which eventually yields to science. Taking up one of his several ruralized metaphors for magic, Freud discusses the ritual of imitating or "playing at rain"[95] in order to evoke rain for crops. As he predicts, after the fact,

> at a later stage of civilization, instead of this rain-magic, processions will be made to a temple and prayers for rain will be addressed to the deity living in it. Finally, this religious technique will in its turn be given up

and attempts will be made to produce effects in the atmosphere which will lead to rain."[96]

In Freud's clear progression narrative, the triumph of science not only renders abject many (racialized, ruralized) ways of knowing, but also demands a correlative change in the spatial life of the interrelationality of bodies. In what Freud characterizes as the "magical" period, "distance" has an entirely different affective economy than it does in modernity. In what he calls "imitative" magic, "the element of distance is disregarded . . . telepathy is taken for granted . . . the operative factor [is] the *similarity* between the act performed and the result expected."[97] The physical proximity between the desiring subject and the object of desire is not required in this model—an idea of space that throws cause and effect into the more indeterminate world of affect, of imperceptible and inexplicable connections between bodies and raindrops. In the second, "contagious" category of magic, "what is believed to be their effective principle is no longer similarity but spatial connection, contiguity, or at least *imagined* contiguity—the recollection of it."[98] Freud offers two examples of this kind of "magical" thinking, each of which suggests that magical thinking is the stuff not just of magicians but also of the most everyday banal moments: first, he mentions a woman who, after injuring her foot with a nail, kept only the *nail* clean and not her foot, and second, he reports that there are "English country people" who "even today . . . if they cut themselves with a scythe carefully keep the instrument clean, to prevent the wound from festering."[99]

These images constitute a different way of thinking about the possibilities of animate and inanimate bodies relating through space. To reclaim another point Freud intends as less than complimentary, we might revel in his idea that those who believe in magic—rather than shore up the tightly closed-off boundaries of the subject's body—consistently assert (the importance of) "contact"[100] both "real" and imagined. The "backwardness" variously attributed to "savages," to rural dwellers, and to magicians entails not just the antirural attitudes Herring so aptly draws out; it also rejects certain notions of interrelationality and contact that might be worth saving. On the most concrete level, at a time when cities are thought to have an almost intuitive queerness, a theory of transgender magic or "contact" holds special significance for rurality because it stakes a claim to the vitality of building relationships and genders on the indeterminate foundations of impossibly "backwards" (nonurban) forms of knowledge. The practiced abjection of magic, geographical and otherwise, works to shore up the notions of "civilization" and "sophistication" on which the supremacy of the urban, as a category and a fantasy, depends. Reclaiming the usefulness of magic is to live out the concurrent critical negativity and counterintuitive hope it takes to become even more backwards—to keep defying gravity at a heavy time of queer settling and the concurrent institutionalization and urbanization of transgender.

NOTES

1 Pugh, "'There Lived in the Land of Oz Two Queerly Made Men,'" 218.

2 Ibid., 217.

3 Ibid., 226.

4 Ibid., 92.

5 Ibid., 71.

6 Ibid., 101.

7 Ibid., 221.

8 Baum, *The Marvelous Land of Oz*, 63.

9 Cited in Pugh, "'Are We Cannibals, Let Me Ask? Or Are We Faithful Friends?,'" 326.

10 Deleuze and Guattari, *A Thousand Plateaus*, 27.

11 Ibid., 18.

12 Pugh, "'There Lived in the Land of Oz,'" 218.

13 Deleuze and Guattari, *A Thousand Plateaus*, 471.

14 Ibid., 470.

15 Weston, "Get Thee to a Big City," 253.

16 See "Pride Toronto 2010: All of Our Coverage in One Place" for *Xtra*'s extensive archive of the "Queers against Israeli Apartheid" controversy. See also Jenn Ruddy's "Edmonton Police Service's Queer Liaison Committee is Out of Touch."

17 Žižek, *The Plague of Fantasies*, 7.

18 Ibid., 9.

19 Ibid., 29, emphasis mine.

20 Baum, *The Marvelous Land of Oz*, 46.

21 Dean Spade has made vital critiques of these state-based struggles for rights to citizenship. See especially "Trans Law and Politics on a Neoliberal Landscape" and his portions of "The Identity Victim," in which he aptly points out that "well-resourced LGBT organizations . . . too often choose symbolic victories and victories that disproportionately benefit white people and people with property" (274).

22 Aizura, "Of Borders and Homes," 289.

23 Ibid., 293.

24 Baum, *The Marvelous Land of Oz*, 135.

25 Aizura, "Of Borders and Homes," 296.

26 Gray, "From Websites to Wal-Mart," 53.

27 Baum, *The Marvelous Land of Oz*, 21–22.

28 Ibid., 23.

29 Ibid., 13.

30 Ibid., 24.

31 Ibid., 25.

32 Ibid.

33 Ibid., 17.

34 Ibid., 40.

35 Herring, *Another Country*, 13.

36 Ibid., 17.

37 Baum, *The Marvelous Land of Oz*, 40.

38 Ibid., 39.

39 Baum, *The Wonderful Wizard of Oz*, 109.

40 Prosser, *Second Skins*, 177.

41 Aizura, "Of Borders and Homes," 295.

42 Baum, *The Marvelous Land of Oz*, 46.

43 Ibid., 47.

44 Ibid., 48.

45 Ibid.

46 Ibid., 47.

47 Ibid., 49.

48 Ibid., 135.

49 Ibid., 137.

50 Ibid., 13.

51 Ibid., 134.

52 Ibid.

53 Ibid., 138.

54 Ibid., 46.

55 Ibid., 136.

56 Gray, "From Websites to Wal-Mart," 49.

57 Baum, *The Marvelous Land of Oz*, vii.

58 Pugh, "'There Lived in the Land of Oz,'" 226.

59 Edelman, *No Future*, 4.

60 Baum, *The Marvelous Land of Oz*, vii.

61 For more on Baum's explicitly American outlooks, see Jack Zipes, "Oz as American Myth."

62 Baum, *The Marvelous Land of Oz*, vii.

63 In 2013, he was killed off of the show after he sustained injuries in a car accident, which occurred because he was texting (his conservative Christian girlfriend) while driving.

64 Žižek, *The Plague of Fantasies*, 8.

65 Edelman, *No Future*, 21.

66 Kincaid, "Producing Erotic Children," 10.

67 Ibid.

68 Ibid., 15.

69 Edelman, *No Future*, 18.

70 Deleuze and Guattari, *A Thousand Plateaus*, 240.

71 Baum, *The Marvelous Land of Oz*, 25.

72 Ibid., 24.

73 Ibid., 27.

74 Deleuze and Guattari, *A Thousand Plateaus*, 243.

75 Baum, *The Marvelous Land of Oz*, 76.

76 Pugh, "'There Lived in the Land of Oz,'" 221.

77 Nancy, *The Inoperative Community*, 1.

78 Ibid., 4.

79 Ibid., emphasis mine.

80 Baum, *The Marvelous Land of Oz*, 54.

81 Ibid.

82 Freud, *Totem and Taboo*, 79.

83 Deleuze and Guattari, *A Thousand Plateaus*, 247.

84 Ibid., 246, emphasis mine.

85 Becoming, in Deleuze and Guattari's words, is "a verb with a consistency all its own; it does not reduce to, or lead back to, 'appearing,' 'being,' 'equaling,' or 'producing'" (ibid., 239). Rather, it "concerns alliance" (238), "involution" (238), and "always involves a pack, a band, a population, a peopling, in short, a multiplicity" (239).

86 Baum, *The Marvelous Land of Oz*, 14.

87 Ibid., 133.

88 Ibid., 20.

89 Adorno and Horkheimer, *Dialectic of Enlightenment*, 3.

90 Herring, *Another Country*, 114.

91 Ibid., 103.

92 Ibid., 114.

93 Ibid.

94 Ibid., 106. For another queer account of "backwardness," see Heather Love's *Feeling Backwards*.

95 Freud, *Totem and Taboo*, 80.

96 Ibid., 81.

97 Ibid.

98 Ibid., 83, emphasis mine.

99 Ibid., 82.

100 Ibid., 85.

7

Outside Forces

Black Southern Sexuality

LATOYA E. EAVES

Asheville is really not the place to have a problem being a lesbian. Asheville has one of the largest lesbian populations per capita. It's as if San Francisco was as small as us, we'd have more than San Francisco. So Asheville is not a problem with that. . . . But it is interesting, though, being black and lesbian. Because believe it or not, there are lesbians who are also racists.

In the quotation above, my informant, Stephanie, is describing how the intersections of her identity as a black lesbian coalesce in the place she calls home—Asheville, North Carolina. Taken from our interview in May 2013, Stephanie's remarks provide a clear rationale for examining the nuances of identity in place. This essay examines the interplay of race and sexuality among black women who experience same-gender desire, intimacy, and love and asks: How is race realized and expressed by black queer and lesbian women? What role does region play in consciousness about race and sexuality? Does the interplay of race, place, and sexuality have the same meaning among the population? Drawing on interviews with three participants to answer these questions, this chapter contributes to the growing body of literature that focus on black southern sexualities and the ways they recast ontologies of race and region. It also adds to discussions of sexuality and space, which are more often focused on white LGBTQ people in major urban areas.

The sociocultural mythology of the South often homogenizes its regional discourse as a site of abjection, or a culturally backwards space that reeks of plantation culture, Jim Crow, and Bibles. This mythology is

problematic because it insinuates a strict regionalism that does not acknowledge the opportunities, realities, and experiences of the entire U.S.
South that can be differentiated from other communities and regions
across the nation. Thus, it becomes important for empirical work to disrupt the cultural narrative that represents the South as a place where all
whites are racists, all blacks are subservient, and all lesbians and gays are
in the closet and to offer another narrative in which agency, freedom,
and possibility exist.

At the same time, southern history reminds us that we must pay attention to the intricacies of race and racism in the region. In researching
the ways southern identity manifests in black and white Southerners,
Thompson and Sloan observe that "the experience of race for these
[white] southerners is an experience of racial privilege."[1] They do not
think of their identity as white southerners; they see themselves as simply southerners. Scholars of the South have to be conscientious when
examining and describing the region and its people to avoid creating a
monolithic regional discourse.

In western North Carolina, and especially Asheville, race is made invisible and declared to be "not a problem." However, race and racism
most certainly do have legacy here. As Darin Waters notes,

> In Asheville and western North Carolina, Blacks were virtually invisible—
> especially politically—and were thus marginalized in all areas of the city's
> post–Civil War development. This marginalization might have been missed
> by the casual observer because the city's white leaders were successful in
> constructing a veneer that suggested the city was peaceful and progressive
> in all areas of life. The reality of white racial attitudes in Asheville and the
> surrounding region, however, hampered the ability of Blacks to fully par-
> ticipate in the city's social, political, and economic structure after the war.[2]

Processes of racialization and the perpetuation of racism as significant areas of empirical investigation remain relevant to the study of the
South.

Moreover, as Beverly Greene argues, "Just as race defines sexuality,
sexuality defines race in a range of ways and in a reciprocal fashion."[3] As
a result, "Blackness and gayness are rendered alternately visible and invisible depending on the social context."[4] At the same time, most scholar-

ship on southern gay life tends to highlight gay men. Thus, for example, in *Sweet Tea: Black Gay Men of the South*, E. Patrick Johnson argues that "the sexual other . . . is implicated in both the region's guts and its glory, its horrific past and its present graciousness. And yet, Black gay southern-ers have co-existed in communities throughout the region for as long as there has been a 'South.'"[5] Researching individuals at the intersections of race, sexuality, and womanhood extracts the complexities of a peripheral experience that is different from that of men. Gay men are able to congre-gate in different areas of visibility, through church and work, for example.[6] However, "the visibility of queer Black women . . . is limited in two key ways. Firstly, in the extent of her own embodiment as a 'carrier' of her sexuality, and secondly, limited to the ways her racialized or cultural iden-tity influences her way of life."[7] The purpose of this essay is to centralize the intersecting social categories of race, gender, and sexuality in order to gain a more enriched perspective of identity in place.

Asheville, North Carolina

Asheville is Cherokee ancestral land. Cherokees lived there relatively undisturbed until Hernando de Soto appeared in 1540. After European colonization began, trade routes were formed throughout Western North Carolina in the seventeenth century. In 1781, Colonel Samuel Davidson, a man of Irish descent born in Lancaster, Pennsylvania, settled his fam-ily and a female slave near the Swannanoa River (just east of Asheville's present city center). Davidson is considered the first white settler in Western North Carolina. A decade later, the Davidsons and other settler families petitioned the state to form Buncombe County, where Asheville is currently the county seat. The city of Asheville became incorporated through a land grant petition to the state of North Carolina in 1797.

Since its incorporation, Asheville has grown considerably while maintaining southern small-town charm. Today, nearly 85,000 individ-uals call Asheville home, and the area attracts visitors from all around the world year round. Asheville's official tourism website provides the following description:

> Asheville is that type of unique, special place that lingers sweetly in your
> mind and memories for years to come. The city's rich architectural legacy

with its mix of Art Deco, Beaux Arts and Neoclassical styles is the perfect retro-urban backdrop to the edgy energy that emanates from the locally owned shops and art galleries, distinctive restaurants and exciting entertainment venues. Known as an art colony, a healing resort and a home to notable luminaries, statesmen and bohemians, Asheville is one of the most welcoming, vibrant cities in America.[8]

As someone who grew up in Western North Carolina and visited Asheville regularly over the years, I can affirm that this description is true. Asheville is a diverse and inclusive city for its residents and visitors, and it is frequently listed as one of the most LGBTQ-friendly places to live in and visit, as this excerpt from a gay travel site indicates:

> Generally, the adage about not going to small towns when you're looking for queer-friendly travel is a smart one, however, there are some small towns that welcome and charm gay travelers with a relaxed and laid-back vibe. Asheville, North Carolina, is one of those places. If you're looking for a romantic getaway with your Mister or Misses Right instead of cruisin' the local scene for a Mister or Misses Right Now, you might consider Downtown Asheville. There are some unique bars and clubs to whet your whistle."[9]

Asheville offers a rich and nuanced nonmetropolitan spatial scale from which to discuss LGBTQ life. Situated in the Blue Ridge Mountains, it provides a corrective to the assumption that urban spaces are the only utopias for LGBTQ individuals. On the contrary, with its southern and mountain culture, Asheville supports tight-knit communities that are racially, socioeconomically, and sexually diverse, while also welcoming travelers seeking respite from urban life. This is where the experiences of those whom I interviewed were grounded.

Methods

This essay draws on qualitative fieldwork conducted in Western North Carolina between 2011 and 2013. The female participants, who were solicited through purposive and snowball sampling, had to identify as black and as lesbian/gay/queer/same-gender loving and live in Western

North Carolina in order to be eligible to be interviewed. I conducted semi-structured interviews with the women during the summer of 2013. Informants responded to questions about their background and their ideas and experiences of "identity," "community," and "home." The interviews utilized for this essay represent women who live in the same town or county, thereby allowing for the opportunity to compare experiences across individuals in a discursively and quantitatively bounded space.

The Women

This essay analyzes the interviews of Vern, Stephanie, and Nicole,[10] each of whom self-identifies as a lesbian. Vern is a fifty-four-year-old substance-abuse counselor and is completing a master's degree in counseling at a regional university. At the time of the interview, she had lived in Asheville for approximately ten years, having moved from Long Island, New York, to be with her partner. Stephanie is a forty-nine-year-old stay-at-home parent and a co-founder of a nonprofit performing arts collective that seeks to produce theatrical and artistic work that supports the diversity of talent in western North Carolina. At the time of the interview, Stephanie, who had moved to Asheville because of a personal need for a "change of scenery," had lived there for sixteen years. Nicole is a twenty-three-year-old student, artist, and founder of a local organization that focuses on the empowerment of black and Latino communities and engaging in dialogue about issues affecting them in the greater Western North Carolina region. At the time of the interview, Nicole had lived in Asheville for around nine years, after having moved to the area with her mother following her parents' divorce.

Analysis

For the women in my project, visibility and affirmation of their full selves were challenging to achieve in the public sphere. When describing herself, Stephanie noted, "I feel like I'm a strong woman. I don't necessarily have the need to attach my sexuality or my race to that because I don't need those qualifiers." Indeed, while all of my participants were distinctly comfortable in their identities, they recognized that their normalized experiences reflected influences from social forces, particularly with regard to race, and resulted in heightened race consciousness. Vern, who came out in her forties after being married to a man for over twenty years, recalled that she was unclear whether it was her identity as a lesbian that shocked her family or whether their reaction also had something to do with race. In fact, Vern's race consciousness was the most apparent of all of my interviewees, which could be due to her being a more recent southern transplant. Nonetheless, I see race conscious-ness as being almost second nature for people of color in the United States, even as racism operates in more dynamic and explicit ways in the South. For Vern, who attended a historically black college, obtained a master's degree in history, studied black film, and is currently enrolled in a second master's program, it was important to highlight race and the experiences of living as a racialized minority.

Stephanie, whose wife, Trish, is white, described a situation in which race consciousness rose to the fore:

> "[Trish and I are] foster parents. And we had a sixteen-year-old white girl in our house first. And she's pregnant. And her mom was still in the pic-ture because the whole thing was getting her to go back home.... And it's funny that whenever Trish was with me and we would be talking to her, she would not have a conversation with me. She would only talk to Trish."

This particular situation of being explicitly ignored connects to a state-ment Stephanie made earlier in her interview: "So my identity is I'm a strong woman. Outside forces recognize or remind me that I'm a black woman." Stephanie thus recognized the impact of the dominant culture on her life, which is not bounded by her lesbian identity but at her spe-cific intersections of race and sexuality.

Nicole described her involvement with a local LGBTQ advocacy group as she was entering her twenties, saying that she enjoyed and val-ued the experience, but that there were no other people of color. As a result, Nicole noted that the visible marker of her racial identity led her to feel and be tokenized in the group, and she was often, and still is, called upon to be the connection to and the voice of people of color in queer spaces around Asheville. She highlighted a constant tension be-tween her desire to integrate herself into the city's fabric and feeling as if she did not belong as a person of color trying to support the LGBTQ community. In her interview, Nicole recalled a voter registration event at a local nightclub organized by a friend of hers. The budget for the event was minimal and the entertainment (a drag show) was organized on a volunteer basis. Those who volunteered all turned out to be African American. The next day, a complaint was made to her friend that the entertainment was not "diverse enough." Nicole remarked, "It was hurtful to see that if it's not white enough, it's not good enough."

Place is made and unmade by people and their sociopolitical experiences. Asheville is a peculiar fixture in the American South boasting global popularity for tourism and retirement and a reputation as a progressive, open, and affirming town for a diversity of people. In fact, I would hypothesize that some visitors and new residents in the region attempt to distance Asheville from the mythologies of the South. But as Nicole stated, "Asheville seems so progressive . . . beautiful and open," but when you "get down to the nitty gritty, it's not diverse at all." By "not diverse," Nicole means the limited racial and ethnic diversity of predominantly white Asheville, which is accompanied by a lack of exposure to perspectives brought about by those lived experiences. Asheville may be home and host to a unique collection of peoples not commonly represented by small cities and towns, but as Nicole reminds us, being welcomed into certain spaces requires access to a certain set of privileges. Moreover, to revisit Stephanie's observation from the opening of this essay, "there are lesbians who are racists" even in a town that has an active lesbian population.

In my interviews with Vern and Stephanie, the topic of tension and disconnection within and between black people was expressed in two distinct ways. In Vern's interview, she noted that she did not feel connected either to the LGBTQ community in Asheville or to the black community. "[I'm] not sure if it's because I'm a northerner living in the South," she said, but "I haven't found acceptance here as a black woman, let alone a black lesbian woman. . . . That brings me a lot of sadness. . . . The friends I do make are usually black northerners." While it is unclear exactly how Vern has attempted to connect with black and/or LGBTQ communities in Asheville, it is evident that she understands a characteristic of Southern regionalism that involves suspicion of outsiders. She has also had to deal with the experience of being black in a region that has maintained a "sundown town" reputation and noted that she did not feel safe outside of Asheville. None of this heightened Southern regionalist consciousness came up as "negative" for any other women interviewed.

Stephanie spent a significant number of years in Atlanta, Georgia, both as a child and as an adult. Situated approximately three hours to the southwest of Asheville, Atlanta is a thriving metropolis that informally operates as the center site of reverse migration, the contemporary phenomenon where significant numbers of black people in the United States, especially younger generations, are making a return to the South from the North and the Midwest. The return is largely influenced by an interest in retracing the paths of their elders and connecting to the heritage and spirit of their ancestors who were enslaved in the region. Additionally, Atlanta is unofficially known as a mecca for black gay people, and LGBTQ people of color are visibly integrated in the city's landscape. Growing up in Atlanta, though, was difficult for Stephanie, as she explained. "I had, you know, the dark-skinned/light-skinned thing. . . . I got called 'oreo' all the time. You know that whole black on the outside, white on the inside. . . . I got called 'tar baby.' . . . I got called 'wannabe.' . . . [The] first time I experienced racism was from my own race." In referring to "the dark-skinned/light-skinned thing," Stephanie is recalling how her phenotypically darker skin caused her to be subject to ridicule on the part of her peers. What Stephanie was explicitly describing was a variation on internalized racism, a phenomenon that equates whiteness as the most privileged human embodiment. Internalized racism is deeply embedded in colonial legacies and still found on a global scale. Skin-whitening products, plastic surgery, and hair products (such as hair weaves and extensions) are objects of consumption that lend themselves to the systemically preferred and heralded standard of aesthetic whiteness. To utilize Nicole's words, "if it's not white enough, it's not good enough." In this case, Stephanie was ridiculed for being phenotypically darker than her peers, while at the same time being accused of trying to "be white," and although she was not seeking to change her complexion or features, she was called "oreo," a pejorative term for a black person said to be somehow ascribing to whiteness or white culture. In addition to the aesthetic attributes of whiteness listed above, characteristics that could be considered "white" include being in the drama club, having a "white" accent, and listening to "white people's music" (such as country, rock, or heavy metal). It could also mean having a social circle inclusive of white people or an otherwise racially mixed milieu. In Stephanie's case, I can infer from her interview that her being targeted as trying to "be white" is a conglomerate of her social activities, social circles, and accent.

Nicole stated that she felt ambivalent about living in Asheville as a black lesbian. She discussed the complexities of being the only black person in white LGBTQ spaces and consequently having to speak on and for the black experience in Asheville, something she said she was growing weary of doing. At rallies and gay pride events, she said that racially diverse people came together "in packs." For her, there was a disconnection between LGBTQ people of color and other LGBTQ groups and people in the community at large, and several times, she noted the importance of Atlanta, where she could "be herself" and not just "the black girl" in white spaces. While she continues to consider her place in Asheville as a black lesbian, Nicole has nevertheless embedded herself into activist work with black and Latino communities in the region and into creating a life with her partner.

All three of the women interviewed thus indicated some level of feeling that they had to fight for a sense of belonging. Fortunately, there was no indication that their families rejected them or that there were other long-term problems. To be sure, Vern noted her family's shock when she came out, and also described the difficulty her daughter experienced initially, but, said Vern, she had "come around." Stephanie has maintained a very close relationship with her parents and her sister, who is also a lesbian. Nicole's family relationships are rather amicable, though she is much closer to her mother than to other family members. Instead, it was in church where tensions arose, and each of the three women recounted experiences of rejection and dissension in and around Christian spaces. Both Vern and Stephanie were asked to leave their leadership positions in the church after coming out. Nicole considers herself to be a "nonpracticing Christian" and struggles with supporting her friends who both hold strongly to their church ties and maintain a stance outside of church that is more liberal and more accepting of Nicole's and their own sexualities—and is therefore contradictory to what is preached in church every week. This kind of tension has broader resonance, given the passage in May of 2012 of Amendment One, a legislative measure that was decided by popular vote and criminalized the recognition of same-sex marriage in North Carolina. During the campaign for passage of the amendment, special attention was paid to African American communities, particularly the black church, whose members were largely expected to support it.[11] In this context, then, the authenticity of blackness was contingent on one's allegiance to heterosexuality.[12] When I interviewed participants in this research project, I never brought up race directly. Instead, each one discussed how her life intersects with race and place in ways that were individually nuanced. As Ann duCille writes, "Where gender and racial difference meet in the bodies of Black women, the result is the invention of an other Otherness, a hyper static alterity."[13] The interviews with Stephanie and Nicole, in particular, reveal an experience of this "other Otherness." Or, again, as Stephanie said, "believe it or not, there are lesbians who are also racists."

While Asheville has traditional sites for gay identity—namely, in bars, clubs, enclaves, and organizations—and while Asheville presents itself as an open and inclusive community, there remain distinct ways in which lesbian and queer women of color commune and experience living in Asheville, where a variety of complications and microaggressions limit their full integration into the communities to which they are connected. As Katherine McKittrick argues, "recognizing Black women's knowledgeable positions as integral to physical, cartographic, and experiential geographies within and through dominant spatial models also creates an analytical space for Black feminist geographies: Black women's political, feminist, imaginary, and creative concerns that respatialize the geographic legacy of racism-sexism."[14] Here, McKittrick is arguing for the centering of black women in order to create visibility and extract alternative modes of understanding geographic phenomena. Similarly, attention to variations of sexuality and desire among black women are necessary to creating productive knowledge in support of black geographies. The richness of the lived experiences of these three women can theoretically and empirically expand understanding of black women's lives. Race foregrounds itself in very different ways for Nicole, Vern and Stephanie, even as their identities as black lesbian women are shaped by racial articulations. This essay positions black feminist geographies with queer of color analysis to highlight the inseparability of race, gender, and sexuality in lived experiences. Vern, Stephanie, and Nicole's stories function as critical possibilities in the social investments that are produced by and in space. By centralizing Asheville, the research underscores the problem of essentialism by providing alternative narratives of a complex geography. As a site with LGBTQ life and politics embedded into its makeup, the small city still is almost exclusively white. If one assumed that a town with a tight-knit sense of community would unquestionably incorporate all sexual minorities, then this essay should counter that assumption. While LGBTQ life is diverse and varied in Asheville, its accompanying representation and levels of acceptance do not often include everyone. Local LGBTQ life mirrors LGBTQ life on the national scale in that it is difficult to bring solidarity across difference when major LGBTQ spaces privilege whiteness. Moreover, Asheville's reputation for being open and inclusive is complicated by the understanding that nonwhite residents are connected to their own race consciousness and thinking about what it means to be constantly be racialized. Clearly, then, the intersection of race and sexuality in the context of ostensibly open and inclusive spaces warrants more in-depth investigation.

Conclusion

In this essay, I have briefly discussed identity as illustrated by individuals living at the intersections of blackness, womanhood, and lesbian sexuality in Asheville, North Carolina. The discussion in this essay highlights the complexity of race and region through the lenses of gender and sexuality, as it acknowledges differences in the ways these concepts manifest through different bodies. As E. Patrick Johnson notes, "there is no master narrative of southern Black gay experience. And yet, there is a note of commonality that rings through these narratives that exemplify the roots and routes of the South."[15] Neither this essay nor my research in general attempts to homogenize the experiences and articulations of race and sexuality in Asheville or, more broadly, the U.S. South. Instead, my analysis offers some insight into the complexities of black women's lives as expressly considered from a racial lens and with a focus on one specific population. As someone who grew up in a small town sixty miles to the east of Asheville, I have always seen it as having a special place in my life. Likewise, the women I interviewed have unique and deep connections to their lives and homes in Asheville. Their narratives constitute critical knowledge that underscores the necessity for incorporating black LGBTQ people, in varying locales, into popular and empirical representations of queer life in the United States.

NOTES

1 Thompson and Sloan, "Race as Region, Region as Race," 80.

2 Waters, "Life beneath the Veneer," 6.

3 Greene, "African American Lesbian and Bisexual Women," 247.

4 Johnson, *Sweet Tea*, 3.

5 Ibid., 1.

6 Ibid.

7 Eaves, "Space, Place, and Identity in Conversation," 115.

8 Asheville Convention and Visitors Bureau, http://www.exploreasheville.com/about-asheville/.

9 GayCities, "Gay Asheville: Small Town Boys and Girls," http://asheville.gaycities.com/overview/.

10 The interview participants were asked if they preferred using their own names or a pseudonym for this project. Each woman gave me permission to use her real name.

11 See, for example, http://www.wcnc.com/news/Black-churchgoers-break-with-leading-Democrats-on-marriage-amendment—148405205.html.

12 Hill Collins, *Black Sexual Politics*; Ferguson, *Aberrations in Black*; and Moore, *Invisible Families*.

13 duCille, "The Occult of True Black Womanhood," 592.

14 McKittrick, *Demonic Grounds*, 53.

15 Johnson, *Sweet Tea*, 547.

PART III

Back and Forth

Rural Queer Life in Circulation and Transition

8

"We Are Here for You"

The It Gets Better Project, Queering Rural Space, and Cultivating Queer Media Literacy

MARK HAIN

Throughout autumn of 2010, a distressingly large number of reports made national news of teenage boys, either out as gay or perceived as gay by their peers, who had committed suicide after having been the targets of sustained anti-gay bullying, in some cases for years. Harassment and violence against gay youth became the focus of considerable media attention and purported social concern—for a brief while. The It Gets Better Project, created in September 2011 by advice columnist Dan Savage and his husband, Terry Miller, was intended as a more lasting response to the suicides and the circumstances that caused them. Savage and Miller initiated the project by posting a video of themselves on YouTube, in which they told their stories of being picked on and bullied during their adolescence, but promising queer youth that "it gets better" and urging them not to give in to despair.

As its own YouTube channel, the It Gets Better Project now offers viewers over fifty thousand video messages of support, as well as opportunities to add commentary and upload video messages of their own. In total, the videos have been viewed over fifty million times.[1] While numerous celebrities and politicians, including President Barack Obama, have added their voices, "everyday" people have contributed most of the videos, including the most emotionally resonant ones. The project has thus become a forum for redirecting sorrow, frustration, and rage into well-intentioned messages of hope.

The It Gets Better (IGB) Project has also become an archive of memories and emotions underrepresented in other media. In her important study on the intersection of affect and archiving in lesbian public cultures, Ann Cvetkovich recognizes LGBT peoples' need to "address trauma through witnessing and retelling."[2] As so many of the IGB videos attest, emotional and/or physical trauma appears to be a virtually inescapable component of life for queer children and adolescents—a trauma that Cvetkovich sees, in spite of the pain of recollection, as "a point of entry into a vast archive of feelings, the many forms of love, rage, intimacy, grief, shame, and more that are part of the vibrancy of queer cultures"[3] and that unify individuals across contexts of culture, place, and time. Thousands of LGBT people have told their own stories of mistreatment, struggles with depression, or suicide attempts through IGB videos, sharing their experiences, good as well as bad, as a way of encouraging others through difficult life stages. The project therefore not only archives individual stories but also documents an alternative history, telling a collective story of enduring and overcoming adversity, as communicated by a multicultural, multiperspectival, intergenerational, and international range of voices. At the same time, it also records a historical moment in which reevaluation of the past, personal as well as societal, becomes a way of collaboratively negotiating the present and striving to better the future.

The mass catharsis chronicled by the project externalizes and makes more visible the internal, individual processes of negotiating difference that LGBT people undertook long before the advent of new media and social networking. This essay examines the differences, but more importantly the similarities, in what new and "old" media provide gay and lesbian audiences in terms of identity construction, emotional support, and hope. I will explore how a specifically queer form of media literacy— the exercising of greater control over one's interaction with mediated messages and exerting more agency in the meanings one extracts from media texts—can help gay and lesbian youth in rural environments locate and create queer space, even if only interior space. Looking at the messages explicitly and implicitly conveyed by IGB videos addressed to gay and lesbian youth, I supplement these case studies with my own experiences of popular music sustaining me through difficult times during my adolescence and coming out in 1980s Nebraska. I locate a substantive distinction in how commercial media and user-generated media alter perceptions of celebrity and the "sexual imaginary," the embodied reassurance described by Kath Weston that someone else "like me" is "out there somewhere." The IGB videos created by rural gay men and lesbians for rural gay and lesbian youth emphasize that queer presence, even if hidden, is already *there*, as opposed to the commercial media in which I was vested as a teenager and which further alienated me from my environment. With these matters in mind, my intent is to think through some of the "survival strategies" that may be available to rural gay and lesbian youth whose circumstances do not allow them to leave problematic environments by observing how IGB videos and viewer responses contribute to a repository of coping mechanisms by queering rural spaces and depicting accessible sexual imaginaries.

In many ways, this essay is also an externalization of the self-reflection and impulse towards autoethnography prompted by the It Gets Better Project and the tragic events behind its formation. As the stories and photos of Justin Aaberg, Asher Brown, Raymond Chase, Tyler Clementi, Billy Lucas, Seth Walsh, and the other young people driven to suicide circulated through the media, I, like many, recognized a disconcerting amount of myself in their stories and their faces. That recognition compelled me, again like many, to revisit dark places in my memories. Rather than just dredging up the hurts of the past, personal as well as collective, or losing hope because of the challenge these deaths pose to a sense that things may actually be "getting better" at a societal level, I contend that pondering the questions of "how *we* made it through" may yet give us insight into ways that we might be able to improve the circumstances of young people who are labeled "different" by their communities, peers, and families.

Getting What You Can: Queer Media Literacy

My focus on ways queer youth in rural areas might use media to their benefit is not meant to suggest that popular culture and the media are necessarily the most productive means of alleviating loneliness and anxiety or of attaining a sense of self-worth and hope. Nonetheless, I contend that idiosyncratic engagement with popular cultural artifacts can have positive effects on the lives of young people who are made to feel like outsiders. In times and places where any sense of "gay community" is absent, media texts and consumer cultural products may be the only means by which some young people begin a process of negotiating queer identity. Moreover, social conditions in which queer youth are made to feel excluded or threatened often lead to periods of isolation in which engagement with media may take the place of interaction with peers. In this vacuum of human contact, overinvestment is likely, with media assuming a position of tremendous influence and impact, and the capacity to both help and harm. This alone means that queer use of the media is a topic of pressing concern.

Cultivation of self-fulfilling queer media literacy, however, requires more than using media texts like a life raft in treacherous waters. The crucial matter, I argue, is developing awareness of media uses that include, but also extend beyond, pleasure, solace, identification, or even establishing connections with others, leading instead to explorations and determinations of self-representation. Amateur-created IGB videos in particular model a vital component of this exploration by showing media use as a way of re-presenting, disseminating, and archiving what one deems meaningful—including one's own history and perspectives.

The sincerity and good will of most IGB videos are abundantly apparent, yet there are many problematic aspects, especially for rural queer youth. One of the criticisms leveled against the IGB campaign has been its frequent variations on a "just stick it out" theme. While this is not to dismiss the importance of the user-created videos, which offer powerfully affecting words of hope and empowerment that may indeed save lives, it is to endorse at least thinking about something more we might offer young people in crisis than "wait." To thirteen-year-olds like Seth Walsh or Asher Brown, the prospect of five years of "sticking it out" may seem beyond endurance.

Further, a message communicated very clearly in many of these videos reinscribes a familiar belief that part of getting *better* is getting *out* of the narrow-minded rural area, the oppressive small town, the unenlightened "flyover" states, because happiness, acceptance, self-fulfillment, and others like you are to be found only in coastal urban centers.[4] The idea that life for LGBT people is better in cities has been accepted as axiomatic, and for many it may be true. However, the ubiquity of this message can also do a great disservice to LGBT people living in environments consistently represented as hell on earth for queer people.[5] "Escaping" to someplace else is a matter inextricably bound to issues of class, education, family relations and obligations, age, and other factors that may root individuals in rural areas, small towns, or conservative central states. With limited options, the sense of isolation and of feeling trapped can only be compounded by the implication that there must be something wrong with the gay person who does not migrate to the city, further alienating those who are already othered by heteronormativity.

Reflecting broader patterns of neglect by the media, the voices of people in these environments remain underrepresented in IGB videos. Because of the sheer number and variety of these videos, however, they are a particularly informative means for addressing questions about how place, sexuality, and sense of self coalesce in queer use of mass media, including an individual's ability to mine media texts for coping responses. In her valuable study of queer rural youth's engagement with media, Mary L. Gray finds that her informants not only "search online to determine what's 'expected' of queer boys and girls,"[6] but also use media technologies to strategize how to "bring home" performances of queer identity, "anchor them locally, and transform them into experiences of self/senses of identity that can and do happen to youth 'just like them.'"[7] IGB videos provide ample material for this kind of exploration—indeed, it seems to be precisely the intent of most of the noncelebrity videos.

The opportunities afforded by current communications technologies and social networking make acts of self-depiction, "talking back" to the dominant culture, and personalized archiving more apparent, and arguably more accessible to a wider range of participants. Such activity, though, has a long and important place amongst LGBT groups and individuals, as evidenced by the rich but often hidden history of queer lives and cultures—a history that would easily have been lost if people had not taken matters into their own hands to collect, archive, and preserve remembrances and artifacts ignored by institutional entities. Whether tangible or virtual, artifacts, memories, and stories take on a particularly queer cast, I contend, in moments of contextualization and reception that complicate standard assumptions about the past and open history up to reinterpretation and reuse. The engagement with memory and history so prominent in many of the videos prompts consideration of the past's impact on the present, and of older generations of LGBT people's capacity to affect the lives of younger generations. IGB videos have the potential to elicit this kind of consideration, and perhaps some aspect of my own remembrances might, too.

Sweet Dreams (of Somewhere Else): Identity Formation and Popular Culture

Media texts that connect us with historical representations may provide access to a queer usable past, as well as resources for identity work. Historical inquiry, however, is reduced to cold statistics and speculations if it does not maintain some sense of the historical individual. Although we can never know each unique history of how all queer people made their way through adversity and invented their sense of self, we *can* listen to the stories audible all around us and extrapolate how social, political, historical, regional, and mediated influences have established parameters enabling or impeding acts of self-determination.

The time and place of my adolescence had a strong influence on how I understood and apprehensively, falteringly, but eventually accepted what it meant to be gay. I grew up and went to school in a semirural suburb of Omaha. Farmland was within walking and olfactory distance. I am just one generation off the farm myself; my father's large family were farmers in a predominantly Catholic, Czech, and conservative part of Nebraska. From earliest memory, I recall experiences and sensations, both positive and negative, from time spent in the small towns where my parents grew up.

As is the case with too many queer kids of any time or place, my high school years were difficult. Teenagers, as many gay and lesbian youth become painfully aware, seem to have a distressingly acute gaydar, which can manifest in attack. I got harassed, humiliated, tripped, pushed, hit, and—it goes without saying—called "fag" and other slurs. I had bouts of suicidal thoughts, but fears of hurting my parents, eternal damnation, or screwing it up and living on in some even more damaged state stayed my hand more than any sense of hope for the future.

The time and place of coming out to myself also heightened a reliance on popular culture, particularly music, as emotional support. Records, the radio, music videos, and my favorite stars provided a glimpse of a wider, thrillingly weirder world. Rock culture, transmitted through magazines, posters, buttons, T-shirts, and other promotional ephemera almost as much as recordings and videos, was the primary source of queer representation for me, albeit mediated through a thick filter of ambiguity, codedness, and equivocation. Significant scholarly attention has been paid to the larger cultural effects wrought by the AIDS crisis and its prevalence in the media of the 1980s. News reports, made-for-TV movies, and tabloid sensationalism brought homosexuality into average Americans' living rooms. A far less explored matter, however, is the part popular music and music video played in bringing gays into the media spotlight in this period, although often in such a way that homosexuality was equated with gender transgression.

The visual and stylistic images of many 1980s pop stars involved cross-dressing or adoption of an androgynous appearance. In the mainstream press, performers such as Boy George of Culture Club, Annie Lennox of Eurythmics, Grace Jones, Prince, and so-called "hairspray metal" bands like Twisted Sister and Poison, were all labeled "gender benders." While many of these gender bender pop stars were heterosexual, their transgender or gender ambiguous appearance marked them as queer. These stars' teasing suggestion of minority sexuality riled conservative sensibilities, while appearing overly coy and irresponsibly evasive to supporters of gay and lesbian equality. But they could also be a wellspring of fascination and inspiration to people who responded favorably to the music and image of these performers—people such as myself.

I became perhaps overly invested in what my taste in music said about me, not only to others, but also to myself. Already somewhat conscious of living out a gay stereotype, I was particularly drawn to New Wave "divas" such as Siouxsie Sioux, Kate Bush, Lene Lovich, and Nina Hagen—but none more so than Annie Lennox, for whom I harbored something close to mad adoration.[8] Lennox's image and inventive play with gender and identity embodied the fabulous and cosmopolitan, the implacably cool, the sexy yet slightly sinister traits that were so desirable but seemingly unattainable to a gangly fourteen-year-old Nebraskan with untamable cowlicks and oversized glasses.

Adolescence is a crucial period of identity formation, and at a time when little else is within their control, many individuals gain a sense of agency from choosing their likes or dislikes in commercial media. Assertion of choice in one's engagement with cultural products becomes a way of figuring things out, looking at the world, recognizing and rejecting certain ideologies, imagining the self, and locating a sense of self-worth in a time and place where some audiences may be starving for any remotely positive representation of "difference." In a safe yet still meaningful act of identity work, the intensity of my attachment to Lennox increased as I became aware that most of my peers regarded her as a "freak," prompting me to "own" and feel better about my own freakishness.

Pioneering gay media scholar Richard Dyer provides some ideas by which I have attempted to better understand my adolescent fascination with Lennox. According to Dyer, audiences prone to experiencing "a peculiarly intense degree of role/identity conflict and pressure" and a sense of exclusion from the dominant cultural order often form more intense "relationships" with stars. He specifically mentions both adolescent and gay audiences as among those who might find special significance in their attachment to certain stars.[9] Although stars are commodities whose range of meanings marketplace conventions attempt to constrain, queer media literacy involves being able to adapt and repurpose popular culture to fulfill needs and desires ignored or ineptly addressed by the marketplace. Describing stars as inadvertently open signifiers, Dyer regards the polysemy of their images as raw material "that an oppressed group can take up and use to cobble together its own culture."[10] This is significant considering Dyer's argument that stars, as embodiments of social categories such as race, gender, and sexual orientation, are never able to completely erase the ambiguities, instabilities, and contradictions of categorization, which, in turn, furthers their usefulness to marginalized groups.

In many ways, I regard my adolescent devotion to popular music as contributing positively to my emotional stability and sense of self. "My" music was a refuge, a respite from a cultural surround, exemplified for me by John "Cougar" Mellencamp's odious and omnipresent paean to small-town heteronormativity, "Jack and Diane," that seemed intent on invalidating the person I was growing to be. Because commercial media prohibited open acknowledgement of actual homosexuality, however, even with readably gay performers like Boy George, Morrissey, or the B-52s, I could not look to pop stars as sites of identification or even sexual imaginaries.

Explaining the role of media in creating the sexual imaginary, Weston notes the greater diversity of media texts within urban areas. Significantly, many of these texts that help to create a sense of the sexual imaginary also suggest that life for gays and lesbians is better in urban areas, encouraging the perception that one has to move to the city to "be gay" and putting the lives of gays and lesbians in rural areas further "under erasure."[11] In my case, the fact that so many of the performers to whom I was drawn were British sparked an Anglophilia that, while making the wider world seem exciting and more accepting, further alienated me from my own environment, amplifying the sense it was a place I would never fit in. Thus, while the rock culture in which I was invested played a significant part in queering my private and personal spaces, it was of little use in queering my social space for the better.

Listening to my records in my bedroom, I waited for high school to end, anticipating that things would "get better" at the university—even if it were in Lincoln, Nebraska. The university was indeed a positive change, and my ongoing self-invention was aided by making friends with other young people in various stages of their own coming out processes. Many of my new friends were from small towns and rural areas in Nebraska and South Dakota, and most of them also found music to be a way of imagining a better time and place. For some, who had endured a greater sense of isolation or level of harassment in their hometowns than I, the attachment to certain bands or performers was perhaps even more meaningful. Music also became the means of connecting with others: Eurythmics, Cocteau Twins, Diamanda Galás, and other shared favorites became a way of bonding with a fashion design major from a small South Dakota town, who is still one of my closest friends.

My affective attachment to particular performers has done more than help me connect with peers, though. It has also made me recognize my place in a lineage of gay male fandom of iconic female stars, from Judy Garland, Barbra Streisand, and Diana Ross before my time, to Björk, Christina Aguilera, and Lady Gaga after. My affection for Annie Lennox provides a sense of a queer history and shared culture that further legitimates my feeling that my popular cultural attachments are both personally and culturally meaningful.

Seeing Who's Out There: Rural Production of It Gets Better Videos

Although recounting my teenage use of the media implies a "now versus then" scenario, a thorough inquiry into the use value of media for contemporary rural queer youth demands a more wide-ranging assessment that avoids creating false binaries. Certainly, the use value of the media "then" appears to suffer in contrast with the promise "now" of making connections and alleviating isolation and loneliness, as facilitated by communication technologies and online culture, plus more frequent, overt, and positive representation in the mainstream media.

While this suggests that conditions have indeed gotten better for even those LGBT people in the most constrained of circumstances, I believe there is more value in uncovering the *connections* rather than *differences* with past modes of reception and media use. By avoiding the facile polarization of "old" media and audience practices in the past as lesser, and new media and its myriad current applications as superior, we are better able to identify queer audiences' ingenuity in rearticulating and adapting media use to better fit changing contexts of time, place, technologies, and individual identity constructs. This mode of inquiry also elucidates ways in which the IGB Project's archiving of feelings and memories can forge a connection to a usable past that might inspire new ways of imagining and working towards improved social conditions.

For individuals in marginalized social positions, seeing something of oneself, or something pertinent and compelling, in media representations can require a determined assertion of will and motivated repurposing. The proliferation of online self-presentation, including IGB videos, raises intriguing questions about viewer reception of amateur media productions, with their presumably more "authentic" depiction of LGBT realities. In creating arguably more accessible sexual imaginaries, the people appearing in their own videos queer rural space by "representing" gays and lesbians leading sometimes difficult but also fulfilling lives outside urban environments.

Through acts of self-representation, the producers of IGB videos perform some of the functions that Dyer theorizes stars do, especially the challenge they pose to restrictive social categorizations. The sheer diversity of people represented creates hundreds of new ways of perceiving and making sense of how race, gender, class, ethnicity, location, age, and other traits intersect with sexuality in the ongoing processes of identity formation and performance. While it would indeed be a stretch to consider these individuals "stars," the risks they take in making their stories, their emotions, and their faces public lend them a microcosmic level of celebrity in online forums. Like stars, they can serve as role models, as points of identification, and as sites of desire, with viewer comments often reading like fan mail.

Unlike stars, though, they complicate our vision of an "idealized self," shifting our perception of what constitutes success, beauty, happiness, authenticity, and a life well lived. Unlike the stars that intrigued me in my youth but did little to help me think through affirming ways of being gay, the producers of these videos do not equivocate on matters of gender and sexuality. As Gray discovered, amateur-made online representations of "real" queer peoples' lives resonated more deeply than fictional gay and lesbian characters with rural youth who were formulating queer identities.[12] Further unlike our relation to mass media stars, we have a greater expectation of interaction and belief that individuals we have come to empathize with or admire may respond to our written comments. Rather than presenting stars, IGB videos present people identifiably "us" for a diverse range of viewers, expanding the range of choices of what and from whom to learn far beyond what is available in commercial media.

Most of the IGB videos that I watched and were created by and addressed to people living in rural areas and small towns, follow the format initiated by the Savage and Miller video, describing negative experiences, generally during the high school years, and then talking about how life improved afterwards. The everyday traumas detailed are familiar to many LGBT people who have endured mistreatment, from being shunned, called names, assaulted, and standing by with conflicted feelings while others are being bullied, to negative messages and threats from churches, schools, and family. The producer of one video, from a "really small town," where "if you weren't involved in sports, you were basically a loser," says that his environment caused him to feel "a lot of contempt for myself."[13] Another speaks to the justifiable distrust many queer youth have of adults, saying that on seeking help from a school counselor, he was dismissively told to "toughen up."[14]

In addition to reporting the expected problems of a queer person in rural areas, though, many of the videos' producers also discuss how to make a good life for oneself in these spaces. In her ethnographic study of gays and lesbians living in rural Michigan and Illinois, Emily Kazyak found that most of her informants either wanted to remain in these areas or had returned from urban areas to a place that felt more like home. In fact, one of her interviewees said that it was not until after he moved *away* from a city and back to his small hometown that he was able to determine that "this is who I am and this is what it means for *me* to be gay." As this informant told Kazyak, he felt rural areas offer "more flexibility in terms of how he makes sense of his sexuality."[15]

The individuals she interviewed, Kazyak maintains, distinguish between rural and urban ways of being a gay man or lesbian and understand "rural" in nuanced ways that "provide them with resources to modify cultural narratives that deny the possibility of being gay in the country."[16] By drawing on their "attachments to small town life," her informants have constructed multiple ways of living as gays and lesbians while still being part of their rural communities, in which familiarity, kinship ties, and being perceived as a "good person" may be valued more than sexual difference is condemned. While this does require some circumspection, though not closetedness, her informants told Kazyak that they are more comfortable living their lives in a more private, low-key manner, regarding this as one of the distinctions between rural and urban homosexuality. Other scholars studying gay and lesbian lives in rural areas have come to similar conclusions about the opportunities as well as the constraints of constructing queer identities in nonurban spaces, in which negotiation of those identities expands ways of being beyond media representations that "genericize" queer identity and politics along an urban model.[17]

Much of the impact of IGB videos derives from such revision of cultural presumptions to recognize and document multiple ways of being gay and lesbian in diverse geographical contexts. Several videos queer rural spaces by acknowledging the presence of not only LGBT individuals but also allies in small towns and farming communities. In one, a woman reminds viewers, "There's more open-minded people, even in a state like South Dakota."[18] In another video, a young man from a small town in Ohio, "where gays arent [sic] accepted at all," tells of being "astonished" when going to a gay pride event and recognizing people he sees "on a daily basis": "I was actually happy to know all these people were around me and I didn't even know it. . . . You just don't know who's around you."[19]

Videos by members of Gay-Straight Alliances (GSAs) in central states are prevalent, although almost all are university-affiliated. For queer youth in rural areas, this could evoke conflicted responses. On the one hand, seeing college students not much older than themselves testifying that life gets better post-high school can convey the message to youth in crisis that positive change is not far off. On the other hand, for younger teens or preadolescents, that change may seem all the farther away, and for young people not interested in or able to attend college, such representations may alienate them further by implying that moving away to pursue higher education is the only "escape." Videos by high school GSAs in small towns and rural areas are far scarcer, but have the potential to resonate with a broader audience in a particularly powerful way. One such example, titled "It Gets Better, Small Town Unity," features eleven members of a GSA "in a small town community, where it isn't accepted very well."[20] In telling their "stories that we want you to hear," these young people from an unnamed town are candid about their circumstances, revealing problems with bullying, parents, depression, and self-cutting, but ultimately emphasizing that their lives have already improved because of the companionship and understanding they have found through joining their GSA. One young woman, acknowledging the difficulties the group faces, remains defiant yet supportive: "We are leaving our mark. We aren't backing down. We are here for you." To underscore this point, another young woman states emphatically: "We all have a voice, and we are making ours heard."

As the video's title implies, the young people onscreen model unity in a manner that conveys hope. Even for young viewers who have no access to GSAs and are experiencing a sense of isolation, videos such as this can perform the function of the sexual imaginary by "being here for you," and demonstrating that other queer youth are "out there," successfully negotiating difference in similarly constrained circumstances. This takes on even greater consequence when considering the observation made by many new media scholars that distinctions between online and offline life have become increasingly artificial, in part because online activities so often precipitate offline realities. In her study of the IGB Project, Amber Muller emphasizes that "virtual and physical realities are forever impacting each other," with unpredictable ramifications. She notes incidents "where makers of It Gets Better videos have become new targets for discrimination and harassment both online and in their real lives."[21] But she also discusses the Make It Better Project, which was established in response to the dearth of practical advice found in IGB videos. Actively striving to "facilitate positive change in the physical world,"[22] the Make It Better Project seeks to "let students, parents, teachers, school administrators, and adult allies know that there are concrete actions they can take right now to make schools safer for all students" and offers advice on how this can be done.[23]

Raising further concerns about the IGB Project's effectiveness, Muller describes most of the videos as "closed discourse" unable to "engage in dialogue with the different subject positions of the multiple viewers." Her criticisms speak to the largely bourgeois and urban points of view presented in the videos, many of which reinforce the notion that supportive communities exist only in cities or universities. By failing to recognize that these options may not be "viable to all youth," Muller sees them as "making the message of hope . . . exclusive" to a privileged few.[24]

Almost all of the producers of IGB videos living in rural areas, however, spoke of finding strength and support from friends and loved ones within their own communities. Billyraymccabe, the maker of a video titled, "It Gets So Much Better . . . Even If You Are from a Small Town!" tells viewers that although he lives in a conservative part of a conservative state, he nonetheless has friends who "love me for who I am" and reassures viewers, "no matter where you go . . . you are gonna find people who love you for what you are."[25] Likewise, a video by "a small town farm boy" in "religiously oppressive" Mississippi attests that while his life sometimes can be lonely, he also has friends he can count on to stick up for him.[26] In contrast to video-maker Billyraymccabe, a recent high school graduate from "kind of a closed-minded" small town in Wisconsin tells of the support and understanding he received from teachers at his high school.[27]

Among the videos proffering a sense of hope through positive representations of life as a queer adult in rural areas, one has gained particular attention and is as interesting for the comments it has generated as for the content of the video itself. At well over twenty-three thousand hits (as of March 2014), "It Gets Better, Rural Dykes!" is by far the most viewed of the videos examined here, and its maker, Krissy Mahan from upstate New York, was included in the book Savage and Miller compiled on the project. Addressing "young lesbians who are not in cities," Mahan writes, "Being a rural dyke has some challenges, but it is really cool, and totally worth sticking around for."[28] While acknowledging that rural life does have its own set of issues, Mahan focuses instead on the positive aspects of country life, especially ones beneficial to people who regard themselves as independent individualists. In the video, she proposes that one of the pluses of rural life is that "you don't have to deal with people all the time," and in her written piece for the book, she remarks on "the long tradition of support for unconventional people in rural areas," which, as supported by Kazyak's study, means that rural gays and lesbians are often evaluated for character traits and abilities completely separate from sexuality or politics. "People are more concerned with what I can do and what skills I have, rather than who I'm involved with," Mahan reports.[29]

Unlike most other IGB videos, Mahan addresses the class issues that are tightly bound to rural life, commenting on the frequent depiction in the media of gays and lesbians as affluent, but making it clear that as "a person who doesn't have a lot of money," she is content with her life and what it has to offer. She upholds the virtues of country life in the comfort and pleasure provided by the natural world, which revitalizes and reminds us "how great it is to be alive."[30] In this view, connection with nature is perceived as vital identity work, completely independent of consumer culture and the media.

The belief that nature has special healing potential and spiritual significance for queer people has been echoed by many, from participants in lesbian separatist back-to-the-land movements, Radical Faeries, and neo-pagans, to vacationers at gay campgrounds. Reflecting on Tyler Clementi's suicide, Alex Johnson advocates outdoor activities and time alone in nature as a way for bullied queer youth to make "space in which to accept themselves," adding that he himself overcame his "fear of others' hate and meanness" by "connecting with nature . . . recognizing that there's a whole world that accepts me for who I am." Based on life histories recorded in his ethnographic study of gay men raised on farms, Will Fellows surmises, "The lack of human diversity in the social experiences" of his informants in their youth "appears to have been offset to some extent by their rich experience of the diversity of the nonhuman world."[31] The isolation that is inherent to farm life, Fellows maintains, meant that some of his informants had more freedom to "invent themselves according to their inclinations and standards."[32] In these viewpoints, nature allows space for the self-reflection and self-invention that

Michel Foucault saw not as "a luxury or a pastime for lesbians and gay men," but as a necessity.[33]

The numerous responses to Mahan's video continue the work of representing queer rurality and attesting to the presence of LGBT people in small towns and farmland. One commentator affirms Kazyak's findings on gays and lesbians who choose a rural life: "I got to know many (semi) out farm dykes and gay men after coming out in Missouri, and as far as I could tell, they loved their way of life and wouldn't have it any other way."[34] Other commentators go beyond testifying to mere presence, recounting the success gays and lesbians have had in finding a place in rural communities, such as the lesbian couple who run a small town coffee shop: "The main customers are the local farmers (straight men) who go in every morning for coffee and sit around to chat."[35]

As an IGB "star," Mahan also represents another aspect of the sexual imaginary: the object of erotic desire. She herself humorously addresses how rurality evokes the lesbian icon of the stalwart, casually androgynous, ultracapable woman of the land by saying, "everything that's frustrating about right now, being in the country . . . rockin' the flannel shirt every now and then, those are gonna be totally hot to somebody."[36] Indeed, her own embodiment of this fantasy image, seated in a barn amidst hay bales, wearing a baseball cap and, yes, flannel, has elicited *many* viewer comments about her desirability, comments that speak to the link between a romanticized impression of country living and the eroticization of distinctly queer, distinctly rural American icons. One commentator states, "I kind of want to move out of the city and be a dyke now,"[37] while another, remarking that Mahan is "totally cute," writes that her video "almost makes me think I should leave Brooklyn for the boondocks."[38] With the country also the site of gay male desire in iconic figures such as the rugged cowboy, the rough trade trucker, and the tanned-and-muscular naïve farm boy, the rural is just as likely a place to picture the eroticized sexual imaginary as the urban.

Conclusion

IGB videos hold potentially high value for the cultivation of queer media literacy and negotiation of queer identities for those with access to computers, Internet connection, time for online exploration, and enough privacy to explore broadly—things that can be hard to come by for rural queer youth. Seeking ways in which media use is most beneficial to queer youth in crisis therefore requires more than setting up a distinction between passive consumption of "old" media and active production enabled by new media. The production of meaning, affective attachments, and idiosyncratic uses of media are influenced but not determined by technology or media platform. Moreover, locating meaningful coping responses from small, ordinary pleasures and solaces in one's environment may or may not involve engaging with media.

That said, new technologies unarguably introduce many layers of complexity into questions of how media can most productively be exploited by vulnerable individuals. For me, popular music transmitted by various "old" media was a vital part of surviving my difficult adolescent years. This is certainly not something exclusive to alienated queer boys in the Midwest, and gay and lesbian investment in popular culture as a coping strategy is pervasive enough to be a source of humor. The musical short "Shit I Love," by Jake Wilson and Alysha Umphress, frames the song with a narrative in which a guy, referring to himself as "the gayest," is harassed by kids on a city street. Instead of being angry or trying to retaliate, his friend urges him to think of the things that make him happy, kicking off a rap number name-checking everything from kittens and chocolate truffles to pop music stars Britney Spears, Beyoncé, Robyn, and Rihanna. Comic artist Ellen Forney, in her contribution to the IGB book, lists among "high school survival tools" for "quirky misfits, oddballs, and the divinely unconventional" music by queer-oriented bands such as Scissor Sisters, Gossip, the Smiths, and Queen.

Several IGB videos, too, indicate how gays and lesbians in nonurban locations enlist music as a "survival tool." In one video, a man talks about the "little steps" through which one "gains confidence," which for him as a teenager included listening to Destiny's Child while working out with his mother's five-pound plastic weights—a reminiscence that prompts him to quip, "so gay."[39] Two young men in another video wear rock T-shirts, one of which, for the band Joy Division, would have been a signifier of teenage angst and "alternative" tastes even back in my youth.[40] In many of the videos, pop music is used as a backing soundtrack to add emotional weight to the speakers' words, in some cases played so loudly that it interferes with the speakers' intelligibility.

While my own history suggests that popular culture can have some positive influence on queer youth, I can hardly call my teenage "relationship" with my favorite stars completely satisfying. I believe more effective benefits will be found in the words of the nonfamous, in the extraordinary strength, insight, and love to be found right here in the ordinary. One of the most remarkable contributions of the IGB Project is its demonstration of the sociopolitical import of queer historiography and the power generated by listening to individuals telling their stories and speaking for themselves. IGB videos, for producers and viewers alike, satisfy "the emotional need for history" that Cvetkovich proposes is particularly acute with gays and lesbians.[41] Functioning as an archive in these terms, the videos also become what Kate Eichhorn regards as "an apparatus that can be effectively wielded in a reparative manner,"[42] transmuting the hurts of the past into especially powerful ways of communicating encouragement and strength for an improved today as well as tomorrow.

The IGB Project, Savage notes, was driven by the need to create a space for dialogue in which homophobic parents, teachers, and school administrators could no longer prevent adult LGBT people from reaching out to LGBT youth and letting them know the things that we wish we had known as we struggled through adolescence.[43] The archiving of a deeply personal alternative history, along with the deployment of queer media literacy, might help us to realize Foucault's conviction that homosexual subjectivity should not be regarded merely as an expression of individual desires, but as a means to imagining new ways of interacting with others.[44] The unique, vital, but often overlooked ways of inventing and living queer identities in rural spaces, as communicated by an important minority of IGB video producers, hold unlimited possibilities for new ways of being and new forms of interaction that will make rural spaces not merely safe for queer youth, but places to thrive.

NOTES

1 "What is the It Gets Better Project?" *It Gets Better Project*, n.d., http://www.itgets-better.org/pages/about-it-gets-better-project/ (accessed April 19, 2013).

2 Cvetkovitch, *An Archive of Feelings*, 241.

3 Ibid, 7.

4 One of the most unequivocal examples of this message comes in New York City Mayor Michael Bloomberg's video for the project. Bloomberg directs his words

expressly to "gay teens" who feel that they have no hope and are not wanted where they are, telling them emphatically, "New York City wants *you*. New York has always been the place where anyone can go and be who they are supposed to be, regardless of ethnicity, religion, gender, or sexual identity." Although Bloomberg quickly adds that there are "lots of other places in the country and the world" where gay people are welcomed, he says this with far less conviction (http://www.itgetsbetter.org/video/entry/2876/).

5 In his study of gay men who grew up in farming communities, Will Fellows lists the issues that contribute to the impression that rural areas are inhospitable to LGBTQ people: "rigid gender roles, social isolation, ethnic homogeneity, suspicion of the unfamiliar, racism, religious conservatism, sexual prudishness, and limited access to information." He adds, "While none of these conditions is unique to farm culture, they operate in a distinctive synergy in that setting" (*Farm Boys*, ix).

6 Gray, *Out in the Country*, 117.

7 Ibid., 130.

8 I didn't realize quite what a gay stereotype Annie Lennox fandom is until years later, after seeing the 1998 film *Edge of Seventeen* (Moreton), in which the teenaged main character's coming-out process in 1980s suburban Ohio is set against a background of 1980s pop music, represented largely by Lennox.

9 Dyer, *Stars*, 32.

10 Dyer, "In Defense of Disco," 410.

11 Weston, "Get Thee to a Big City," 282.

12 Gray, *Out in the Country*, 121.

13 KindaGayBlog. "It Gets Better: Sam from Small Town, USA," YouTube, August 3, 2011 (accessed May 20, 2013).

14 Billyraymccabe. "It Gets So Much Better . . . Even If You Are from a Small Town!" YouTube, October 2, 2010 (accessed May 20, 2013).

15 Kazyak, "Disrupting Cultural Selves," 571 (her emphasis).

16 Ibid., 563.

17 Gray, *Out in the Country*, 38.

18 Brittany Buell, "It Gets Better (USD 10% Society)," YouTube, June 20, 2011 (accessed May 20, 2013).

19 Brandon Hostetter, "It Gets Better—Brandon Hostetter," YouTube, September 20, 2012 (accessed June 1, 2013).

20 saggerG, "It Gets Better, Small Town Unity," YouTube. December 15, 2010 (accessed May 20, 2013).

21 Muller, "Virtual Communities and Translation into Physical Reality in the 'It Gets Better' Project," 273.

22 Ibid., 275.

23 "About," *Make It Better Project*, n.d., http://makeitbetterproject.org/about (accessed May 20, 2013).

24 Muller, "Virtual Communities," 275.

25 Billyraymccabe, "It Gets So Much Better."

26 ZydaneJeremiah, "It Gets Better! Cory from MS," YouTube, May 9, 2012 (accessed May 20, 2013).

27 Ross Pearson, "It Gets Better: Ross from Wisconsin," YouTube, August 22, 2011 (accessed May 14, 2013).

28 dykeumentary1, "It Gets Better, Rural Dykes!" YouTube, October 2, 2010 (accessed May 20, 2013).

29 Mahan, "Rockin' the Flannel Shirt," 71.

30 Ibid., 72.

31 Fellows, *Farm Boys*, 15.

32 Ibid., 16.

33 Halperin, *Saint Foucault*, 81.

34 Vinomazzei, response to dykeumentary1, "It Gets Better, Rural Dykes!" YouTube, n.d. (accessed May 20, 2013).

35 dja1062, response to dykeumentary1, "It Gets Better, Rural Dykes!" YouTube, n.d. (accessed May 20, 2013).

36 dykeumentary1, "It Gets Better, Rural Dykes!"

37 lovedisaster69, response to dykeumentary1, "It Gets Better, Rural Dykes!" YouTube, n.d. (accessed May 20, 2013).

38 D Avraham, response to dykeumentary1, "It Gets Better, Rural Dykes!" YouTube, n.d. (accessed May 20, 2013).

39 KindaGayBlog, "It Gets Better."

40 Buell, "It Gets Better (USD 10% Society)."

41 Cvetkovich, *An Archive of Feelings*, 251.

42 Eichhorn, "Archiving the Moment," 26.

43 Savage, "Introduction," 4.

44 Halperin, *Saint Foucault*, 78.

9

Queer Interstates

Cultural Geography and Social Contact in Kansas City Trucking
Co. *and* El Paso Wrecking Corp.

RYAN POWELL

By the mid-1970s, media representations of gay men were becoming
increasingly fused with dominant metropolitan iconographies of fashion, style, and taste. As historian Dennis Altman notes, this period saw
the rise of a new kind of gay man, one who was "non-apologetic about
his sexuality, self-assertive, highly consumerist and not at all revolutionary, though prepared to demonstrate for gay rights."[1] Similarly,
Stephen M. Engel asserts that "by the end of the decade, gay politics
appeared to be subsumed by an every-expanding gay cultural lifestyle."[2]
Offering further reflection on the place of gay life at the decade's close,
Edmund White notes in his travelogue, *States of Desire: Travel in Gay
America*:

> New York gays are justifiably proud of their status as tastemakers for
> the rest of the country, at least the young and up-to-date segment of the
> population. Our clothes and haircuts and records and dance steps and
> décor—our relentlessly evolving style—soon become theirs.[3]

Simply put, the urgent project of making gay life visible, a bedrock of
the early liberation movement, was increasingly subsumed by a consumerist fixation with celebrating the *most* visible, so often dictated
by the fickle fashions and styles of the metropolitan marketplace. As
Rosemary Hennessy notes, investment in "lifestyle" promotes "not
only individuality but also a more porous conception of the self as a
'fashioned' identity" that is indicative of a "heightened involvement in
consumption and the promotion of the cosmopolitan."[4] Thus, for the

"young and up-to-date," aesthetic investment becomes a means not only of affirming identity, but also of asserting class position, demonstrating through material investment in "clothes," "haircuts," and "records" one's place as an informed and sophisticated consumer in the marketplace.

Nationally distributed magazines such as *In Touch*, *The Advocate* and *After Dark*—which acted as the primary venue for the promotion gay films—also became increasingly urban-centric, shifting coverage from socially oriented national issues to localized urban-specific life-style themes. Emblematic of this shift is *The Advocate*, which went by the slogan "Newspaper of America's Homophile Community" from its inception in 1967 until 1975, when the slogan was revised to "touching your life style." Likewise, while in the early 1970s, prominent issues of the magazine featured nationally vital cover stories like "Dallas Attorney Murdered" and "New Orleans Memorial," by the mid-1970s the cover stories tended towards topics such as: "Good News For New York," "New York's Octogenarian Artist Minna Citron," and "In New York Linda Hopkins talks about "Me and Bessie."[5]

However, contrary to popular stereotypes of gay men as having un-limited access to social and economic mobility, gay men in the mid-1970s did not dwell only in the "gay ghetto" of the metropolis, but were often confined to the spaces in which they could find employment, wherever this put them. Also, many men who did live in "friendlier" metropolitan areas still maintained relationships with the towns and smaller cities from which they came, while others chose to stay in the region where they were raised. In an oral history of his experience with coming out in the late 1970s, Richard Kilmer writes:

> I'd heard that gay people lived in big cities, mostly San Francisco and New York, so I moved to San Francisco. My plan was that I would get in con-tact with my family eventually, and if they came to visit I would pretend I was straight. . . . I lived in New York for a year. . . . It felt claustrophobic like there was no way that I could get out. . . . It was really hard, I felt so far away from the country. . . . I came back to Wisconsin. . . . Here in Madison, people know each other. It feels like it's kind of an in-between spot for me. I can have a garden here. . . . I like having lesbians and gays around me, having that sense of community. So I'm kind of on the fence, not a farmer but not a city slicker either.[6]

Kilmer's account provides a good example of the complex series of relocations some male-desiring men undergo in the search to reconcile their identity, interests, and personal needs with their environment. Ironically, in moving to places where he felt he could come out, he simultaneously felt "claustrophobic" and that he couldn't "get out." More importantly, Kilmer explains that it was in an "in-between spot," between rural and urban, where he felt most at home.

Such a desire for in-between-ness provides the basis for Joe Gage's *Working Man Trilogy*, a series of hardcore porno-romances that countered the rapidly emerging dominance of metrocentric gay representations in the United States during the early to mid-1970s. The three films that comprise the trilogy—*Kansas City Trucking Co.* (1976), *El Paso Wrecking Corp.* (1977), and *L.A. Tool and Die* (1979)—invite viewers into a world where the buddy-couple antics of the road movie, hardcore sex, and Hollywoodian romance come together to create an unlikely portrait of trucker life along the interstate highway system. With all three films following the combined sexual, romantic, and occupational pursuits of a trucker named Hank (Richard Locke) as he moves across the Southwest, the trilogy constructs the American road as a site rich in a variety of forms of sociosexual contact. In contrast to the popular genres they draw on, which tend to be characteristically stable in their adherence to a heterocentric perspective, Gage's *Working Man* films and the promotional materials used to publicize them stand as imaginative reworkings of a whole range of generic materials. Through a self-conscious mobilization of the idea of a crossover film, the trilogy elaborates the queer potential of numerous kinds of crossovers, merging and collapsing taken-for-granted distinctions among genre, sexual orientation, gender, class, age, and region.

Looking at *Kansas City Trucking Co.* and *El Paso Wrecking Corp.*, this essay explores how these films self-reflexively build on this crossover status and, most importantly, function as gay hardcore films engaging with the codes and conventions of more popular, mainstream genre material. Unlike the final film in the trilogy—which is more focused on the resolution of a love plot between the film's leading men—these first two films dwell on unresolved and in-between positions in their representations of U.S. road space, both in terms of more fluid or unsettled models of sociosexual practice and in terms of cultural spaces that are less clearly organized around fixed, hegemonic constructions of gender and class. In the case of *Kansas City*, I explore how advertisements for the film work to appeal to a heterogeneous audience through a cross-over address that explicitly situates the film as being of interest to both male-desiring men and male-desiring women as well as gay identifying and non-gay-identifying men. I then consider how the film's representation of the U.S. highway system furthers this address through a careful engagement with popular road movie conventions. Turning to *El Paso Wrecking Corp.*, I explore how the film builds on the figure of the cross-over to offer a vision of the interstate highway system as a space that fosters nonmetropolitan forms of desire between men, and ones that may even be inclusive of women. Throughout, I am concerned with how the trilogy uses hardcore porn as a site for formally inventive elaborations of queer desire that may resonate with the cultural geographic contours of life as lived by many male-desiring men but seldom put to screen.

"It's All Here": The Marketing of *Kansas City Trucking Co.*

The theatrical trailer for *Kansas City Trucking Co.* opens with images of truckers traversing through vast unpopulated landscapes of sprawling mountain ranges under blue skies, creating a panoramic framing of American highway life reminiscent of the road movie iconography of contemporary releases like *Two-Lane Black Top* (1971) and *Thunderbolt and Lightfoot* (1974). However, any allusions to the straight road movie rapidly give way to intermittent images of men, sexually engaged with one another in truck cabs, bunkhouses, and rest stops, combined through montage editing with images of the western landscape. As a young trucker steps up into a MAC truck, the sultry voice of a female narrator asks, "Have you ever wondered about truckers? Or about how men get it on—with each other?" She continues, "My old man did, and then he did something about it." Accompanying images of hardcore male-male sex as they flash in a succession of quick edits, the woman's voice announces: "Wichita, Amarillo, Albuquerque, Bakersfield, San Bernardino, L.A.—It's all here . . . and it's all real and it's real hot."

The deceptively small phrase "it's all here" is packed with a playfully sophisticated set of sociopolitical implications, particularly with regard to how geographic and cultural boundaries come to take on various meanings across local, regional, and national scales. Insofar as "it's all here" is combined with iconic images of the rural Southwest, "here" denotes the presence of male-male desire in a geographic space that is different from where it is often assumed to be, thereby countering the myth that it is only in the "grittiness" of the metropolis that such desires reside, or are perhaps even bred, as well as encouraging a departure from what Thomas Waugh has termed "minoritizing cosmopolitan iconography."[7] The phrase "it's all real" adds a further layer, suggesting this is not merely your average road movie, but a site where something actual and more "true" is on offer.

When compared with marketing strategies used for erotic film and video today—which tend to target *either* a straight or a gay audience— *Kansas City* appears surprising in its textured mix of hetero- and homo-motifs, leading current viewers to a whole series of questions. Most pressingly, how and why did this presumably heterosexual female narrator come to be the tour guide for a rural underground network of gay male desire? Adding to the complexity of this question, the positioning of the leading man as the female narrator's "ol' man" sentimentally tropes the couple within a heterosexual matrix, while her encouragement of his gay sexual exploits suggests a complete inversion, or perhaps even an "outing," of this trope. In describing how the identity of the heterosexual male is often "authenticated" in popular film, Lee Edelman notes that "the gay man is . . . *necessary* to confirm the 'integrity' of the face of male heterosexuality."[8] With this in mind, we can see how the double signification of the film's leading man as being bound to both hetero-sexual and homosexual relations in effect negates the Othering potential of his male-male desire. Moreover, given his "lady's" encouragement of these desires, there is the absence of any sort of "Jekyll/Hyde" narrative that might work to explain away this behavior as form of "passing" for straight. Thus, heterosexual coupling is presented as just another role that can be crossed over and, in a complete inversion (and perversion) of heteronormative imperatives, cannot be located and/or authenticated by the "appearance" of heterosexuality.

Should it not follow that this transgression of binary oppositions would have risked alienating a wide range of potential viewers— diminishing gay male interest with the presence of a female and pro-voking anxiety in straight female viewers about the (latent) homosexual desires of straight males? I would suggest that, paradoxically, these seemingly incongruent alignments are integral to the film's popular appeal—that it is specifically because of the assertion that male-male desire is not a closed circuit, appealing and/or available only to gay men "in the know," that the film may work to attract a whole range of subject/ viewer positions across lines of sex and gender. As Joe Gage recalls in a discussion of the film's popularity, "It was the public that made this happen, the guys who watched the film and the girls who watched the film. I remember when *Kansas City* was first playing in Manhattan there were always women in every show in the afternoons."[9]

Promotion for *Kansas City* also worked to attract a wide male viewership with its panoramic vision of male-male desire. Countering the increasing dominance of gay representations focused on the young, urban, and aspirational, the widely circulated poster and magazine campaign stridently asserted the film's working-class appeal, at the same time stressing how trucking—as a vocational site of independent and semi-independent labor—can be cultivated as rich site of sociosexual contact. Alerting audiences to the variety of male types on offer and building anticipation for the way in which these types may come together, these advertisements turned on a photograph of actors Richard Locke and Steve Boyd posed casually in front of a MAC truck, highlighting the world of trucking as a domain rich in possibility for male-male contact (figure 9.1).

The black-and-white documentary aesthetic of the photograph suggests that the underlying fantasies of ordinary working men will be unleashed as they pursue relations that cross over the dictates of appropriate workplace behavior—a phenomenon made all the more accessible to the trucker by the relative privacy of the truck cab. Accordingly, as John R. Burger puts it, in the trilogy "homoeroticism slips out of the closet and into the gravel pits, truck stops and work sites of America."[10] At the same time, however, the inverse also holds true. That is, the trilogy can also be understood as an instance in which the filmmakers have slipped into environments where male sexual companionship is implicitly present and may even to a certain extent be facilitated by the "all-male" exclusivity of the work site. Bringing into visibility working-class males who share sexual companionship with other males of similar class and vocational backgrounds, the trilogy vitally widens the representational scope of gay cinema.

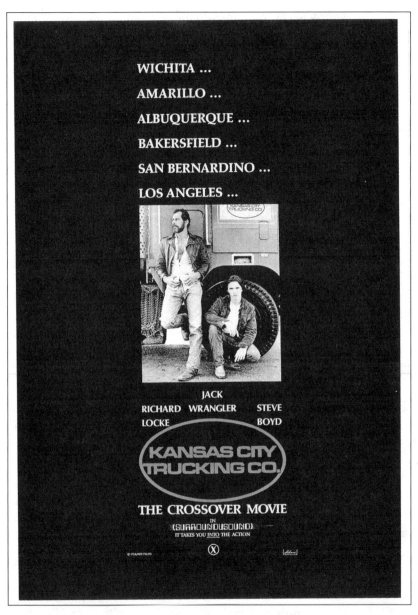

Figure 9.1. Poster for *Kansas City Trucking Co.* (1976)

While the simplicity of the photograph establishes a sense of everyday work life, the poster as a whole generically contextualizes the film within a road movie register, prominently foregrounding locations that move west from Kansas to California and stressing the western frontierism that comprises the film's narrative arc. In reconfiguring one of the road movie's most familiar tropes, the buddy couple, to include male sexual companionship, the marketing foregrounds the film's cache: to render an implicit (and highly specific) set of relations between the homosocial and the homosexual. In doing so, the film offers a correction to what Eve Kosofsky Sedgwick has termed "the radically disrupted continuum, in our society, between sexual and nonsexual male bonds."[11] It follows that when the trailer asserts "it's all here" and "it's all real," the viewer is cued into the fact that *Kansas City* contains what has been prohibited, extracted from, or sublimated in the mainstream buddy film, as well as in society at large.

Before looking directly at the textual features of the trilogy's first two films, it is useful to consider some of the ways in which its status as theatrically exhibited gay hardcore informed the context of its reception at the time. As explored by scholars such as David A. Cook, Eric Schaeffer, Jon Lewis, and Thomas Waugh, the early 1970s saw the rise of a new kind of sex film that featured uncensored versions of numerous sexual acts within the context of a feature-length format.[12] While introducing new kinds of imagery to the screen, feature-length hardcore also carried with it many of the same qualities as classic Hollywood cinema, such as an emphasis on narrative and plot development, continuity editing, and scripted dramatic action. By the late 1970s, the genre fell into steep decline with the onset of the VCR and the increasing closure of downtown porn theatres (the result of a combination of factors including the advance of anti-porn laws, gentrification, and the effects of suburbanization on urban infrastructure), although it did for some time between the early and late 1970s hold a lucrative corner of the commercial cinematic marketplace.

While no single study has been devoted to the subject of the audience for hardcore films, a few accounts do suggest the ways in which audiences for gay hardcore could be surprisingly diverse. In his study of New York porn theaters, *Time Square Red, Time Square Blue*, for instance, Samuel R. Delany provides one such example through his own chronicling of the period:

The population was incredibly heterogeneous—white, black, Hispanic, Asian, Indian, Native American, and a variety of Pacific Islanders. In the Forty-Second Street area's sex theaters specifically, since I started frequenting them in the summer of 1975, I've met playwrights, carpenters, opera singers, telephone repair men, guys on crutches, on walkers, in wheelchairs, teachers, warehouse workers, male nurses, fancy chefs, guys who worked in Dunkin Donuts, guys who gave out flyers on street corners, guys who drove garbage trucks, and guys who washed windows on the Empire State Building.[13]

While no other account to date has provided such remarkable specificity, others also suggest a similar range of heterogeneity. Through a series of questionnaires distributed as part of the data-set for his 1975 doctoral dissertation on gay porn cinema in Los Angeles, Paul Siebenand discovered that the audience at the then popular Palace Theatre was similarly comprised of viewers from across vastly different backgrounds and geographic locales, with patrons hailing from places as varied as El Paso, Beverly Hills, and San Diego, spanning in age from teenagers to the elderly, and coming from a variety of socioeconomic and cultural backgrounds.[14] While Siebenand's pool of participants was far too small to stand as conclusive evidence of who the audience for gay hardcore was in any definitive sense, it does, in concert with Delany, suggest a notable degree of diversity.

These spaces existed as sites of diversity not only on a level of individual film reception but also in terms of group social contact, where reaching across cultural and geographic lines, a variety of patrons came to know one another as a consequence of the social and sexual interaction facilitated within the bounds of the adult film theater. What Delany has described as the "inter-class" and "inter-race" make-up of the adult theater is not only a matter of audience demographics but resonates on a textual level with some of the most popular 1970s gay hardcore films, with many of them giving ample screen time to stories and images that feature a surprising level of complexity and nuance in terms of how they represent character interaction at the levels of individual, couple, and group. Vividly demonstrating that gay hardcore involved far more than images meant exclusively for sexual gratification, films such as *Bijou* (1972), *The Erotic Films of Peter de Rome* (1973), and *Navy Blue* (1979) took their time to elucidate the dynamics between the various kinds of individuals and groups comprising American social life and sometimes even with a critical and conscientious eye for problems of classism and racism.

Considered within this context, the multidirectional address extended in the promotion for *Kansas City Trucking Co.* at least anticipates, if not coincides with, a moment when theatrically screened gay hardcore could function as a site of social inclusivity. As if to embrace such a phenomenon, the statement "it's all here" may be understood as a vindication of the panoply of sociosexual possibilities inherent in the heterogeneous make-up of the audience—a sort of knowing wink stressing potential affinities between on-screen performance and off-screen interactions within the space of the theater. A similarly playful slipperiness is evident in the poster's listing of cities that Hank is to travel through, which upon first glance may appear to be places in which the film is screening—a not uncommon marketing strategy in the nationally circulating gay newspapers and magazines during the period, such as the *Advocate*, *Drummer*, and *After Dark*.

The Undeflected Buddy Tension of *Kansas City Trucking Co.*

In exploring the representation of male-male desire in the trilogy, it is useful to contextualize the films in relation to the popular road movie conventions they make use of. A staple trope of the 1970s road movie was a narrative focus on relationships of desire, passion, and love between men. Looking closely at some of the specific ways in which *Kansas City* reconfigures the visual and narrative conventions of the road film, in effect turning them back on themselves, will illuminate how the film elaborates a rhetorical critique of both cinematic norms and the sociopolitical climate in which these norms were produced.

Discussing the generic features that most strongly mark the road movie, Julian Stringer writes:

> The road movie differentiates itself from other genres by defining distinct parameters of action and aspiring to complete a particular emotional trajectory. The progression is towards a unified and fulfilling subjectivity.

Road movie logic maintains that the further [sic] you drive from civilization the more easily you can shake off its constraints, the more people you
leave behind the closer you can get to yourself.[15]

Despite how closely the narrative adheres to the generic inscription of
the road movie, the introduction of uncensored male-male sexual activity into this formula reconfigures the genre into a self-reflexive mode.
As Stringer further notes, a staple of the genre is the way in which "the
fragility of the masculine identity requires that sexual tension between
men be deflected."[16] *Thunderbolt and Lightfoot* (1974) stands as an excellent example of a film that relies on such a deflection when the sexual
tension between the film's leading buddies (Clint Eastwood and Jeff
Bridges) is transferred into such acts as the procuring of women for sex
as an affectionate gift from one buddy to another. In the *Working Man
Trilogy*, not only is this deflection self-consciously performed as a trope,
but the trope itself becomes the signpost for where male-male desire
can be located and actualized. Just as the repression of gay desire in the
straight road movie appears, through its overly plotted deflection, to be
a symptom of unconscious or latent homoeroticism, here that desire is
brought to bear on the plot itself—the homoerotic subtext carried into
the text.

As Joe and Hank set out on their drive westward, the viewer is presented with a series of iconic images, which nod to the popular generic
conflation of the road movie and western. Shortly into their drive, Hank
comments to Joe, "Looks like you could use some action, kid," to which
he replies, "Guess so." Following his rather nonchalant reply, the shot
stays with Joe's perspective as he turns to look outside the truck window
across barren desert vistas under a harsh sun, evoking Jane Tompkin's
description of the opening shot of a western as "defined by absence: of
trees, of greenery, of houses, of the signs of civilization, above all, ab
sence of water and shade."[17] However, as the plot develops, contrary to
the road film/western format, we find that it is not the absence from
civilization that the road provides, but rather an entry into social experience. Throughout the film, the American interstate dramatically shifts
from being a place that is barren and sparsely populated to one that is
full of well-established social networks.

Figures 9.2–9.5. Male-male desire along the interstate in *Kansas City Trucking Co.*

As a Stetson-hatted man follows alongside Joe and Hank's truck in a convertible, he gives the two a quick "knowing" smirk and a thumbs-up (figure 9.2). Hank instructs Joe that he is a friend who "works the pit stop outside of Wichita." Joe asks, "Is he a mechanic?" to which Hank wryly replies, "Not exactly." The shot then follows the man as he picks up a hitchhiker, with whom he engages in hardcore roadside sex (figures 9.3, 9.4). Farther down the road, the two truckers pass another convertible with two collegiate looking boys, smoking grass and giving each other hand jobs while driving. Hank explains that it "looks like a couple of jack-off buddies." The shot then follows the boys while they pull over upon discovering an abandoned house beside the road, with a tattooed and undressed older man with a moustache awaiting their arrival. Once inside, the men engage in a plethora of group sexual activity (figure 9.5).

Within the bounds of this American interstate journey, the viewer is provided with a selection of stock masculine types, such as the trucker, the mechanic, and the college kid, to name only a few. At the same time, the trilogy works against the normalizing processes of typology by disrupting, dismantling, and deconstructing the "truth" of the "widely recognizable" working-class man whose labor-intensive vocation is so often posited as an index of his authentic heterosexuality. Instead, each given type deviates from its usual hetero-affirmative function and comes to denote an ironic blurring between the way the men in these films identify with their profession and the way they identify with their private pleasure, while using the same terms of signification for both—"working the pit stop," for instance. This inversion of tropes, rather than perpetuating fictitious figurations, which attempt to negate homoerotic desire, acts instead to productively index the actual social conditions of life for many gay men. As Vito Russo notes:

> Gay people are born into a heterosexual world and spend a lot of time being raised as heterosexual. We therefore know a hell of a lot more about being straight then straights know about being gay. We needed training to effectively "pass." Consequently, we see the culture with a dual division and a particular "aliveness" to the double sense in which some things can be taken.[18]

Still, what of the many viewers who sexually and/or romantically engaged with other men but did not choose to identify as gay? With this question in mind, it is important to note that the non-gay identifying man is also socialized under the hegemonic reach of heteronormative ideology, that he also undergoes "training" to meet the requirements of heteronormative manhood and to have a solid grasp of the heterosexual sign system that asserts it. Thus, it follows that male-desiring men who occupy spaces outside of the clearly delineated confines of "out" urban gay culture might use their expertise in the shared system of masculine signifiers "ironically" as a cue for sexual desire.

Cultural Geography and Utopian Space in *El Paso Wrecking Co.*

The trilogy regularly makes good on its crossover promise not only in terms of genre but also in terms of how space and, in particular, in-between space are figured. In a way that resonates with Kilmer's desire for a more ambiguous in-between—neither gay nor straight, city nor country—*El Paso Wrecking Corp.* utilizes a distinctly utopian schematic, opening up a dialogic space where incongruities, contradictions, and irreconcilable forces that directly comprise the lived reality of life for many male-desiring men are taken up as a site of representation. In *Utopics: Spatial Play*, Louis Marin notes that:

> In the imagination utopic discourse functions not like an icon, but as a schema. Utopia is singled out as a figure. Produced in the distance between contradictory elements, it is the simulacrum of the synthesis, while yet signifying the contradiction that produced it. It stages a fiction of the reconciliation and offers it up for view in a text.[19]

In the *Working Man Trilogy* this schema is made up of a chain of signifiers that speak to the contradictory forces of homosexuality, masculinity, and romanticism as positioned within hegemonic heteronormative conditions. Kilmer's description of his life "in-between," as well as the film trailer's portrayal of underground networks of male-male desire that exist in the unmarked, uncharted, and ambiguous "here" of spaces that are literally in-between (the road, the desert, the truck-stop) carve out ideological spaces where contradictory modes of gender and sexuality can flourish.

By the mid-1970s, dominant cinematic representations of gay social life across genres presented the viewer with a world where gay culture appeared reliant on, if not defined by, the absence and exclusion of women. The stylized and eroticized woman, so central as a correlative to gay desire in the work of filmmakers like Kenneth Anger and Andy Warhol, was becoming more and more rarefied. Reflecting the growth of an increasingly fraternalized commodity culture, which posited the urban, male-only space as the apex of gay cultural value, representations of women and gay men as related subject positions under heteronormative patriarchy began to slip away.

In contrast, the *Working Man Trilogy* not only continued to include representations of women but also took the erotic potential of these representations further than many of its predecessors, showing the ways in which women can exist as an inclusive and central aspect of gay male desire, broadening its utopic rendering of gay social networks and ideologically refuting reductive versions of fraternalized gay culture as the privileged domain of "true" and "authentic" gay identity. In this sense, the trilogy's utopic schema works as a means of reimagining, refitting, and redefining the architecture of gay social space, moving it away from the register of cosmopolitanism and towards the expanse of a less certain and identifiable figuration of gay desire.

The utopic visualization of how women and men can co-invest in male-male sexual activity is taken up as a major turning point in the second instalment of the trilogy, *El Paso Wrecking Corp*. Continuing with a series of roadside discoveries, Hank and his new buddy, Gene (Fred Halsted), join up on a journey from Kansas City to El Paso. Early on in their drive, the two men pull over at a roadhouse tavern marked by the single word "food" on a sign above the door (figure 9.6). Once inside the space, the naturalistic colors of the evening outside give way to low-lit images shot through a red filter (figures 9.6–9.10).

While talking with a female bartender, Gene finds himself cruised by a young male/female couple, Millie and Will, who, after an affirmative counterglance from Gene, follow him through a darkly lit doorway to the basement storeroom of the tavern. Once downstairs, Gene pulls Will up close to him by his belt and they begin to talk.

> GENE: Now what are you two up to?
> WILL: I heard about this place, and you know, everything goes right? She wants to see me get off, um, she gets, um, she wants to see me make it with another guy.
> GENE: Have you ever made it with a guy before?
> WILL: Uh-uh.
> GENE: Is she gonna join us?
> WILL: She gets off watching.
> GENE: Yeah, she ever seen you kiss a man?
> WILL: No.

Just as Will replies "no," the shot cuts from a close-up of the two men about to kiss to an extreme close up of Millie's eyes as she gazes longingly at them (figure 9.7). The shot then cuts to a close-up of the men, which aligns the viewer with Millie's point of view. Punctuated by an extra-diegetic increase in the ambient background noise of men and women socializing upstairs, the two men begin a slow and romantic kiss (figure 9.8). After several quick edits between the men kissing and

Millie intently watching, the camera pans slowly down from a close-up of Millie's eyes to reveal her open mouth as she licks her lips.

After the men undress one another, Will kneels down on the floor and begins to fellate Gene, while a close-up of Millie shows her licking her fingers and moving them down and across her now bare breasts. Shifting back and forth in a triangular fashion, images continue to cut, for several minutes, between Will providing oral sex, Gene's eyes as they watch Will, and Millie's eyes watching both of the men. This formation is further emphasized by an image of the two men, framed in the triangle of Millie's legs (figure 9.9).

As the men continue to sexually engage one another, trading off oral sex and hand jobs, Millie is shown standing and masturbating while she watches. As Will nears climax, masturbating above Gene's face, quick edits cut between images of all three faces in shared ecstasy, picking up momentum and moving in faster succession, visually punctuating the build-up towards the point where all three characters are shown climaxing together. Capping off the scene, the shot cuts back upstairs to Hank socializing with the female bartender, Billie. As Gene makes his way back to the bar, Billie greets his return with a smirk and asks, "Back already?" (figure 9.10).

While the red filtration of the images sets the scene within a fantasy space, creating a division between everyday life and the eroticized space of the tavern, the scene also gives a series of signals that work to merge codes of reality and fantasy. The red coloration denotes a hypersexualized atmosphere, while the commonplace sounds of social banter along with images of men and women casually drinking beer serve as a reminder of the ordinary and everyday atmospherics of the space. In combining these elements, the scene blurs distinctions between what Thomas Waugh has formulated as "Everywhere" and "Elsewhere" in gay erotic imagery. Delineating the two, Waugh describes the "Everywhere" as part of "a documentary sensibility" based in an "appreciation for the nitty-gritty of the familiar, grungy or mundane," and the "Elsewhere" as a space for exotic dreams, of "Other places and people."[20] The way in which the scene blurs the distinction between these terms establishes yet another instance of crossover, where within the space of the tavern Everywhere and Elsewhere merge together harmoniously through the use of dialogue and other sound elements: the

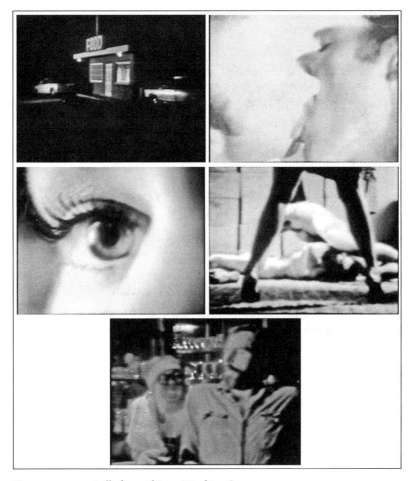

Figures 9.6–9.10. Stills from *El Paso Wrecking Corp.*

ambient sounds of bar banter spilling over into the storeroom; the casual tone of the conversation between Will and Gene sustaining the friendly social register of the patrons upstairs (despite its deeply erotic content); Billie welcoming Gene back to the barroom just after his sexual encounter.

Within this context, the sexual and the social are continually bound together, rather than opposed, representing what screens more like a cinematically fantastical version of a possible reality than the heavily eroticized and mystified fantasy scenarios that characterize much of 1970s gay hardcore cinema. For its crossover audience, particularly those who patronized the film in smaller towns and cities where access to overt representations of male-male desire were harder to come by, these images could offer a "blueprint" for social networks yet to be found or developed. In *Public Sex: The Culture of Radical Sex*, Pat Califia discusses how such networks have tended to develop in semipublic places, where, like the basement storeroom in *El Paso*, some sort of "barrier screens out the uninitiated".[21] She argues that citizens opposed to such activities are often unreasonably afraid of coming into contact with them, explaining that

> If people are going to see what is going on in these places, they must intrude. They must actively look for things that will offend them, either by penetrating physical barriers, by setting up covert surveillance, or by posing as potential participants.[22]

Paradoxically, these dynamics work quite well to describe the kind of "intrusive" perspective constructed within *El Paso*'s portrayal of public sex. However, instead of "penetrating physical barriers," the camera penetrates social and cultural-geographic barriers, allowing previously uninitiated viewers into a space where they are invited to "actively look for things" that excite them. Moreover, for the viewer who comes into the film weary of stereotypes about the "coldness" of public sex, the physical warmth and affection displayed in the scene may act as a corrective to this preconception. As Samuel R. Delaney puts it in discussing the dynamics of public sex amongst male-desiring men within the confines of the 1970s porn theater, "a glib wisdom holds that people like this don't want relationships. They have 'problems with intimacy.' But the salient fact is: these *were* relationships."[23]

In introducing the viewer to a male/female couple who are in pursuit of an encounter with male-male buddy sex, the scene turns the normative inside out, suggesting a world where, instead of gay men assuming a minority position, anyone and everyone's sexual desire, gay and straight alike, is brought into question. Reinforcing this sense of the open and inclusive, the scene's roadhouse setting stands as a distinct counterpoint to commonplace 1970s film representations that continually assert gay space as a discernibly urban space, such as the apartments, bars, and homes that shield gay men from the greater social world and vice versa in films such as *The Boys in the Band* (1970), *Some of My Best Friends Are . . .* (1971), and *Saturday Night at the Baths* (1975). As a counterpoint to gay metropolitanism, the scene presents viewers with a utopic challenge, resonant with Krishan Kumar's comment that "utopia's value lies not in relation to present practice but in its relation to a possible future."[24]

At the same time, "present practice" is not objectively determinable; proof of what does and does not exist is very much reliant upon experience, exposure, and knowledge, all of which differ among various subject positions and according to the particular ways in which different subjects occupy, access, and utilize various spaces. Representational norms in both gay and mainstream cinema in the mid-1970s asserted the "present practice" of gay men as minoritized, ghettoized, fraternalized, and often highly commercialized. This representation is a direct result of how notions of the city worked in tandem with gay identity, coalescing in an easily locatable, map-able, and discernible gay sector—in other words, a space that could easily be identified as "where gay men belong." As Elizabeth Grosz has noted:

> The city's form and structure provide the context in which social rules and expectations are internalized or habituated in order to ensure social conformity, or position social marginality at a safe or insulated and bounded distance (ghettoization).[25]

Conversely, the less specifically marked territory of the American highway system in *El Paso* presents a space where, far from the organizational city-grid of government, commodity culture, and metrocentric dictates of "social conformity," sexuality can go untagged, uninsulated, and unregulated, and where men and women as individuals make up their own rules in terms of social organization, unimpeded by the socially policed norms and expectations of metropolitan life.

El Paso takes up an imaginary space outside of the bounds of the taxonomizing imperatives of the city. In particular, the sociosexual dynamics that play out in the basement where Gene, Millie, and Will meet contradict any minoritizing subject position as each one of the players resists any simple taxonomization based on either appearance or behavior. Instead of searching out an inclusive space or being told "where they belong" by others, the three characters define the space around them by their actions, leaving out questions of sexual identity or territory (such as who this space belongs to, whether it is meant exclusively for gay men, or can it include straight men and women?). Thus, as Gene provocatively asks the couple, "What are you two up to?" the film insinuates the space is one in which many potential scenarios may play out. As Will explains that Millie has a desire to "see him with a man" and Gene enthusiastically responds, "Is she gonna join us?" it becomes even clearer that the specific decorum of this site of public interaction is one of implicit fluidity, malleability, and openness as the erotic endeavor of all three characters comes to define the space according to their desires on individual and collective terms.

Through the formal construction of the scene the viewer is constantly reminded that, although they are in a basement, this is not a closed off or hidden space, but simply a private space, separated from the bar area yet close enough to be filled with the talking and laughing of the other patrons just up the steps. The momentary cut from the sex downstairs to Hank casually drinking upstairs contextualizes the sex within the larger scenario of the bar itself, reminding viewers that sexual interaction is itself a social act. Likewise, the long pause on Hank's beer establishes the banality of the scene, meshing the nearby sexual interaction with the sight of the mundane and everyday and ultimately demystifying the erotic. Taking this demystification even further, while the dialogue that precedes the sexual encounter implies that hardcore male-male sex is likely to ensue, what is delivered is anything but. Instead, *El Paso*'s version of sexual action is remarkably tender and romantic; slow panning camera movements follow the two men gently kissing, carefully embracing, and attentively touching each other's whole bodies. Accordingly, Millie's response to the sight of the men, tracing her hand lightly over her lips, breasts, and vagina, privileges the "soft" and sensual over the "hard" and sexual.

Despite the emphasis on self-stimulation, all three are shown as intimate and bonded, foregrounding the way in which bodies function not only as agents of individual sexual exchange ("you give me pleasure/I give you pleasure") but also as a means of social and experiential interchange ("my pleasure *is* your pleasure"). Working in accord with the networking dynamics of the interstate highway life established in *Kansas*

City Trucking Co, El Paso both sustains the trilogy's conceptualization of this space as an ideal opportunity for moving between and crossing over both generic and social conventions and norms and expands upon the scope for doing so by including an even greater range of subject positions as it moves along. In the process, the film demonstrates the numerous ways human desire can play out, calling to mind Delaney's assertion that "there are as many different styles, intensities, and timbres to sex as there are people."[26] In offering a version of the rural Southwest where the rules and codes of the city simply do not apply, the *Working Man Trilogy* demonstrates a version of road-buddy desire as something so vast and unbound in possibility and circumference that any entrance or exit is worth consideration.

NOTES

1 Altman, *Homosexual*, 45.

2 Engel, *The Unfinished Revolution*, 46.

3 White, *States of Desire*, 259.

4 Hennessy, *Profit and Pleasure*, 132.

5 Thompson, ed., *Long Road to Freedom*, 81, 129.

6 Kilmer, "Farm Boys," 178.

7 Waugh, *Out/Lines*, 31.

8 Edelman, *Homographesis*, 238. Emphasis in original.

9 Morris, "Keep on Truckin.'"

10 Burger, *One Handed Histories*, 40.

11 Sedgwick, *Between Men*, 23.

12 Waugh, *Hard to Imagine*; Schaefer, "Gauging a Revolution"; Lewis, *Hollywood vs. Hardcore*; Cook, *Lost Illusions*.

13 Delany, *Times Square Red, Times Square Blue*, 15.

14 Siebenand, "The Beginnings of Gay Cinema in Los Angeles," 263–81.

15 Stringer, "Exposing Intimacy," 165.

16 Ibid., 173.

17 Tompkins, *West of Everything*, 71.

18 Russo, "All about Camp,"139.

19 Marin, *Utopics*, 11.

20 Waugh, *Hard to Imagine*, 33.

21 Califia, *Public Sex*, 76.

22 Ibid.

23 Delany, *Times Square Red, Times Square Blue*,40.

24 Kumar, *Utopianism*, 3.

25 Grosz, "Bodies—Cities," 250.

26 Delany, *Times Square Red, Times Square Blue*, 45.

FILMOGRAPHY

Bijou. Wakefield Poole. 1972.

The Boysin the Band. William Friedkin. 1970.

Easy Rider. Dennis Hopper. 1969.

El Paso Wrecking Corp. Joe Gage. 1978.

The Erotic Films of Peter de Rome. Peter de Rome. 1973.

Kansas City Trucking Company. Joe Gage. 1976.

Navy Blue. John Amero. 1979.

Saturday Night at the Baths. David Buckley. 1975.

Some of My Best Friends Are . . . Mervyn Nelson. 1971.

Thunderbolt and Lightfoot. Michael Cimino. 1974.

Two-Lane Black Top. Monte Hellman. 1971.

10

Epistemology of the Bunkhouse

Lusty Lumberjacks and the Sexual Pedagogy of the Woods

PETER HOBBS

Along with red-coated Mounties and pictures of Niagara
Falls, one of the abiding images of Canada around the world
has been a shaggy, lonely figure swinging an axe amid the
snow and evergreens of the north woods.
—Donald MacKay, *The Lumberjacks*

When the workers came out of the woods most townspeople
avoided them. They were "timber beasts," foul men in filthy
clothing who had no place in respectable society.
—John E. Haynes, "Revolt of the Timber Beast"

Since Canada's confederation in 1867, the lumberjack has played a prominent role in both the country's history and mythology. His popularity as
an icon of both masculinity and the Canadian interior is a direct consequence of the remote camps or shantytowns where the country's logging
industry was developed. While these all-male communities seemed
to present an ideal backdrop for the social inscription of masculinity,
citizenship, and whiteness, they also presented the possibility of homosexual desire. With whom, if not with each other, were these men going
to have sex? Although this question remained for the most part unasked,
it can be seen as a major source of anxiety and the driving force behind
the concerted efforts of religious and civil authorities in early Canada
to educate the workers in these homosocial communities about importance of physical and moral hygiene. In turn, these efforts contributed
to the collective discourse of Canadian nationhood and proper forms of
citizenship.

I should admit up front that much of my motivation in examining the lumberjack is exceedingly personal: I am sexually drawn to this historic figure. Consequently, what I am proposing is more of an emotive and discursive journey through the woods and less of a conventional historical analysis. In this journey, Eve Kosofsky Sedgwick's *Epistemology of the Closet* (1990) serves a guide, providing a number of helpful signposts. Of primary value is her central claim that "many of the major nodes of thought and knowledge in twentieth-century Western culture as a whole are structured—indeed, fractured—by a chronic, now epidemic crisis of homo/heterosexual definition, indicatively male, dating from the end of the nineteenth century."[1] An essential point for Sedgwick's claim has to do with the unstable nature of the homo/heterosexual pairing, which means that our attempts to embody or inhabit one or the other of these figures, to perform as a homosexual or a heterosexual, can never be unequivocal. Instead, our performances of identity/selfhood are always subject to doubt, as they persist in the shadow of this homo/heterosexual schism. The shadow also destabilizes other fundamental binaries so that ideas of the natural and the artificial, the authentic and the forged, become entangled and impossible to parse out. Perception and paranoia—understanding and fearing—also become muddied. It is against this fractured background that I want to pursue the lumberjack as both a fictive and a real figure, who manages simultaneously to inspire masculinity and doubt, pride and shame, desire and panic.

The Sexual Typology of the Woods

Alongside Sedgwick's text, I am also guided by Peter Boag's *Same-Sex Affairs: Constructing and Controlling Homosexuality in the Pacific Northwest* (2003), which provides a detailed history of the various ways same-sex desire and relations manifested in logging camps and similar work sites in the late nineteenth and early twentieth centuries, during what he identifies as "a golden age" of casual labor.[2] Boag explains how the resource economy and woods conspired to bring large numbers of men and boys to remote camps and provided them with a sexual milieu that was very different from the closely monitored confines of the city:

Natural resource-based industries throughout the region's hinterland depended on a multitude of men and youths migrating to them for work. . . . The constant movement of males to such locations where they concentrated in large numbers did more than make sexual contact likely: it provided the milieu in which sexual contact occurred. Thus rather than having to travel from one site to the next for sexual relations, men found that the hinterland itself was a sexual space.[3]

Drawing testimony from police files and first-person accounts, including Nels Anderson's 1923 study, *The Hobo: The Sociology of the Homeless Man*, Boag details the various types of personas and forms of behavior that were adopted (and modified) by men and boys to help fashion their identities and interrelations with one another. While these figures include the wolf, the lamb, the urban fairy, the yegg (a transient who lives by thievery), and the bum, Boag's main focus is on the relationship formed between the jocker and the punk, which was a common bond held by an adult male and a younger male companion. Although both of these figures could find themselves incarcerated for their transgressions, the pair was more or less accepted within the camps as a recognized form of same-sex desire and male bonding.

Whereas Anderson sees this coupling of the jocker and the punk as an aberration that results from a combined lack—the lack of women, education, and community—Boag emphasizes the pervasiveness and openness of these same-sex relationships. "Migrating men and youths," Boag insists, "constructed an elaborate same-sex sexual culture that was anything but anonymous and furtive. . . . Indeed, their *community* provided for and reinforced same-sex activities. Thus openness, acceptance, and common practice rather than obscurity, disdain, and infrequency were responsible for transient same-sex sexuality."[4] Boag's point is to underscore that sexual bonding between men and boys was prevalent in the camps and that the combined notions of the closet and shame would be for the most part out of place, or imposed, if at all, by outside interests.

While I appreciate Boag's detailed account, it does not speak to the fracture and anxiety that Sedgwick posits as definitive of modernity. Indeed, much of this anxiety seems mitigated or absent in Boag's treatment of the work camps as prototypes of gay communal life, rather than sites of illicit or forbidden pleasure. My point is not to dispute or confirm Boag's text, but to show how the lumberjack and the bunkhouse are not easily folded into conventional histories of the logging camps. To echo Michel Foucault, I am interested in how the lumberjack and the bunkhouse constitute slippery indices or fissures in normative relations of power that are capable of "mobilizing groups or individuals in a definite way, inflaming certain points of the body, certain moments in life, certain types of behavior."[5] My aim, in other words, is to delineate the conflicting sentiments that mobilize my attraction to this figure.

The Invention of the Lumberjack

Despite the ubiquitous popularity enjoyed by the figure of the lumberjack, he did not emerge from the forest and enter the social imagination of early Canada fully formed and untroubled. In his economic survey of colonial Canada, a British diplomat named John McGregor described loggers in New Brunswick consuming "immoderate quantities of ardent spirits [to] sustain the cold," and engaging in scenes of public drunkenness. He further complained that the loggers' "moral character, with few exceptions, is dishonest and worthless."[6] Similarly, in a published collection of colonial letters, *The Hargrave Correspondence, 1821–1843*, a fur trader gave an account of communities along the Ottawa River living in fear of the loggers, who would "commit every species of cruelty and injustice on the peaceable settler" and were "the most depraved and dissipated set of villains on earth."[7] The lumberjack's poor reputation was further fueled by newspaper stories of violent clashes between rival logging companies.

In his 2006 history of logging in the Ottawa Valley, David Lee chronicles a company of Irish loggers using strong-armed tactics to secure control of the region. The company was led by an unsavory timberman, Peter Aylen, who, after having established control over the region's logging, turned his interest to Bytown (Ottawa) itself. Recruiting an army of "about 200 men," Aylen "launched a reign of terror in the town, highlighted by beatings, arson, jail-breaking, extortion, intimidation of magistrates, and political interference."[8] Such stories were repeated to such an extent that the lumberjack was generally seen as an uncompromising strong horse who would never shy away from a fight. For many people living in local logging towns, these unruly "timber beasts" would have inspired considerable fear and anger.

From the late nineteenth century onward, however, animosity for loggers was replaced by sympathy and respect. "Some people," Lee explains, "began to feel that the shantymen were more to be pitied than maligned; that they were, in truth, more victims than villains."[9] No doubt this reversal of public sentiment was a result of the consolidation and subsequent growth of the logging industry. Stories began to circulate of the harsh conditions of the logging camps. Some of these stories took the form of folksongs and folktales in which the hardworking lumberjack was easy prey for ruthless businessmen and the predatory practices of the company store. And rather than a thug or hooligan who was brought into the region, the lumberjack was fashioned as a naïve and kind-hearted soul who was representative of the local population. Regardless of the accuracy or exaggerations of these stories, they indicate a radical shift in the public image of the lumberjack. He was now seen as an inchoate national hero, someone who should be praised and emulated rather than criticized and shunned.

As a part of this shift in public opinion, stories of the lumberjack's heroism—tall tales—circulated throughout nineteenth-century North America as a form of regional pride and boasting. "In Quebec," states Lee, "nationalist writers embellished the fighting exploits of a real-life Valley raftsman, Joe Montferrand (1802–1864), and made him a legend. . . . He was later adopted in English Canada as Joe Mufferaw, a giant who performed mighty deeds in the wilderness. He may have also been the model for the American folk hero Paul Bunyan."[10] For most of the population of early Canada, these tales also provided vicarious and reassuring experiences. It is important to remember that despite Canada's wilderness mythology, for most of the population of Upper and Lower Canada the woods would have been an extremely alien space.[11] As a result, these tales were an important form of psychological comfort. Rather than portraying the woods as a dark and forebidding space, they featured a champion from the region, who, by using only his strength and his moral compass, is able to make the wildness his home.

The Grammar of the Woods

Hyperbole, the most common trope associated with lumberjack tales, is used to transform the everyday life of the lumberjack so that his actions and the objects that surround him take on gigantic proportions. The stories of Paul Bunyan provide the best-known example of the lumberjack-giant, who, in the tradition of Gargantua and Gulliver, has an insatiable appetite and excessive habits that serve as a recurring source of spectacle. In other words, the lumberjack's feats occur as the result of accidents as he attempts to satisfy his hunger or to carry out his daily routines. For example, Paul Bunyan is celebrated for accidentally creating trails and riverbeds by dragging his axe behind him. Similarly, there are recurring suggestions of ejaculation, in which the lumberjack-giant cannot contain his bodily fluids, resulting in the mythic creation of streams, lakes, and bodies of islands. The source of the Mississippi is attributed to the sweat of both Paul Bunyan and Big Joe Mufferaw. In this fantastic play of the gigantic and the everyday, the lumberjack is constituted as a grotesque figure of masculine excess.[12]

Beyond his miraculous feats and gigantic size, the mythical lumberjack is not that much different from his nonfictional counterpart. In both fiction and nonfiction, the lumberjack is presented as a bigger-than-life character who has an insatiable appetite for life. Like his fictional counterpart, the nonfictional lumberjack lives outside the constraints of civilization, and, as such, he represents an untainted/untamed version of manhood. To reinforce this idea, nonfictional authors often adapt a robust, folksy vernacular to convey the lumberjack's manly character. J. E. MacDonald's 1966 regional history, *Shantymen and Sodbusters: An Account of Logging and Settlement in Kirkwood Township, 1869–1928*, provides a typical example:

> When spring rolled around and the camp "break-up" loosed the boys upon civilization, many of them went on a rip-snorting spree. And not a few of them turned some of the energy that they had used for logging all winter to fighting. Occasionally, too, differences that may have simmered during the winter came to a head and resulted in some very lusty brawling.[13]

Through this mimetic strategy of using a seemingly unaffected prose style to reflect the language of "common folk," both the lumberjack's behavior and the author's text acquire a feeling of authenticity. Such a text presents itself as a faithful depiction, a window onto the past.

Donald MacKay similarly adopts a folksy/woodsy vernacular in his popular history of logging in Canada, simply entitled *The Lumberjacks* (1978). I want to draw particular attention to his treatment of the common practice in which loggers would dress up as women for regular dance parties held in the bunkhouse. "The men," MacKay explains,

> usually had Sunday off so when they came back to the camp at nightfall on Saturday there was usually horseplay and laughter and perhaps something special for supper. . . . The best fun was the stag dance. . . . Since there were rarely any women in the early camps, half the men sported flour sacks around their waist or handkerchiefs around their arms to show they were dancing the lady's part. "They'd tie a dish towel around a fella's arm, and away you'd go."[14]

What I find interesting in this description is how quickly MacKay dismisses the gender play of the stag dance. Rather than pausing to offer any analysis or comment, he demonstrates what Sedgwick describes as a potent and purposeful ignorance, in which the very thing that is understood as an aberration, the source of tremendous anxiety, is both acknowledged and brushed aside as inconsequential.[15] In MacKay's version of bunkhouse life, loggers could casually don flour sacks and take the lady's part without any slight to their manliness. The stag dance is presented as just part of the fun of a typical Saturday night, a simple case of tying "'a dish towel around a fella's arm, and away you'd go.'" By adopting this vernacular and projecting this blindness/ignorance, MacKay in effect sidesteps the homosocial intimacy shared by lumberjacks.

Historians and folklorists have also offset the homosocial conditions of the camp by extoling the lumberjack's reputation for traveling to the nearest town and spending all his year's wages in acts of heterosexual debauchery. Time and again, the reader is told that carousing lumberjacks sought out brothels and female prostitutes. For example, Edmund Bradwin's 1928 text, *The Bunkhouse Man: A Study of Work and Pay in the*

Camps of Canada 1903–1914, refers to men seeking the "companionship of women" and engaging in "all-night orgies, the drunken sprees lasting for days in the top room of a hotel or lodging house."[16] The sheer repetitiousness of these accounts naturalizes the lumberjack's heterosexuality and female prostitution, presenting both as simple consequences of the environment. In turn, this dual naturalization renders homosexuality the farthest thought from the lumberjack's mind and, in effect, as literally unthinkable.

Despite this concerted denial, homosexual desire manages to insinuate itself into such accounts in the form of an unruly subtext involving the lumberjack's excessive masculinity. In his insatiable lust for life, the lumberjack presents a cultural impasse or struggle. Another excerpt from Bradwin's text provides a graphic example of how it is impossible to focus on the lumberjack's body and not suggest homosexual desire:

> Few men physically are so splendidly endowed as the workers in the frontier camps. . . . Abounding health is theirs with something heaven-sent in their laughter and the freedom of untrammeled ways. [With] massive thighs [they are a] mighty resource of sinew and strength . . . fit to bear the grapes of Eschol. In mackinaw well-clad, with heavy shirt hung loose, his muscled limbs begirt with socks and pliant packs, the bunkhouse-man with easy stride confronts the sun.[17]

Bradwin's profuse celebration of the lumberjack's body is striking in part because it is very much out of line with the rest of his study. However, this type of fetishism—the fixation on the lumberjack's muscles and virility—is extremely common in the lumberjack literature. In both fiction and nonfiction, the lumberjack's body and the landscape are described as rich metaphoric expressions of one another. As a result, this fetishism naturalizes the lumberjack so that he is seen as a product of the natural environment, rather than as an intruding agent. But it also presents an imaginary landscape that is overwrought with homoeroticism.

The fulcrum for this battle between propriety and excessive masculine vitality/lust is the logging bunkhouse, with a great deal of attention being paid to its rough and overcrowded living conditions. The general lack of hygiene is seen as a disgraceful hardship unworthy of the hardworking lumberjack. However, alongside this image of squalor and neglect is the idea that the bunkhouse is an essential hub in the very making of the lumberjack. Often being the sole place for socializing, the bunkhouse is presented as the main site in which the lumberjack's persona, as a rugged man among men, is fashioned. Thus, two opposing images of bunkhouse life are simultaneously presented: (1) the rough and crowded conditions of the bunkhouse place the loggers in physical jeopardy; and (2) the rough and crowded conditions are what help shape the simple and manly character of lumberjacks.

The sleeping arrangements of the bunkhouse are a recurring cause of anxiety. Many bunkhouses featured one long bed that all the loggers shared. These beds were called "muzzle loaders" because the loggers had to get into them from the one end and all at the same time. MacKay provides an anecdotal description:

> Smaller camps had field bunks where everyone slept in a long row. There were two decks to it and, oh, the arguments because those up top sweated to death and those down below froze. If somebody got steamed up and wanted to turn he would call 'spoon!' There was always one fellow who wouldn't turn at the same time as the others and threw the whole lot out of kilter.[18]

This excerpt, with its spooning, steaming, and sweating bodies, presents something of the unavoidable intimacy shared by the men. I should clarify that I am not focusing on the sleeping arrangements of the bunkhouse as proof of the loggers' homosexuality. Instead, I am arguing that the sleeping arrangements served as a recurring source of anxiety—a slippery index or fissure—that worked against the efforts to portray the lumberjack as an unequivocal model of both manhood and citizenship.

Archival photographs of the bunkhouses also depict a space of unavoidable male intimacy (figure 10.1). These images show primitive and overcrowded dormitories and typically feature rows of bearded men posing for the camera, sitting together on their shared bunks. Plumes of smoke and makeshift clotheslines further augment the squalor. The men stare into the camera, with their arms folded across their chests. And while the loggers' deadpan expressions are no doubt the result of the lengthy exposure time that early photography required, this does not

Figure 10.1. Interior of an old-time bunkhouse common on frontier works during the period 1890–1925. (Source: Library and Archives Canada)

prevent viewers from seeing their facial expressions and poses as signs of possible defiance/deviance.

The bunkhouse—like all open dormitories—is designed so that all of the bunks are in public view. In light of this fact, it would be difficult for bunkmates to have any sort of sex without the rest of the bunkhouse knowing of it. This idea conjures two opposing scenarios: (1) a panoptic scenario of normativity in which the loggers police each other's behavior; and (2) a homoerotic scenario in which the bunkhouse colony as a whole agrees to shun the rules of prudish civility and to let their masculine urges run amuck. Even if we refuse to acknowledge any suggestion of homosexual desire in these photographs, they still show a hypermasculine space very much removed from—if not resistant to—the influences of moral reform.

The Schoolroom in the Bush

No doubt the sleeping arrangements of the bunkhouse and the routine coupling of men and boys, jockers and punks, would have been a major concern for Reverend Alfred Fitzpatrick, who was an iconic figure in the Canadian campaign to educate and reform loggers. In his polemic from 1929, *The University in Overalls*, the reverend rallied his fellow Protestants to bring dignity to the logging bunkhouse by way of literacy. Fitzpatrick was the founder of Frontier College, which began in 1899 as an early version of an open university with the idea that instead of being in one location, the classrooms of Frontier College would be taken into the bush. The reverend's stated goal was to instill Christian values by teaching the loggers to read and acquire a general education.

Lurking within the subtext of Fitzpatrick's text are the twin figures of the jocker and the punk, who pose an essential dilemma wherein which Fitzpatrick struggles to name the sin that is unmentionable, the mere suggestion of which would pollute his text and impugn his thoughts. His moral rectitude and authority, in other words, would become suspect if he were capable of naming/recognizing the relationship between the jocker and the punk as a sexual one. As a way to map some of the contours of this restrictive principle, this rhetorical closet, I want to rehearse more of the historical context or background that the reverend would be responding to and writing against. I also want to isolate moments in the reverend's polemic where his struggle with homosexual desire—to name or recognize it—becomes more or less apparent.

As part of his polemic, Fitzpatrick vehemently chastises Canadian universities for producing a generation of dull and pale men who suffer as of result of being overly educated and urban. In his eyes the typical university student is a "tenderfoot" who would greatly benefit from the physical and mental demands of manual labor. Applying the metaphor of a hardy stalk of grass or grain, he complains that for the student "there is not sufficient storm to stiffen the tender blades and freshen the soil about the roots. The plant savors of the hothouse. Like semi-recluses, they are pale in the spring and their muscles so lax that they are unfit for manual labor until a fortnight or more has passed."[19] Thus, the reverend's version of the urban student is the cliché of the hothouse flower, a young man who has spent too much time at rest and is, subsequently, far too delicate for the demands of manual/manly labor.

Fitzpatrick himself is shown in a portrait as a bespectacled and well-groomed gentleman, far removed from the lauded woods and the toils of physical labor. His demeanor suggests a critical stance toward sweeping changes that were taking place at the turn of the twentieth century and resulting in a sharp decline in the economic and cultural influence enjoyed by the middle-class businessman. In his comprehensive history of *Gay New York: Gender, Urban Culture, and the Making of the Gay Male World, 1890–1940*, George Chauncey documents this transition in terms of the way people imagined typical forms of masculine and feminine behavior. He explains that whereas in the economy of the Gilded Age of the late 1800s, middle-class entrepreneurs were essential to forming and backing small private businesses, by the turn of the century, as large corporations were formed and monopolies were established, opportunities for independent companies and businessmen were drastically reduced. Under the circumstances, many middle-class men were forced to give up their sense of economic freedom and became the salaried employees of these corporations. And even though they took on managerial positions, such positions nevertheless undercut the public persona of the self-sufficient patriarch.

Moreover, the arrival of women in the workforce further challenged this image. As Chauncey writes, "More and more women began working . . . and although they took on different and usually subordinate tasks, their very presence . . . seemed to feminize the culture of the corporate workplace and to diminish its status as a masculine domain."[20] In addition to this intrusion, women were also forming temperance movements across the United States and Canada to combat vices associated with male entertainment and bonding, such as alcohol, gambling, and prostitution. One of the biggest of these organizations was the Woman's Christian Temperance Union, which was primarily made up of middle-class women. These groups, Chauncey asserts, "had identified alcohol as a male vice and campaigned to shut down the saloons and private clubs where men gathered to socialize and drink."[21] Thus, many of the privileges and freedoms that men had long assumed to be their natural rights were now under siege. "On every front," continues Chauncey, "women seemed to be breaching the division between the sexes' proper spheres and to be claiming or challenging the prerogatives of men."[22] The idea that these men could no longer keep their wives and daughters in check also came to be seen as an obvious affront to their masculinity.

In her 1995 work on *Manliness and Civilization: A Cultural History of Gender and Race in the United States, 1880–1917*, Gail Bederman also focuses on this historical shift in the public sphere. Echoing Chauncey, she explains that the self-restraint and sacrifice to which bourgeois men had aspired were no longer considered so admirable. Instead, the characteristics and habits associated with working-class men were being championed as a source of a natural or undiluted masculinity. For example, sports that were associated with working-class men and stressed physical strength—like boxing, weightlifting, and football—were widely praised as worthy pastimes that helped to build male character. During this time the Young Men's Christian Association (YMCA) formed sports clubs and financed the construction of gyms to encourage young men to take up athletics. In contrast, the activities and characteristics normally associated with the middle-class gentleman, such as education, appreciation for the fine arts, and a restrictive display of one's body in public, became markers of a molly-coddled or effeminate man. As Bederman explains, this reconfiguration of masculinity was evident in the everyday vernacular:

> As men worked to remake manhood, they adopted new words which could express their dynamic new understandings of the nature of male power. During the 1890s, they coined the new epithets "sissy," "pussy-foot," "cold feet" and "stuffed shirt" to denote behavior which had once appeared self-possessed and manly but now seemed overcivilized and effeminate. Indeed, the very word "overcivilized" was coined during these years.[23]

This notion of being too civilized put men in a difficult and suspect position. Not only was their public image marred by a decline in their economic and social status, but this image also aligned them with the traits and behaviors that were currently being used in both institutional and vernacular discourses to identify a new aberrant social figure: the homosexual.

Here, then, is historical context or framework—the broader cultural closet—in which Reverend Fitzpatrick struggled to name the ills of the logging camp. Not only does it help us recognize the dilemma that he would face personally as the embodiment of the refined (and thus feminized) urban gentlemen, it also underscores the college's dilemma in finding appropriate candidates to send into the woods as instructors. As the reverend explains, these recruits would need to be young educated men who were able to work alongside the loggers during the day and then provide classes in the evening. Fitzpatrick believed that this combination of being both able-bodied and educated was very rare and that one of the clear benefits of bringing education to the camps would involve exposing this workforce of educated, urban men to their working-class peers and to the hardy conditions of living in the woods. "To carry the university to the worker," he stated, "a new kind of teacher is needed, a man whose hands are trained as well as his mind and soul, and who possesses that intangible quality which gives leadership. He must be a university man who can satisfy not only the foreman with his daily work, but can awaken enthusiasm in a gang of men."[24] In Fitzpatrick's praise it is not clear who would be benefitting the most from this arrangement, the satisfied foreman, the gang of illiterate lumberjacks, or their physically fit and well-liked instructor.

This idealized scene of the successful integration of the university man in the logging camp reveals something of the potential danger Fitzpatrick saw in bringing young men in contact with older, more experienced loggers. In an essay entitled "The Instructor as Canadianizer," he also spoke of the young recruits functioning as agents of nationalism, helping to instill Protestant values in what he called a "Canadianizing process"[25]— a priority for the reverend and his colleagues especially after the end of World War I, when a large influx of European immigrants arrived in Canada's logging and mining camps. As James Morrison explains, "To many Canadians, spooked by the Bolshevik revolution sweeping Europe as the War ended, work camps represented veritable hotbeds of revolution."[26] But it is also apparent that beyond fears of Bolshevism, embodied in the steady arrival of Poles, Rumanians, and Russian Jews, Fitzpatrick was also "spooked" by another sort of "hotbed": the idea that these foreign men represented an unchecked source of sexual corruption. After listing black flies, smallpox, boredom, and alcohol as part of the lumberjack's torments, Fitzpatrick was compelled to leave little doubt that his most pressing anxiety was the unholy union of male bodies. "The Bunkhouse," he finally declared, "is a curse to the inmates, to the employers, and to the public. Why should young lads with comparatively clean minds be tumbled promiscuously into bunks with filthy-minded men?"[27] Unable to help but invoke a scenario in which innocent Protestant boys are bedding down for the night with lusty, older strangers (possibly of Eastern European origin), Fitzpatrick provided his less conventional readers with excellent fodder for homoerotic fantasy.

It is important not to gloss over the fact that despite his effort to enforce propriety and restraint, Reverend Fitzpatrick invokes scenes of impropriety and sodomy. In this way, his polemic illustrates the connotative trace or supplement that haunts our binary thinking. Again to echo Sedgwick (and Jacques Derrida), this is the layered and slippery character of language: it gives rise to the play of signifiers, of saying and not saying, of invoking something by saying its opposite. For Reverend Fitzpatrick and his fellow moral watchdogs, the fluidity of language presents an essential irony: each time they sound their battle cry and champion a Christian worldview of fortitude and salvation, they inevitably plant new seeds of temptation and sin in the minds of their parishioners.

The binary nature of language goes a long way in explaining why the heroic inscription of the North American lumberjack enters the social imagination at roughly the same time as the medical and criminal inscription of the homosexual. Both were nineteenth-century constructions or inventions that relied on each other for definition. To fully appreciate the constitutive relationship of the lumberjack and the homosexual it is important to stress that while the two figures helped to define the limits of what Judith Butler refers to as "gender ontology," or an embodied mode of being, such a binary relationship could not help but be a tremendous source of homophobic anxiety and masculine insecurity.[28] But just how could these two figures, the lumberjack and the homosexual, both secure and trouble nineteenth-century notions of masculinity? The answer is that the two figures functioned as a discursive framework rather than as two fixed positions that individuals would embody or exemplify to the letter. Rather than occupying opposite poles, these figures are better understood as part of a continuum of gender performances, for as Butler insists, gender is a form of, and forum for, serial imitation that undermines the very idea of a singular or authentic performance. Each performance of manhood, womanhood, boyhood, and girlhood is a copy of previous copies, and it is in these variations of sameness that discontinuity and trouble emerges.

To show how the figure of the lumberjack has been enrolled into this play of sameness, discontinuity, and trouble, I turn to a segment in Martin Levine's history of gay life in the 1970s, *Gay Macho: The Life and Death of the Homosexual Clone*, which provides an anecdotal account of how the figure of lumberjack served as a recognized vehicle-persona that gay men could adopt in fashioning a personal and shared identity. As Levine explains, the care that gay men took in refashioning/repurposing the lumberjack's garb so that it would read simultaneously as genuine and parodic was essential to taking on this persona. "Take Frank for example," states Levine, referring to one of his informants: "Everything he wore was tailored and matched. His jeans and plaid Pendelton shirt fit perfectly. His black, wool, watchman's cap matched his black Levis and the black in his shirt. . . . No real lumberjack ever looked so well put together, so coordinated in color, his outfit fitting so perfectly. Frank, then, *signified* the lumberjack—appropriating the gender conformity that is traditionally associated with lumberjacks, but not actually having to cut down trees to do it."[29] As a result of the popularity of this figure, variations of brawny lumberjacks populated the streets and gay bars of San Francisco, New York, and Toronto.

Alongside this appropriation (or performed integration) of the lumberjack into the gay culture of the 1970s, it is important to reemphasize that the pairing of the lumberjack and the gentleman emasculated by cultural changes strengthens Sedgwick's argument that the twin specters of homosexual desire and homophobia, which mark modernity and contemporary notions of sexuality, make it impossible to inhabit codes of behavior—normative and otherwise—without falling under suspicion or being subject to self-doubt. Monty Python even makes fun of this ubiquitous culture of sexual ambiguity in their Lumberjack Sketch, in which the ultra-masculine lumberjack is shown to be subject to disreputable thoughts of cross-dressing. The sketch begins with the lumberjack introducing himself by praising the virtues of manly work done in the fresh air and forest of British Columbia. With his gal in his arms, and accompanied by a chorus of Mounties, the lumberjack launches into a music hall song about the woods. But by the third verse he has revealed that he is not the man that his gal and the chorus of Mounties made him out to be:

> I chop down trees.
> I wear high heels,

Suspenders and a bra.
I wish I'd been a girlie,
Just like my dear papa.

As I have pointed out above, such scenes of bearded and brawny woodsmen in drag have historical precedent. But the humor of this sketch does not depend on knowing this precedent. Instead, like most of Monty Python's humor, the skit is overtly camp, purposely over the top. As purveyors of camp, Monty Python never tired of making fun of propriety, of showing how the proper itself constitutes a performance or grammar that we learn to inhabit. The Lumberjack Sketch also reveals how easily this grammar of propriety can be ridiculed and how it is never far from betraying itself as a parodic performance—and in ways that can have violent repercussions for those who stray too from their assigned parts/roles.

The Death of the Lumberjack

The solid forests of Glengarry have vanished, and with the
forest the men who conquered them. The manner of life and
the type of character to be seen in those early days has gone
too, and forever.
—Ralph Connor, *The Man from Glengarry*

By way of a conclusion, I want to look at Ralph Connor's 1901 moral tale, *The Man from Glengarry*, which was a best-selling novel of the period. Set in Upper Canada during the mid-1800s, *The Man from Glengarry* chronicles the life of Ranald Macdonald, a simple but hardworking woodsman who eventually becomes a successful businessman. Connor presents the lumberjack as a manly figure, who, despite his penchant for carousing and violence, has been wrongly criticized and undervalued. Being representative of the good folk of colonial Canada, the lumberjack is also presented as someone who is out of step with progress and industry, and, as such, in need of protection and guidance. As a narrative of transition, the novel is very much about the demise of the lumberjack, who is presented as a necessary casualty of modernity and the march of progress.

"Ralph Connor" was the penname of Reverend Charles William Gordon, a Presbyterian minister and instructor at Upper Canada College. Like Reverend Fitzpatrick, Reverend Gordon saw the Canadian wilderness as the ideal setting for rehearsing the moral lessons of manliness and nation-building. Under this penname, Gordon produced a series of novels set in the woods and frontier towns of early Canada,[30] which offered tales of heroism and responsibility and quickly acquired a popular readership in Canada and abroad, where they were translated. Indeed, "Ralph Connor" sold more than five million copies of his works in his lifetime, making him one of the most popular writers of the early twentieth century.[31]

The primary relationship in *The Man from Glengarry* is between the young Ranald and Mrs. Murray, the wife of the local minister. Early in the story, Mrs. Murray decides to take Ranald under her wing to make sure he lives up to his potential as a model of Christian manhood. Much of the plot meanders from one season to the next, as Ranald attempts to win Mrs. Murray's approval by giving up his former life as a lumberjack. At the novel's conclusion, Ranald marries Kate, a younger version of Mrs. Murray, while also transforming himself into an honest lumber executive and a civic leader. By chronicling Ranald's social development, the novel presents a clear parallel between the protagonist's transformation and the country's transformation as a fledging nation.

Yet by focusing on the lumberjack's assimilation and eventual disappearance, rather than his former glory, the plot presents a paradox: Why does Ranald need saving? At outset of the novel, he is already represented as an exemplary young man. Had he been left to pursue his family tradition of working in the bush, it stands to reason that his faith would be as strong as that of the next God-fearing woodsman. In contrast to both his father and uncle, who both rose up through the ranks of their fellow loggers to become highly respected camp leaders, Ranald succeeds by virtue of his willingness to leave his former life and the woods behind him. He is also encouraged by Mrs. Murray to find a middle-class bride thoroughly removed from his Glengarry circle of acquaintance. Thus, Ranald's story repeats a tragic lesson that runs throughout much of the lumberjack literature: the lumberjack who is championed as a masculine role model is also shown to be thoroughly obsolete. Like Ranald, turn-of-century males were simultaneously asked to emulate and respect the

values and masculine characteristics embodied by the lumberjack—the
frontier life, the freedom, the rewards of manual labor—and give them
up in the name of social progress and propriety.

Much of the lumberjack literature is centered on the disappearance
of both the frontier and the heroics of the lumberjack. Similarly, I have
traced some of the ways in which this contradictory cultural message
of emulation and loss gave rise to conflicting and unruly expressions of
masculinity and desire. I hope I have made it apparent that the thrill or
titillation of these historical texts and tall tales comes from the scenes
in which the queerness of the lumberjack cannot be sidestepped or ignored. Instead, they call out to the avid gay reader, luring him onto the
dance floor and into the hotbeds of the timber beasts.

NOTES

1 Sedgwick. *Epistemology of the Closet*, 1.

2 Boag, *Same-Sex Affairs*, 17.

3 Ibid., 41–42.

4 Ibid., 39. Italics in the original.

5 Foucault, *The History of Sexuality*, 96.

6 McGregor, *Historical and Descriptive Sketches*, 167.

7 Hargrave, *The Hargrave Correspondence*, 33.

8 Lee, *Lumber Kings and Shantymen*, 189.

9 Ibid., 159.

10 Ibid., 160–61.

11 As exemplified in Susanna Moody's pioneer memoir from 1852, *Roughing It in the
Bush*.

12 For examples of lumberjack folktales, see Michael Edmonds, *Out of the Northwoods*.

13 MacDonald, *Shantymen and Sodbusters*, 80.

14 MacKay, *The Lumberjacks*, 240.

15 Sedgwick., *Epistemology of the Closet*, 4–8.

16 Bradwin, *The Bunkhouse Man*, 137.

17 Ibid., 291.

18 MacKay, *The Lumberjacks*, 230.

19 Fitzpatrick, *The University in Overalls*, 104.

20 Chauncey, *Gay New York*, 111.

21 Ibid., 112

22 Ibid.

23 Bederman, *Manliness and Civilization*, 17.

24 Fitzpatrick, *The University in Overalls*, 33.

25 Ibid.,138.

26 Morrison cited in ibid., 16.

27 Ibid., 45.

28 Butler, *Gender Trouble*, 43.

29 Levine, *Gay Macho*, 61. Italics in the original.

30 These novels include *The Sky Pilot: A Tale of the Foothills* (1899) and *Corporal Cameron of the North West Mounted Police: A Tale of the MacLeod Trail* (1912).

31 See the *Canadian Encyclopedia*, www.thecanadianencyclopedia.com.

11

Rethinking the Closet

Queer Life in Rural Geographies

KATHERINE SCHWEIGHOFER

In our contemporary understanding of LGBTQ[1] identities and communities, the binary of visible gay community versus closeted individuals is mapped on to American geographical and cultural divisions. Simply put, we associate urban with out and proud, and rural with closeted and homophobic. Scholars of queer rurality have explained this geography of the closet as one in which the rural United Sates "is made to function as a closet for urban sexualities"[2] and "operates as America's perennial, tacitly taken-for-granted closet."[3] One scholar has even specifically dubbed the state of Mississippi as the nation's closet.[4] This foundational "metronormativity" in LGBTQ identities and communities has been undermined by recent work in rural queer studies. This work emphasizes that representing the country as the closet elides flourishing LGBTQ communities and individuals in rural spaces. Additionally, the country-as-closet construct reinforces an urban definition of LGBTQ identity and visibility that may not be compatible with rural LGBTQ lifestyles, in effect rendering rural queer life impossible. This essay problematizes the metaphor of the closet relative to rural gay and lesbian identities to identify new directions for scholarship on queer identity and community. I challenge the closet's reliance upon binary divisions between public and private space and visibility and invisibility by locating other forms of gay and lesbian community and identity that flourish across and beyond these binaries.

Given its centrality in this essay, a brief explanation of "the rural" is in order. Geographic identities are shaped as much by cultural ideologies as by physical landscapes, and the constructed division between the "country" and the "city" is a particularly powerful and naturalized formation in American culture. I turn to material that builds upon Raymond Williams's early examinations of the British construction of "city" and "country"[5] and reframes the rural idyll to reveal its homoerotic content, complicating the perceived sexual conservatism of rurality with evidence of an omnipresent queerness.[6] In the United States, specific regionalisms produce a variety of ruralities from which scholars continue to tease out specific implications for queer identities.[7] As Scott Herring points out, the distinction between urban and rural is "as much context-specific, phantasmatic, performative, subjective, and . . . standardizing as it is geographically verifiable"[8] Yet geographical identity clearly shapes the lived experiences of LGBT individuals, often prompting migrations, relocations, dislocations, circulations, and other movements between and within rural and urban spaces.[9] Within the source material used here, respondents are predominantly located in the Upper Midwest and Appalachian regions, and the "rural" in which they live is characterized by small towns and unincorporated townships with sparse population density, an emphasis on crop and dairy farming, white working- and middle-class politics, and religious and social conservatism.

For source material, I have used collections that center first-person narration as evidence. Will Fellows's *Farm Boys* is an ethnographic collection of stories of gay-identified men who grew up on farms of various sizes in the Midwest. These men experienced adolescence between 1940 and 1980 and were in various stages of outness at the time of their interviews. Fellows found his subjects by placing ads in gay circulars in Chicago, Minneapolis, and Iowa City, effectively limiting his pool of interviewees to those men visiting, if not living, in these urban areas and thereby suggesting a metronormative bias to his study. Fellows addresses this and other restrictions on his narrators, including his realization that men who were completely in the closet were not easily found. His sample therefore skews to those who engage in visibly out gay communities to the extent that they have access to and read gay circulars. Thus closeted individuals in both rural and urban locales with similar farm-based upbringing were excluded from his collection, an omission that both suggests an area for future scholarship and, as will be explored in this essay, points to the problematic ways in which rural homosexualities are identified.

For a glimpse into the experiences of lesbian and bisexual women in rural spaces, I turn to three sources: *Lesbian Land*, Joyce Cheney's 1985 collection of narratives from women's land members, which is one of the only publications on that movement;[10] *Country Women* magazine, a periodical that ran for most of the 1970s and was written by and for women living in rural areas; and materials from the Lesbian Herstory Archives subject files.[11] These sources provide a rare window into the life of rural-living lesbians between 1960 and 1990. As an additional geographic twist, many of Cheney's narrators originate from urban or suburban backgrounds and are drawn to the country as part of a radical lesbian feminist ethos; their readings of lesbian identity and the lives of the local women they encounter provide unique snapshots of the role of geography in women's identities.

As a point of contrast, Mary Gray's *Out in the Country: Youth, Media, and Queer Visibility in Rural America* (2010) provides a more recent perspective. Gray focuses on coming out and queer identity issues faced by a younger generation than Fellows and Cheney, as well as considering the impact of greater access to media on queer identities. Despite the availability of gay-themed entertainment and cultural resources such as PlanetOut.com, *Brokeback Mountain*, and *Will & Grace* for these teens, their stories reveal important problems with the concept of the closet for rural queer identities and offer a new generation's perspective on the teen struggles also described by Fellows's narrators.

These sources are particularly useful here because they are primarily, and in some cases entirely, told in the participants' own words; instead of being written about, these rural gays and lesbians are writing about themselves. It should also be noted that the source material used here addresses primarily a Midwestern, white, Protestant and Catholic, mostly male, middle- and working-class experience, and the resulting analysis likely applies best to this particular setting. Despite intentional efforts to add women's perspectives to this analysis, lesbian, bisexual, and queer women's experiences differ from those of gay and bisexual men in ways that often leave a less readily apparent historical record of their communities and lives. Additionally, the identities, relationships, and closet/coming out experiences of LGBTQ and Two-Spirit Native Americans, Southerners and Westerners, people of color, itinerant or poor persons, or transgender persons in rural spaces will differ from the stories driving this analysis. These stories of queer experience in rural space I suspect further destabilize the structure of the closet, and deserve future exploration.

Building the Closet

Since the coalescing of theories of homosexuality into sexual identities, the concept of coming out has been a major part of gay life and culture. As early as the late 1860s, German homosexual rights advocate Karl Ulrichs advocated disclosure of one's sexuality as a positive step toward acceptance.[12] The phrase "coming out," however, was originally understood as contextually similar to debutant traditions; "coming out" into gay society was a joyful and social event. After the 1969 Stonewall riots, the understanding of "coming out" was linked with the idea of "skeletons in one's closet," and thus, "coming out of the closet" became a move of resistance to oppression and isolation.[13] Queer theorists have dug even deeper into this metaphor. Eve Sedgwick's landmark *Epistemology of the Closet* begins by describing the power of the image of the closet, not only declaring it the fundamental feature of homosexual social existence but also delineating its importance in heterosexual culture as well. Sedgwick argues that the "epistemology of the closet has given an overarching consistency to gay culture and identity throughout this century" and has been "inexhaustibly productive of modern Western culture and history at large."[14] Sedgwick also outlines the contradictory demands placed on homosexuals in relation to the closet. In one case, a high school teacher is fired as a result of his homosexuality, with the legal verdict hinging on an illogical decision stating he both revealed too much about his sexuality (by coming out) and not enough (that he had not indicated his homosexuality on his application for the position).[15] Thus, the closet is formed by conflicting impulses to secrecy and proclamation, private knowledge and public display.

Other scholars examine the construct of the closet with specific attention to geography. In the opening lines of his geographical analysis *Closet Space*, Michael Brown gives his own definition of the closet, again, referencing contradictory elements: "The closet is a term used to describe the denial, concealment, erasure, or ignorance of lesbians and gay men. It describes their absence—and alludes to their ironic presence nonetheless—in a society that, in countless interlocking ways, subtly and blatantly dictates that heterosexuality is the only way to be."[16] Brown's attention then turns to the geography of the closet, addressing the impact of space on desire. Brown maps the gay bars and bathhouses in the city of Christchurch, New Zealand, to examine of the production of the closet in urban space.[17] He argues that the closet "enables gay [male] desire to be commodified for profit."[18] The successful presence of a handful of gay bars, strip clubs, and bathhouses in one particular commercial sex district is due to their subtle and minimal advertising methods. Brown believes that by not making a grand show of their presence (particularly compared to the advertising methods of heterosexual strip clubs in the area), the gay clubs multiply their business, drawing both closeted and out gay men. What Brown has potentially uncovered, even if he does not address it, is a different way of constructing gay community. The clubs *undo* binary assumptions about gay community and space: they are both anonymous and also frequented by a small and identifiable set of residents (Christchurch being a city of only 228,000); they are hidden yet obvious to the knowing; they are both right in the center of a busy commercial sex district in the middle of the city and tucked down quiet alleyways and up dark flights of stairs. These gay bathhouses and sex clubs are *both* closeted and out, suggesting that queer geographies are already more complicated than can be captured by the metaphor of the closet.

In addition to organizing social and economic elements of gay and lesbian community, the construct of the closet has also been an integral part in defining and understanding modern gay identity. Structurally part of the gay coming-of-age narrative, closetedness precedes an adult state of openness, acceptance, and happiness. This chronological narrative is also mapped onto a geographical one: a rural-to-urban migration is overlaid upon the child-to-adult and closet-to-out movements. Thus the tale is told: the young gay subject lives outside LGBTQ community in a nonurban space, one day realizes he is different, and leaves his rural upbringing to head to the big city where he comes out into adult gayness and lives happily ever after, embraced by his urban-based gay community. Even as the lived reality of many lesbian, gay, and especially bisexual, trans, and queer lives deviates from this fictional narrative, its structuring elements continue to inform individuals, communities, and theories of queer identity.

This narrative also provides structure and connection for lesbian and gay lives, grounding them in ritual and history. Sharing coming out stories is a common practice among new friends or partners, and might even turn competitive, with each participant telling an even worse tale than the one before of family and friends' reactions to the news. Recounting the details of one's time in the closet and coming out moment(s) also often affirms or provides a space for sharing parts of an individual's past that he or she may otherwise prefer to avoid, stories of changed relationships, hurtful memories, or feelings of disconnection and unbelonging. Coming out stories provide a space to engage with potentially difficult pasts and find positive connections with the present.

This tradition of sharing stories creates not just individual history that is valued by other LGBT community members, but a larger communal history of resistance and perseverance in the face of oppression. LGBT histories are full of coming out stories, and readers often connect to the material through their own experiences. The entire LGBT movement has been given a closet/coming out story as well; historians frequently refer to the movement's more visible moments (Stonewall and sometimes the Compton's Cafeteria riots[19]) as coming-out moments, with earlier decades (particularly the 1940s–1960s) as times characterized by secrecy, hiding, and loneliness. Ironically, although the closet metaphor is usually intended to acknowledge and respect the difficulties faced by earlier queer generations, it also forces individuals who lived beyond an in/out binary into an anachronistic closet, instead of truly reflecting the way sexuality shaped their lived identity.

Lesbians and gay men establish a personal history through coming out stories that resonates with and grounds them in a collective past, something they are precluded from within heteronormative culture. Finding a sense of belonging might heal years of feeling out of place, of constantly feeling different and uncomfortable. Though the community exists primarily in opposition to the closet—the individuals who are "out" primarily make up the community—it is also dependent upon the closet as its originating location (a state of not knowing or presumed heterosexuality must by definition precede a state of known homosexuality). The binary is also not a clean division, as individuals exist at various states of outness, might have to come out over and over again,[20] and may move in and out of participation in the community. As Diana Fuss so simply put it, "the problem of course with the inside/outside rhetoric . . . is that such polemics disguise the fact that most of us are both inside and outside at the same time."[21] LGBT groups and organizations recognize this complexity and are thus often sensitive to privacy and the need for secrecy. In some ways, LGBT communities might be seen as the logical outcome of the closet, the very result of groups of people making the same decision to come out. The closet can equally be seen as the result of a visible LGBT community—if there are some people who are noticeably and publicly queer, then those LGBT individuals who are not visible become a group in need of a separate designation. Thus the closet and visible LGBT communities operate in a mutually reinforcing relationship through which individuals may move back and forth over time and space.[22]

Public Space, Private Space: Breaking apart the Rural Closet

As part of the structure of contemporary lesbian and gay identity, coming out of the closet requires several elements. Mary Gray suggests that "discovering a sense of one's queer self requires three things: the privacy to explore one's queer differences . . . a visible [queer] community . . . and the safe space to express queer difference."[23] Under scrutiny here is the first item on Gray's list, privacy. Secrecy, private space, and time to oneself are critical to the closet's functionality. The queer individual, whether youth or adult, might write in journals, draw pictures, or reflect on questions concerning desire and identity. She might collect clues to existing constructions of gay identity, including porn, pulp fiction, mementos from same-sex crushes or experiences, or even sexological literature. Secret stashes, time to pore over them, and time spent in quiet reflection all require physical and emotional space not always available in busy households or small residences. Fellows's Midwestern farm boys talk extensively about their lack of privacy as children and teens in the 1950s through the 1980s. For many, life on the farm entailed almost zero privacy. Constantly being surrounded by family members, often sharing a bedroom and usually a bed, meant no individual could lay claim to a private physical space. Several narrators spoke of the fear that their siblings, particularly brothers, might reveal shared sexual experiences or find treasured queer items. On family-run farms, the intense workload meant everyone had to chip in, often resulting in morning-till-night cycles of chores.[24] School offered a respite from farm work for children, but certainly not any sort of privacy or individual time. Instead, school often heightened young gay men's exposure to others who might detect their queerness.

Simultaneously, the isolation and space of farm life created pockets of privacy, or at least opportunities for making private moments. Some farm boys spoke of being able to disappear into fields, barns, or the woods during chore times for a respite from their families. The large number of family members might mean it was easier to sneak off, as busy parents lost track of who was doing what. Increased numbers of siblings meant more sources of information on sexuality and desire, and a few men even mentioned having other gay siblings. Yet the isolation of individual farms and farming communities meant a higher level of homogeneity and an intensification of focus on difference. Young gay men felt high levels of scrutiny from neighbors and community members who knew who they were, what their car looked like, and who their parents were.

Rural farm life thus creates spaces that are simultaneously extremely public and private. A wide-open back pasture, with no one watching but a few grazing horses or cows, is a space that defies clear public/private divides. These places are always available, yet must be sought out by the queerly desiring subject. They are both far from the hustle and bustle of everyday family life, yet structurally central to that world. Remote fields, empty barns, or a stretch of woods might become just as conducive to queer sexual exploration as San Francisco's Castro or New York's Greenwich Village.

This type of queer space is not limited to farms, but might also appear in small cities with rural characteristics. Brown's analysis of the gay club scene in Christchurch demonstrates how urban/rural and public/private lines are blurred; these clubs are urban enough to be easily identifiable as gay community (they are anonymous, public, within particular city blocks), yet they also present contradictory elements (people know one another, the clubs are private and hard to find) that suggest something more complicated. If spaces like the back pastures and the Christchurch clubs are queerly both public and private, if they are both rural and urban, hidden and visible, then they undermine our cultural expectations for the spatialization of homosexual identities and communities. The closet model, in its strict adherence to in/out, private/public divides, does not allow for these sorts of queer spaces, and this limitation suggests that the closet model is not only metronormative but also homonormative, reinforcing a notion of gay life as striving toward a heteronormative married consumer lifestyle. If the closet is a major structuring element in identifying LGBT communities, and it cannot conceive of queer geographies, then it also cannot imagine the queer identities and communities that circulate in those spaces. Queering the rural closet allows us to imagine that two farm boys having sex in a back field are using both the public *and* private elements of that space to create their own gay community, even if it is one that is difficult to align with dominant notions of LGBT community centers and pride parades. Slowly, the rural closet begins to break apart.

"Everybody Said They Were Brothers": The Rural Closet's Visible Invisibility

Woven into the closet's public/private divide is the binary of visibility and invisibility. Coming out of the closet is understood as a proclamation in which one makes publically known one's desires, thereby becoming a visible member of the LGBT community. Yet this visibility binary, in ways similar to the public/private space binary, is problematized by the lived realities of gay rural existence. Returning to Fellows's *Farm Boys* makes this clear.

One trend among the *Farm Boys* narrators was the pattern of recognition by the people around them. Even prior to modern-day media bombardment by *Queer Eye*, *Will & Grace*, and other TV shows awash in gay culture stereotypes, certain family members often developed suspicions about a young boy's sexual identity. Mothers in particular seemed to pay more attention to the gendered behavior and potential sexual identity of their children than fathers, siblings, or other relatives. Many of Fellows's farm boys believed that their mothers knew they were gay long before they knew themselves, perhaps as a result of the increased time spent caring for children that fell to women in a gendered division of labor. They recall being treated differently than their brothers, mothers protectively intervening when their gender deviance was being policed, or coming out to their mother who simply nodded in agreement, as if she had been waiting for the official declaration for years. Mothers and grandmothers often encouraged boys whom they suspected to be gay to explore traditionally feminine activities, such as gardening, sewing, or knitting, or welcomed the additional help with household labor.[25] Certainly not all children have mothers who recognize or defend their queer behavior but many found refuge under the care of women. Mothers kept young children in the home with them, and even those sent to work in fields or barns for the day would return to her care at mealtimes and in the evening. As families grew larger, mothers had even more reason for keeping a male child working with her throughout the day, if only to deal with the unending household labor; some mothers even created chores to keep a particularly effeminate boy near her side instead of sending him to the group of fathers, uncles, and older male siblings working in fields.[26]

In today's rural communities, young children—and their families—are more than ever connected to a worldwide network of media, entertainment, news, and pop culture information flow. Cell phones, Internet, magazines, movies, and television funnel an incredible volume of information on gay "lifestyles" and LGBTQ identity to children and adolescents, particularly those searching for it. As a result, many gay and lesbian teens raised in rural spaces today no longer suffer from the information gap that Fellows's narrators describe. Instead of not knowing about homosexuality, today's LGBTQ kids often already know who and what they are from a very young age. In her ethnography on the impact of media on queer rural youth, Mary Gray's teen narrators address their visibility in an age of hypervisibility. The result of their own self-recognition, combined with increasingly visible LGBTQ media representations, is that these teens grow up in communities where the lack of privacy means everyone "always already knows" they are queer. She writes, "Most of the youth I spoke with talked about their unacknowledged status as the 'town gay kid.' As one 15-year-old from a township of 3,000 noted, 'What do I have to be afraid of? Someone finding out? They all know.'"[27] Yet despite this high level of visibility, gay and lesbian youth are simultaneously expected to remain what Gray calls "functionally invisible."[28] Not expressing affection for a same-sex partner in public, not dressing or acting in gender deviant ways, not being "too gay"—in short, actively working to make themselves *in*visible—are the unspoken rules these teens feel pressure to follow. Gray writes that these "tensions among familiarity, visibility, and knowability . . . shape public recognition in rural settings."[29] Despite what seems an unjust system of social pressure on vulnerable gay and lesbian youth, the fluid visibility these teens demonstrate and the lives they create between visibility and invisibility are also undermining the very system that restrains them; for each gay youth who decides exactly when and where he "swishes," the expectation that gay individuals are always easily identified by such behavior is further undermined. The structural relationship between hetero- and homosexual that requires that homosexuality reveal itself is upset by the selective visibility/invisibility of these rural gay teens.

This demand for invisibility that Gray's teens negotiate demonstrates the inconsistency of the visibility characteristic of the closet model in dictating the behavior of rural gay and lesbian identities. One of Fellows's narrators describes varying levels of gay and lesbian invisibility in his Midwestern town:

> "There were two women that lived together in our town, and they were accepted by the community. Mom said, 'Well, one of them's got to be the man.' So I realized as a kid that women did that, but there weren't any men that I knew of. There were two guys, two miles from us, that lived together for years and died together, but as a kid I just passed that off. When Dad needed help at harvest time he told me to go get them, because they didn't have a car. Everybody said they were brothers, but they didn't have the same last name."[30]

The politics of visibility, of who becomes identified as queer and who flies below the radar, is complicated by the social structures of small towns. Other hierarchies and power dynamics—family connections, class status, gender, local conflicts and disputes between neighbors— play a large role, and perhaps may be more likely to determine the level of acceptable gay or lesbian visibility than any particular gendered or sexual behavior.

The demand for gay invisibility described by Gray's contemporary teens echoes that faced by Fellows's narrators as much as forty years prior. Some of the farm boys suggested that invisibility meant they had trouble understanding their desires and difference; without basic information and a definition of homosexuality, much less visible gay or lesbian role models in their communities, some of these men spoke of feeling confused for a long time. Others were able to find information on homosexuality, yet still felt confused. For many of these men who were born and raised in rural areas, learning about what they perceived as urban-based, flamboyant, swishy, effeminate, and in-your-face gay gender identities left them feeling even more isolated and out of place. "'It seemed like I was the peg that didn't fit. I wasn't a queen; I didn't like to dish. I always tended to feel more at home with some of my non-gay friends. I still feel that way, but less so.'"[31] Fellows writes of a double alienation, of rural-raised gay men feeling they do not belong in their rural communities of origin and then finding they feel equally out of place in urban-based gay communities.

Other scholars note similar experiences. In a study of gay and lesbian subjects from rural areas in San Francisco, Kath Weston found large numbers eventually returned to rural living as a result of a similar feeling of incompatibility with urban gay cultures.[32] A fair amount of this discomfort seems to stem from differences in public/private boundaries and flamboyant gender-deviant behavior. One narrator addressed both in explaining his perspective, "'I don't go for guys who are trying to prove a point by holding hands and walking through the mall. . . . I would never take part in a gay pride parade. If I see somebody being ostentatious . . . I think it's too much. I believe in being yourself, but there's a proper time.'"[33] Ironically, for individuals who bemoaned living in communities described as involving no privacy and extremely limited gay visibility, these men end up policing their own behavior, enforcing the same restraints on visibility that some of them found oppressive and difficult to negotiate as younger teens.

Closet Resistance

In addition to privacy and models of queer desire that might enable awareness of one's gay or lesbian identity, the model of the closet also depends upon not just identifying as gay, but on gayness being a major focus of one's identity. Two cases illustrate the conflict with this element of the closet model.

The closet, on a basic level, requires identification as gay, lesbian, or bisexual.[34] Yet nearly all of Fellows's narrators spoke of sexual contact with other men and boys that was never discussed or acknowledged, and certainly was not identified as "gay" or "homosexual." At times these relationships took the shape of long-term affairs. Other men included stories of unacknowledged and unpursued homosexual desire shared with various men in their lives. In fact, Fellows's collection suggests that a great many rural men were having sex with other men who never acknowledged their queer desires, much less incorporated any sort of homosexuality into their identities. Urban-focused sex researchers and outreach programs have designated these men as "MSM," short for "men who have sex with men," eking out a space not clearly delineated as heterosexual, homosexual, or bisexual. However, MSM are often viewed as closeted about their sexual activities and queer identities, particularly by the heterosexual mainstream and (out) homosexual communities. The hetero-/homo- binary demands these individuals be classified somewhere within the schema, even if they problematize both heterosexuality and homosexuality. MSM and men with unacknowledged homosexual desires also upset the notion of the closet because they disrupt the narrative movement of the trope—the concept of the closet does not apply if there is nothing to reveal or no change is imminent. Someone who does not see an identity element at play or does not incorporate homosexual sex acts into an understanding of self cannot be said to be in the closet. At the same time, individuals having homosexual sex without claiming gay or bisexual identities do not operate separately from the construct of the closet, as they are woven into the social and sexual networks of closeted and out individuals. Without individuals seeing themselves as gay, lesbian, or bisexual, they cannot engage in the closet's narrative of coming out, even if they are up front ("out") about their sexual practices.

A second group of rural gays and lesbians pose a slightly different challenge to the closet, however. This group may be more directly a product of the cultural specificity of small-town rural existence, particularly for earlier generations. These individuals are fully aware of lesbian and gay elements as part of their identities, but choose to identify themselves primarily as something else—farmers, mothers, church deacons, writers, land owners, and so on. They actively resist "coming out" because they see sexuality as private, because they do not identify with urban, gender-non-normative stereotypes of gay and lesbian identity, or because other parts of their identities are much more central.

Again, as with MSM, this group is very difficult to identify in literature, specifically because they are resisting a searchable identity category. With rural women in particular, finding first-person accounts from those who might engage in lesbian sexual activity, relationships, politics, or community membership and still do not identify as lesbians or queer women is difficult, but not because they are not present. Additionally, the demands of rural or agricultural living often meant a different set of gendered expectations for women than their urban or suburban counterparts experienced. As the time period under consideration also overlaps with the second-wave feminist and lesbian rights movements, rural women often appear as a confusing mélange of rural gender patterns, feminism, lesbian activism, and staunch pioneer independence.[35] Glimpses into the lives of these women can be found, however, in a handful of places. *Country Women*, a magazine published from 1973 to 1980 is one. *Country Women* was "devoted half to sharing the personal experiences of women living in the country and half to exchanging new found skills with each other" and quickly became a point of connection for women with a variety of sexual identities who were interested in meeting others through farming and rural living.[36]

Connections like those in *Country Women* flourished in the 1970s and 1980s among some radical feminists who believed rural spaces offered an opportunity to escape the constraints of patriarchy. The lesbian separatist movement and the rural-based "lesbian land" movement included women who identified as lesbian as well as those who preferred "political lesbianism,"[37] meaning they dedicated their energies to other women but refrained from sexual relationships with them. Lesbian land collectives founded during this time period were usually populated by women from cities, who often found themselves quickly in need of the knowledge and skills of local women.[38] In an archive of writings from the lesbian land movement, one new country resident wrote about her beginnings as a dairy farmer, thankful for the network of women she stumbled in to: "The women from the Christmas tree farm come down to teach us to butcher. The vet's receptionist answers questions the vet cannot."[39] Another new country resident relied on assistance from both straight and lesbian neighbors: "Other neighbors could care less that a lot of us are lesbians. They help me out a lot. We get our eggs from them, and they helped me when my goat got sick. . . . It was nice that first winter, to have a set of wimmin on the land that aren't close friends, and yet they're there for support. Neighbors who happen to be dykes."[40]

Many of these neighborly rural women are soon revealed to be lesbians as well, often helping connect newcomers to substantial networks of lesbian women. ("There are ten lesbians that we know of within 80 miles."[41]) Others, though, are less easily understood, but still affecting women exploring feminism and lesbianism. New rural resident Barbara Lightner described one woman she met as both incredibly similar to herself but also strikingly different, "Thelma: never been out of the state. Never stepped out of her role. Living way back in, down such a long gravel road, where so few come to tell her of her own fine strength."[42] Here the lack of mobility and lack of visibly enacted feminism of a local woman both reinforce a rural stereotype (she "never stepped out of her role") while simultaneously problematizing the author's assumption that any strong woman would actively seek out others and not remain "hidden down such a long gravel road." Though we cannot know if Thelma identified as a lesbian, she lived in queer ways that seemed unimaginable to urban lesbians.

The snapshot of Thelma echoes a 1995 article that was published in a gay and lesbian periodical and took issue with representations of rural lesbians.[43] Author Lee Lynch responded specifically to a survey of lesbian readers, presumably by the magazine, which was so poorly organized that it did not identify any lesbians living in nonurban spaces. Lynch countered the assumption that this meant there were no such lesbians by explaining that reasons for living in rural spaces could include a desire *not* to get involved in lesbian community: "It's cheaper and I can spend a little more time writing. The air is clean. It's easier to be a hermit. I like the distance from gays and straights alike. I like the independent spirits of my peers. It smells like pine trees."[44] Lynch's passionate essay went on to record an extensive list of roles occupied by lesbians in the country, "We have: editors, realtors, teachers, entrepreneurs, retirees, artists and writers, performers, big businesswomen, bus drivers. . . . Don't tell me that there are no dykes in the country."[45] Other women writing about their fellow rural lesbians took a similar approach; one women's land included the following membership:

We have two owners of wimmin-owned alternative business, an architecture student who uses this as her vacation home, and wimmin truckers who are here a week and then away a week. We have a machinist, a wommon with inherited money, and an artist who makes a living with her art. We have old-time dykes and dykes who came out thru feminism.[46]

Lynch and others made their point that the country has plenty of lesbians, yet by identifying them via their professions, they suggested these women might have chosen *not* to identify as lesbian, preferring to be seen as a teacher, for example. In Lynch's self-description, it is clear that she was both out of the closet (she was publishing a piece about her lesbian identity in a national magazine) but also simultaneously preferred the privacy and lack of visibility she found in quiet rurality. Lynch's essay suggests the concept of the closet may not be useful at all for understanding the identities of lesbian and queer rural women like her.

Rural space permits many more variations of queer lifestyles than one might presume: there are individuals who engage in nonheterosexual sex acts with no apparent impact on their ostensibly heterosexual identities and those who may well recognize their sexuality as gay or lesbian, yet choose to prioritize other aspects of their identities. Mary Gray addresses the politics of visibility and outness in reflecting on her experiences with queer youth in Kentucky and Indiana, noting that "rural youth do the collective labor of identity work differently than their urban counterparts not because rural queer youth have it inherently harder, but because they confront different heteronormative/homophobic burdens. They also bear the weight of a politics of visibility that . . . was built for city living."[47] This visibility—being out—is not only a metronormative phenomenon with limited applicability for rural gay and lesbian experiences, but in its monolithic application, it erases the possibility of other types of queer existence. Building upon the theme of the country-as-closet explored earlier, Gray writes, "A politics of visibility needs the rural (or some otherness, some place) languishing in its shadow to sustain its status as an unquestionable achievement rather than a strategy that privileges the view of some by eliding the vantage point of others."[48] Despite the injustice perpetuated by the invisibility of the rural queer subject, complex queer lives and experience nevertheless thrive in this "shadow" of visible, urban LGBT identity.

Beyond the Closet

If the closet contains too many metronormative elements to function as a useful metaphor for rural gay and lesbian identity, how might we address diverse sexualities and identities in rural spaces? Given the above concerns, we need a model that does not rely on urban concepts of privacy and space or on a monolithic model of the gay or lesbian lifestyle. It must be separate from narratives of child-to-adult growth, rework the visibility/invisibility binary, and find a way to better incorporate other identity elements and different lifestyle patterns. It must not demand homosexuality as the primary identity element.

Opening up the closet allows us to broaden our understanding of what lesbian and gay identity in general might look like, and where it might be found. Here again, rural-based examples are fruitful. The practice of men cruising and engaging in sex acts in public bathrooms is prevalent in both urban and rural parts of the United States and internationally. Particularly in rural locations, public rest stops along highways are popular sites for men seeking sex with other men. These anonymous sexual encounters suggest an example of both a location and a community that informs and shapes queer (male) identities in ways not normally recognized by traditional definitions of identity and sexuality. Particularly in sparsely populated rural areas, where rest stops or other gay cruising sites may be fewer in number, the chances for recognizing or being recognized by someone is much greater. One of Fellows's narrators recounts frequent visits to a local rest stop as part of his adolescent homosexual explorations and the complications to this secret pleasure caused by an encounter with the father of a classmate.[49] Networks created by less-than-anonymous but never discussed sexual encounters are not understood as "gay community" in the same way as the rainbow-clad populations of twinks, leathermen, and drag queens parading down New York's Fifth Avenue. Yet they are as much a part of rural gay lives and identities as those urban-based behaviors. David Bell and Gill Valentine briefly suggest something similar, noting that a "community of the cottage" (cruising for sex at rest stops is called "cottaging" in the United Kingdom) might exist among rural queer men, along the lines of a "community of the closet."[50] Bell and Valentine connect the binding ties of secrecy between those in the closet and those in the rest stop. Yet the implication in equating those "communities" is that the attendant notions of shame, misery, and loneliness that are associated with the closet must be similar for the rest stop. As some studies of rest-stop culture have suggested, the "community of the cottage" is *not* necessarily one of secrecy, shame, and loneliness; on the contrary, many men find care and connection in brief moments of intimacy with others, particularly when repeat visits result in smiles from familiar faces.[51] These interactions might not fit a homonormative vision of a monogamous, married couple, but these relationships are also not necessarily meaningless to their participants.

Alternative versions of lesbian community sometimes occur through nonsexual encounters. Lesbian periodicals, including magazines focused on rural living such as *Country Women* and *Maize*, listed mailing addresses for "contact dykes" in the personals section. These women were available for information on local lesbian community and resources; according to some, they served as pen pals, tour guides, or friendly new neighbors, enabling contact between women who otherwise would not have found other lesbians to connect with. Taking the periodical-based community a step further, many women on lesbian lands saw themselves as connected, pieces of a larger "Lesbian Nation" that empowered women across space: "All across the country these islands of the Amazon Nation exist, standing strong and proud, a sign of women's power. They offer the needed space for women to retreat to and regroup when the pressures and paranoia of living in the patriarchy become too overwhelming. . . . There are no boundaries in the Amazon Nation."[52] The "community of the catalog" and the Lesbian Nation pose additional challenges to boundaries of space and time we expect of a lesbian or gay community, as they foster lesbian identities and relationships without necessarily sharing physical space or sexual contact—or even requiring direct knowledge of one another. If different geographies of sexuality pose different sets of constraints on the individuals within them, it follows that the identities and communities produced cannot be read through the same rubric. Whether through quick sex in a bathroom stall or long-running written correspondence and visions of a network of others doing the same, lesbians and gay men in rural spaces create their own forms of identity and community, ones far outside any urban-based expectation of the closet.

NOTES

1 In this piece, I aim to use terms like "LGBT" and "queer" with as much specificity as possible. Thus, I most often use "LGBT" to discuss broader queer communities and identities, but do so with recognition that the "B" and "T" individuals often experience these formations differently. As the examples used here are dominated by gay- and lesbian-identified individuals, but also include those who practice same-sex desire but may not identify as such, I will occasionally use "queer" to include these individuals. However, the "queer" used here does not necessarily indicate a particular radical political identity nor contemporary forms of nonbinary gender identity but instead references earlier meanings of "queer" as either an implication of homosexuality or sexually uncertain forms of oddity, deviance, or difference.

2 Halberstam, *A Queer Time and Place*, 37.

3 Gray, *Out in the Country*, 4.

4 Howard, *Men Like That*, 63.

5 . Williams, *The Country and the City*.

6 See, for example, Bell, "Eroticizing the Rural," Phillips, "Imagined Geographies and Sexual Politics," and Shuttleton, "The Queer Politics of the Gay Pastoral."

7 For examples, see regional analyses of the South in Johnson, *Sweet Tea*, and Howard, *Men Like That*; the "Queering the Middle: Race, Region, and a Queer Midwest," special issue *GLQ* 20, nos. 1–2 (2014); the specifically western analysis in Bell, "Cowboy Love," and even Anzaldua, *Borderlands/La Frontera*, for a southwest or border region-specific analysis.

8 Herring, *Another Country*, 8.

9 For work addressing lesbian and gay movements in and out of rural geography, see Weston, "Get Thee to a Big City"; Raimondo's study of gay men dying of AIDS returning to rural family homes, "'Corralling the Virus'"; Oswald, "Who Am I in Relation to Them?"; Annes and Redlin, "Coming Out and Coming Back"; and even Hoffert's recent memoir, *Prairie Silence*.

10 "Women's land," also called "lesbian land," describes a movement from the 1970s and 1980s, which merged lesbian feminism, identity politics, environmentalism, anticapitalism, and a back-to-the-land, do-it-yourself ethos. Women, often from urban areas, relocated to rural spaces to live alone, in pairs, or in collectives as a strategy for escaping patriarchal oppression.

11 Lesbian Herstory Archives Subject Files, Lesbian Herstory Educational Fund (2004): reel 80–81, folder 07390, "land," April 20. 2009. All sources from "land" subject file include the tag "land" in footnotes, while all sources from "rural lesbians" subject files include the tag "rural" in footnotes. Henceforth, all citations of materials from these archives will specify author, document title (if any), and either "land" or "rural."

12 Kennedy, *Ulrichs*.

13 Tamashiro, "Coming Out."

14 Sedgwick, *Epistemology of the Closet*, 68.

15 Ibid., 69.

16 Brown, *Closet Space*, 1.

17 While Brown's study takes place in New Zealand, and not the Midwestern United States, there are striking similarities between Christchurch and many Midwestern small and mid-sized cities, such as Fort Wayne, Indiana, or Des Moines, Iowa. These include a small but moderately dense downtown, the strong presence of religious organizations in local culture, the "neighborly" or "small-town" attitude of citizens toward one another, and the social positioning of these small cities as secondary or outside U.S. metropolitan centers, which are often coastal, larger, and understood as more "modern" centers of culture and business.

18 Brown, *Closet Space*, 56. Brown notes the near absence of lesbian bars or commercial establishments, saying that his sources indicated women gathered in private homes, often via a dinner-party circuit (ibid., 81).

19 Susan Stryker and Victor Silverman, dirs., *Screaming Queens: The Riot at Compton's Cafeteria*, 1988 (San Francisco: Frameline, 2005).

20 For example, as Judith Butler writes, "being 'out' must produce the closet again and again in order to maintain itself as 'out'" ("Imitation and Gender Subordination," 16).

21 Fuss, *Inside/Out*, 5.

22 Fuss adds that coming out constructs both the closet as well as the "true" identity it reveals (Ibid., 4-5).

23 Gray, *Out in the Country*, 5.

24 Fellows, *Farm Boys*, 15.

25 Ibid., 117.

26 Ibid., 172.

27 Gray, *Out in the Country*, 96.

28 Ibid.

29 Ibid.

30 Fellows, *Farm Boys*, 69.

31 Ibid., 157.

32 Weston, "Get Thee to a Big City," 49.

33 Fellows, *Farm Boys*, 132.

34 Certainly trans people also come out (as trans as well as other identities); since trans coming out deals more centrally with sex and gender rather than sexuality, I'll set those coming-out experiences aside here.

35 For more on the impact of gender on an earlier generation of rural women, see Colin Johnson, "Hard Women," in his *Just Queer Folks*.

36 Claudia Scott, "An Unassuming Little Magazine," *Lavender Woman*, March 1974, land.

37 Also sometimes referred to as "women-identified women"

38 It should be noted that some women in the lesbian land movement came from the very rural spaces the collectives sought; these women brought particularly valuable experience in negotiating small-town and rural community dynamics, and often challenged middle-class urban-originating women to examine their classism. One trio of

rural-raised women determined to live in the country despite not owning land wrote, "our views of country living are decidedly political, and a combination of country working class / hick lower middle class" (Brown, Wright, and Dragon Fire, "Lesbians on Land without Land," 169).

39 Lightner, "O! We Are Just Begun!," 3, land.

40 Adobe and Mint Judith, "Adobeland," in *Lesbian Land*, edited by Joyce Cheney, 27–28.

41 Panzarino, "Beechtree," 44.

42 Lightner, "O! We Are Just Begun!," 3, land.

43 Lee Lynch, *In the Life*, April 1995, rural.

44 Ibid.

45 Ibid.

46 Pelican and Hard, "Maud's Land," 93. All original spelling.

47 Gray, *Out in the Country*, 21.

48 Ibid., 9.

49 Fellows, *Farm Boys*, 293.

50 Bell and Valentine, "Queer Country," 117.

51 Many of Fellows' narrators spoke fondly of men whom they encountered in rest stops, saying they were caring and gentle, particularly when they were still new to gay sex. It should be noted, though, that rest stops in particular are *not* seen as places to find a boyfriend. For rest-stop culture analysis, see van Lieshout, "Leather Nights in the Woods," and Flowers, Marriott, and Hart, "The Bars, the Bogs, and tje Bushes."

52 Mary O'Sullivan, "Politics of Wimmin's Land," n.d. land.

12

In Plain(s) Sight

Rural LGBTQ Women and the Politics of Visibility

CARLY THOMSEN

Jene Newsome, an Air Force Sergeant stationed at Ellsworth Air Force Base in western South Dakota, didn't tell. And no one asked. Until November of 2009, that is, when local police officers visited Newsome's home and spotted a marriage certificate on her kitchen table. The officers subsequently reported this piece of information to the military, essentially "outing" Newsome, who was honorably discharged in 2010 under "Don't Ask, Don't Tell," the military's former policy that dictated that lesbian, gay, or bisexual individuals could serve in the military so long as the military remained unaware of their sexuality. With assistance from attorneys at the American Civil Liberties Union, Newsome filed a complaint against the Rapid City Police Department, stating, "I played by 'Don't Ask, Don't Tell.' . . . I just don't agree with what the Rapid City police department did. . . . They violated a lot of internal policies on their end, and I feel like my privacy was violated."[1] Newsome directed her criticisms at the individual police officers involved with her case, rather than the military or its policies.

Despite Newsome's position, various liberal media sources, as well as national lesbian and gay rights organizations working to abolish "Don't Ask, Don't Tell," used Newsome's story to express and foment opposition to the policy. One such liberal news source wrote, "MEET JENE NEWSOME . . . The repeal of 'Don't Ask, Don't Tell,' pending in Congress, can't come quickly enough."[2] The remainder of this report argued for the need to completely do away with "Don't Ask, Don't Tell" and, in the interim, make the policy less stringent so that third-party "outings"— such as the one that occurred in Newsome's case—would not lead to the dismissal of military service members. Readers did not actually "meet"

Jene Newsome in this article, as its opening line promised; her story was coopted to support a broader fight against "Don't Ask, Don't Tell," despite Newsome's own refusal to critique the policy.

In this essay, I document and analyze an estrangement between the discourses and strategies used by many national lesbian and gay rights organizations and those used by LGBTQ women in the rural Midwestern United States.[3] I look to various online sites, including websites, Facebook pages, blogs, and Flickr accounts, to argue that such an estrangement encourages a critical consideration of calls for LGBTQ visibility, a strategy seen as appropriate for community-building and as a desirable form of political activism that overemphasizes an essentially urban ethos and does not represent the discourses and communication strategies of rural LGBTQ women.[4] I further argue that a critical analysis of contemporary visibility politics is crucial for rural queer studies because the abjection of the rural, based as it is on metronormativity, informs and is informed by cultural and (LGBTQ) subcultural ideas regarding the political potential of visibility. In taking up Jene Newsome's story, along with other sites I consider here, I examine the logics informing the illegibility of rural LGBTQ women's subjectivities and, in so doing, focus on a demographic and region that have been largely overlooked in queer studies scholarship and LGBTQ activism.[5]

Scholars and activists have problematized the totalizing discourses of international lesbian and gay rights organizations, pointing out that many of their assumptions do not necessarily apply in non-Western contexts. These scholars highlight, for example, the ways in which the deployment of Western categories *creates* sexual subjectivities as well as backlash to them,[6] the mutually constitutive nature of contemporary Western and non-Western LGBTQ identities,[7] and the normalizing of Western lesbian and gay subjectivities so that non-Western (Muslim) subjects can occupy the space of the abject.[8] A critique of visibility politics undergirds much of this scholarship, which calls into question the assumption that non-Western identities, representations, discourses, and strategies will be progressively influenced by Western intervention—to which visibility politics are central.[9] In this essay, I extend the kind of argument made by scholars of transnational LGBTQ sexualities—their challenge to the deployment of Western discourses, categories, and strategies—to suggest that it may be paralleled *within* Western, and particularly rural, spaces. J. Jack Halberstam, following Tom Boellstorff, has called for "translocal" analyses, arguing that such examinations could complicate our understandings of sexuality within and outside the West.[10] Bridging the literatures on rural and non-Western sexualities creates opportunities to dismantle both the urban/rural and global/local binaries and to examine the relations at play within each binary as well as the ways in which the binaries themselves are mutually constitutive. Assumptions about the rural are, of course, as informed by ideas about the urban as they are by the global, a point crucial for understanding the centrality of visibility politics to metronormative logics.

Rural queer studies scholars challenge the idea that same-sex sexual desire in rural spaces is rare, invisible, dangerous, or isolated; posit that the goals and strategies of rural LGBTQ people differ dramatically from those of urban LGBTQ people; and critique the narrative that pairs closeted, violent, and homophobic with the rural and liberated with the city.[11] This dominant cultural narrative cloaked in metronormativity persists, in part, because alternate modes of inhabiting and articulating LGBTQ identities and experiences—including those emerging from the rural or existing outside of the "out, loud, and proud"—are not recognized as legitimate modes of LGBTQness. Rethinking the centrality of metronormative narratives to both hetero- and homonormative cultural imaginaries requires examining ideologies and strategies that have rendered visibility, identity, and community indistinguishable, challenging the assumption that visibility and "outness" are indispensable to identity and community,[12] and questioning the notion that visibility is requisite for liberation.

This argument builds upon important queer theoretical interrogations of visibility. In *Epistemology of the Closet* (1990), which is considered one of the founding queer theory texts, Eve Sedgwick points out that visibility is treated as the binary other to invisibility, the abjection that visibility then must work against. Scholars have argued that visibility politics are "a trap" because such approaches create the potentiality of surveillance[13] and, via claims to a victimized identity, increased state power.[14] Despite these critiques, invisibility continues to exist in the cultural imaginary as apolitical, abject, and that which visibility must expose and extinguish.

I take off from such theoretical examinations of visibility, as well as the literature on LGBTQ sexualities in rural U.S. and non-Western contexts, to consider an additional problematic of visibility politics: calls for visibility reassert the dominant narrative of the history of sexuality that Foucault has so famously argued against, a history that suggests we have moved from the repressive Victorian era, in which we could not talk about sex, to the present day, where we are liberated enough to do so freely. In other words, visibility is the mechanism through which a progress narrative is both made possible and articulated. That LGBTQ people today can be "out, loud, and proud" functions as evidence that our society has progressed beyond the backward ideas of other eras, when people were presumed to be less open-minded and liberated, and LGBT people were closeted or sexually repressed.

Such understandings of our contemporary moment are as bound to the geographic as they are to the temporal. Certain spaces, including the rural and the non-Western,[15] exist in the cultural imaginary as inherently more regressive. Ideas about visibility often undergird such framings; the ostensible inability of LGBTQ people to be "out" *there* serves as evidence for such narratives, which simultaneously elide geographic and historical nuance. The closeted, afraid, and embarrassed LGBTQ people who inhabit non-Western and nonurban spaces today are imagined to exist in much the same way as did LGBTQ people in the urban United States in prior (less advanced) historical periods.

Those who are "out, loud, and proud" simultaneously serve as embodied representations of their own liberation and the progressive nature of the time and place in which they live. By extension, then, those LGBTQ people who do not fulfill (dominant and subcultural LGBTQ) cultural expectations for visibility exist in opposition to progress. According to this logic, if one does not confess, come out, and become visible, one must not be liberated enough to do so, or must not live in a time or place in which doing so is allowable. In this way "gay visibility is simultaneously given a spatial location and a social value."[16] Assumptions about visibility, then, are central to progress narratives of this variety—through which the rural and non-Western are reproduced as abject, normative understandings of time-space relations are reiterated, and LGBTQ people become conceptually inseparable from the time and place they inhabit. This "naturalization of both time and space" obscures the ways in which visibility is a *constructed* spatial practice with ramifications for how we conceptualize the very spaces from which such practices emerge.[17]

In an attempt to elucidate the damages of calls for LGBTQ visibility, I examine here three cases: the lack of representations of rural LGBTQ women in cyberspace, the self-presentations of board members of Equality South Dakota, one of the state's lesbian and gay rights organizations, and the discourses surrounding Jene Newsome's outing and military discharge. Considering the common assumption that rural LGBTQ people are increasingly finding community via the Internet, one might expect to find an array of online representations of LGBTQ women in the rural Midwest. Following this line of thinking, I scoured the Internet for representations of this demographic and found remarkably few. While my analysis of online representations of LGBTQ women in the rural Midwest might, then, seem counterintuitive, this absence functions as part of the story, as evidence itself of the limits of visibility politics. The online "invisibility" of LGBTQ women in the rural Midwest, far from constituting a dilemma in need of fixing, speaks to the problematic and overdetermined nature of expectations for visibility.

Absence as Evidence: Suburban and Rural Gay Life at Flickr.com

Flickr.com is an image-hosting website to which participants can upload photographs or videos, communicate with fellow group members, and view over five billion images from around the world. The site's "Suburban and Rural Gay Life" group is not attached to a particular locale. In conflating the rural and suburban, the group positions both in relation to the urban and suggests that nonurbanness is a commonality around which LGBTQ people might gather. Its 124 members posted 388 photographs; of these, 190 overtly evoked a sense of place: landscapes, flowers, foods, and animals suggestive of rurality dominated the photographs, speaking to the importance of place to group members' articulations of their sexualities.[18] The group's photographs construct representations and represent constructions of rural sexuality, creating new ideas and reflecting current ones regarding rurality and sexuality.

The very existence of this Flickr group makes visible the presence of LGBTQ sexualities in nonurban places; ironically, it does so through the erasure of sexuality. The prominence of place in the photographs informs the contributors' constructions of rural gays as wholesome, normal, and deeply connected to their rural communities. The images of people on the site feature nonsexual same-sex relations, rather than any explicit sexual content. It is through the simultaneous erasure and visibility of sexuality within the Flickr.com group that posters come to constitute good rural folks *and* good gays. This presentation of the rural gay is, of course, intentional and mediated, as indicated by the group moderators' direction: "Please avoid pornography or nudity. There are plenty of other groups available on Flickr for that. If they are posted, they will be deleted." Rural gayness, here, involves constructing gays as normal and unthreatening and the rural as idyllic and unthreatening. If the rural is understood as unsafe or homophobic, gays cannot plausibly exist there happily. Likewise, images that construct rural gays as non-normative challenge representations of the rural as wholesome. These images recapitulate hegemonic ideas of the rural with the effect of disrupting metronormative narratives that frame the rural as homophobic and backward. In so doing, group members make evident the importance of the politics of space to the construction of their sexual identities.

But whose rural gay sexualities are represented on this site? The vast majority of the photographs were posted by men, the top five contributors to the site are men, and images of men dominate the site. Of the site's 388 photographs, 124 contain men, often as the sole person in the photograph. Forty-five of these images include two men who are presumably meant to be read as coupled based on the contents of the image, comments provided by the photographer or other group members, and within the context of other photographs on the site.

By contrast, only twenty images contain people recognizable as women, including two of young girls and one each of flag dancers, a mixed-gender group of friends, a family, and an LGBTQ political activist. Aside from the activist, none of these images of women connote same-sex sexuality or desire. Even more striking, only one photograph of affectionate or coupled women is posted.[19] In this image, two women enjoy a moment of intimacy outside in the rain, hidden from the camera by a bright blue umbrella, rain drops falling into the puddles filling their (rural or suburban) street, complete with cookie-cutter homes, a U.S. flag, and a nondescript car—a picture of normalcy that is fully in line with the group's representation of rural and suburban gay people as firmly rooted in their communities.[20] The kissing women stand in the

Figure 12.1. Love(EXPLORE): An image posted in "Suburban and Rural Gay Life" at Flickr.com.

center of a neighborhood's flooded street, taking the time to kick up their feet and enjoy a moment of intimacy. The position of the umbrella at once shields the lovers from the viewers and makes them visible to their rural or suburban community. These women are not concerned with the neighbors. They own this street. They are not in a rush. They belong here.

Yet, in other ways, this anomalous image exists outside of the norms established by the Flickr group and challenges their stated purpose: "While suburban and rural gay life might not be quite as visible as gay life in the cities, we are out there and we are living our lives. Here's your chance to show it off."[21] The women in this image are not exactly showing it off. They are not using this site to increase the visibility of rural and suburban gays. In the only photograph of two women together, in which sexuality is hinted at but not made explicit, the women are veiled behind an umbrella. Viewers are, of course, meant to assume their intimacy. The genders and sexualities of the women are ambiguous, made clear only in a comment on the photograph. Jackson H., the photographer who posted the image, wrote: "love(EXPLORE) . . . hahaha i didnt [sic] have a guy with me so is [sic] used 2 girls hahahah." Within the context of this particular site, Jackson's light-hearted comment suggests that he would have preferred to have been in the photograph with another man. It also suggests that Jackson found that posting a photograph of two women on this site, an obvious rarity, required an explanation.

The dearth of representations of women on the Flickr site, as well as the shielded women in the site's sole image of two intimate women, suggests that visibility on such a site is not important to rural LGBTQ women, a trend evident online more broadly. That the Flickr site is symptomatic of a lack of online representations of rural LGBTQ women further crystalizes the tension between calls for LGBTQ visibility and the approaches of LGBTQ women in rural places. I have yet to locate, for example, a single blog or website authored by an LGBTQ-identified woman from the rural Midwest. Of course, it is possible that these women are blogging and creating websites without writing about their sexuality or that their blogs and websites are not open to public viewing. In either of these speculative cases, the women would not be utilizing this medium as a way to increase visibility or gain the rights to which increased visibility ostensibly leads. The absence of websites run by and for LGBTQ rural women as well as the lacunae of representations of LGBTQ rural women on sites dedicated to rural gay life, here exemplified through the Flickr group, is an argument for the significance of a null set: the invisibility of rural LGBTQ women, from the Midwest or otherwise, suggests that this demographic is not using the Internet as a site to increase their visibility, that rural LGBTQ women relate to calls for visibility differently than other LGBTQ folks, and that visibility politics are complicated in ways that lesbian and gay rights organizations have not acknowledged.

Lesbian and Gay Rights Organizations

For lesbian and gay rights groups, becoming visible is both a means and an end; visibility, it is assumed, will lead to further progress and is always already evidence of progress. The Human Rights Campaign, the largest lesbian and gay civil rights group in the United States, relies upon such positions. In their "Event Ideas for National Coming Out Day," the HRC urges people to

> Make a commitment to be *honest* about your sexual orientation or gender identity to those who know you. *Coming out and living openly* as a gay, lesbian, bisexual, transgender or supportive straight person is an act of *bravery* and *authenticity* . . . . Polls continue to show that people who know someone gay are more likely to support *full equality*.[22] (Emphasis added.)

In this passage, the HRC connects increased visibility to greater political rights. It assumes that to be "honest" and "authentic" one must accept a single definition of "being out," which includes explicitly telling friends, family, and coworkers about one's sexual preferences. The bravery associated with doing so ostensibly leads to the HRC's vision of "full equality," or more accurately, the rights to participate in the military and, above all, marry.[23] Although queer studies scholars and activists have long critiqued the normalizing logics at the heart of this vision of equality, such analyses have rarely focused explicitly on visibility—a remarkable oversight considering that visibility is one mode through which normalcy is compelled and articulated.[24]

Equality South Dakota is South Dakota's version of the Human Rights Campaign.[25] Much like the HRC, Equality South Dakota assumes that political rights and visibility are mutually constitutive.

> The mission of Equality South Dakota is to secure and protect the rights and well-being of LGBT . . . South Dakotans and their families through full *engagement in the political process*. We seek dialogue with elected officials and invite them to use us as a resource in their decision making. In doing so, we give a *voice* to families that have been silent and fearful.[26] (Emphasis added.)

The group's deployment of "voice" and "full engagement in the political process" points to an ideological connection between Equality South Dakota and the broader cultural narratives that assume a relationship between visibility and rights; using one's voice for political purposes is, after all, precisely the form of visibility for which the Human Rights Campaign calls. Yet, Equality South Dakota makes no explicit claims about the political benefits of visibility. For Equality South Dakota, the "voice" of South Dakota families emerges out of *the organization's* struggle over political rights—a result that is tethered to the organization, rather than individual LGBTQ people. Unlike the HRC, the group does not argue for the benefits of hosting a "Coming Out Day," and instead urges its supporters to get involved by, for example, assisting with the organization's website, hosting a house party, or speaking with their legislative representative—a far cry from urging people to come out to "those who know you."

Despite the group's production of discourses not fully in line with the ideologies of national lesbian and gay organizations, their approaches—which implicitly frame visibility as being in opposition to silence and fear—arguably impact women's engagement with the organization. According to Equality South Dakota's website, only two of their board members in 2013 were women. These women explained their board positions in terms of their families' connections to the state, utilizing discourses markedly different from those of the men board members.[27] Sharon Ludwick Warner, one of the women board members, mobilized a rural familial history, describing herself as "a *third generation family owner* of Rain Bird Corporation, a manufacturer and provider of irrigation products and services" (emphasis added). The biography of Amy Richards, the second woman board member, similarly stated that she "grew up on a ranch east of Sturgis, SD, on the Belle Fourche River. She is the *granddaughter of a Methodist minister*, Reuben Tanquist, and a great uncle, Dr. Benjamin Rush, signed the Declaration of Independence" (emphasis added).

Warner's and Richards' accounting of their positions on the board is indicative of Mary Gray's finding that rural LGBTQ people deploy discourses of family and localness in order to gain community support.[28] It is through the histories of their upstanding (business-owning and religious) families, which have given a great deal to South Dakota and to the nation, that Warner and Richards legitimate their localness. They are from here. They can expect things of this place that is theirs. This approach relies on a framing of LGBTQ people as *similar to* the people in their rural communities. Indeed, as Gray argues, rural LGBTQ folks prioritize solidarity and loyalty to the familiar over public declarations of difference.

Such strategies and priorities mark a significant departure from national lesbian and gay rights groups' expectations that their constituents come out and be visible, which requires articulating oneself as *different from* others, a point that explains why such strategies may not be desirable for rural LGBTQ people. According to the logics of lesbian and gay rights groups, it is though this articulation of difference that we become known to those who are unlike us, convincing them that we, too, are deserving of rights. This tension between sameness and difference represents a paradox of homonormative rights-seeking approaches: we are compelled to express like-ness through centralizing our difference, a difference so crucial that it is impossible to be authentically known without an articulation of this difference. We are compelled to articulate our difference so that others may cast it aside as unimportant, simultaneously rendering us similar to them and producing themselves as the type of "flexible subjects" who are tolerant of such difference.[29] In short, becoming recognizable as similar requires an articulation of sexual difference, which functions to make one knowable. Visibility is both a goal and effect of the expression of such difference.

The two women on the board of Equality South Dakota, by contrast, feature their multigenerational attachments to the state, working to construct their subjectivities within discourses that suggest sameness. They are knowable through their families and communities, rather than via an articulation of difference.[30] This desire for similarity—without prerequisite difference—suggests that calls for visibility do not resonate in rural places, and that such approaches are sites of negotiation and contestation for LGBTQ women in the rural Midwest, as exemplified in the Jene Newsome case.

Newsome in the News

In October 2009, Jene Newsome and her partner, Cheryl Hutson-Newsome, got married in Iowa, the only Midwestern state that had legalized same-sex marriage at the time. Just weeks later, Rapid City police officers came to Newsome's home looking for Hutson-Newsome, who was wanted on theft charges in Alaska, and saw the couple's marriage certificate. This incident led to Newsome's discharge from the military. Newsome subsequently filed a complaint against the city of Rapid City in which she asked for $800,000 in damages, a policy change to prohibit police officers from releasing personal information to the military in the future, a reprimand for the officers involved with her case, and a formal apology. Despite the applicability of "Don't Ask, Don't Tell" and same-sex marriage rights—two issues that have recently dominated the efforts of national lesbian and gay rights groups—to Newsome's case, Newsome continually aimed her criticisms at the Rapid City Police Department, rather than commenting on either of these issues or the governmental institutions responsible for such policies.

The vast majority of local and regional press coverage of Newsome's case similarly focused on the Rapid City Police Department, with little mention of same-sex marriage rights or "Don't Ask, Don't Tell." Of the thirteen articles in the *Rapid City Journal* regarding Newsome's case, none focused primarily on "Don't Ask, Don't Tell" or even mentioned marriage. An editorial written by the *Journal*'s board began, "The Rapid City Police Department has changed its policy on sharing information with Ellsworth Air Force Base officials. The new policy states that only the department's records custodian can turn over official documents to the military."[31] The editors went on to describe this policy change, which emerged out of Newsome's encounter, as "sensible," without addressing the national policies responsible for making Newsome's case notable in the first place; the word "marriage" is absent, and "Don't Ask, Don't Tell" is mentioned once. Much like Newsome's own approach, the editors decoupled Newsome's story from both national politics and from her sexuality, stating, "We don't see how the case would have been handled any differently regardless of Newsome's sexual orientation." It seems obvious that the case would have been handled differently had Newsome been heterosexual—in fact, there would have been no case. Had Newsome been married to a man sought by local police, officers could have plausibly contacted the military, but reporting Newsome as married would have had no repercussions. In suggesting that Newsome's sexuality was extraneous to the officers' decisions, the editors depoliticized the case's connections to national debates and shifted the focus to the politics of policing in the context of the local community—thereby repoliticizing the case in ways that mirror Newsome's concerns.

By contrast, Newsome was tertiary in the coverage of her story by urban non-Midwestern news sources and national lesbian and gay rights groups, which used the story to argue for same-sex marriage rights and repealing "Don't Ask, Don't Tell," framing these issues, rather than the Rapid City Police Department, as the roots of Newsome's problems. Even in an article titled "Military Discharges Sergeant after Cops Out Her," posted to the *San Francisco Chronicle* website, national lesbian and gay political issues occupied as much space as Newsome's actual story.[32] The article ended by reasserting the "heinous" nature of third-party outings, marking a significant departure from the framings of Newsome's case by local and regional press and by Newsome herself.

The complexity of Newsome's story is not captured, however, by viewing her case as a simple cooptation of rural stories for the fulfillment of urban goals. It is certainly plausible to consider Newsome's desires as in line with the goals of mainstream lesbian and gay groups; she was, after all, married and a military employee. Furthermore, her demands for compensation included public reprimands of the officers and a public apology. However, even in this case, Newsome's desires were never for her own visibility, nor to gain rights or further a movement—facts that point again to the distance between Newsome's approaches and those of national organizations.

This is nowhere more evident than on the "Justice for Jene!" Facebook page. The anonymous creator of the site, who went by the name "Justice for Jene!," posted forty-eight messages between March 13, 2010, the day of its inception, and June 3, 2010.[33] The group's first wall post, which mimicked the group's mission, stated, "Jene Newsome was outed by the Rapid City Police Department for no apparent reason to the United States Air Force. Because of the outing Jene, a nine year service member, has been removed based upon the military's 'Don't Ask, Don't Tell' policy. Let's end DADT and get justice for Jene!" Although the initial post called for ending "Don't Ask, Don't Tell," and implied that doing so would result in local recompense, none of the subsequent posts by "Justice for Jene" even refers to the policy, and nor do the posts of the group's 5,135 fans. During the time when the Facebook page was active, Congress was considering legislation regarding "Don't Ask, Don't Tell" and the policy was consistently in the national spotlight. But neither Newsome herself nor her Facebook supporters conceptualized Jene's justice in relation to national lesbian and gay politics, and, thus, challenging this policy was not the intended purpose of the page. That "Justice for Jene!" never again mentioned "Don't Ask, Don't Tell" in any of the forty-seven subsequent posts—despite the ban being referenced in the mission statement and initial post—speaks to the difficulty of discussing Newsome's case outside of the logics of lesbian and gay politics as well as the desires of rural LGBTQ folks to do so.

The function of the "Justice for Jene!" Facebook page was to raise support for Newsome's battle against local authorities and institutions. Forty-one of the forty-eight wall posts made by the page's creators commented on the Rapid City Police Department, City Council, or mayor. On April 6, 2010, for example, "Justice for Jene!" posted:

> The Rapid City Council discussed the situation with Jene last night but they are still not taking any official action. It's been three weeks since Jene's story went public and the Rapid City Council has not made a single statement. It looks as if they are simply going to allow the Rapid City Police Department to act and do what they want too [sic].

Such posts are in line with Newsome's public statements documenting her frustration with the officers' violation of what she viewed as a set of unspoken local norms that allowed her to presume that her marriage was a private matter, rather than with local politics that might appear to preclude her from being "out" or visible. In many ways, Newsome was "out"; her family and friends knew about her sexual orientation, and she is married, which, as scholars have argued, itself "forces people to be out" and reflects desires for "visibility and recognition of their partnerships and families."[34] Assumptions regarding the value of visibility, and the impossibility of being authentic or honest without marriage and military rights, undergird contemporary struggles for lesbian and gay rights. But such positions do not resonate with those posting to the "Justice for Jene!" Facebook page or with Newsome, who is married and out, but exists in ways that do not satisfy the demands of calls for visibility. As Newsome said, "I'm not an activist. I hadn't planned to be changing my life. . . . If I hadn't been discharged I'd be making the Air Force my career."[35] Newsome refused to frame her case in relation to the military or federal government, or to work to change these institutions so that she might exist in alternative (more visible) ways.

Despite Newsome's lack of interest in a certain type of (lesbian and gay) politics, the "Justice for Jene!" site comments on an otherwise over-looked dimension of the case: the politics of race. Newsome is black and part of an interracial couple, two points rarely mentioned in de-ployments and coverage of her case. The final two Facebook posts on "Justice for Jene!" addressed racism. On June 2, 2010, "Justice for Jene!" posted, "Continued race problems haunt policing in Rapid City," along with a link to a *Rapid City Journal* article that described a protest against the Rapid City police department's refusal to punish an officer for killing a young Native man one month earlier. The following day "Justice for Jene!" posted a link to a 1963 report on racism in the Rapid City Police Department, stating,

> Rapid City, South Dakota has a fairly extensive past of racial discrimina-tion. In 1963 the United States Government investigated allegations of racism against African-American Airmen from Ellsworth Air Force Base and found systemic racism. Racism continues to be an issue that haunts Rapid City.

Such posts worked to historicize ongoing racism against Native people and to suggest that racism was involved in Newsome's case—a marked difference from the approaches of lesbian and gay rights groups, which ignored Newsome's race in their attempts to increase opposition to "Don't Ask, Don't Tell" via deploying Newsome's story, and often, ironi-cally, her photo. Similarly, the ACLU disregarded the influence race may have had on the case. Although the discourses Newsome utilized—her critique of the Rapid City Police Department, rather than the U.S. military or government—directly reflect the history of police brutality against black communities, Newsome also refrained from discussing her case through explicit discourses of race, focusing instead on how local police officers violated her privacy.

Marriage and intimacy are, for Newsome, private matters. In many ways, desires for privacy exist in opposition to calls for certain (homo-normative) intimacies to be made visible. While Newsome's deployment of privacy discourses reflects the ways in which the contemporary neo-liberal moment compels individualization, privacy also becomes the mode through which Newsome both expresses a distancing from national lesbian and gay rights groups and also carves out a place through which she can connect her case to histories of police brutality against communities of color without explicitly addressing the potential racism involved in her case.

These complexities are flattened when sexuality is not examined in relation to race or when race goes unacknowledged altogether. Such a problematic is especially evident in South Dakota, a state largely imagined as white, but with particular racial dynamics that require serious consideration. For example, Native Peoples comprise 8 percent of the state's population, the history of radical Native Peoples' activism continues to influence how race is understood in the state, and Native leaders such as Cecilia Fire Thunder have made national headlines by discussing race in relation to contemporary political issues, including abortion and land rights.[36] The framing of the Midwest as white allows for such intricacies to be left out of analyses, resulting in the further marginalization of racialized subjects. In ignoring Newsome's race, lesbian and gay rights organizations, the ACLU, and local, regional, and national news unintentionally participated in constructing the Midwest as white and its racial minorities as "others." In Newsome's case, the representation of the Midwest as white meant that groups deploying Newsome's story could not comment on her race because racialized subjects are always already outside of hegemonic representations of what constitutes both the (good) queer and the (good) rural Midwesterner—and yet Newsome was (even if temporarily) both.

Such avoidance of Newsome's race, then, informs and is informed by metronormative narratives that construct the rural as backwards, homophobic, and stifling, always lacking the glamor, lights, and diversity of the big city. Metronormativity is enabled by constructions of the rural as white, which come to stand in for the ostensible safety *and* backwardness of the rural; the rural's presumed whiteness is what makes it both wholesome and dangerous. Indeed, its wholesomeness makes it dangerous—not only for those who disrupt rural wholesomeness, but also for those with liberal political commitments, including those reminiscent of lesbian and gay movements, who desire to be understood as flexible subjects and require various forms of (racial, gendered, sexual) otherness in order to perform their ideological flexibility. While metronormative narratives require that race in the rural must be erased, race remains central to narratives of Western-global and urban-global relations. Non-Western LGBTQ subjects who move to the urban United States are compelled to retain their "otherness" in order for urban liberal subjects to assert a (nationalist) progress narrative and present their own flexible subjectivity. The rural's failure at multiculturalism, then, comes to represent the inability of its people to be "inclusive" and thus its backwardness.

The approaches of Jene Newsome and her Facebook fans depart from this metronormativity, as well as the broader ideologies of lesbian and gay rights groups that rely on and reproduce metronormativity. Such partings might best be understood as disidentificatory practices, which, as José Muñoz argues, allow marginalized people to simultaneously work on, within, and against dominant ideologies, neither assimilating into nor dogmatically opposing such structures.[37] Newsome and her supporters at "Justice for Jene!" neither reproduce the discourses and strategies evident within national lesbian and gay groups nor engage in oppositional approaches to position themselves outside of struggles for lesbian and gay rights. Had Newsome and her supporters at "Justice for Jene!" identified with contemporary gay rights logics, they might have blamed federal policies for Newsome's problems. Had they counteridentified, they might have rejected dominant logics and critiqued the military, government, and marriage as oppressive institutions. Newsome and her Facebook fans disidentify, working on, within, and against dominant logics, power structures, and institutions.

Conclusion

Global and rural sexualities scholars have argued that the strategies of contemporary lesbian and gay movements—including calls for visibility—are incongruous with the lives of LGBTQ people beyond Western metropoles. In this essay, I extend this argument by considering what the estrangement between lesbian and gay rights groups and LGBTQ women in the rural Midwest suggests about the relation of calls for visibility to metronormative ideologies. As Mary Gray explains, the "reliance on family, local power dynamics, class and racial politics, and the cultural marginalization that structures these specific rural communities render them *ill-suited* to strategies of visibility."[38] The ill-suited nature of visibility politics to the rural tells us at least as much about the problematics of such strategies as it does about the nature of the rural and the relationship of the rural to the urban and the global. Rural queer studies must remain critical of such rights-seeking approaches, not because they are untenable in rural places, but rather because they implicitly produce the rural as abject. For the purposes of my argument, the ill-suited nature of visibility politics to the rural is, perhaps, less important than what this estrangement points toward: the ill-suited nature of the rural to the urban. Attempts to rectify the predominance of metronormative ideologies are futile without a critical engagement with the modes through which such ideologies s come to exist in the first place. Visibility politics—far from a simple reflection of the nature of rural communities or an effect of the hegemony of the urban—aid in the very existence of metronormativity.

NOTES

1 Newsome's remark, made to the Associated Press via telephone, circulated widely in stories about the case. See, for example, "Jene Newsome Discharged: Rapid City Police Told Air Force that Sergeant Was Lesbian," *Huffington Post*, March 13, 2010, http://www.huffingtonpost.com/2010/03/13/jene-newsome-discharged-r_n_498134.html.

2 Steve Benen, "Political Animal," *Washington Monthly*, March 14, 2010, http://www.washingtonmonthly.com/archives/individual/2010_03/022853.php.

3 For discussions of the difficulty of defining terms such as "rural" and "Midwest," respectively, see Herring, *Another Country*, and Osborne and Spurlin, *Reclaiming the Heartland*. Following these scholars, I use "rural" and "Midwestern" to gesture to geographic locations as well as perspectives and positionalities, a use that insists on the fluidity of these terms not wholly unlike the fluidity scholars have argued exists in regards to other markers of social location and identity, including gender, sexuality, disability, class, race, and so on.

4 I use "lesbian and gay" to refer to national organizations whose politics are primarily geared toward lesbian- and gay- (rather than bisexual, transgender, or queer) identified people. I use "LGBTQ" as an acronym for lesbian, gay, bisexual, transgender, and queer in regards to visibility politics to suggest that visibility is compelled of people with an array of identifications by both mainstream and queer groups. I also use "LGBTQ" to refer to those women who make up the representations I examine because it is a fairly inclusive approach to describing the potential sexual identifications of those I do not know.

5 Rupp, *Sapphistries*, and Halberstam, *In a Queer Time and Place*, have commented on the lack of analysis of gender in LGBTQ studies and queer theory, a point particu-

larly relevant in regard to rural queer studies. In terms of activism, the metronormativity of lesbian and gay rights groups is reflected in the make-up of the Human Rights Campaign's board of directors, foundation board and board of governors, as listed on the organization's website in 2012: of the 201 individuals serving on these boards, five claim to live in rural places. For a current list of HRC board members, see http://www.hrc.org/the-hrc-story/boards

6 Massad, *Desiring Arabs*, 183.

7 Boellstorff, *Gay Archipelago*; Manalansan, *Global Divas*.

8 Puar, *Terrorist Assemblages*, xxvii.

9 Massad argues that the Egyptian government has attempted to repress the *public nature* of gay identification, rather than same-sex sexual activity, a point in line with Puar's position that for non-Western LGBTQ people, the promises of "identity-based narratives of queerness, especially those reliant on visibility politics" are quite limited (*Terrorist Assemblages*, xxvii).

10 Halberstam, *In a Queer Time and Place*, 38.

11 See Gray, *Out in the Country*; Herring, *Another Country*; Howard, *Men Like That*; Johnson, *Just Queer Folks*.

12 For critical analyses of gay identity and community, respectively, see D'Emilio, "Capitalism and Gay Identity" and Joseph, *Against the Romance of Community*.

13 Foucalt, *Discipline and Punish*, 200.

14 Brown, *States of Injury*.

15 Said, *Orientalism*.

16 Gray, *Out in the Country*, 9.

17 Halberstam, *In a Queer Time and Place*, 8.

18 These numbers were accurate on September 22, 2010. The images posted on Flickr.com change daily, so while the numbers I cite may differ on another day, the importance of rural place to the group is a trend I recognized after following the site for several months.

19 My breakdown does not total 388 photos. I classified eight photographs as gender-neutral because they include people with ambiguous genders. This is clearly not a quantitative analysis; I provide these numbers to highlight men's dominance on the site.

20 While this photo does not connote particular rural aesthetics, it is posted on a site dedicated to "suburban and rural gay life." An assumption that the photo is not of a rural space reflects the limited cultural representations of rurality.

21 "Suburban and Rural Gay Life," Flickr.com, http://api.flickr.com/services/feeds/groups_discuss.gne?id=662371@N22&lang=en-us&format=rss_200 (accessed May 28, 2013).

22 Human Rights Campaign website, http://preview.hrc.org/issues/3374.htm (accessed June 11, 2013).

23 Of the thirteen issues on which HRC claims to work, no other occupies the position of same-sex marriage, captured in statements such as, "Only marriage can provide

families with true equality"(http://www.hrc.org/americansformarriageequality/impact, accessed June 11, 2013).

24 A great deal of queer theoretical scholarship critiques the normativity of gay rights groups. See, for example, Berlant, *Intimacy*; Conrad, *Against Equality*; Muñoz, *Disidentifications*; and Warner, *The Trouble with Normal*.

25 Up until this point, I have made claims about (representations of) rural LGBTQ women without focusing on any specific region or area; the absence I have documented clearly exists beyond a locale. As I move forward, I locate my analysis in South Dakota—a site that, while indicative of the understudied nature of the Midwest, is not meant to represent the region.

26 Equality South Dakota website, http://www.eqsd.org/about.html (accessed June 11, 2013).

27 While the men also work to articulate their connections to South Dakota, each relies solely on his own life. "Board of Directors," Equality South Dakota, http://www.eqsd.org/about/board.html (accessed May 28, 2013).

28 Gray, *Out in the Country*, 28.

29 McRuer, *Crip Theory*, 17–18.

30 Neither woman stated her sexual orientation or gave clues that gesture toward an identity. Their sexual identities are largely irrelevant for this analysis, as I am interested in the discourses that circulate *by, about, and through* LGBTQ women and politics in the rural Midwest.

31 "Editorial: Police Policy Change Makes Sense," *Rapid City Journal*, April 16, 2010, http://rapidcityjournal.com/news/opinion/editorial-police-policy-change-makes-sense/article_1f1d892c-4966-11df-b6e3-001cc4c03286.html.

32 Timberly Ross, "Military Discharges Sergeant after Cops Out Her," *San Francisco Chronicle*, March 14, 2010, http://rapidcityjournal.com/news/opinion/editorial-police-policy-change-makes-sense/article_1f1d892c-4966-11df-b6e3-001cc4c03286.html.

33 While the creator of the site was anonymous, the content of the posts made clear that the creator was extremely familiar with South Dakota politics.

34 Bernstein and Taylor, *The Marrying Kind?*, 18, 5.

35 Frank Pizzoli, "Lesbian Air Force Sgt. Jene Newsome in DADT Grinder," *Central Voice*, March 20, 2010, http://centralvoice.wordpress.com/2010/03/20/lesbian-air-force-sgt-jene-newsome-in-dadt-grinder/.

36 Thomsen, "The Politics of Narrative, Narrative as Politic,"

37 Muñoz, *Disidentifications*, 11.

38 Gray, *Out in the Country*, 30 (emphasis added).

PART IV

Bodies of Evidence

Methodologies and Their Discontents

13

(Dis)locating Queer Citizenship

Imaging Rurality in Matthew Shepard's Memory

E. CRAM

Something substantial can be made from the outline left
after the body has disappeared.
—Peggy Phelan, *Mourning Sex*

As leaves turn to shades of crimson, amber, and gold, the cold winds
of fall settle in every early October, and so does the ritual of remembering Matthew Shepard. In a memorializing narrative, the story enacts
familiar markers of time and place. After attending a pre-homecoming
meeting of the University of Wyoming LGBTA on the night of October
6, 1998, Shepard met two Laramie locals at the downtown Fireside Bar.
On October 7, 1998, a mountain biker discovered Shepard's disfigured,
struggling body near its end, tied spread eagle to a buck fence in a sub-
division past Laramie's Walmart.[1] The story that unfolded between the
temporal markers of beers at the Fireside and the discovery of Shepard's body in the frigid morning hours would be framed in the national
media by a tragic public narrative of homophobia, rural cowboy culture,
drugs, sex, and violence.

Although Shepard's community experienced the private ritual of grief
and loss, Shepard's story traveled through national and transnational
networks. Strangers from San Francisco to New York paused their daily
routines for public memorials, political funerals, and moments of silence and outcry to grieve and politicize the loss of a body framed as
America's gay son. Shepard's face was soon affixed to the national gay
and lesbian agenda and to demands for recognition and visibility that
spanned the realms of institutional policies, media representation, and
community attitudes. As grievers mourned Shepard's body across the

nation, catalyzing the otherwise inert debate over the Hate Crimes Prevention Act, vigils enacted a transformative space for publics to mobilize and connect Shepard's story with other experiences of interpersonal gay and lesbian violence. Yet, as the circulation of news media and public discourse began to sediment a particular narrative of the case, Shepard was transformed into an iconic and metonymic articulation of queer bodies in pain.

I watched the story work its way through the circuits of television, public radio, photojournalism, community gossip, and public memory for years, even after verdicts had been rendered, and Aaron McKinney and Russell Henderson had been shuffled away in orange jumpsuits to the state penitentiary in Rawlins, one hundred miles west from where they left Shepard to die. In 1998, fifty miles east of that fence, I was nearing my sixteenth birthday in Wyoming's capitol city. I thought about Matt as my queer body shuffled through the hallways of my high school, and how uncanny it felt to hear Tom Brokaw and other voices of the national press use words like "Laramie" as the camera lens panned across scenes of railway cars or dry grassy plains. Like others in Wyoming, I sensed the media harbored a strategic curiosity about our lives. For those less intimate with the physical and cultural landscape of Wyoming, we were a place where horses still roamed freely through dirt roads and downtowns and cowboys wrangled on the open range. Our predominately rural western culture did not have an explicit presence in the discursive streams of national publics, save for a few nostalgic looks toward what was supposed to be seen as a place that reflected a long lost ethos of American life: idyllic, hard-working, but just a little bit rowdy.

In order to understand the motivations of that sudden and virulent fascination, I grapple with visual technologies of Shepard's iconicity. I explore how meteronormative optics of Laramie constitute public memory in order to see the violence committed against Shepard as an effect of living in rural places. Within dominant public memory, *place* is ascribed with a sense of agency that marks Shepard's murder in substantially different ways in comparison to narratives of gay and lesbian violence entangled within urban imaginaries. In the U.S. public discourse of the late 1990s, Shepard's memorialization was exceptional in the context of gay and lesbian violence. Shepard's murder was one of the 1,260 sexually motivated hate crimes reported in 1998.[2] And although interpersonal violence encompasses one important dimension of broader social violence, his murder continues to be remembered with each passing year, sometimes as the zenith of anti-gay crimes, for the (un)imaginable brutality done to a body seen through the lens of youth, white fragility, and fraught innocence.

To make sense of Shepard's visual archive means situating conditions of grievability relative to space, place, and imagined communities.[3] Normativities sediment sociality in relation to the modalities of race, class, gender, and sexuality, and enable and constrain civic orientations of friendship or enmity. Accounting for emotional culture—why a national and international community could emerge to denounce the spectacle of homophobia, yet embrace the repetitive conditions of everyday acts of violence—articulates the logics of understanding and resolving Shepard's trauma.[4] For urban queer publics, Shepard illustrates the normative safety of the anonymous city juxtaposed to the horror and violence of the rural as a place for queer citizenship.[5] For imagined non-queer urban publics, identification with Shepard normalizes particular queer bodies as citizen-friends and treats those bodies as capable of being mourned; it also involves a dis-identification with the acts of McKinney and Henderson and with the modalities of violent homophobic practice. In essence, non-queer urban publics are able to evacuate their complicity in homophobic practices and culture in their grief for Shepard and condemnation of McKinney and Henderson.

Metronormative optics negotiate stranger relationality within the complexities of an emotional culture of anti-gay and lesbian violence. In turn, the place of the imagined rural American West is consumed as an acutely volatile space for queer bodies, displacing attention to articulations of violence in the spaces of cities and suburbs. *Homophobia* becomes spatialized to the rural and the possibilities for queer *citizenship* move to the urban, foreclosing the possibility of a queer rural citizenship and a scope for collective queer politics. The making of Shepard into an icon raises concerns about the erasures of race, class, and gender-queerness from non-queer publics' identification with queer bodies and invites a critically queer reconsideration of citizenship grounded in the politics of envisioning space.

Metronormative Optics and the Troubled Places of Queer Citizenship

Questions of citizenship encourage scholars to consider the relationships that comprise civic orientations.[6] This may mean forms of identification—wherein strangers share interests, obligations, or civic visions—or, they may take up modes of agonism—wherein dissent expands the possibilities of belonging to a political community.[7] Conceptualizing citizenship as a mode of political relation exceeds the term's containment by a liberal imaginary that privileges formal relationships among individuals, the state, and institutional formations.[8] Yet, liberalism's optics elide relationships among citizen-bodies who inhabit and share spatial formations. In this vein, I consider the emotionality of citizenship.[9]

My interest in *cultural* citizenship emphasizes how emotional culture matters in response to violence against marked bodies within a community. We can imagine citizenship as a negotiation of belonging. The emotionality of citizenship suggests that the affective (de)attachments we have toward others create the conditions from which citizens participate in violent practices or the conditions from which citizens respond to acts of violence. In Shepard's case, political emotions such as grief, queer fear, rural shame, and urban disgust are negotiated through the management of spatial relationships, particularly the rural/urban imaginary.[10]

The emotionality of citizenship is dynamic and a critical interest for rural queer studies in marking the felt presence of metronormativity. Initiated as a rubric of the spatialization of sexuality in the United States, metronormativity has been identified by J. Jack Halberstam as a way of valorizing urban cityscapes and political investments for queer and trans-folks, in contrast to the simultaneous horror and impossibility of rural queer and trans- existence.[11] Scott Herring amplifies this conception, marking the discursive and material undercurrents that sediment metronormative attitudes and affects alongside narratology, racialization, socioeconomics, temporalization, epistemology, and aesthetics.[12] Following the spirit to mark particulars, I illustrate how metronormativity is animated by structures of feeling.[13] Here, the feeling of "rurality" takes up space as an aesthetic and cultural discourse more than it may encompass modes of dwelling. As such, in national cultures of circulation, photographs that depict perceptions of environmental precariousness manage emotional culture.

What I call "metronormative optics" sees the interrelation of imagined relationships among the country and the city and political emotion. Metronormativity can be considered as an affective relationship made intelligible by emotional displays.[14] When grief publics emerge, the ensuing public discussion illuminates complex affective and spatial politics between urban and rural publics. Naming the power of metronormative optics challenges the mobilization of queer fear, or a sudden felt threat of violence enacted against queer bodies; doing so also calls attention to rural shame and urban disgust, engendered by demeaning temporal tropes and in which urbanism is lauded as progressive and spatially privileged for the desirable queer/trans- life.[15]

The emotionality of metronormativity challenges how queer critics approach "citizenship." Isaac West implores queer critics to adopt a sensibility of citizenship as a "cultural practice of managing stranger relationalities."[16] West argues that practices of stranger relationality often disobey the inherent normativities embedded within an instrumental legal imagination. Situated within cultures of circulation that manage geographic imaginations, stranger relationality becomes a problem of place, as both lived and abstracted. The confluence of visual culture, public emotionality, and metronormativity elucidates the process by which "country" and "city" accumulate feelings in contemporary scenes of violence.

Shepard's national memory is primarily visual, animated by familial snapshots and photojournalistic depictions of place. I distinguish Shepard's visual archive from considerations of "gay visibility." My engagement with photography moves beyond the problematic of representation within dominant culture.[17] Instead, I highlight the interplay of emotion and visuality in creating conditions for locational stranger relationality. Photography's relational and political dimensions reimagine the value of photographic performances beyond representation, such that the optics in which we engage images become central to the generation of meaning.

The shift from visibility to optics gestures toward the failure of "visibility" as a mobile tactic of recognition across place, race, class, gender, and sexuality. Critics of metronormativity emphasize visibility's particularity. Mary Gray argues that visibility is contingent upon one's geography, and not a tangible way to establish connections in rural areas because of norms of rural familiarity.[18] E. Patrick Johnson questions "the closet" for black gay men in the South, insisting that it reflects instead a white gay politics of visibility.[19] And Herring resists visibility by his diagnostic of aesthetic metronormativity and the generation of cultural capital.[20] Rather than treat space and place as mere background for particular phenomena, Gray, Johnson, and Herring illustrate why space and place must be considered as constitutive of subjectivity in addition to a location or orientation.

The movement from photography as representation to *relationality* marks how photojournalism puts the *terms* of citizenship on display, such that members of a community see and imagine themselves acting as citizens. Danielle Allen argues that civic photography is one of the modalities through which citizens imagine "habits of citizenship," or ways in which we relate to one another.[21] To this end, photojournalism is a critical technology for managing the temporal, spatial, and affective dimensions of public life.[22] The extent to which certain images become memorable or iconic speaks to how images become central to public life and to constituting public identities and collective memory.

Visual communication scholars Robert Hariman and John Louis Lucaites argue that iconic images are "moments of visual eloquence that acquire exceptional importance within public life . . . and . . . motivate public action on behalf of democratic values."[23] Hariman and Lucaites emphasize how visual memories "activate strong emotional identification or response."[24] The critical term here is "identification." Forms of identification that emerge in the circulation of the visual archive, such as Shepard's grievability and iconization, unearth how the images are articulations of a cultural understanding of the relationship between queer bodies and imagined rural places.

Thus my concern, well over a decade after Shepard's death, is how the ritual circulation of the same photographs animates the contingency of grievability. Public memory emerges alongside metronormative optics, in effect constraining conditions of grievability. Experiences of loss, mourning, and trauma are "laden with creative political potential. . . . The politics and ethics of mourning lie in the interpretation of what remains—how remains are produced and animated, how they are read

Figure 13.1. On October 12, 1999, participants of "Hike for Hope" visit the fence where Matthew Shepard was beaten. (Source: photograph by Ed Andrieski, Associated Press)

and sustained."[25] The stakes of the metronormative optic, or a way of seeing that privileges an urban narrative of queer citizenship, involve how we understand the politics of grief. If photographs display civic habits and enable a confrontation with "corporeal vulnerability and the task of mourning," optics that enable an identification or dis-identification with certain places over others produce another iteration of violence. Images of damaged bodies in public culture enable us to "see" "whose lives count as lives."[26]

I supplant the metronormative narrative that understands queer rurality as the primary condition in which Shepard was murdered. In dominant visual memory, guilt for violent acts is evacuated from urban publics as the metronormative narrative elides the struggle over place in city spaces. Rather than seeing Shepard's story as one of many violent actions enacted against queer bodies, his story and his whiteness are seen as transforming into a sense of place and universal claim of rural queer experience. Moved by class normativities that constrain rural bodies to the space of the threatening domestic other, national publics are absolved from their collective obligation to address conditions of violence animated by differential precariousness.

The technologies that enabled such a reading are embedded in the affective circuits mobilized through iconic photographs of the fence circulated to memorialize Shepard. As a structuring element in the narrative of the crime, the fence is invoked as object of discipline and violence, especially given that the aesthetic of the buck fence is quintessentially rural and western. Accounts of the positioning of Shepard's body on the fence relied on religious iconography, effectively constituting a crucifixion image.[27] The fence's instrumental function as a boundary transforms symbolically as an illustration of the borders that sediment with heteronormative attitudes towards gender and sexuality. Thus, in the memory of Shepard, we are able to find judgments about life in the city, life in the country, grievable queer life, and a body that matters.

Bodies in Pain that Matter

A slender young white man pauses awkwardly in the kitchen for a spontaneous photo shoot. His body engulfs almost the entirety of the frame, which has been cropped to include objects familiar to the center of a middle-class home. To the side of his forehead, we can see an installed microwave oven nesting within finished wooden cabinetry. White canisters hide behind a glimpse of his forearm, nearly blending into the white painted wall. Small Tupperware, filled to the brim, gently grace the edges of his shoulder blades. And in the center of the frame, we see the whole of Shepard's torso adorned in a bulky blue and white plaid button-down shirt.

Digital red numbers in the lower right hand corner stamp the time as a witness of a moment now indexed as the past: click, flash, roll. For a moment, we might remember how flannel dominated fashion in the late 1990s. We might also identify with the scene of the kitchen as a

Figure 13.2. One of many personal snapshots of Matthew Shepard that circulated.

space of everyday rituals. Perhaps this moment in the kitchen is one of friendly or familial congregation. We might register Shepard's kitchen in terms of our own, as an insulated space that comforts us with an aura of sense-making practices, a space in which we enjoy the sensory pleasures of cinnamon, basil, or pumpkin pie and engage in the labor necessary to indulge our hungry appetites. Yet it seems as though those kinds of sense-making practices are also classed in peculiar ways. Why a hanging nestled microwave and not one that sits on the counter? Why wooden cabinets instead of painted ones? The image is a queer combination of simplicity and ornament. Shepard after all, was a college student. Yet the presence of containers gives pause. His confident look makes it seem as though this kitchen is a space in which he finds comfort—yet, we cannot be sure to whom it belongs. Him? His parents? A friend in Casper or Laramie or Denver? Despite these questions, in this image, we encounter Shepard in an intimate moment, a domestic space, and most importantly, one that is marked by objects of middle-class whiteness.

The use of personal photographs such as the kitchen snapshot enable a kind of intimacy with Shepard's life, in which we are able to imagine

Figure 13.3. Matthew Shepard senior photo.

everyday practices as either similar or dissimilar to our own. Other images circulate as well. Black and white high school senior photos are distributed to family and friends strewn across time and space, much as they are in a ritual common to middle-class families. In figure 13.3, an earnest young man, ready and waiting to engage the world, looks at the camera directly, with a slightly tilted head. His boyish good looks make him seem like he is well kept: his trendy haircut emphasizes the movement of light in the image across the lines of what looks like highlights. The artistic control of the lighting in the image—generated through the bright tones of window in the background—also enable access to a sense of time, evident in the division of his face by lightness and shadow. The image tightly frames his face and includes only a small section of his shoulder. Even so, in this image, Shepard seems small, even though we have no ability to make comparisons according to scale.

In another black and white photo (figure 13.4), Shepard crouches down, hugging his knees in deep contemplation. We are able to see fully the smallness of Shepard's body compared to the world around him. The framing is different in terms of the space that surrounds his body. Here, Shepard looks away from the camera, perhaps towards the future or at the world with uncertainty, in a way that is common for gay and lesbian youth. The low tones of black and white fused with the senior-portrait genre comprise a level of sophistication and polish. He wears tennis shoes, giving the somewhat somber image a feel of playful youth.

Nearly every "captioning" of Shepard's photographs includes commentary about his size and fragility. Shepard was "slight of stature, gentle of demeanor."[28] Brian Ott and Eric Aoki eloquently explain how images of Shepard's body performed and indexed cultural tropes of whiteness, middle-classness, and nonthreatening queerness.[29] For his friends, like Jim Osborn, then LGBTA student president, Shepard was "someone we can identify with. Shepard was the boy next door. He looked like everybody's brother and everybody's neighbor. He looked like he could have been anyone's son."[30]

If Shepard's photos enable a kind of identification that makes him look like *everybody's brother* or *anybody's son*, we must ask why a gay white middle-class body is capable of transcending the corporeal markers of race and class.[31] In effect, Shepard's whiteness becomes invisible and his queerness is diminished, yet still present. Such a strong moment of identification is provocative in comparisons to claims that position queer subjects as sexual strangers that comprise the constitutive outside of the national imaginary as contaminants.[32] What about Shepard's body enabled the championing of identification over division?

Photographs of Shepard that circulate in the national press privilege middle-class whiteness as the grounds for identification. The melodramatic account of extraordinary violence juxtaposed with Shepard's "ordinariness" mobilizes modes of identification relative to what bod-

Figure 13.4. One of many senior portrait–style photos of Matthew Shepard circulated online.

ies constitute a grievable life. This is not to say that racialized acts of violence such as the lynching-by-dragging of James Byrd, Jr., in Jasper, Texas, do not receive national attention. The horrific acts of violence enacted upon Shepard's and Byrd's bodies are doubly memorialized by the 2009 Hate Crimes Prevention Act. Yet, why are extraordinary acts of violence "what it takes" to cultivate the conditions of national grief? Why can we not be moved by the everyday violence of systemic heternormativity, homophobia, and racism?[33]

When national publics are moved by everyday trauma, mobilizations of disgust are most palpable if mapped into rural places. Nonmetropolitan places are characterized as insufferable because of their lack of queer spaces like bars, community centers, or other mass queer enclaves and because of their restricted codes of visibility. The effect of making violence exceptional, rather than a dimension of everyday lived experience in both urban and rural spaces, is that acts of violence are too easily individualized and spatialized. In essence, they are exceptional problems, committed by an isolated individual. They are characterized as irrational acts committed by unstable or evil persons who operate outside of the scope of the sociocultural field rather than materializations of the cultural attitudes that make queers and racialized bodies strange from the start. From the auspices of citizenship, the deflection of communal responsibility to individual culpability is fraught with risk. In Shepard's case, it means that the homophobic violence committed against him is a rural problem rather than a national cultural problem for which we are all responsible.

Since the national culture of grief emerges because of the spectacle of predominantly exceptional rather than everyday violence, it is important to consider what resources enabled such a strong identification. Although personal photography constitutes Shepard as somewhat ordinary and identifiable, the narrative of a body tortured, viciously beaten, and left alone to die over a long period of hours in the cold, Wyoming October night engenders another way in which we imagine Shepard's body: as a wounded gay body in pain.

Images of bodies—whether damaged, vulnerable, or at risk—act as a powerful rhetorical resource for political appropriation.[34] In one of the more powerful and visceral narrations of the image of Shepard in pain, Romaine Patterson, a close friend to Shepard, writes:

When I closed my eyes and tried to sleep I saw the disgusting scene played out in dark colors—dark reds, dark blues, dark blacks. My mind had glommed on to the most gruesome details from the news and created a picture that ran on a loop: *I'm an invisible presence on the prairie, set back from a scene shrouded in darkness. Matt's strung up on the fence, the truck's headlights on him like spotlights. He's tied crucifixion style. There's blood everywhere—caked in his eyes and dried in his hair on the side of his caved-in head. Fresh wet blood rolls down his body over purple bruises and exposed bone. Just outside the light on either side of Matt I see the black outlines of two men, crouching beside him, each holding a lighter. Simultaneously they click their flames to life, press them to his flesh, and watch the skin curl.* My brain flashed, and I saw it from Matt's perspective: *The chafe against my wrists as I try to free myself, the crack of my bones with each blow of the bat.* Then my brain flashed again, and I saw it from the attacker's perspective. I felt his rage and his sense of power as he looked on the body of that tiny little man: *I swing back my foot and kick him again and again, making him bleed, scream, and beg for his life.* Suddenly I sat up and turned on the light, terrified of the dark. Then I collapsed and cried into my pillow. It was a violent cry, the kind that makes you feel like you're going to vomit. I prayed out loud, "God, please make it go away—whitewash my mind. Make it so I see nothing."[35]

In this visceral narration, we are witnesses to Patterson's telling the story of Shepard becoming undone. Previous images illustrate how Shepard's body is disciplined symbolically through coding and inscription. However, with the image of a fragile body in pain, we are confronted with the image of a body undone by more than discursive whips and lashes. The torture narrative made its way through a variety of imagistic cultural productions: songs such as Melissa Etheridge's "Scarecrow," poetry like E. Patrick Johnson's "The Scene in Wyoming," and national productions of the Tectonic Theater's *The Laramie Project*.[36] The circulation of cultural production asked us to confront what is to be made of witnessing the unmaking of a human being.

If Shepard's body enabled such a strong sense of identification, then witnessing the process of "unmaking" is profoundly horrific. The pains of such torture exceed the capacity to understand and articulate them in an accessible language.[37] Perhaps this is why image practices and their production of affective excess are so central in the elevation of Shepard to iconic status. And yet, what is so remarkable about the Shepard archive is the lack of circulated photographs that physically witness his undoing. The image of Shepard being beaten and tied to a fence is largely a mental image produced through the telling of verbal narrative.

A number of factors may explain the lack of access: perhaps it would violate prudent decision-making to photograph a crime scene when Shepard was clinging to life; perhaps photographs taken in the hospital after his death to document his injuries do not circulate in order to respect the wishes of the parents or to be in accordance with norms of public propriety. Regardless of the motive that kept *photographs* of the damaged body out of the public sphere, others continued to invent the image through the retelling of the story in a process that illustrates the close intimacy of verbal narrative, photographs, and the human imagination. Where there was no *physical* body to cling to and grieve, no photograph to tell what happened, we were able to invent its presence in the imagination.

Imagining Shepard as a white middle-class gay body in pain enabled strong modes of identification across queer and non-queer publics. Accounting for Shepard's uptake in public culture, Ott and Aoki cite journalist JoAnn Wypijewski as remarking: "Shepard is the perfect queer: young, pretty, and dead."[38] But Shepard's becoming the type of an innocent and fragile body left to suffer does not account for the scope of Shepard's iconicity. The white, middle-class, and fragile body was located in a specific space. The memory of Shepard's murder is grounded in a temporal and spatial narrative, one not evident in the images of his face and body. Would the ghost of Shepard have haunted public memory if it did not have a space in which to become grounded? Just as we met Shepard through images, so we also met the sparse, but sparkling lights of Laramie, Wyoming.

Abject Spaces: Metronormativity and the Horror of the Rural

A buck fence in the middle of a dry prairie has bark that appears to be peeling away from the cycles of time. A basket of fresh flowers hangs lopsided from one of the posts, in a remarkable juxtaposition of life and death, new and old. The unfettered wind rushes between the wooden

Figure 13.5. *Time* magazine
cover, October 26, 1998.

posts, through the petals of each flower. Sandy reddish tones of prairie dust are juxtaposed to the electric blue sky, touched only by clouds, seeming to go on endlessly. We are in the middle of nowhere; we are not even sure what purpose the fence might serve. We are encompassed by space, division, dust, and the cold Wyoming wind. More so, we are haunted by the specter of Shepard's body. The framing of the photograph cuts away the bottom of the fence below the basket of flowers. Perhaps that is the marker of where Shepard's body was left behind?

In another image, a friend clings to the fence, as if trying to hug any remnant of a body left to die, but no longer physically present. Her body grips the fence, as if to do so could ease something that is shaking inside of her, or perhaps touching the point where a body once was lets her imagine the splintery wood was something a bit more human. This time we see more of the ground, more flowers left in tribute, a ritual of grief, mourning, and remembrance. Yet, in this instance, the image is centered on Patterson at the fence, and we get the impression of the fence's belonging to a community of people who have just lost someone.

Figure 13.6. Romaine Patterson grieves at the fence where Matthew Shepard was beaten.

The buck fence where Shepard's body was found was one of the most haunting images that circulated in popular press each year of his remembrance, having found its way to places like the cover of *Time*'s October 26, 1998, edition, popular online "retrospectives" of the *New York Times*, and the front of playbills for productions of *The Laramie Project*. The fence served the immediately symbolic function of articulating a physical site to grieve and memorialize the loss. But the symbolism of the fence extends beyond pure memorial. Rather, the image of the fence, I argue, is situated within the mythos of the horror of the rural and appropriated by queer publics in a maintenance of meteronormative visions and affects of queerness, constituting articulations of urban disgust and rural shame. Consequentially, the rural becomes the imagined space of homophobic violence, while urban spaces are valorized as progressive safe havens.

The rural/urban binary is enabled by both the material specificity of geographic location and the discursive imaginary that marks certain places in peculiar ways.[39] The urban imaginary represents the unmarked public constituted by its own set of norming practices, or "queer urbanisms."[40] Bound to the urban imaginary are representations of the rural, "replete with such devices of exclusion and marginalization by which mainstream 'self' serves to 'other' the positioning of all kinds of people in the socio-spatial relations of different countrysides."[41] Untangling the politics of rural representations disturbs otherwise monolithic articulations of queer bodies bound by space and time.

The mythos of the rural is bound by two dominant narratives. On one hand, narratives of the rural centralize places of escape and renewal for those caught in the chaos of urban space. The rural is "cherished as an innocent idyll of bucolic tranquility and communion with nature—a place to retreat from the ever-quickening pace of urban living."[42] This narrative works particularly well for imagining the rural as a place of arrival for mobile elites. For the urban office rat, visits to the countryside enable a sense of freedom and calm. This was the case for Jim Gladstone, who made a visit to Jackson Hole in 2010. Jackson, which lies in the midst of the Teton Mountains south of Yellowstone, is one of Wyoming's wealthiest towns, in part because of a lucrative tourist industry. In an assessment of his experience, Gladstone shares how his trip to Jackson was spurred by a feeling of being "soul-worn by daily life in my own cubicle. . . . I would head to the land where the elk roamed free!"[43] Escaping from his urban cubicle created feelings of rejuvenation through the use of services intended for wealthy travelers like Gladstone—not folks who populate the state.

The image of rural idyll also characterizes the image Donna Minkowitz, a self-proclaimed New York yuppie and writer for the *Nation*, found when she visited Laramie in 1999, a year after Shepard died. Minkowitz writes,

> Comfort is easy to find in Laramie, if you're a yuppie like me. I feel like I am on vacation because luxury restaurants are so cheap here; my bed-and-breakfast is the nicest I have ever stayed in. By my standards, it is cheap: $57 a night. And how does it feel to be a lesbian here? Fabulous. Annie Moore's is not only a Victorian filled with sensuous period furniture, it has a copy of *Rubyfruit Jungle* on the guest bookshelf. Lesbian and gay lovers stay in these sexy little rooms all the time, along with the University of Wyoming's most prestigious visitors. Sometimes the town's yups come to stay for the night just to feel well-off and taken care of. The charming innkeeper, Ann Acuff, who is straight, makes me feel at home by telling about the night she spent at a lesbian bar the last time she was in New York.[44]

Though Minkowitz paints an attractive image of Laramie, complete with quaint hospitality, camp aesthetics, and lesbian literature, this is not the image that resonated in public culture. Dialogically paired with images of a rural idyll are those that "move away from positive, romantic images of rural communities towards images of fragmentation and backwardness."[45] In this context, rural perversion is cast as an iteration of rural shame and queer fear to enable the temporal demonization of non-queer folks as explicit threats to queer bodies. Doing so relies on the conventions of tropes that see rural and working-class bodies as incessantly and intrinsically violent. The intersections of rural perversion and shame and urban disgust can be illustrated by ways the press attempted to mobilize images of Laramie's backwardness. Thus, *Guardian* writer Gerard Wright characterized the everyday trauma of queer rurality as an effect of stereotypical Western practices: "To be gay in the American West, a land of pickup trucks, dipping tobacco and concealed firearms, is, say club patrons, to have a secret that can only be shared with the most trusted confidants and to live two separate lives."[46] Wright articulated the management of queer practices and performances exclusively to rural western places because of his belief that trucks, tobacco, and firearms are incommensurable with queer desires. (Clearly, Wright has never spent much time around queer rodeos or cowboy fetish bars.) The normalization of queer aesthetics and classist judgments relative to potential violence enacted by rural folks evokes the affect of queer urbanism in the register of transnational cosmopolitanism.

Even as Wright expressed disdain toward the symbolic economy of the West, and even more broadly, toward class symbols of American consumption, we must consider space as dynamic and invented, in that it is produced by the bodies that inhabit its ever-shifting boundaries.[47] For every narrative of secrecy as an example of the constraint of agency, there are even more narratives of the creative refashioning of dominant culture to cultivate feelings of place-based resilience and regeneration. If "space is a practiced place," as Michel de Certeau notes, then how does queer practice generate queer space?[48] More so, what does queer practice *look* like? It is at this point in which the meteronormative valences of queer visibility foreclose the possibility of imagining queer country.

The horror of the rural and its status as a closet for the more socially "intelligible" forms of queerness are evident in the appropriation of the fence's image in multiple iterations. The fence becomes the way in which the spectator imagines the whole of the crime: through the appropriation of the fence, we see the image through its other clustered images that evoke such strong meanings and responses. Perhaps this is indicative of the position at which the fence is reproduced: each original image, along with its ensuing reproductions, imagines a relationship to the fence wherein we see what McKinney and Henderson see. In these images, we do not see through the eyes of Shepard. Consequently, the photograph and its geographic circulation invite and implicate extant publics within McKinney and Henderson's point of view, reiterating feelings of domination constituted by the initial scene.

With the appropriation and circulation of such a horrific image, most apparent in the use of the fence in playbills for the performances of *The Laramie Project*, how is it possible to imagine queers in rural places? The popularity of the "The Great Gay Migration," in which queers left their small, oppressive towns for the lights, glamor, and safety of anonymous city space constitutes the possibility for rural subjectivity through the movement of bodies across space and narratives of exile and escape. In essence, we hear a popular coming-out chant articulated in a different way: "Out of the country (closet) and into the city (streets)!" Acknowledging the limits of urban visibility means accounting for the limitations of metronormativity in queer histories and in reconstituting what bodies make for a grievable life.

Imagining the Possibility of Queer Country

The study of images of Shepard and of the fence, as well as their circulation, troubles how optics and effects of metronormativity constitute public memories of queer trauma. These images become iconic because of their clustering: we identify with Shepard because of his fragile and innocent body, imagined as a body in pain, left to die at a fence in the cold. Their intertextuality illustrates how emotions such as grief, queer fear, rural shame, and urban disgust mobilize, given various identifications or dis-identifications. How each photograph gets read, or what fragments of the series are emphasized over others, seems to be contingent on their uptake by either queer or non-queer publics. By looking at these images as a cluster of separate but intertextually meaningful images, we are able to see how queer and non-queer publics engage the memory and grieve Shepard in different ways. For non-queer publics, Shepard is a son, a boy whose life was cut short because of banal evil, typified by the actions of two rural "locals" who murdered a college kid trying to find his place in the world. The way that he could have been *anyone's* son illustrates the constrained conditions of grievability. For queer publics, Shepard was murdered in a specific space, motivated by rural perversion and hatred. McKinney and Henderson are not merely individual actors. They are "local boys" whose actions are indicative of a place and reiterate the danger of the country and the supposed safety of the city. In sum, bias against rural communities and bias against queer articulations collide in the piecing together of Shepard's memory.

Given that images of Shepard still perform affective labor, how might we be able to use those images to contest the cartography of the queer rural entangled within normative discourses of white cosmopolitan queerness and reimagine queers in the rural after a confrontation with violence? If bodies are produced by the spaces, myths, and practices that they inhabit and perform, then the scope of queer cultural politics can be imagined as a dynamic and open process. As Elizabeth Grosz reminds us, "There is no natural or ideal environment for the body, no 'perfect' city, judged in terms of the body's health and well-being. If bodies are not culturally pregiven, built environments cannot alienate the very bodies they produce."[49]

Deterritorializing queerness from the exclusive purview of the urban imaginary enables a less impoverished reflection on conditions of trauma and violence in the United States. To confront the structure of feeling that enables metronormative optics would mean to confront a collective responsibility to alter the conditions that legitimize violence against queer, trans-, and bodies of color within and outside of cityscapes and countrysides. If queerness is supple, shifting, and capable of multiple performances and articulations, queering citizenship enables a way to see queer country and call attention to the limited scopes of our capacity to grieve bodies that matter.

This case also demonstrates a need to be regionally diverse in the emerging field of rural queer studies. Rather than make universal claims about the operations of rural culture or practices, we must be more attuned to the ways particular topographical and regional relationships enable and constrain queer practices or formations. The visual memory of Matthew Shepard circulates relative to aesthetics and mythologies of the nonmetropolitan American West. Queering the rural necessitates a consideration of multiplicities of rural spaces and their constitutive historical contingencies. Each space has dynamic and often competing historical myths, and critics must explicate the contexts, places, and tactics that articulate queer presence in relation to material cultures. In so doing, critics can articulate a sense of how particular environments produce queer feelings, intimacies, and kinships, as well as identify how they matter in the politics of place and belonging.

In the context of Shepard's case, it also means remembering depicted moments that did not receive heavy circulation. For example, after Shepard's case consumed the nation, when Fred Phelps and the Westboro Baptist Church traveled to Laramie to engage in a notorious "God Hates Fags" style of anti-gay activism, a large group of local queer students and their allies participated in "Angel Action" in order to block his protest from public view. (Such an action involves production of yellow armbands with green circles meant to symbolize peace and acceptance in the face of viciousness.) In 1998, the armbands were in high demand for homecoming activities, and the symbol also found its way to the backs of the helmets of the University of Wyoming's football team. In 2003, on the five-year anniversary of Shepard's death, the armbands were seen again, in resistance to Phelp's return to Laramie. The armbands continue to be used as a symbol of resistance and peace-making, animated by the local memory of Shepard. But for national public memory, queer and non-queer, these images are long forgotten.

These acts of local grief, forgotten by the national melodrama that encompasses Matthew Shepard's memory, constitute another version of public memory worthy of scholarly inquiry. Although Shepard became an icon in the national imaginary, generating decades of cultural production, we have yet to truly consider the ways in which *local* cultures of grief were constituted in Laramie, Wyoming, and the larger Rocky Mountain region. Future scholarship might attend to the hidden transcripts of Matthew Shepard's memory, examining how rural queer formations in Laramie interact with queer urbanisms and gestures of disgust or sympathy. My analysis of dominant public memory illustrates how the place of rurality, typified by the rural West, becomes consumed by urban publics who desire to remove themselves from responding to conditions of violence. Yet to say that Shepard's loss destroyed possibilities for rural queers in Laramie is far from the truth. In turning to local queer performances and productions of space, perhaps scholars can better understand how queer cultures emerge through trauma—in both the exceptional and the everyday.

NOTES

1 Loffreda, *Losing Matthew Shepard*, viv.

2 FBI Hate Crime Statistics, 1998, https://www.fbi.gov/about-us/cjis/ucr/hate-crime/1998/hatecrime98.pdf.

3 In reading the image, I think "queer public" attempts to illuminate a sense of belonging to an imagined community. Anderson, *Imagined Communities*.

4 These two perspectives on trauma are inspired by Cvetkovich, *An Archive of Feelings*.

5 Generally, I situate Matthew Shepard's public memory in relation to gay and lesbian politics because the iconization of Shepard circulated in relation to these discourses. When I evoke the term "queer," I do so to mark an "umbrella" public and imagined community that includes many forms of self-identification, rather than as a term of explicit identification or anti-essential positionality.

6 Miller, *The Well-Tempered Self*; Berlant, *The Queen of America Goes to Washington City*; Berlant, *The Female Complaint*.

7 Isin, *Being Political*.

8 Schudson, *The Good Citizen*.

9 By "emotional relation" I am taking up how Sara Ahmed imagines queer emotion as an orientation. See Ahmed, *The Cultural Politics of Emotion*.

10 Herring, *Another Country*; Halberstam, *In a Queer Time and Place*; Weston, "Get Thee to a Big City"; Gray, *Out in the Country*.

11 Halberstam, *In a Queer Time and Place*, 36–37.

12 Herring, *Another Country*, 15–16.

13 Williams, *Marxism and Literature*.

14 Gould, *Moving Politics*.

15 On how metronormativity emerges temporally, see Herring, *Another Country*, 16.

16 West, *Transforming Citizenships*, 21.

17 Walters, *All the Rage*; Phelan, *Unmarked*, 11.

18 Gray, *Out in the Country*, 30–31.

19 Johnson, *Sweet Tea*, 109.

20 Herring, *Another Country*, 16.

21 Allen, *Talking with Strangers*, 4.

22 Hariman and Lucaites, "Visual Tropes and Late-Modern Emotion in U.S. Public Culture."

23 Hariman and Lucaites, "Public Identity and Collective Memory in U.S. Iconic Photography," 38.

24 Hariman and Lucaites, *No Caption Needed*, 9.

25 Eng and Kazanjian, preface to *Loss*, xiii.

26 Butler, *Precarious Lives*, 20.

27 Dunn, "Remembering Matthew Shepard," 611–52.

28 Ott and Aoki, "The Politics of Negotiating Public Tragedy," 487.

29 Ibid., 489.

30 Loffreda, *Losing Matthew Shepard*, 27.

31 On race as a "regime of looking" see Seshadri-Crooks, *Desiring Whiteness*. For the visualization of class as a habitus, see Bourdieu, *Distinction*.

32 I use identification to understand a particular mode of persuasion. See Burke, *A Rhetoric of Motives*, 21; Bennett, *Banning Queer Blood*, 3.

33 These are questions inspired by my reading of Cvetkovich.

34 DeLuca, "Unruly Arguments," 9–21; Harold and DeLuca, "Behold the Corpse," 267.

35 Patterson, *The Whole World Was Watching*, 141 (emphasis in original).

36 Johnson, "The Scene in Wyoming," 122–24.

37 Scarry, *The Body in Pain*, 35.

38 Ott and Aoki, "The Politics of Negotiating Public Tragedy," 495.

39 Herring, *Another Country*, 8.

40 See Calhoun, "Imagining Solidarity," which is pertinent for Calhoun's treatment and delineation of marked publics, unmarked publics, and counterpublics. "Queer urbanisms" is a phrase used by Herring, *Another Country*, 22.

41 Cloke and Little, Introduction, 1.

42 Bell, "Anti-Idyll," 94.

43 Gladstone, "Jackson, Wyoming."

44 Minkowitz, "Love and Hate in Laramie."

45 Bell, "Anti-Idyll," 106.

46 Gerard Wright, "Gay Grief in Cowboy County," *Guardian*, March 27, 1999, http://www.guardian.co.uk/books/1999/mar/27/books.guardianreview7?INTCMP=SRCH.

47 See Massey, *For Space*; Lefebvre, *The Production of Space*.

48 de Certeau, *The Practice of Everyday Life*, 117.

49 Grosz, *Space, Time, and Perversion*, 109.

14

Queering the American Frontier

*Finding Queerness and Sexual Difference in Late Nineteenth-
Century and Early Twentieth-Century Colorado*

ROBIN HENRY

It is not only time for queerness and gender-nonconformity scholarship
to leave the city; it is time for it to leave the twentieth century. Recently,
scholars such as J. Jack Halberstam, David Bell, and John Howard have
begun to challenge the concept of metronormativity for queer spaces
and to examine rural areas as locations of queerness and gender nonconformity.[1] The majority of this work focuses on the United States after
1945, a period of time on the cusp of contemporary sexual politics and
queer activist movements. This scholarly rural turn illuminates the ways
in which men and women use and identify the countryside as a space
of queerness.

This rural turn is also a romantic one, featuring bucolic farmland and
small towns, which represent only a portion of the rural. The countryside can also be a space of temporary leisure, ripe for sexual freedom. As
Linda McCarthy points out, however, we need to question the dichotomy between rural and urban, look beyond Rhoda Halpern's "shallow
rural," and examine more closely the "deep rural"—a locus that accommodates for class, race, and region in multiple narratives of sexuality.[2] In
this essay, I follow Nicholas Syrett and Colin R. Johnson, who examine
prewar queerness, but push the temporal line farther back into the late
nineteenth and early twentieth centuries, when Americans sensed that
the frontier, if not entirely closed, was more settled.[3]

Additionally, I question assumptions of rural-as-farmland and rural-
as-idyllic by examining queerness in turn-of-the-century Colorado
mining and resort communities. Containing elements of both urban
and rural, leisure and work, the Colorado frontier presents a com-

plicated arena in which to examine queerness and its connections to capitalism and the state. Off the farms and away from the weekenders, frontier queerness and gender nonconformity challenges notions of the rural as idyllic, while simultaneously confronting more commonly held perceptions—void of industry, multiculturalism, and sexual plurality—that Americans and scholars still have of the American West.

Though the New Western History addresses issues of gender, class, race, and sexuality, Americans continue to hold a false image of the trans-Mississippi West. Stereotypical cowboys, Native Americans, covered wagons, and homesteaders existed, but so did lawyers, judges, and courthouses. The image of lawlessness, however, rarely included queerness. With frontier Colorado as my historical landscape, I examine how three communities—the mining camp of Georgetown, the tourist town of Steamboat Springs, and the company town of Pueblo—dealt with sexual difference. As Colorado transformed from a mining frontier into an industrial state, communities cracked down on gender nonconformity and queer spaces disappeared.

Sexuality represents one of the newer frames of investigation in the history of the American West, with newer work examining masculinity, and queerness in the West. By examining gender nonconformity along the Colorado frontier, as well as the language used to describe it, I intend to complicate both the history of the American West and queer studies. Even with source limitations, the late nineteenth- and early twentieth-century American West provides an interesting landscape in which to observe same-sex relations and changing reactions to queerness over time. These reactions come in two main forms: state and non-state responses. Though recent works by Margot Canaday and Pippa Holloway discuss the origins of state-sanctioned homophobia in the postwar United States, I suggest that state and non-state institutions advocated for closing queer spaces in the West at the turn of the twentieth century.[4] Looking closely at three queer experiences of the time, I suggest possibilities for a more complex narrative of rural queerness and masculinity in the American West.

A note about the word "queer": this is a word that is both broad and narrow and has transitioned from a slur to a word of empowerment and identity. In a scholarly context, "queer" most often describes post-twentieth-century gender nonconformity in relation to identity politics, which, as Eve Sedgwick observes, comes out of a growing field of gay and lesbian criticism.[5] While I intend to examine spaces of gender non-conformity, the men I discuss did not identify as "homosexual." "Same-sex," a term Leila Rupp prefers to "queer," "gay," or "homosexual," may also be misleading, particularly with respect to activities that are sexual, such as kissing and touching, but that fall short of intercourse.[6] Thus the word "queer"—a space situated outside of accepted sexual norms—seems more appropriate.

From "Harmless Incident" to "Unspeakable Crime"

In 1870, Charles Emerson, a lawyer from Portland, Maine, headed west to Colorado. In Portland, he had worked for the family law firm, which specialized in monetary reclamations.[7] In the course of tracking down western-bound debt evaders, Emerson developed the desire to migrate himself. Like many men of his generation, he had grown up reading stories about life on the frontier, and now he sought his own adventure.

With his family's support, Charles Emerson left Portland and traveled by train to Leavenworth, Kansas. Two days later, he took a stagecoach to Georgetown, Colorado. Upon arriving, Charles staked a claim and panned for gold. In addition, he studied the business and science of mining, and eventually developed and invented.[8] Over a period of twenty years, Emerson grew as a miner, an inventor, and a businessman. He also engaged in same-sex relationships.[9] Because mining district laws and social customs in 1870 did not specifically address sexual behavior or sexuality, for Charles Emerson, the mines became a place where hard work and personal freedom coexisted. Though individual freedom lay at the center of the construction of western masculinity, same-sex relationships did not.

In 1877, Edwin Emerson joined his brother. Like his brother, Edwin saw many possibilities in Colorado—wealth, business opportunities, and personal freedom.[10] From Charles's letters, Edwin knew about the possibilities that awaited him. Charles had described life in Colorado as "exhilarating and hard, carefree yet filled with worry." Charles remarked that he was able to "work hard and make money, and, more importantly live as [he chose] away from New England women who harbor eternal winter in their stare, demeanor, and endless demands."[11] To both Emerson brothers, "Mother" Emerson (as they referred to her) represented one such demanding, New England matron. Throughout her letters, she appears concerned that her sons not fall into the rough life she had heard about in Colorado, and to take care to associate with "the same type of men that [they] knew in Portland."[12]

Like many miners, the Emersons came from a middle-class family. They had worked as bankers and lawyers, and through correspondence, maintained their business and family connections from afar. Adventure may have lured them westward, but pragmatic concerns consumed their days. While both men worked seven days a week in the mines, Charles involved himself in engineering, leaving Edwin to oversee the business. The Emersons' story is not remarkable. While it challenges a myth perpetuated by dime-store novels, their lives of hard work, ingenuity, and risk follow a typical narrative of frontier economic development.

What makes their story, and Charles's in particular, different is that Charles Emerson had several sexual encounters with men, and this leads us to examine individual freedom along the frontier anew. Nineteenth-century male friendships had a more emotional tone than contemporary friendships do, as scholars such as Jonathan Ned Katz and Donald Yacovone have shown.[13] Letters, expressing friends' yearnings to be closer to one another, demonstrate male friendship as a bonding emotional connection made in boyhood, but one that did not, in most cases, included a sexual bond. In the case of Charles Emerson's relationships with other men, there are limits to what we, as historians, can know. Nonetheless, in his writings, Charles described his experiences with different men using different language. Additionally, he never mentioned women or the desire for a wife, and he never married. Of course, this fact alone does not suggest that he desired men, but letters exchanged between Edwin and "Mother" Emerson note his lack of interest in women and marriage, going so far as to identify it as a "sign [he is] not trying to stop [his] socially delinquent behavior."[14] Charles Emerson's sexual behavior demonstrates what Katz acknowledges as a part of a broad spectrum of male sexuality in the nineteenth century, without using the twentieth-century nomenclature of "homosexual" and "heterosexual."

Both Charles's diary entries and Edwin's alluded to Charles's same-sex activity, although whereas Charles mentioned several same-sex sexual encounters, Edwin never discussed sexual activity explicitly.

Correspondence, however, does reveal disapproval, particularly in letters exchanged between Edwin and 'Mother' Emerson and Edwin and F. Bradford. Both "Mother" Emerson and Bradford, a trusted family friend and business partner, refer to Charles's "personal sin" and "sinful habit" and to his behavior as a "misunderstanding God's law."[15] Returning from a trip to Colorado, Bradford wrote to a mutual friend, Charles M. Harris, disclosing that "Charles appears to be in the same habit of living with men." Harris responded that "he vowed to keep perfectly quiet about the actions of [Charles and his] habits with other men." While Charles's family and friends never mentioned Charles's sexual activity as a liability to his work or their economic security, their comments suggest that, while they did not vilify their brother, son, and friend, they also did not condone his behavior.

Though anti-vice and reform movements held sway in many American cities and towns, their success depended on local support. In the 1870s, for example, an anti-sexual vice movement gained support in New York City, where it sought to ban public sex, such as prostitution, and the solitary vice, masturbation. Reformers such as Anthony Comstock derided such activities as "nothing more than thinly veiled acts of sexualized play and mutual stimulation in public."[16] Though Portland, Maine, was no New York City, it fell under the mantle of reform. "Mother"Emerson, participated in several anti-vice campaigns, and attended public lectures on eliminating vice from society. From New York to Portland, however, a social and civic infrastructure and a well-established middle class proved essential for reform movements to take root and advocate change in the community. In the 1870s, Charles Emerson's "immorality" would not matter in Colorado unless it threatened industrial production or private property, but even if it did, Georgetown did not have the infrastructure to successfully prosecute him.

In 1871, Charles Emerson recorded his experiences visiting his mines in central Colorado. These week-long trips meant spending a few days at each camp before moving on to the next mine. On September 17, he wrote that he walked twenty miles to Georgetown for a mine inspection, where he stayed at the McCleory house. Overnight, he slept with John Fillius, a miner who worked for the Emersons. In itself this was not unusual since men often slept together when space dictated.

Other comments, however, show subtle differences between Charles's encounter with Fillius and experiences with other men that demand a second look. For one thing, he slept with Fillius more than once, including at his own home in Georgetown. In fact, every time he mentioned sleeping with Fillius, or later with Mr. Van, Charles wrote that he "had a pleasant time," "enjoyed [him]self immensely," "relaxed well with him," and "spent an emotional evening with him."[17] Juxtapose these entries with those recording work trips with Edwin: When Charles and Edwin shared a bed, Charles's wrote in his journal, "bedded with Edwin." The entries do not contain comments concerning pleasure. Moreover, when Edwin traveled without Charles, he noted that he spent the night with other men; but unlike Charles, Edwin's entries do not mention pleasure or sentiment.

What allowed Charles to live outside of accepted nineteenth-century sexual norms? We can extrapolate only limited information from these brief diary entries by looking at the patterns of exposition as well as the silences of the Emersons. Being part of the middle class helped; Charles had greater access to private spaces and institutional power that might, if needed be persuaded to turn a blind eye to Charles's sexual habits. Additionally, as in many other mining towns, Georgetown laws focused on property and less on social propriety, with the exception of a broad, ill-defined nuisance law, stating that "every act of commission or mission which may affect the public health or convenience shall be regarded as a nuisance."[18] A staple of western jurisprudence, the nuisance law reflected more of a holdover from common law than a tool of social control. The 1870 mining towns, not wanting to get a reputation as inhospitable, used nuisance laws to protect property. For the moment, Georgetown residents who knew about his sexual behavior did not view it as a threat to property, and therefore it did not warrant discussion outside the private exchange. In addition, his status as an upstanding resident and businessman of Georgetown granted him a level of protection from scrutiny if it had become known more widely.

Finally, Charles and Edwin's diaries reveal aspects of Charles's sexual activity, not only for what they say, but for what Edwin leaves out. Both Emersons typified male diary-keeping in the nineteenth century. While Charles's diary contains emotional entries, Edwin, by contrast, did not expound on emotions and sentiments, but used his diary as a way to keep track of appointments. Any additional information, no matter how small, marks a departure from the ordinary. Between 1877 and 1898 both Charles and Edwin remained consistent in their writing style and use of diaries. Charles's entries express pleasure, emotion, and enjoyment in his encounters with John Fillius and Mr. Van. Edwin's entries note when he "beds with" traveling partners, but do not display emotional overtures.[19]

On December 1, 1873, Charles Emerson took a business trip to New York City for the mines. According to his journal, he first settled into his hotel, wrote a quick letter to "Mother" Emerson, and then went for a walk to Forty-Second Street, where he "looked for a boy—unsuccessfully."[20] In the geography of prostitution, Forty-Second Street was a place of interest for men seeking sexual pleasure, including from other men.[21] Upon returning to Colorado, Charles Emerson made several more entries during 1873 and 1874 referring to sleeping with men, but by mid-1874, he mentioned only sleeping and staying longer periods of time with Mr. Van.[22] In his entry for November 25, 1874, Emerson wrote that he "spent another wonderful evening with Mr. Van. We slept together and took a mint bath in the morning. We had much pleasure and joy in our encounter."[23] Not only was this account lengthy for Emerson, but it represents one of his most personal entries. Though Charles Emerson's subsequent journals either did not exist or were lost, his brother continued to refer to him living in Colorado, sometimes living and spending time with Mr. Van.[24]

Charles Emerson's situation is particularly interesting because of its location. Georgetown, Colorado, in the 1870s was undoubtedly frontier living. However, the development of mining into an industry juxtaposed the rural with the urban. There is nothing bucolic about mining sluice and industrial sills. It was also a place for simultaneously escaping and embracing freedom and capitalistic endeavors, which gave Emerson personal freedom at the time, although, as we will see later in this essay, a process of closing down queer spaces along the frontier in the name of economic development and propriety soon set in. Finally, Emerson's story challenges long-held ideas about the American West. Outside of the 2005 cinematic adaptation of Annie Proulx's story *Brokeback Mountain*, most Americans do not incorporate queerness in to western masculinity. Even when gay cowboys, a staple in the gay club scene, surfaced briefly in mainstream lexicon, western and frontier queerness remained on the outskirts, more as titillation than as serious endeavor to complicate the narrative about western masculinity.[25]

As Colorado's economy flourished, boosterism, or the practice of enthusiastically championing a cause, or in this case, the economic opportunities of this growing territory, helped transform Colorado from a frontier state into a national economic and tourist powerhouse. But at what cost? When long-term residents and business proprietors boosted their state to the nation, they inevitably encountered the belief that Colorado was the lawless frontier. Community leaders believed that in order to compete for eastern investors, they needed to begin addressing this image problem themselves. Curbing rumors of social and sexual license in the West was high on the list. In February and March of 1884, Denver police arrested men on four separate occasions for "dressing in women's clothing and parading around town in a disorderly fashion." On March 2, the *Rocky Mountain News* reported, "these men had been seen in such a state several times prior. . . . There [was] now felt a need to crackdown on such behavior."[26] When they were arrested under Denver's vague nuisance statute, it became clear that the interpretation of "nuisance" had shifted. Though cross-dressing did not directly destroy property, Denver leaders interpreted this action as an indirect threat to the potential economic gain and property development from eastern capital.

Cases like this one demonstrate a change in the interpretation of nuisance laws in Colorado in the 1880s and 1890s to include sexual crimes. Newspapers accounts and police dockets show that under the original interpretation of nuisance laws, these men did not commit a crime. But reading social disruption as an economic threat, Denver police viewed the challenge to established sexual norms as potentially costing the city and the state national investments. Thus, Coloradoans began to infuse sexual activities with the potential to disrupt economic, social, and political infrastructures. At the same time, the capitalist principles of efficiency, productivity, and control of energy defined increasingly manhood in the American West, replacing the image of "rugged individualism" mythologized in early accounts and stories of the West. As Denver resident Robert Dickinson observed in the *Rocky Mountain News*, "Since the railroad, the people who come are soft and without patience. They don't come to work, but to buy and rule. It's a new breed, maybe even a new man that now inhabits the Colorado gold fields and towns."[27] As Dickinson's criticism suggests, not all Denverites welcomed this new breed of capitalist frontiersmen, but as more businessmen and entrepreneurs arrived in Colorado, sentiments like Dickinson's took a backseat to expanded economic visions that emphasized the connections between the local and national economies. The 1880s and 1890s were crucial decades for those Coloradoans who believed that the state's reputation as a rough-and-tumble frontier community hindered large-scale economic growth and development. As Thomas Andrews points out, however, when the economic tide turned away from the miners toward businessmen and outside investors, local attitudes about miners' characters changed as well.[28] This shift included a reinterpretation of nuisance laws and adoption of statutes designed to align sexual and social behavior with the middle-class capitalist values of efficiency, production, and control.

Panic at the Bathhouse

Robert Dickinson's musing in the *Rocky Mountain News* notes that the skills needed to succeed in Colorado had changed. He also observed that instead of coming to work side by side with other miners, a "new breed" of men came to "buy and rule" in a way that emphasized class distinctions. Applying the marketplace principles of efficiency, production, and control to a definition of manhood required more supervision, more top-down monitoring that conflicted with western men's recognized level of privacy. While these changes were felt in mining towns, pressure to present a lawful image of Colorado affected tourist towns as well. In the 1880s and 1890s, the town of Steamboat Springs became one of the first communities to attempt to look beyond mining and to capitalize on western tourism by developing resorts for this "new breed" of investor.

A man by the name of James F. Crawford was influential in this process. In 1874, Crawford discovered the snowy, isolated land between the Yampa River and the Elk River Valley that would later become the ski resort town of Steamboat Springs. Crawford was not the first to discover this area; for almost fifty years, the Ute Indians had been feeling the pressure from migrating trappers, ranchers, and miners.[29] Disregarding the Utes and migrating backwoodsmen, Crawford had big visions and large plans for the fledgling mining community. He imagined Steamboat Springs catering to middle-class tourists, who wanted to experience the wilderness of the West, but did not necessarily want to leave their comforts and values behind.

Immediately there were problems, however. Steamboat Springs's leaders had decided that they wanted to build a bathhouse to compete in the growing market of natural springs spas and resort hotels that were popular along the East Coast and to provide economic stability to the town in the hopes of increasing its population. In order to carve out a niche for Steamboat Springs in this market, the bathhouse needed to cater to both the region's industrial investors and out-of-state visitors. The leaders also knew that in order for Steamboat Springs to prosper, they needed to present it as a safe, clean resort community, not a frontier town.[30] In fact, Crawford's vision for Steamboat Springs became a reality only in the latter part of twentieth century.

From the beginning, the town faced obstacles to becoming a world-class resort town. First and foremost, geography created obstacles. While Crawford believed that the remote location would appeal to travelers, Steamboat Springs remained virtually inaccessible to all but the heartiest frontiersmen and women until the railroad arrived in 1909. Second, founded by a joint-stock company, it was built, developed, marketed, and run by committee. In order to foster interest in Steamboat Springs, the town company decided to sell stock to outside investors. In a letter to A. J. MacKey, a town officer and original investor, another Steamboat Springs investor, P. A. Burgess, noted that there were problems getting the stock issued in a timely manner, and that this anomaly would cost the company a lot of new investors. At the same time, the problem with the stock also chased away old investors, who left the town underdeveloped, with marshy streets and partially completed buildings. Therefore, Steamboat Springs offered few conveniences to attract either investors or visitors.[31]

In 1884 the Steamboat Springs town company decided to build the bathhouse anyway to improve investment possibilities, and within three years, prospects for the town appeared to improve. Two years later, MacKey received a letter from investment advisor J. W. Crawford suggesting that an office should be installed at the bathhouse to oversee the business:[32]

I am persuaded it would be for the best for the bath building by keeping it clean and in order. Hoodlums and vandals would not conduct themselves distastefully in shameful ways that I shall not discuss nor disfigure the building and occupy the baths and buildings for hours at a time to the exclusion of dozens of good people who may be waiting on the ground for needed baths—as is and has been the case many times. This would call for a very small outlay for building an office at the bath.[33]

There were two reasons for this reaction. First, the baths had developed a reputation for attracting men who "engaged in unnatural sexual encounters while bathing."[34] Though correspondence of town-company investors indicates that only a handful of such indents actually occurred, they made quite a negative impression on investors—so much so that even when they ceased occurring in 1887, Crawford and MacKey continue to worry and write about the incidents for almost another decade. Crawford believed that hiring a bathhouse keeper and building an office would ensure, "behavior improper for a bathhouse of our caliber" would not happen again. The investors worried, however, that the stories would leak out to tourists, who might forego visiting Steamboat Springs on their tours of Colorado, deeming it "too rowdy."[35]

The second reason for the reaction is that when an outside investor attempted to build a saloon in town, MacKey received requests that the town officers block the saloon. Thoughts turned again to the bathhouse "incident" and to the general reputation of Colorado and Steamboat Springs. In a letter to MacKey dated July 2, 1895, Crawford wrote that the saloon intended to sell "whiskey and other lowly liquor generally associated with ruffians."[36] He was concerned that even though the saloon would make money for Steamboat Springs, it would undoubtedly limit Steamboat Springs as a tourist destination for elite travelers. Steamboat Springs resident Mrs. Jenny Bennetto seemed to feel similarly about the saloon. In a letter to MacKey dated January 2, 1896, she wrote

I here take the liberty to inform you that the saloon element are circulating a petition for consent of Co. to retail intoxicating drinks, on the other hand property owners *and* many residents are strongly opposed to it— not only for its moral blight, but as a financial disadvantage. This being a natural health resort—to be visited by a class of people who would find saloons with their victims a great drawback to the comfort and gratitude of the place.

Some of the real estate owners say they would proceed to legal protest. I think a petition will be sent to you soon against the saloon blight. . . . I learn you have an annual meeting soon. I trust you will pardon the liberty I take to apprise you of the feeling of many against license.

What Bennetto expressed in her letter was not just her own anxiety, but a general concern for the direction of development in the community. She believed that if Steamboat Springs was going to cater to an elite crowd, it could not present itself in the "shadow of Leadville," notorious Colorado mining town with a national reputation for gambling, fighting, and prostitution.[37] The baths and the community needed to be clean and display a level of control in order to place visitors at ease.

In Colorado, the first wave of behavior regulation came with enforcing local anti-vice and anti-prostitution laws. Even though the Colorado General Assembly had passed several laws that targeted vice, they remained virtually unenforced. By the 1890s, local reformers from Boulder, Cripple Creek, Denver, Aspen, and Steamboat Springs took the lead in vice regulation and gained real sway in local politics and law enforcement.[38]

Like Steamboat Springs, Aspen turned to tourism at the close of the nineteenth century to boost its economy. Though Aspen had had success as a mining town, its fortunes were tied entirely to the silver industry, and when Congress repealed the Sherman Silver Purchase Act in 1893, Aspen's economy plummeted. According to police records prior to 1894, arrests were primarily for public nuisances against property or drunken disruption, resembling arrest patterns in other mining communities. Beginning in 1894, however, two incidents occurred that concerned Aspen officials. First, on February 18, Aspen police arrested Perry H. Storer and John W. Atkinson for acts of buggery and sodomy.[39] In itself, this incident, the first arrest of its kind in Aspen, marks a change in policing behavior in Pitkin County. Moreover, there was an additional twist in that the police recorded Storer as being "better known as Eliza Fisher" and also charged him with "dressing counter to gender." Over the next few months, there were a string of arrests for "dressing counter to gender."[40] In the newspaper Aspenites discussed these incidents with concern for the reputation of their town.[41]

Like Steamboat Springs, Aspen wanted to compete as a tourist destination for wealthy Coloradoans and eastern tourists. Incidents like cross-dressing helped reinforce reputations for lawlessness that stigmatized mining communities. The communities of both Steamboat Springs and Aspen communities realized that even rumors of sexual indiscretions could dissuade tourists. Their attempts to harness sexual behavior remained focused on using the nuisance laws, though in an expanded form. Now they interpreted the phrases about protecting property not only to mean the tangible destruction of property, but also the economic destruction wrought by sexual misconduct.

In Order to Form a More Perfect Worker

In the wake of the labor strikes that took place at the Colorado Fuel and Iron Company (CF&I) in southern Colorado during the winter and early spring of 1913–1914, John D. Rockefeller, Jr., came to see his workers' social, cultural, and sexual differences as contributing to an overall sentiment of unrest. In 1914, John D. Rockefeller, Sr., transferred majority shareholding of CF&I to his son, John D. Rockefeller, Jr., Unfortunately for Junior, he also acquired blame for years of mismanagement and built up frustration toward mine leadership over low pay, weights and measurement supervisors who favored management, dangerous work conditions, and unionization. For months following the strikes, the deadliest in the nation's history, he received letters from the public, some expressing sympathy with an anti-union stance, but others increasingly deriding his callous treatment of his workers and their families. In these letters, Americans such as J. W. Ogden of Lynchburg, Virginia, questioned not only his business acumen, but more hurtful to Rockefeller, his commitment to his Christian values. Like many Progressive-era businessmen, Rockefeller believed that his business ventures were guided by the Protestant ethos, and so it was with great horror that he found himself having to defend his business and his faith in the wake of these events.

In the aftermath of this public and personal crisis, Rockefeller attempted to present a new image to the American public by transforming himself into a hands-on business owner. Immediately following the labor strikes known as the Colorado Coal Wars, he visited his western mines annually, but his visits became less frequent by the 1920s. Instead, he relied on men such as Dr. Peter Roberts of the YMCA's Industrial Department to send reports on relations between management and labor. Rockefeller became interested in introducing his workers to the Young Men's Christian Association (YMCA). In one of his reports, Roberts observed that by 1918 "the whole town revolve[d] around CF&I, but the social life revolved around the YMCA baseball club."[42] He concluded that the popularity of the baseball team and of the YMCA in general accounted for the decline in crime. He also observes that, "sexually suspect and undesirable citizens are eliminated [from CF&I and its company towns] as soon as possible. They are a threat to the stability of the community. Anything that threatens the stability of the community threatens the efficiency of the work week and the company."[43] Through social, economic, and cultural means, Roberts wanted to pressure "sexually suspect and undesirable citizens" to either reform their ways or leave CF&I and its company towns.

What Roberts meant exactly by "sexually suspect people" remains unknown, but this statement marks a difference from earlier attitudes and methods of dealing with queerness. First, he identified "sexually suspect people" as a problem that CF&I needed to address. Second, Roberts acknowledged the role that sexual behavior had in the construction of a stable community. Where earlier mining communities ignored aberrant sexual behavior in order to attract as many people as possible to their towns, mine owners now understood sexual behavior had the potential to threaten the stability and growth of their company.

While the Rockefellers and the YMCA had similar goals, the workers had mixed feelings. Many did participate in YMCA programs, such as baseball teams, Bible groups, and English and hygiene classes. But it is difficult to know what impact participating in these events had on the workers' sexual behaviors. Maybe the largely immigrant workforce took the opportunity to Americanize—the process of acquiring the personal and work habits of the white, Protestant middle class—and maybe they participated because of overwhelming pressure. Anecdotal evidence supports the latter. According to the final report on conditions in CF&I company towns, while pressure to shop at the company store decreased after 1914, the workers still perceived pressure to participate in company-run activities.[44]

Arrest records and court documents from Pueblo, Colorado—the largest CF&I company town and seat of the largest YMCA in southern Colorado—also demonstrate changes in criminal activity after the strike. Between 1916 and 1922, arrests for public intoxication, prostitution, and cross-dressing declined. A closer look at the punishments for these crimes, however, reveals a more complex story. During this seven-year period, arrests might have declined, but the punishments and fines increased in severity. Fines for public intoxication increased from $1.25 to two dollars; fines for prostitution increased by seventy-five cents, and in two cases resulted in a night spent in jail. The arrests of two men, John Darby and Daniel McCourt, for the "crime against nature" require a bit more explanation. Like most states, Colorado had adopted a sodomy law, but local police and state officers had never used it. As the vague wording of nuisance laws proved unhelpful to prosecutors, cities, under pressure from civic and social improvement organizations, began to explore alternative legal avenues. The Pueblo police chose to arrest Darby and McCourt very explicitly under the state statute "crime against nature." Choosing to use the more specific, more severe state sodomy law, and not change Darby and McCourt with a lesser charge of vagrancy or public nuisance marked a clear departure from the ways in which known same-sex activity had been dealt with before.[45]

The reference to the "crime against nature" sparked debate in both the police docket and the court of public opinion. The notes are limited, and there is no trial transcript because there was no trial. The fact that the "crime against nature" statute was being used, however, created an argument. One officer wanted to "invoke Colorado's law specific to this crime," the state sodomy statute, and the other officer wanted to deal with Darby and McCourt with local vagrancy and public nuisance laws His solution was to have them pay a fine of twenty dollars each, spend a week in the local jail, and banish them from town. In the end, Pueblo used the threat of law enforcement as deterrent, but it is clear that sodomy no longer was a crime that could be ignored. The *Pueblo Daily News* wrote a brief opinion piece about the arrests, declaring Darby and McCourt "disgraces to Pueblo and all that Mr. Rockefeller has done for us!"[46] This sentiment declared that the Jenny Bennetto of Colorado had won the war over regulating queerness.

Rockefeller's reconstruction plan worked in decreasing the number and severity of future labor strikes, but his support of cultural and social Americanization programs helped curtail vice and limit expressions of sexual and gender nonconformity in Colorado mining towns. Though miners continued to go on strike from time to time, the unrest never reached the same levels as 1914. The years following the implementation of Rockefeller's Industrial Employment Representation Plan and the cultural reconstruction efforts reflected the growing power of the middle class and Rockefeller's management class on the mores and behavior of the towns in southern Colorado. Though Pueblo officials chose not to prosecute Darby and McCourt under the state sodomy law, the changes that Rockefeller implemented allowed sexual reform and anti-vice organizations to gain power and continue to mount pressure not simply to regulate sexual difference in the state, but to use the powers of the state to eliminate queer spaces. In 1922 they proved successful. Colorado used its sodomy law for the first time in *People v. Wilkins*, sending Charles Wilkins to jail for a year.

Conclusion

These examples demonstrate the existence of queer life in late nineteenth- and early twentieth-century American West, though not always in ways that scholars of the twentieth century might identify readily as queer. In fact, piecing together the stories requires an extra keen eye for the details of people's lives, but even after careful reading, large parts of the sexual activity and desire of men like Charles Emerson remain elusive. Clearly, identifying queerness at the turn of the twentieth century is possible, but with limitations that do not define a specific political or social consciousness of identity. In the case of the Steamboat Springs bathhouse, Jenny Bennetto's decade-long struggle to eliminate same-sex activity remains a one-sided argument; we do not know anything about the men involved. In fact, beyond the rumors and her letters, no evidence exists that anything actually occurred at the bathhouse. John Darby and Daniel McCourt's arrest records are more apparent as evidence of queer behavior, as is the trial transcript for *People v. Wilkins* because they are part of the public record.

Police and court records, however, also tell only one side of the story; neither Darby nor McCourt left a testimony, a diary, or statements regarding their arrests. At his trial, Charles Wilkins spoke in his defense, but within the context of the court, his statements were clouded by the criminal justice system; we have only his courtroom testimony, with answers to the prosecutor's questions, not a personal statement. Though Wilkins alluded to previous same-sex encounters—making his story more closely recognizable as queer—he did not take on the newly defined identity of homosexual or attempt to hold on to a sexually free space that was quickly disappearing. What becomes clear is that the increased involvement of the state makes the existence of same-sex activity more evident, but it also signals the end of whatever tolerant space for queerness and gender nonconformity existed along the frontier. As the frontier closed down, so too did its ability to contain multiple sexualities comfortably.

Though limits exist as to what we can know about queerness along the frontier, any discussion challenges scholars of both queer studies and western U.S. history to expand their horizons and rethink long-held ideas of metro- and heteronormativity. However, what work in queer rural studies suggests in general, and this essay does in particular, is that the larger institutional trappings of progress—economic, social, political, and cultural—that we often identify with providing the opportunity for queer spaces to develop and mature and for political activism to take seed and flourish also have tendencies to shut down spaces of freedom and personal expression that were operating just fine without the help of civilizing forces.

NOTES

I would like to thank the participants of the Queering the Countryside Conference, held at Indiana University in November 2010 for their thoughtful insights.

1 Halberstam, *In a Queer Time and Place*, 36–37.

2 Halperin, *Cultural Economies Past and Present*, 150–52. McCarthy, "Poppies in a Wheat Field," 76-78.

3 Syrett, *The Company He Keeps*; Johnson, *Just Queer Folks*.

4 Canaday, *The Straight State*; Holloway, *Sexual Politics and Social Control in Virginia, 1920–1945*.

5 Sedgwick, *Epistemology of the Closet*, 47.

6 Rupp, "Toward a Global History of Same-Sex Sexuality," 288.

7 Charles Emerson (CE) to unknown correspondent, Portland, Maine, March 4, 1870, Emerson Family Papers (EFP), Western History Collection, Beinecke Rare Books and Manuscript Library, Yale University (hereafter referred to as Beinecke).

8 CE to F. Bradford, Colorado, April 6, 1871; CE to George P. Cahill GPC, November 30, 1871; John Lourillo to Edwin Emererson (EE), September 30, 1871, EFP, Beinecke.

9 CE diary, 1870–1882, EFP, Beinecke.

10 EE diary, March 8 and April 15, 1877, EFP, Beinecke.

11 CE to EE, September 13, 1873, EFP, Beinecke.

12 "Mother" Emerson to CE, October 5, 1879, EFP, Beinecke.

13 Yacovone, "Abolitionists and the Language of Fraternal Love"; Katz, *Love Stories*.

14 "Mother" Emerson to EE, April 4, 1880, EFP, Beinecke.

15 F. Bradford to EE, March 10, 1874; "Mother" Emerson to CE, April 13, 1870, July 23, 1870, and March 2, 1874; F. Bradford to Charles M. Harris, March 2, 1874, EFP, Beinecke.

16 Anthony Comstock, as quoted in Halttunen, *Confidence Men*, 56.

17 Diary entries, December 21, 1871–April 14, 1872, CE, EFP, Beinecke.

18 Nuisance law, *Georgetown Mining District Laws*, Georgetown, CO, 1859, Beinecke.

19 Diary entry, October 17, 1872, CE; diary entry June 20, 1878, EE, EFP, Beinecke.

20 Diary, December 1, 1873, CE, EFP, Beinecke.

21 Timothy Gilfoyle, *City of Eros*, 103–34.

22 Diary, February 4, 1874, CE, EFP, Beinecke.

23 Diary, November 25, 1874, CE, EFP, Beinecke.

24 Diary 1877–90, EE, EFP, Beinecke.

25 Annie Proulx, "Brokeback Mountain"; Ang Lee, "Brokeback Mountain" (2005), DVD.

26 Denver County Police Dockets, March 1, 1884, Western History Collection, Colorado State Historical Society; *Rocky Mountain News*, March 2, 1884, Western History Collection, Denver Public Library (hereafter referred to as DPL).

27 Robert Dickerson, "The Effects of Railroads on Our Towns," *Rocky Mountain News*, May 3, 1885, 2:1, DPL.

28 Andrews, *Killing for Coal*.

29 Crawford, *The Crawford House of Steamboat Springs*, 15.

30 Steamboat Springs Town Company founding documents, Western History Collection, Special Collections, University of Colorado, Boulder (hereafter referred to as UCB).

31 Letter exchange between P. A. Burgess and A. J. MacKey, November 14 and 25, 1880, and December 2, 1880, UCB.

32 James Hoyle to A. J. MacKey, December 31, 1887; J. W. Crawford to A. J. MacKey, January 11, 1889, Steamboat Springs, UCB.

33 J. W. Crawford to A. J. MacKey, February 16, 1889, Steamboat Springs, UCB.

34 Crawford to MacKey, April 29, 1889, Steamboat Springs, UCB.

35 Letter exchange, MacKey to Crawford, September 14, 1895, Crawford to MacKey, July 2, 1895, Steamboat Springs, UCB.

36 Crawford to MacKey, July 2, 1895, Steamboat Springs, UCB.

37 Mrs. Jenny Bennetto to MacKey, January 2, 1896, Steamboat Springs, UCB.

38 Citizens' Reform League," *Boulder County News*, 2:2, April 21, 1893;"Women's Temperance Meets Tonight," *Colorado City Iris*, 4:1, December 3, 1891, DPL.

39 Arrest of Perry H. Storer and John W. Atkinson, February 18, 1884, Pitkin County Policy Dockets, Pitkin County Sheriff's Office Archives, Aspen, CO (hereafter referred to as PCA).

40 Ibid.

41 "Man-Woman Arrested," *Aspen*, February 20, 1884, 3:2, Special Collections, Aspen Historical Society/Aspen Public Library.

42 Roberts, 2-4, Rockefeller Archives Center (hereafterRAC).

43 Roberts, 5, RAC.

44 Robert, 6–8, RAC; Winters, *Making Men, Making Class*, 47–50.

45 Arrest record for John Darby and Daniel McCourt, Pueblo Police Dockets, 1915–1920, 1920–1925, Colorado State Archives.

46 "Crime against Nature Arrests," *Pueblo Chieftain*, January 10, 1922, 4:2, DPL.

15

Digital Oral History and the Limits of Gay Sex

JOHN HOWARD

As the old joke goes, "If you're one in a million, there are ten of you in New York." And for good and for ill, this critical mass logic—intellectually validated by the rural-to-urban great gay migration narrative—has centrally informed place-based conceptions of queer sexualities, gender non-conforming lives, big city enclaves, and affinity groups organized around specialized erotic proclivities. Further, it has materially enabled queer studies research clusters at universities from San Francisco to London and, happily, Indiana. Still, like people, ideas travel, in multiple directions. Communication and transportation technologies have always mitigated distance, and though I may personally prefer real-time meetings one-to-one or in groups, I know virtual proximity also shapes my subjectivity. Even before new media, queer networks have spanned vast stretches. Though longer journeys may be infrequently undertaken, dependent in particular upon class and race, a savvy rural queer cosmopolitanism—on the road and ever more online—holds out extraordinary analytical promise, especially as set against a hegemonic urban gay provincialism.[1]

The hegemonies nonetheless persist. White. Gay. Male. Metropolitan. Elites. The oft-noted lamentable dominance of these groups within our wonderfully diverse, polymorphously perverse queer communities begs the questions: How did it happen? Why do these types and their tastes continue to hold sway? Whence cometh homonormativity?

In cultures organized primarily around gender and sexual dissidence, two key visual-textual products prove crucial: sex manuals and introduction services. Near the end of the twentieth century, one of each came to thoroughly dominate its genre. They remain in the ascendant today. As this essay argues foremost, though oppressive urban norms often circulate through them, radical rural resistance likewise can be—

and is—positioned from within, in part by marshalling rural critical masses, which is a technologically enabled but ethically vexed process. As such, this essay constitutes an experiment in crafting new ways of accessing previously inaccessible, non-white, non-normative, rural queer pasts—its principal methodological intervention. Thus, I first deconstruct one metronormative gay cultural product, the sex manual *The Joy of Gay Sex*, before demonstrating how we might reappropriate another, the website Gay.com, as we press new social media platforms into the service of illuminating our always highly mediated, always highly varied queer histories.[2]

In four sections, the essay first critiques the urbanist homonormative assumptions of this most influential gay sex manual ever published, performing a careful calculus of its exclusions and elisions and exposing the way in which a sexual act's purported infrequency is maligned as a normative inferiority: fewer equals lesser. Second, analyzing its illustrations, the essay argues that not only region and rurality but also race and class figure prominently in the manual's stigmatizing, pathologizing, and marginalizing discourses, which are redoubled by a second-person imperative voice, a rhetorical device producing insidious truth effects to bolster its problematic truth claims. Third, after a brief critique of the late twentieth century's most formidable gay website and after drawing a sample of rural and small-town "oral history" narrators therefrom, the essay examines three chat room digital histories to argue that rural sex practices including sitophilia and zoophilia can be—and are—on the one hand, successfully promulgated, and on the other, historically recuperated, via the site in a mutually-informing pair of queer counter-hegemonic interventions. Fourth, with reference to one particular narrative, the essay explores the advantages and potential pitfalls of this new digital queer history methodology, arguing that the paramount benefits are the capacity for rural narrators—on their own, at their computer—to participate in far-flung queer historical projects and to negotiate with greater accuracy and precision both aspects of *informed consent*. Finally, by way of conclusion, I position the intrusive scrutinizing habits of institutional review boards within the broader context of multiple constituent investments in queer scholarly projects, forcing a meditation on competing agendas and researchers' collectively constructed ethical agency.

A Very Small Percentage of Gay Men

Charles Silverstein and Edmund White's *The Joy of Gay Sex* was the first gay sex manual to be published by a major trade press, Crown of New York, in 1977. It has remained in print ever since. Many of its 120 alphabetized entries chronicle casual sex between friends and strangers in language that still reads as refreshingly liberationist. About BEAUTIES, the authors note: "People . . . like to slur someone who's very good-looking; beauties are often branded 'sluts' or 'whores,' though these words make little sense in a sexually permissive age. What, in fact, do they mean? That someone likes to have a lot of sex with a lot of people? What's so bad about that?" Many of the categories themselves suggest a libertinism born of 1960s and 1970s radicalism: CRUISING, DIRTY TALK, DOGGY STYLE, HALLUCINOGENS, MASTURBATION AND FANTASY, MIRRORS, NIBBLING AND BITING, NOISE-MAKING, ONE-NIGHT STANDS, PORNOGRAPHY, TEAROOMS, and BACK-ROOMS. The entry on BATHS, or bathhouses, perhaps best evidences the manual's urban bias and critical mass logic: "For sheer efficiency, the baths can't be bettered. At the baths making out is certain and more sex can be packed in per hour than anywhere else." As this entry suggests, more is more, and as we shall see, that evaluative judgment reigns, as it rules out rural spaces with less people, less capital, less public resources.[3]

As its second title boasts, *The Joy of Gay Sex* is moreover *An Intimate Guide for Gay Men to the Pleasures of a Gay Lifestyle*. There are entries on CIVIL RIGHTS, CONSCIOUSNESS RAISING, DEPRESSION, LONE-LINESS, SELF-ESTEEM, and MONEY MATTERS—which, interestingly enough, is not about sex work, but rather income disparities in coupled relationships. Here is manifested a tension running throughout the text. Is the book about gay sex or about gay men and their "lifestyle"? Does gay sex a gay man make? Can a straight man have gay sex? If so, does that necessarily make him one of the BISEXUALS? Is the book about sexual acts or sexual identities? Of course, it is about both. And more.

The book title suggests a dialectic between the two, mirroring the acts/identity dichotomy at the heart of lesbian and gay historiography. On the dedication page, first Dr. Charles Silverstein offers his tribute, "To William," his life partner. Edmund White dedicates his efforts to his numerous sex partners: "To all my tricks from Ed." Throughout the text, this productive contradiction looms: the homonormative imperative of a long-term monogamous dyadic relationship versus the queer desire for uninhibited sex with multiple partners, more readily located in the cities. But my concern here lies not so much with the potential normalizing force of monogamy—nor with the identity construction offered by a newly out-of-the-closet gay psychologist with an agenda for combating, in the words of one entry, the EMOTIONAL PROBLEMS OF GAYS. Rather, I want to understand how advice about intercourse—especially sex with abandon—can have an ascendant impact upon subjectivity for nonconformists and how it can stigmatize and foreclose options, even among those ostensibly committed to sexual liberation. Simply put, I want to ask how queer queer instruction can be.[4]

While offering descriptions and recommendations of various sexual practices, *The Joy of Gay Sex* purports to measure them. "There is a small minority of gay men," we are told in the entry on SCAT, "who like to make feces a part of the sex scene." By contrast, "almost every gay encounter" will include a BLOW JOB. "Facing your partner while you fuck," we are told (*contra* DOGGY STYLE), "is the position preferred over all others by most gay men"—heralding a homo missionary position. Though it may aspire to a statistical legitimacy modeled by Alfred Kinsey in the 1940s and 1950s, *The Joy of Gay Sex* cannot deliver reliable gauges of sexual acts. Proportional values are never presented as numerical percentages. Ostensible majority behaviors are asserted by an unsubstantiated "most": "most men do not come more than once or twice a night"; "most men fear that their cocks are not large enough"; and "if we are honest, most of us will admit we know what it's like to run on that [compulsive CRUISING] treadmill." "Many gay men—perhaps the majority—smoke dope at least from time to time." So-called majority views sometimes are made universal: "Everyone secretly dreams of approaching a man in a bar and saying 'Wanna fuck?'"

With or without statistics, a sex manual could never merely describe sexual acts—that is, give a dispassionate account of them in all their great diversity. Through the very selection of topics, the framing of categories, the language employed, and the judgments averred, sexual instruction actively popularizes some forms of sex and stigmatizes others. Thus a *gay* sex manual has the potential to affirm as it molds some gay men, marginalizes others, and helps set the boundaries of gay community. All too often, to assert a quantitative minority is to produce an evaluative minority; it is to equate infrequency with inferiority.[5]

Implicit throughout *The Joy of Gay Sex*, this quantitative-yields-qualitative, fewer-equals-lesser reasoning as applied to radical sex practices is extended to notions of rural homosexuality. Not only must such practices and peoples be fewer in number (inadequate critical masses); they must be lesser in caliber (inferior sexual cultures). As we see in the next section, like the celebratory account of BATHS above, the construction of ORGIES below springs from urban imaginaries and material conditions, which are highly classed and also insidiously raced. In section three, we see that *The Joy of Gay Sex*'s construction of rural archetypes, the lone cave dweller and isolated lumberjack, serves to illuminate not rural cultures but rather urban gay fantasies of a conventional cast.

Occasionally, the discursive assertion of a "minority" practice exposes its own panicky morality, as in *The Joy of Gay Sex* entry on WATER SPORTS. Long sex sessions that involve piss, we are repetitively told in a single brief passage, are "[1.] very much a minority taste and [2.] only a very small percentage of gay men go in for [them]. Indeed, [3.] few gay men are attracted by water sports." Say it three times, wave the magic wand, and it may go away altogether.

While acknowledging that fistfucking "is becoming more and more popular," the authors clearly aren't keen on it. The first words of the entry: "It's extremely dangerous." It's an irony of alphabetization that the entry on the FIRST TIME—not one's first sexual encounter with a man, but the inaugural act of receptive anal sex, specifically—is followed by the entry on FISTFUCKING. Of course, it's reasonable to assume that proceeding from one experience to the next might involve considerable time and practice. But Silverstein and White further valorize majority practices and discredit minority practices through the amount of attention they devote to each. The entry on the FIRST TIME encompasses five verbose pages, including tender ministrations to "breathe deeply and relax," "complimenting yourself" along the way. Fistfucking, particularly if it's so perilous but popular, would seem to require more meticulous instruction and elaboration of technique. Yet, it receives a scant page and a half.

Of further oversights and elisions, the two-and-a-half page entry on SADOMASOCHISM tells you nothing about spanking, flogging, or tying and untying knots. Instead, the authors demonize and pathologize S/M cultures, asserting that "the whole S and M scene is unusually given to taking drugs." Outfitted in "absurd get-ups," "many sadomasochists are also heavy drinkers." But as if to reassure readers, they add that "only a very few leather guys indulge in the scene" and "fewer than half the men strutting into leather bars are actually sadomasochistic"—implying further that majoritized straight-laced normal gays can, do, and should go wherever they want, minority refuge be damned. Still, to avoid being branded as prudes, Mr. White and Dr. Silverstein insist, in a doozy of a Freudian slip, that "only the hopelessly narrow-minded bourgeois or the amateur psychologist could dismiss the [S/M] phenomenon."[6]

The S/M entry, however, does occasion the authors' most significant reflection on societal inequities and power differentials. "Our culture is one based on a hierarchy of power, but in everyday life the power is clothed, not naked, hypocritical, not honest. Nevertheless parents do dominate children, men dominate women, whites dominate blacks, the rich dominate the poor, the boss dominates his or her employees, and straights dominate gays." It conspicuously stops there, just short of the forms of dominance that get played out *within* LGBT communities and as are so well-illustrated and perpetuated by this manual. Then it continues: "In S and M these relationships are dramatized and sometimes reversed," with those cowed by day becoming aggressive sexual players by night. S/M "allows partners to explore some of their previously repressed fantasies of domination and surrender, of cruelty and tenderness, of contempt and adulation. It also creates an exciting arena for ritual and sensual ceremony."

By producing minorities and majorities, norms and deviances, *The Joy of Gay Sex* effects exclusions within a community of the excluded. It further banishes certain behaviors and beings from that community. By cordoning off a statistical and evaluative center—namely, the commercialized youthful gay white male middle-class cultures of lower Manhattan, as we see in the next section—it asserts the right to define and disregard the peripheries: rural netherworlds and queer undergrounds. Some readers are thus left with the counterhegemonic project of reclaiming legitimacy. It is incumbent upon us not only to elaborate those defamed sexual practices, but also to shift the angle of vision back upon these two presumptuous authors of *The Joy of Gay Sex*. For as we see, they are indeed a very small percentage of gay men—a minority of two—who attempt to direct mainstream representations of gay sex, a monopolized gay cultural production.

You are [Edmund] White

As Edmund White is clearly charged with writing entries on sexual practice—as opposed to Silverstein's on "the gay lifestyle"—White's sexual desires and interests, masquerading as objective analysis, underwrite much of the volume's exclusions. This becomes most apparent in the entries on STEREOTYPES, which simply put are a bad thing, and TYPES, which if not a wholly good thing are depicted as immutable and thus fully to be accepted. So societal depictions of the stereotypical homosexual as pathological, for example, are to be denounced and fully exposed as constructed through particular medical and media discourses. But types—that is, the types of people to whom one is sexually attracted—are seen as essential, hard-wired, at the core of one's being—an unsurprising argument for men who have struggled a lifetime to overcome societal stigma and own up to an insistent desire for other men. But must those types of men then become so rigid?

Likewise, sexual tastes are understood as transcendent, culture-independent phenomena. Though White asserts that "there's no accounting for taste," with the help of theorists such as Pierre Bourdieu I argue, quite the contrary, that we must account for taste, that naturalized tastes are among the most insidious mechanisms of dominant cultures. Bourdieu's analysis of taste in his study *Distinction* extends notions developed by Antonio Gramsci about cultural hegemony—those governing ideologies that are so pervasive and dominant as to become forgotten, to be made commonsensical. Similarly, particular sexual tastes, too easily given taken-for-granted status, become the everyday, the accepted, the sexual hegemony of a normative gay community.[7]

By placing tastes outside of culture, *The Joy of Gay Sex* masks its own role in the creation and perpetuation of gay archetypes, in instructing men not only *what to do* but also *whom to like*. Typing is particularly pernicious around race. Edmund White at various points in the text has unwittingly revealed his desire for urban, urbane, salaried businessmen who enjoy mildly perverse pleasures in the evening. He occasionally lets slip his preoccupation with Frenchmen as well—this long before the successful Edmund White of later years relocated to Paris.

In the entry on ORGIES, as White describes one of the "ways to bring the participants together," he may be revealing as much about himself as his readers: "You can invite all the tricks you've met over the last year and tell them to bring along anyone they like. If your sexual tastes are very specific, however, you may end up with a room of six-foot blonds, all of whom like to fuck and refuse to get fucked. That may seem like paradise to you, but it may not thrill them." Might White's use of the word "you" instead signal the word "I"—"your sexual tastes" really mean "mine"? Dependent on location, might six-foot blonds be in short supply? (Or even beyond media lionization?) The thrilling paradisical critical mass of tall blond tops that White (un)imaginatively "bring[s] together" in one room (of one's own)—and the raced, classed "tastes" it exposes—seem difficult to sustain in the sparsely populated regions undepicted in this volume and thus call for a more democratic approach, outlined in the discussion of rural bear cultures below.

White's readership is likewise presumed white, as evidenced in part by the volume's illustrations. For example, a grouping of nine color prints by Michael Leonard seems to portray, in various states of undress, either alone or in pairs, a range of men—blond, red-headed, brown-haired. But all have short hair, none looks older than thirty-five, none is heavy set, and only one is black, perhaps two. But how can we tell? In one pose, the black man's head is cut off by the cropping of the hand-drawn work. In another, perhaps the same black man's face is obscured by the shirt he's pulling up over his head. This illustration, in particular, invites comparison to Robert Mapplethorpe photographs, as critiqued by Kobena Mercer.[8]

Despite any critical mass propensities toward group sex, Julian Graddon's fifty line drawings, scattered throughout the volume, featuring various male models, never depict more than two men together. One drawing accompanying the FETISH entry shows one white midsection sporting tight leather underwear, laced at the sides; another accompanying the MALE SEXUAL RESPONSE entry shows a white midsection in an anatomical cross-section, as in the doctor's office. Two drawings capture a solitary white guy masturbating. The remaining forty-six feature *couples*—a couple of friends, a couple of sex partners, usually on a bed, three or four times on a sofa or chair, a few times standing, once in the shower, all seemingly in a private residence. One drawing suggests an apartment house stairwell. None suggests the out-of-doors poor and working-class street cultures of homelessness and overcrowding or the rural cultures of sex in the fields and woods.

In only eight of the forty-six couplings is one of the guys black, never both—as if the artist cannot imagine black gay cohabitants. Interestingly, of the three drawings in the volume involving mirrors, two include a black subject. In one, the mirror allows the white bottom to see himself getting fucked from behind by the black top, reflecting not black pleasure but white, and further reflecting it to an assumed white audience. In the other, the white man encourages the viewer *and* his black partner to gaze upon the black body. The black subject is centered, standing naked with his back to us. His white mate, in briefs, stands alongside, cut off at the left edge. The reflection in the mirror shows us only the chest and face of the white man; it reveals almost the entirety of the black body and all of the penis. Positioned next to the entry on BODY IMAGE, this illustration hints that the black man needs the white partner and white spectator to corroborate, confirm, and convince him that black is beautiful.

With one or two possible exceptions, there are no Latinos nor Native Americans among the fifty Graddon drawings. There are no Asian Americans. Non-black people of color do appear in *The Joy of Gay Sex*, but only in a set of anachronistic illustrations by Ian Beck. Uncaptioned, uncontextualized, unconnected to the entries, these full-page, full-color artworks are placed willy-nilly in the text, giving the impression of timelessness. Clustered in four groups, they are not direct reproductions, but rather reworkings of homoerotic imagery from otherworldly pasts: pottery from ancient Greece, mosaics from Roman edifices, *shunga* prints from Tokugawa Japan, seemingly patterned after Harunobu Suzuki and Utamaro Kitagawa; and rusticated phallic imagery, as if from India and Persia.

At a minimum, the Beck, Graddon, and Leonard images seem to acknowledge that some of the presumptively white readers of *The Joy of Gay Sex* might find non-white men attractive. The occasional entry suggests that White occasionally finds them desirable, at least as fonts of non-white wisdom, as with the "highly informative . . . small talk that's exchanged during one-night stands"—again, with "you" perhaps standing in for "I." "You've heard about Castro's concentration camps for homosexuals, but only when you meet a gay Cuban who's been interned can you find out the truth." Reflecting middle-class assumptions and anxieties, "you wonder how safe the airports are in L.A. and Boston; then you meet a flight attendant who tells you." Once again exposing the urban, specifically lower Manhattan, biases of the volume, "You want to know the latest slang expressions in Harlem; a black guy you pick up tells you." Thus White's knowledge of non-white worlds is acquired experientially, through sex. White concludes this section with his own reworking of a Whitmanesque egalitarian ethic: "Though gay men, like all other people, tend to remain loyal to their socio-economic group and can't as a group claim to be particularly liberal, nevertheless they are, perhaps, more democratic than most of the population by virtue of their far-flung contacts with every stratum of society." Democratic ideals, in White's vision, are enabled by the wealthy worldliness of an international gay jet set headquartered in Chelsea and the Village—not the more commonplace back roads wanderings and gatherings of ordinary people.[9]

White concedes that some might find black men alluring; still, he warns them in the opening sentences on TYPES: "Many people go on a spree of self-loathing every time someone turns them down. . . . What too many people forget is that most people have definitely preferred types. The black guy turned you down because you are white; if you study him for a few nights you'll see he always leaves with other black guys." Though White then proceeds to imagine a seemingly similar scenario in which a black gay man's desires are thwarted by intractable tastes, he fails to account for the lengthy histories of denigrating racial typing—standards of beauty and hierarchies of desirability—that make such a comparison untenable. The passage well illustrates theorist Roderick Ferguson's directive that the "history of African American sexuality . . . must be written as a materialist history of discursive practices and as a discursive history of material practices."[10]

Exposing the author, such passages also expose the authoritative nature of address from author to audience—what theorists such as Roland Barthes and Douglas Crimp after him have called "truth effects." Certain genres of writing—realist prose, journalism, history, business and legal case studies, and more—cloak their conventions in order to create the aura of a direct unmediated account: not one particular representation or portion of the truth, but *the truth*. Notably, these genres often use a third-person voice-of-god omniscient narration. Thus the author does not, in first-person singular, state: I believe it to be so. Rather *it is so*. Advice literature such as sex manuals can use a *second-person impera-tive* voice to create an even more totalizing, difference-effacing sense of truth-telling. To say that "you do it this way" is to imply that you *must* do it this way or you are not a part of *us*, "us" being the first-person plural "we" that this book constructs as the metronormative gay com-munity. To invite participation in a sexual practice—*this* is how you *do* it—is to subtly, coercively warn against expulsion from a sexual com-munity: this is how *we* do it.[11]

Animal or Vegetable?

If *The Joy of Gay Sex* was an unparalleled print media articulation of urban gay male subjectivities and sexual practices, two decades later a new media technology enabled a discourse of even greater magnitude and breathtaking sweep. In 1996, to own the Internet domain name Gay.com was to have unprecedented influence over gay thought and con-versation. Thousands and soon tens of thousands of people across the United States and select portions of the globe would be connected to one another through its innovative introduction service, the Java-based chat rooms. As their numbers multiplied, they would help shape the more networked—and more Americanized and Westernized—global queer communities many experience today.[12]

While inarguably expanding and accelerating communication among queers with the money and know-how for computer access, Gay.com chat rooms also have served disciplinary functions. Early Gay.com "Chat Guidelines" prohibited "impersonating someone else," a broad stricture of potential offence to transgender persons, as well as theorists and everyday users who have noted the joys of identity recreation, sexual stimulation, and gender proliferation/obliteration though cyber role-play. Gay.com insisted upon the rigid gender binary, thereby perpetuat-ing it.[13]

Under the early guidelines, chat participants had the right to insist that "visitors of the opposite [sic] gender . . . move to the 'Friendly Visitors Room,' 'Bisexual (mixed) Room' or other specified area." While this helpfully allowed lesbians to evict aggressive male interlopers from the Women's Floor, it also meant that male visitors to Gay.com—who greatly predominated—once again got to boss women around. Furthermore, the guidelines did not reveal how this policy might or might not apply to pre-operative transsexuals, to genderqueer people, or to intersexuals. To ignore their distinctive concerns served to further marginalize them, to minimize their significance within queer communities.

In outlining its "Rules Regarding Adult Content," the website indecorously exposed its reductive notions of erotic activity, its limited sense of what counts as sexual. "While some degree of nudity [was] acceptable" in visitors' linked pictures, "images showing erections . . . and sexual contact [we]re not." Thus, with a police-state precision, an erection had to be "defined," as "a penis [that] stands at an angle of more than 45 degrees." As if valorizing hard-ons wasn't enough, Gay.com—with brute simplicity—reduced multifarious queer sexual expression worthy of 240 book pages in 1977 to just five curt words: "Sexual contact" was defined as "any physical contact involving genitals." Monitors clearly fell behind in their patrols, for pictures of erections abounded, as did images of numerous erotically stimulating and satisfying methods of contact *not* involving genitalia—all testament to the inventiveness and assertiveness of human sexuality. Truly, the splashy pictures showed and the countless conversations proved that embedded within the very site itself were the means for its subversion.

Around the turn of the millennium, I began to imagine the potential benefits of chat room technology for queer history. Over the preceding decade, I had utilized oral history as a principal methodology in my research on mostly rural and small-town queer southerners, audio-taping interviews in person or, occasionally, by telephone. Their tales provided needed correctives to the great gay coming-out narrative of migration to the cities that had characterized American LGBT history. Rural southerners in particular painted a picture of queer life markedly different from that of urban gay enclaves, and they helped shift the historiography, at least in part, away from categories of (bounded, confining) gay identity and community toward (potentially more open-ended, liberating) queer desires and acts. Still I worried that in documenting those personal accounts, I was not always sufficiently solicitous of the full panoply of sexual acts. Nor was I able to arrange meetings with the diversity of individuals who practiced them, especially the non-gay-identified men and circumspect trans women who had sex with men. The Internet, associated from its earliest days with sexual candor and exploration, struck me as a logical venue for making contact with these individuals and for retrieving accounts of ever more varied sexual pleasures from the past.

In early 2001, my first online interviews in Gay.com chat rooms quickly revealed the limits of previous approaches. Whereas before, enormous efforts were expended not only enlisting but simply finding rural oral history narrators in the South, both white and non-white, here geographical rooms organized by state, such as historically rural Alabama and Mississippi, insured my access to a very large potential sample. Also especially useful, within the broad southern regional platform, was the demographic room Mature Men, promising contact with elders and stories of more distant pasts; even more so, to help redress an important imbalance in American LGBT historiography, was the Men of Color room. Before the advent of personal profile pages, Gay.com's imperfect mechanisms for parsing out a nationalized and normalizing gay "community" assisted in soliciting stories from men who regularly felt excluded from that very community, especially those outside urban centers. Using the screen name "researcher 4 older" and a simple identifier—"gay author wants chat with mature men from the south"—I entered these rooms. Then I waited for men to strike up a conversation with me—that is, to invite me away from the fifty-person public chat rooms into a one-on-one private chat. And chat we did.

First assuring anonymity and gaining consent to ask a few questions, I ascertained as I ordinarily would the narrator's age and the places he had lived. Dispensing with lengthy life-history approaches that minimized my own interjections so as to avoid scripting the tenor and vocabulary of responses, I found it necessary here to craft a central query and promptly pose it, given the brevity of many private chats. I posed it to a fifty-something, mixed-race-identified, Native and European American, raised in Bossier City, Louisiana (then a small town), who chose the pseudonym Andrew, in a conversation that ended at 4:39 p.m. GMT (10:39 a.m. his time) on May 9, 2001. I typed using the loose grammar and spelling of the net, now tidied up here, "I'm most interested in rural areas. And I'm also interested in forms of sex beside oral and anal. Does any of that apply to you?"

"My first sexual encounter," Andrew typed back with great wit and charm, "was with a warm watermelon in my uncle's garden. A cousin did it and made me do it too. I was about 15." Since Andrew, as a teenager, never had a wet dream—the baleful "nocturnal emission" of McCarthy-era sexual advice literature—the watermelon "was earth-shattering. My first climax. I guess you could say I lost my virginity to a fruit." This young mixed-race small-town sexual adventurer, therefore, had his "first sexual encounter" outdoors, an act of sitophilia taught, encouraged, and accompanied by a male relative, in another male family member's fields. Obviously, this "first" queer male sexual act departs dramatically from *The Joy of Gay Sex* entry on the FIRST TIME.[14]

Other online narrators confirmed what none of the fifty-five interviewees for my previous book project had mentioned: that fruits and vegetables were an obvious, readily available masturbatory aid on the farm. New Yorker Edmund White, in an entry on GADGETS, or sex toys, had mentioned only manufactured objects, many quite expensive. "Fingers, dildos and cocks can be pleasurable and are safe," but he cautioned elsewhere, "*Never* put *anything* else up your ass." That meant no "sweet potatoes." "They may damage you," he wrote with undue alarm, "since they may elude your grasp and get lost in your intestines." Chat narrators from the countryside suggested otherwise. Whereas White worried vegetables might tempt city boys in the supermarket aisle, small-town and rural queers discovered they were *freely* available down the garden row.

With admirable outspokenness, two of the first six chat-room narrators described engaging in what is perhaps the second great rural sex taboo: sex with animals. Among friends and acquaintances, my books on southern queer history had occasioned numerous sniggers about cows and cucumbers, but they had not actually documented them. In a matter of minutes online, this new digital history had. It radically reoriented the rural sexual landscape I had recreated through traditional oral history methodologies. The pre-cam faceless chat room conversations allowed for greater possibilities of self-revelation and collective memory work.

Indeed, chat histories revealed a range of sexual practices virtually undisclosed in American queer history to date. Prior exclusions resulted not only from the bourgeois trappings of interviews but also from the limited scope of questioning in scholars' own agendas. At a 2001 American Studies Association panel on Appalachian studies, for example, one presenter was so driven in his quest to upset stereotypes of hillbillies that he discounted any need to seriously assess the material propensities of rural landscapes that might lead to an increased incidence of bestiality and incest: more cows in the country, fewer acquaintances beyond biological family members. (Likewise sitophilia, though not an exclusively rural phenomenon, has much greater probabilities in the country, with foodstuffs literally thick on the ground.) Sex between adolescent male cousins was so commonplace and implicitly sanctioned in the postwar rural South that oral history narrators had described it to me in a laid-back, matter-of-fact tone. But fruits and animals had remained unspeakable—by most of us historians and (consequently?) by our oral history narrators. My chat interviews with Blackfoot-identified Andrew and other men of color in the South illustrated the centrality of these practices—and the range of others.

They also demonstrated the ways social media platforms would allow access to narrators previously unavailable to queer historians. Initiating a roughly one-hour chat dialogue ending at 5:43 p.m. GMT on May 9, 2001, older white southerner Marcus (a pseudonym) inquired: "Busy?" As the conversation unfolded, Marcus noted that he had been to college, was married early in life, and remained married. Only as a result of the net had he been able to meet many gay-identified men, on the side, late in life. Even so, he had experimented back in his teens and twenties. He declared unprompted that as a farm boy in the 1940s he had had "sex with watermelons." Further, he had "fucked a cow a very few times. I heard at school about [it], so I decided to try it."

These exchanges exemplified the ease of sexual disclosure in Gay.com chat rooms. Whereas Andrew told me about his experiments with FROTTAGE—learned directly from *The Joy of Gay Sex*, purchased in Fort Worth, Texas—he, Marcus, and others described acts unarticulated in the book, acts discovered through the popular discourse of rural men and boys, and the vernacular knowledges circulating on the playground or among acquaintances. A white Tennessean I'll call Jim told me how a new friend had introduced him to "pissing in his ass"—a watersport now known as "pissfuck," unmentioned in the *Joy of Gay Sex* entry. And Marcus carefully depicted an act that neither Edmund White nor American historians had ever chronicled, to my knowledge: "An older cousin [from out of state] used to take me to the woods and play with me. He would take my [erect] dick and wrap his [fore]skin around it. It is called 'docking,' I later learned. It is when an uncut guy withdraws his skin and lays someone else's dick on the head of his, then pushes his skin to cover both." The two can then mutually masturbate.

Though he first discovered it in the woods with his cousin in the 1940s, Marcus had only "learned fairly recently [that it was] a big turn-on for a lot of cut guys." In this way, Marcus's story disclosed how oppressive majority ritual—Judeo-Christian traditions of forced genital mutilation sanctioned by the medical establishment—might produce a minority ("uncut") desirability. Further, Marcus's tale suggested that rural consensual same-sex incest—docking, anal sex, or any number of other acts—amounted to a victimless "crime," with no prospect of congenitally compromised offspring.

Of other homonormative assumptions defied by digital queer history narrators, there is no entry in *The Joy of Gay Sex* on the by-then well-developed gay male bear cultures. The entry on HAIR only spins out more of White's flip observations on the desirability and the *place* of rural queers: "Shaggier beards of lighter hues run the gamut from looking windswept and philosophical (old hermit in a mountain cave) to seeming robust and outdoorsy (lumberjack in town for a day to raise some hell)." Perhaps intuiting the limits of his own research, White eventually would set out for the hinterlands, producing *States of Desire: Travels in Gay America*. But that text too would do little to unsettle urbanist assumptions, beyond easy tropes of "gay cowboys" and the like. The travelogue, as he concedes, amounted to a "city-by-city description of the way homosexual men lived in the late seventies." Outside New York, White assumed, gay Americans of the 1970s could only be found in (smaller, lesser) cities.[15]

Disinclined to accept the standard monikers of "gay," "homosexual," "bisexual," or the more recent "queer"—"I'm just me. I don't discriminate"—Andrew nonetheless identified as a bear. "I've been always drawn to body hair, especially moustaches and beards." He added that he considered bear culture and small-town life to be highly compatible, indeed egalitarian: "really open to all sizes, shapes, [length] of hair, or lack thereof," with a range "of ages." As he also made clear to me, he had sex across a range of races, all found across a broad geographical expanse. Raised in a missionary Baptist church that preached his damnation, Andrew found that the commercial gay establishments of north Louisiana and east Texas worked their own exclusions, not unlike *The Joy of Gay Sex*. Andrew was made to feel older than he actually was. Now, with the Internet, his liaisons were easier to arrange across the rural and small-town South. His sexual practices were "a little too rough for some," but he was not fully "into s/m." He'd had piercings, "mostly to draw attention to my tits, because I like tit work." Mostly, he was a "cuddle bear."

Like Andrew, Marcus enjoyed interfemural sex, the rubbing of an erect penis between the thighs of a partner. Given the briefest of mentions in *The Joy of Gay Sex* entry on FROTTAGE, it is perhaps most fully detailed in historical and locational specificity by Dunbar Moodie in his study of intergenerational male sex in twentieth-century South African gold-mining camps. Interfemural or intercrural sex clearly was commonplace in the rural South as well, suggesting the potential of as-yet underexplored binational, cross-regional comparative queer histories. These connections also forward the larger project of synthesis that historian Leila Rupp has trumpeted in her compelling essay, "Toward a Global History of Same-Sex Sexuality." Perhaps most importantly, these three rural and small-town southerners—Andrew, Marcus, and Jim—suggest that vernacular knowledges of sexual creativity can be shared and explored both on and offline, across great distances, to counter the provincial exclusions of urban enclaves' key cultural texts, thereby proliferating nonhomonormative sexual practices.[16]

A Very Large Range of Queer Acts

In addition to the increased candor of the net and the proliferation of non-normative sexual acts, another benefit of online "oral" history methodologies is the capacity of narrators to talk back—in particular, to dictate the terms of consent. After completing traditional oral history interviews, I had presented narrators with a standardized transfer agreement, in which they generally signed over all rights to the interview, usually only with the stipulation that a pseudonym be used. Most of these gay-identified men, who had agreed to the interview well in advance, wanted their stories told.

Also, the time between agreeing to the interview and the actual interview had allowed them to polish their stories, as oral historians refer to it. They had smoothed out the rough edges, edges they assumed unpleasant, irrelevant, or unprintable. Marcus told his stories spontaneously, warts and all. And near the end of the interview, this family man—married, with grown children—not only questioned me about my project in greater depth than had any previous narrator, in online or real-time settings, but also exercised his own agency and power by precisely stating the terms for publishing his interview. A portion of the chat dialogue is directly cut and pasted here, without correcting phrasing or spelling:

> do u mind if I use some of this in the writing i'm doing?
<MARCUS 2> let me ask
> go 4 it
<MARCUS 2> . . . if you think early childhood experiences cause guys
    to be gay or bi?
> don't know, truthfully
> not really an interest of mine
> why ask why, know what I mean
> i'm much more interested in the what and how
<MARCUS 2> are you trying to prove any point with your writing?
> just that human beings are creative, sexually speaking
[. . .]
<MARCUS 2> there are some things that I have told you that I would
    not want linked to my experiences that I have told you
> no problem, i'll just use a false name if that's ok
> u choose
<MARCUS 2> no that is not the point
> sorry, do explain
<MARCUS 2> I do not want [my children] mentioned [by gender,] in
    number or in any way
> hey, no problem at all
> can I say you went on to have a family, wife and children?
> again, using a false name?
<MARCUS 2> yes that would be ok
> great, thanks a million for that

> so just a couple more questions

<MARCUS 2> but do not mention [the university I attended by name]

> ok, no problem

<MARCUS 2> Do not mention

<MARCUS 2> [a particular state]

> ok

> I don't think u did mention [that state] did u?

<MARCUS 2> say a [regional] state if necessary

<MARCUS 2> yes I did

> ok

> sorry

> of course, the cousin from [that state], i'll just say he lived out of state
[...]

<MARCUS 2> and do not use [my current location by name of town or city] either

> is there anything else you'd like to tell me about?

> (ok, won't use [place name])

<MARCUS 2> I think I have probably told you too much already

> no, trust me, your story is *very* important and i'll treat it with respect

<MARCUS 2> where do you publish?

> i did a book called men like that published by univ of chicago press in 1999

<MARCUS 2> Is this a book primarily for other gays

> primarily, yes

<MARCUS 2> Do you have a partner? when did u have your first experience with another guy?

Thus, having told me all he wanted about his sexual past, Marcus insisted I likewise share my own sexual history. He began by soliciting a well-known polished narrative, repeatedly called up by gay men: the first time.

Unlikely to find or participate in queer historical projects, Marcus well represents that variety of non-gay-identified men who nonetheless have participated, on and off through the years, in queer acts: an adventurous youth given to male homosexual experimentation, as well as "heterosexual, 'heterospecial' endeavour[s]" with female cattle, as Jens

Rydström puts it in his brilliant study of bestiality and homosexuality in Sweden. But Marcus told me that since young adulthood, he had stopped having sex with other men for over forty years. Perhaps only with the introduction of the Internet had he begun to engage with queer men again, primarily via his computer when his wife was away.[17]

To be sure, Marcus might best represent the extraordinary privilege of straight-identified white men in the South to engage in and success-fully cloak queer acts and to minimize or efface non-normative activi-ties. The acts themselves may not be so queer after all, but an extension of the historic sexual license of white male southerners, including the sexual assault, procuring, and coercion of African American females and males. They may further exemplify the fine gradations by which normativity can be measured, calling up class, race, gender, region, and other variables. Certainly, the acts suggest the slipperiness of the gay-straight binary, as well as the need for other analytical continuums, scales, and registers—that is, for a matrix of relevant criteria. Without chat-room technology, they can never be adequately explored.[18]

What pitfalls are apparent in this digital history methodology? They primarily concern potential fabrication, by both historian and informer, as well as replicability of research, a key concern of all historical practice. What is to prevent narrators from concocting fabulous sexual fantasies and passing them off as real? What is to prevent them from taking the elaborate chat stories of sexual exploits, a staple of mutually mastur-batory cyber-sex, and presenting them as actual accounts? As with the analysis of any other primary documents, cyber historians will have to weigh chat dialogues against other types of accounts, with an eye to con-sistency, corroboration, and informed consent. And we can make our transcripts available to other researchers, as oral historians do, by open-ing our files or placing tapes and transcripts in archives.

Just as voice, timber, dialect, and intonation can be important in tape-recordings or digital audio files, the spelling and timing of typed phrases in chat rooms can be revelatory. Also, just as the posture, body language, and material surroundings of the oral history interviewee cannot be wit-nessed by a follow-up researcher, neither can they be witnessed by the primary conductor or secondary verifier of a chat-room dialogue. Nor can the follow-up researcher, from the easily cut-and-pasted transcript, know the rhythm, pace, and complete context of the chat. But these factors strike me as no more nor less difficult than the variables encountered in other forms of primary research.

Shortly after I began conducting these interviews, Gay.com added a new restriction to its chat guidelines: "Research, interviews and therapy are prohibited in chat rooms." After three emails to Gay.com requesting the rationales for this policy, they responded lukewarmly, with hopes I would just go away. Thus, with Gay.com, I decided to bend the rules, relying foremost on the teachings of Martin Duberman in his watershed essay on the antebellum letters of Jeff Withers and James Henry Hammond, withheld from him by archivists. As Duberman comments, "It [i]s essential to challenge the tradition of suppressing information which might prove useful to gay people in better understanding the historical dimensions of our experience, the shifting strategies we have adopted over time to cope with oppression, and varied styles we have developed to express our special sensibilities. If the 'lawless' tactics I've resorted to seem extreme to some, well, so is our need."[19]

Our needs and our obligations extend most to those individuals and cultures too often pushed outside the gay male community frame of "us"—poor and working-class, rural and small-town, queers of color and white farm boys and men pursuing joyous sexual pleasures unimagined by Ed White or Gay.com capitalists. As theorist Miranda Joseph so convincingly argues, "capitalism and, more generally, modernity depend on and generate the discourse of community to legitimate social hierarchies." Digital queer history helps us expose illegitimate hierarchies of productively illicit practices, generating both challenges and possibilities for shattering normative structures of sexual pleasure and desirability.[20]

Conclusion

If defying homophobic archival gatekeepers or profit-motivated gay entrepreneurs can be readily justified, university institutional review boards (IRBs) are a thornier matter. Although the American Historical Association and Oral History Association in 2003 successfully argued to the Department of Health and Human Services that oral history should be exempt from most "research on human subjects" protocols, universities and their legal departments tend to err on the side of caution. This can have stultifying, ossifying consequences for queer research.[21]

Queer studies academicians are answerable to any number of con-
stituencies. Ethical guidelines vary across the varied stakeholders in any
project: the employing institution and its oversight bodies; publishers
and *their* legal departments; professional organizations in the humanities and social sciences such as AHA and OHA; relevant funding agencies; and, as Duberman suggests, popular audiences with a distinctive
cultural investment in the research—the queer activist movements and
networks to whom we are, perhaps ultimately, beholden. As I inform my
own funders, when the inevitable *inconsistencies* in these multiple proliferating guidelines become *incompatibilities*, I seek the advice of colleagues. That means the sort of scholars gathered in this volume—those
well-attuned not only to the distinctive issues in the historiography of
queer genders and sexualities, but also to the histories of institutional
apparatuses that reshape ideologically troubling work into reassuringly
reformist comportment. This is not to shirk ethical responsibilities.
Quite the contrary, it is to ascertain the most appropriate ethical framework with which to judge a project's principles and methodologies.

With the advent of elaborate personal profiles online, researchers
can quickly amass more targeted samples of narrators from particular geographical regions (such as a rural critical mass), with specific
erotic proclivities, with distinctive physical traits (cut/uncut), with ever
more inventive means of crafting their interpersonal relationships and
encounters. Thus, Rydström's largely criminal history of bestiality in
Sinners and Citizens can be supplemented with intentional histories of
zoophilia and of furry cultures. Tim Dean's startlingly important analysis of barebacking in *Unlimited Intimacy* can be augmented by narrators
found across a variety of locales through websites such as barebackrt.
com. Dossie Easton and Janet Hardy's ground-breaking 1997 *The Ethical Slut*, reflecting distinctively West Coast white lesbian and bisexual
women's cultures of polyamory, can be enhanced, as Lee Kham Chuan
has done, by enlisting study participants in "open relationships," as indicated on gayromeo.com profile pages. As more such studies should
make apparent, these kinds of commonplace, emotionally faithful,
sexually nonmonogamous commitments often go well beyond dyadic
couplings to include multinational queer collective households, multi-
racial noncohabiting fuck buddy networks, and numerous other queer

combinations and permutations, again spanning vast distances, rural, suburban, and urban.[22]

I do not propose solely utilizing demographic or personal traits from LGBT community websites to identify larger samples of project participants or to create new critical masses in rural queer studies in the humanities and social sciences. Regardless of obstacles, I advocate the conducting of research on and through the sites, as well as the innovation of fresher methodologies via new media platforms. In fostering these innovations, we cannot expect institutional review boards to lead the way. In fact, I fully expect them to continue to *get in* the way. "Meant to facilitate . . . processes of research production and circulation," as Mary L. Gray notes, IRBs often impede them by "giv[ing] greater scrutiny" to projects on non-normative genders and sexualities and "lack[ing] sympathy for the gains to be made through this research." Thus I encourage us all to ponder just how far we are willing to bend the rules, as we aggressively push unwieldy old institutions in revolutionary new directions. In patriarchal, homophobic, and transphobic contexts, the moral ingenuity we bring to our interpersonal relations—the lessons we can offer to a wider world—must be matched by an ethical inventiveness in our approaches to research and scholarship.[23]

Just as contemporary cultural products have not always imagined the myriad ways in which sex is practiced or organized today, queer history has barely begun to chart them in the past. Much less has it comprehensively measured their relative prevalence, their dissemination, their spatial bases—material, environmental, and ideological. Therefore, we cannot articulate well how sex has changed over time, except to arrogantly assume that we new millennials continue to innovate, continue to propagate ever more elaborate sexual pleasures. I distrust such assumptions. And I long for more sexual knowledge. Improving future conditions for sex and gender outcasts may require us to look more carefully into our pasts. The narrators of digital history challenge the enforced "we" of gay white male urban elites; they provide us with useful alternatives in learning how to do it.

NOTES

1 On rural queer cosmopolitanism, see Howard, "Me and Mrs. Jones."

2 On metronormativity, see Halberstam, *In a Queer Time and Place*, 33–45.

3 Silverstein and White, *The Joy of Gay Sex.*

4 On acts/identities distinctions, see Halperin, *How to Do the History of Homosexuality*, 24–47.

5 On statistical versus evaluative norms, see Warner, *The Trouble with Normal*, 52–61.

6 For a trenchant critique of related discourses, see Downing, "Beyond Safety."

7 Bourdieu, *Distinction.*

8 Mercer, *Welcome to the Jungle*, 171–219.

9 On the myth of gay wealth, see Badgett, *Money, Myths, and Change.*

10 Ferguson, *Aberrations in Black*, 81.

11 Barthes, *The Rustle of Language*, 141–48. Crimp, "Randy Shilts's Miserable Failure," 647.

12 Altman, *Global Sex.*

13 Fortunately, since that time, the imbalance has been offset by Johnson, *Sweet Tea.*

14 These chat dialogues have been easily transcribed and stored—that is, cut and pasted and retained in the files of the author, who makes them available to other researchers upon request.

15 Hennen, *Faeries, Bears, and Leathermen*, 95–133, 181–95; White, *States of Desire.* Quoted passage from White's professional website, http://www.edmundwhite.com/html/statesdesire.htm (accessed February 21, 2011).

16 Moodie, "Migrancy and Male Sexuality on the South African Gold Mines"; Rupp, "Toward a Global History of Same-Sex Sexuality."

17 Rydström, *Sinners and Citizens*, 18.

18 On queer white male southerners and their black companions of varied levels of power and reciprocity, see for example Percy, "William Alexander Percy (1885–1942)."

19 Duberman, "'Writhing Bedfellows' in Antebellum South Carolina," 30–31.

20 Joseph, *Against the Romance of Community*, viii.

21 Linda Shopes, "Oral History, Human Subjects, and Institutional Review Boards."

22 Rydström, *Sinners and Citizens*; Dean, *Unlimited Intimacy*; Easton and Hardy, *The Ethical Slut*; Chuan, "Exploring the Discursive Construct of Open Non-Monogamy Relationships."

23 Gray, *Out in the Country*, 185, 193, 194.

16

Queer Rurality and the Materiality of Time

STINA SODERLING

I first make my way to the "Gayborhood" in the rural U.S. South as a retreat from my day-to-day life in New York City. After a twenty-four-hour bus ride, I am picked up at the Greyhound station, and the journey continues for another hour by car, until we roll into the hollow[1] just after the sun has set. D tells me he's excited I got here after dark. He always loves when people arrive in the pitch black, which is possible only in the absence of electrical lights, loves seeing them discover the place in the morning, wide-eyed at the splendor of what was hidden in the dark of the night. Though this particular home is on the grid and there is electricity in most of the buildings, in between is a night ranging from pitch black to gray, depending on the moon. Night here is a break, a time when one can only venture out safely with a flashlight (the rattle snakes, like the people, migrate from the hills to the hollows). And flashlights are great, but they don't make for any extensive partying, and certainly not work. Life starts again in the morning.

Indeed, I am wide-eyed when waking up the next morning to a time and place where everything is slightly out of kilter. Bucky's,[2] the household where I am staying, located in the Gayborhood, is commonly described by visitors and residents as "magical," a word connoting a time-space beyond the normative.[3] Someone is building a porch wearing a black slip; the shower is in the vegetable patch; the outhouse is the most beautifully painted building on the land. The house I am staying in is painted blue with yellow stars and moons. To the left of the house is a creek, to the right an outhouse shaped like a rocket ship. And everywhere a thick layer of green, the vegetation reclaiming the ground the humans have borrowed. A path leads to the front of the property, past a bridge with paintings of dolphins and unicorns, a silver Airstream trailer, dogs and cats, an old house with the quirkily sloped roofs so common in this region. And then the kitchen, a whole building to itself. Someone is eating breakfast, somebody else frying eggs collected from the chicken coop in the front yard. Outside the kitchen are the gardens, at this time of year—early summer—so lush the rows flow into each other. There are strawberries and basil and eggplants and beans and dozens of other edibles, not to mention stunning flower beds. The early risers are out gardening, enjoying the last hours of mild weather before the midday heat sets in.

Though I do not know it during this first visit, I will end up returning to the Gayborhood repeatedly, both for research and retreat. Here, in this chaotic space, I am faced with new relations of indoor and outdoor, human and more-than-human. Here, too, questions are raised about the role of time in queer life. The rhythms of existence in the Gayborhood are decidedly queer, yet they are far from the conceptualizations of queer temporality we have seen from scholars of urban queer life. Time here is centered not on nightlife, partying, and fleeting anonymous interactions, but on quotidian labor and ongoing community.

In this essay, I formulate a theory of queer temporality located in a rural community. I posit that by focusing our investigation of temporality on rural queerness, we gain new perspectives on the materiality of time. I focus on three aspects of time in the Gayborhood: materiality and "stickiness," temporality's connections to economic structure, and the overlap between rhythms and chaos. Life in the Gayborhood is often messy, out of "order," as the description of Bucky's above indicates. Objects and people are seemingly out of place, yet equilibrium is maintained in the constant reclamation of time, space, and objects by the more-than-human world. This includes time. You can sleep in long past sunrise, but by the time the sun sets, the world will claim you into stillness.

Introduction to the Gayborhood

Before we delve deeper into the question of rural queer time, let me introduce the specific context from which I draw my examples. This essay is based on ethnographic fieldwork in a queer community in rural Tennessee, conducted during stays over the course of five years. Lovingly referred to by its residents as "the Gayborhood" (a term usually associated with urban LGBT enclaves), the community consists of just over a hundred residents, living on about one thousand acres of queer-owned or -rented land. There are also well over a thousand visitors each year, extending the Gayborhood's influence far past its physical locale.

Central to the Gayborhood are five or so intentional communities. The two most visited, and arguably well-known, are "Bucky's" and "Hickory Knoll," both of which I introduce in greater detail below. The intentional communities are open to visitors, and thus serve as an introduction to the Gayborhood and to rural queer life more generally. In addition to this handful of communal properties, there are also private plots of land where individuals and couples live. Many of them started their time in the Gayborhood as residents of, or long-term visitors to, one of the communal projects and later decided that they wanted a more private living situation while still being involved in the Gayborhood.

The biggest and oldest intentional community in the Gayborhood is Hickory Knoll, a Radical Faerie sanctuary. Though some Gayborhood residents-to-be came to the area already a decade earlier, the Gayborhood got its official start around 1980, with the transformation of Hickory Knoll from a hippie farm[4] into a Faerie sanctuary. Radical Faerie sanctuaries are, as the name implies, the nodes of the Radical Faerie movement. The Faeries were formed in the late 1970s as a gay men's earth-centered spiritual movement. They draw on—many would argue appropriate—various spiritual traditions, especially North American Native spiritualities. Rural living, either year-round or during regular gatherings, is central to Radical Faerie life. There are active Faerie groups in cities across the United States, but large-scale gatherings tend to take place at the rural sanctuaries, and these gatherings serve to revitalize urban groupings. Over time, the Radical Faerie movement has opened up to women and gender-nonconforming people, though most sanctuaries are still heavily male-dominated, and some gatherings are for men only.

The other prominent communal land in the Gayborhood is Bucky's. It is here that my fieldwork is based and that most of the ethnographic vignettes in this article are drawn from. Bucky's was founded in late 1993 by visitors enamored with Hickory Knoll. Located on two hundred acres, most of the property is forested; the rest contains houses and extensive gardens. Over the past two decades, Bucky's has developed into a central node in a growing North American phenomenon of mixed-gender queer "land projects."[5] Bucky's started off as an all-male space, but has since, through hard work by women, transpeople, and their allies, become gender integrated. Today, there are just over ten residents of various genders, all of them white, and all of them U.S. Americans, ranging in age from their twenties to fifties. There are also several hundred visitors each year. Most come for festivals, staying only a week, but a significant number come for garden internships lasting from one to five months. Only one of the founders still lives there; other current residents have been there anywhere from a few months to nineteen years.

Colliding Temporalities

Perhaps a meditation on rural queer time is best begun with a trip to the city, where the collision of rural and urban temporalities becomes apparent. Our protagonists are a group of queer folks from Bucky's, living far down in a hollow out in the countryside of middle Tennessee. On occasion, the country queers will make their way into Nashville, the nearest metropolis, preferably when it is karaoke night at the gay bar. It takes hours to get ready: planning out who is going to ride in which car or truck and making sure everyone has a spot, putting on makeup, rummaging around closets and piles of clothes to find sparkly yet mold-free outfits.

Eventually, the crowd does make it out of the hollow. Before karaoke, we go out to dinner, at a medium-sized family-owned restaurant in a strip mall close to the gay bar. It is crowded, but not horribly so, as the group rambles in. The usual shuffling of tables to accommodate a large crowd takes place. Then, waiting. And waiting, and waiting. People are starting to get anxious: we are getting hungry, but there is also the unsettling worry that maybe this is all taking so long not because the staff is busy, but because we look "wrong." Other guests seem to be getting their food. And are we "wrong" because we are queer or country, or both, that mix of rhinestones and dirt? The slow time of the hollow follows us into the city, and here it is so obviously out of rhythm. The food does arrive eventually, and people eat uncomfortably, murmuring about how they should have just eaten at home, in the kitchen.

Finally arriving at the bar, later than planned, we have what turns out to be a fun night. There is karaoke and line dancing and hanging out, beer and fried chicken. We sing, talk, try to learn the dance steps. Then, by midnight or 1 a.m., people are ready to go home, knowing we have at least an hour's drive ahead of us. When we head out, the night is still young for the others at the bar; none of the locals are making any move to leave. We pile back into the cars and trucks, speed down the highway, go slower on the winding roads down the hill, then slow down to a crawl on the dirt road leading down into the hollow, silence engulfing us as the radio signal fades away.

Theories of Queer Temporality

In recent years, queer theorists have taken an increasing interest in the question of time. While illuminating how temporality and sexuality intersect, these theorists have largely limited their focus to urban areas. In the instance described above, rural queer time collides with the model of temporality espoused by metronormative queer theorists, begging for attention to the role of queer time in rural areas.

In the 2005 book *In a Queer Time and Place*, J. Jack Halberstam argues that temporality in the United States is structured according to a heteronormative life course. For most straight people, life is built around a series of life stages: childhood, adolescence, adulthood-marriage-babies, old age.[6] These stages are set up to facilitate reproduction, the creation of new humans through male-female intercourse and cohabitation. Queers, having been excluded from the realm of socially acceptable reproduction, Halberstam argues, do not live according to this time line. Without the pressure to get married, adolescence is prolonged. In this model, queer and straight time differ not only on a grand lifetime scale, but also in its everyday structure. If there are no kids at home that need to be fed and put to bed, there is really no reason to not be out partying all night. Queer life thus takes on a nocturnal quality.

Published the year before Halberstam's book, Lee Edelman's *No Future: Queer Theory and the Death Drive* also critiques heteronormative temporality, what Edelman terms "reproductive futurism"—that is, an imperative to center the child in political and personal decisions. Edelman poses queerness as that which is against reproductive futurism, that which "figures, outside and beyond its political symptoms, the place of the social order's death drive."[7] This argument is not unique to Edelman, or even to queer theory; on the contrary, the trope of queers being against society due to their status outside of reproduction is common in anti-queer rhetoric. Rather than arguing against "the ascription of negativity to the queer," however, Edelman argues for "accepting and even embracing it."[8]

Because of the nonlinearity of rural queer time, Edelman's suggestion of embracing negativity is not easily applicable to rural queer contexts. Futurity does not stand in opposition to the present. Further, I would argue that a space where the connection to more-than-human life is more palpable is less likely to embrace a death drive, or even to pose life and death as dichotomous. Edelman's model is in this regard a metronormative one. This is not to say that cities are "dead," nor is it to say that the rural is somehow more "natural" than the urban, but that the connections to more-than-human materiality are often more immediately recognizable outside of cities, and life and death are viewed less in opposition and more in interaction.

Halberstam's and Edelman's models of queer temporality are useful insofar they suggest that time functions differently in queer and heteronormative circumstances, yet the theories are incomplete, as they assume that queer people reside in cities. This is a common assumption among scholars of LGBT life,[9] but one that recent scholarship, including the contributions to this volume, puts into question. The countryside is not universally heterosexual and hostile to queer people; it is also a space where queer life takes place.

Taking rural queer life into consideration allows us to see alternate models of queer temporality. Life cannot be structured around late-night partying when there are vast spaces with no electrical light. It cannot be about the constant interaction with strangers when one's immediate vicinity contains only a handful of people. We need to think of time in different ways.

One model for thinking differently about queer time comes from José Muñoz, in *Cruising Utopia*, Muñoz questions Edelman's high valuation of negativity, writing instead a text that embraces possibility; in Muñoz's own words, it can be "used to imagine a future."[10] He does this by positing a queer futurity. *Cruising Utopia* starts with the words "Queerness is not yet here. Queerness is an ideality. Put another way, we are not yet queer."[11] But this equation of queerness with a never-reached futurity does not line up with life in the Gayborhood. As one regular visitor to Bucky's told me, "There's something queer going on in each of these hollows." And she does not just mean the hollows populated by out GLBTQ individuals, but the whole region. Rural Appalachia, a culturally and economically marginalized region of the United States, can in many ways be read as queer, outside of properly normative behavior. Activities outside of the realm of the proper are survival mechanisms. Sometimes you just butcher your own deer, sell your milk right from the farm.

While Muñoz's conceptualization of queer temporality as futuristic does not line up with rural queer time as I conceptualize it, his book provides key insights into queer temporality that can be applied to the rural. Muñoz asserts that "queerness's time is a stepping out of the linearity of straight time. Straight time is a self-naturalizing temporality. Straight time's 'presentness' needs to be phenomenologically questioned, and this is the fundamental value of queer utopian hermeneutics."[12] In my case study of rural queerness, this is combined with a focus on cyclicality. I argue, however, that rather than rejecting "presentness" altogether, queer rurality helps us see a different form of it.

Rural queer temporality is thus neither about Edelman's push against futurity, nor Muñoz's longing for it; instead, it is about a present that bleeds into the future and the past, a nonlinear temporality, a utopian sensibility in the current moment.

As Elizabeth Freeman reminds us, time is not neutral. Rather, "manipulations of time convert historically specific regimes of asymmetrical power into seemingly ordinary bodily tempos and routines, which in turn organize the value and meaning of time."[13] She coins the term "chrononormativity" to describe the dominant mode of manipulating time: "a mode of implantation, a technique by which institutional forces come to seem like somatic facts. Schedules, calendars, time zones, and even wristwatches inculcate what the sociologist Evitar Zerubavel calls 'hidden rhythms,' forms of temporal experience that seem natural to those whom they privilege."[14] This chronomormativity is distinctly absent at Bucky's, replaced by another way of interacting with time. It is this other way, this break with chrononormativity, that I refer to as "rural queer temporality."

Through the examples presented in the rest of this essay, I propose that rural queer temporality is *non-normative and material*. My argument here is not that "rural queer time" is applicable to all rural situations, nor that it is exclusive to queer subjects in rural spaces; rather, I am using a case study of queer life in the countryside to explore different ways of situating temporality in queer theory.

Everyday Rhythms

The chromonormative time that Freeman discusses has developed over the past several centuries. Italian cultural historian and anthropologist Piero Camporesi argues that "the precise measurement of time began with the rise of urban mercantile society, and from that measurement arose a stern philosophy of time for work and time for death."[15] With markets came exactitude, a use for dividing the day into hours, rather than times of light and darkness, heat and cold.

A conch[16] is used at both Bucky's and Hickory Knoll as an invitation to dinner. In these two communities, it is the main method for marking time and disciplining behavior temporally. This is how it works at Bucky's: twenty minutes before dinner is ready, the conch is blown once. Once food the food is ready to eat, it is blown again, a little more forcefully. These twenty minutes may or may not coincide with twenty tickings of the minute hands of the kitchen clock, which is broken most of the time, anyway.

Most people do not wear a watch around Bucky's, and since there is no cellphone reception, mobile phones cannot be counted on to tell the time. The only somewhat reliable public timepiece is the clock on the kitchen stove, which goes out if someone slams the oven door too hard, and it will take a day or two before anyone resets it. Hence, there is not a constant knowledge of clockwork time, and this is not an impediment—it does not matter very much if you know the exact minute of even hour.

The lack of clockwork time has been portrayed as a failure of the countryside: rural areas and small towns are often labeled as backward, slow, less "happening" than cities. Scott Herring, in *Another Country: Queer Anti-Urbanism*, argues that this bias against the countryside is a notable feature of metronormative queer theory. Herring lists as one of the qualities of metronormativity "the hierarchized assumption that a metropolitan-identified queer will always be more dynamic, more cutting-edge, more progressive, and more forward-looking than a rural-identified queer, who will always be more static, more backward, and more culturally backwater."[17] Herring questions this notion, and my study of the Gayborhood agrees with his analysis. Life in the Gayborhood may rarely function according to clockwork time, but it still moves, is still dynamic. The conch blows at dinner time, but exactly how this will line up with the clock nobody knows.

According to notions of efficiency and calculability, Bucky's is not doing very well, yet nobody seems especially concerned by this. The non-timed system of food provision, for example, is remarkably well functioning. When I first arrived at Bucky's I was astounded by the meal system. People often take care of their own breakfast and lunch needs, but dinner is always a communal affair. Given that Bucky's feeds a dozen residents and a slew of visitors, I had expected a chore wheel,[18] but none existed. Despite this lack of order, I never encountered a missed meal. There was always food for everyone. And this is not unique to this homestead, but rather representative of a broader queer rurality. Sociologist Peter Hennen writes about the Radical Faeries:

> For example, there is widespread agreement within the group that Faeries never agree about anything, yet their very existence depends to some degree upon consensus. Most Faeries understand their community as intentional, but exactly what this intentionality consists of is an open question. Refreshingly, Faerie culture seems to continually privilege process over results. Faerie enterprises, from preparing a meal to creating a sanctuary, are notoriously inefficient affairs—and this is just the way the Faeries like it.[19]

Part of what makes the meal system work is, ironically, its inefficiency. If people expected to always be fed "on time," a more organized cooking regime might have to be instituted. But because exact times do not matter, people are happy to eat dinner when it happens, and pitch in to cook it when needed.

Time as Sticky

Another defining aspect of time in the Gayborhood is what I have come to refer to as its "stickiness." What is supposed to take a few hours ends up taking weeks or months. Brief moments turn into decades, that which was supposed to be temporary becomes permanent.

Say you want to leave for Alabama on a Saturday morning, but it is just too early for anyone to get up and drive you to the bus station, so your departure is postponed until Wednesday, when the next bus departs. Then on Wednesday, you all simply forget to leave, and it is not until next weekend you actually take off, and then not to Alabama at all, but to wherever somebody happened to be driving.

L and J met only months before J was scheduled to move to Tennessee. Instead of promises of ever-after, they set a September deadline for their relationship. L was happy with his life in Florida, tending bars, making slow progress on his master's degree. No way was he going to move to the Appalachian backwoods. So when September rolled around and J packed his bags and took off, the relationship was over. But L could not get that strange little man out of his head, and one day he made a decision: he was moving. When J came back on a short visit to get the last of his belongings, L asked if he could come to Tennessee. J just smiled—little did L know that he had performed a magic ceremony at Hickory Knoll to make L consider moving. Seventeen years later, L and J are still together.

Others tell stories of coming to the Gayborhood for a short visit and ending up staying permanently. Spree jokingly refers to herself as Bucky's longest visitor, having been there for close to two decades now.

And seven years after he got his job as a bagger at the Food Lion, P is still bagging groceries. Sometimes permanence comes out of magic, and sometimes it comes out of the gnawing desperation of poverty. The median income in the county hovers below $18,000,[20] and unless your grandfather knew somebody else's grandfather, your chances of getting a job are slim.

The particular temporal rhythms of rural life are thus not only the result of a more intimate relationship to the more-than-human, but also of a long process of economic exploitation and abandonment. The lazy days of porch-sitting so common at Bucky's are partly a choice to stay outside of the rigid bounds of nine-to-five capitalist labor, but also the result of not being able to find steady employment.

* * *

In urban-centered queer theorizations of time, the rural is the end, the space-time of death. The rural is approached with fear and presented as an Other at constant risk of demise. Those who are stupid enough to not leave for the city are to blame for their own death. This narrative is constantly retold through stories such as those of Brandon Teena or Matthew Shepard, young white queers who succumbed to the homophobia of the flyover states. As J. Jack Halberstam writes in regard to Brandon Teena, a transman who was raped and killed in small-town Nebraska in 1993, "his story . . . symbolizes an urban fantasy of homophobic violence as essentially Midwestern."[21] And I would argue not just Midwestern, but southern, too. Think, for example, about the documentary *Southern Comfort*, which traces the last year in the life of Robert Eads, a transgender man living in "the back hills of Georgia."[22] The medical maltreatment that leads to Eads's death from ovarian cancer is likened to the racism against black people in the antebellum South, implying that Eads was not living in the modern era and that had he lived in the modern urban North he would have survived. Even the physical process of his death is portrayed as southern, through his increasingly slow, blurred, heavily accented speech. Through the narratives of Teena, Shepard, and Eads, conventional gay/queer scholarship and popular culture portray the southern and Midwestern countryside as a time of queer death; these are environments where queer bodies are supposed to die, not live, survive, thrive.

When AIDS first hit in the 1980s, it was either a death sentence ("In 1986, the average remaining lifetime of someone diagnosed with PCP [a form of pneumonia common among people with HIV] was less than ten months"[23]), or something to be shooed away like an annoying horsefly (Radical Faeries doctrine originally believed that they were too spiritual to need worldly protections such as condoms[24]). Now, twenty-five years later, we know that neither extreme was correct; plenty of people did die, including Faeries, but many have also survived.

And the Gayborhood is a location for survival. A significant number of new residents arrived in the Gayborhood in the mid-1990s expecting to find a quiet place to die. Today, many of them are still alive. They credit medicine, but also space, time, an interaction with the more-than-human world. We see here the stickiness of rural queer temporality, a time and land that will not easily let go of life. We need to write a queer theory of life and death that is more complex than urban = life // rural = death. A dichotomous thinking around space and life/death does not take into account those who live in the countryside (queer separatists, among others) nor those who die in the city (Sakia Gunn, who was killed in Newark, New Jersey, in 2003; Jason Mattison, Jr., killed in Baltimore in 2009; and innumerable unnamed others).

Once again, temporality takes shape in the intersection between materiality and economy. On January 1, 1994, the state of Tennessee instituted TennCare, which by now is "one of the oldest Medicaid managed care programs in the country."[25] Though the requirements have since been tightened, in the early days TennCare was not all too difficult to access, resulting in almost all of the state's five million residents having health insurance.[26] In one swift move Tennessee became a place where those living with AIDS could imagine a future. Spree, who has lived in the Gayborhood for over fifteen years, recalls how he came to move here:

> "So, anyway, one of the reasons why I decided—this is getting to your question of 'why Tennessee?'—was because they were going through this thing where they were starting this whole new program where everybody in the state was going to get healthcare. And they started a special program they called TennCare, and it is basically a whole jumbled up amalgamation of Medicaid and all these different programs put together that the state decided that they were gonna give everyone in the state health coverage. And since I knew I was gonna be needing it, that's why Tennessee was particularly appealing to me. Because it wasn't working out in the Netherlands because of how their system is and it doesn't work the same way and all that kind of stuff, so I was like, I knew that eventually I was gonna be needing medical attention and medical care and that I better, you know, get serious about it and stuff like that, so I was like 'oh! I could give that a try.'"[27]

TennCare is part of the politico-economic history of the region, a history that in multiple ways has facilitated the creation and maintenance of the Gayborhood. Economic structures and the material world come together to create the sticky, unruly time of the Gayborhood.

Holidays, Celebrations, and Spectacles

Life in the Gayborhood follows rhythms that differ from metronormative queer time not just on a diurnal cycle, but also on a yearly scale. The main holidays celebrated in the Gayborhood are those that relate to nature. Winter solstice is a moment for renewal; a few days later, Christmas passes by almost unnoticed. The emphasis on the solstice is partly because of the Radical Faerie influence—the Faeries follow a pagan calendar—but it is also due to what matters, literally. The hollow can be dark; because of the surrounding ridges, the sun sets an hour earlier than in town. So the turning from longer nights to longer days is reason for excitement and celebration. For the first couple of weeks after the solstice last year, a resident reported every day exactly how many more seconds of sunlight there was.

In rural homes with a significant commitment to food production, such as Bucky's, some aspects of life are mundane to a fault, with little if any distinction between workdays and holidays. The reproduction of the more-than-human does not follow a five-days-a-week schedule. The chickens need to be fed, the flowers watered. But this also means that any day is a possible holiday. Birthday parties, "field days" with games and food, and movie nights scatter the calendar at Bucky's, with little attention to weekdays and weekends. If you want to watch a movie, what is important is that it is dark enough outside to project a movie on a sheet on the porch, not what day of the week it is in order to attract an audience.

Retemporalization

Queer rural time, as manifested in the Gayborhood, is also a refusal of modern/industrial time. According to Elizabeth Freeman, "the advent of wage work . . . entailed a violent retemporalization of bodies once tuned to the seasonal rhythms of agricultural labor."[28] Rural queer time is not a return to a pastoral paradise (and it is worth remembering here that agricultural labor is as socially constructed as other forms of work, and often violently strenuous); however, the rhythms of the more-than-human world are closer here than in most urban locales affecting the tempo of human bodies. Regardless of the extent to which one participates in the agricultural labor at Bucky's and the surrounding food-producing Gayborhood plots, the seasonal rhythms affect one's body, retemporalizing it. Because of the lack of outside electrical lighting, winter is by necessity a slower time of year, where there are not as many hours in the day.

The retemporalization of life from one structured by electrical lights and weekly schedules to one more in tune with the seasons is not only one of the romantic dream for a return to the pastoral; as Freeman goes on to argue (drawing on the work of John Borneman) the timeline of normative life "tends to serve a nation's economic interests, too."[29] As Freeman points out, in the United States, the life cycle is carefully monitored by the state, and this benefits the current economic system. Registering births means registering new citizens, "eventually encrypted in a Social Security ID for taxpaying purposes." Marriage and domestic partnership, also under the eye of the state, "privatizes caretaking and regulates the distribution of privatized property." Finally, death "terminates the identities linked to state benefits, redistributing these benefits through familial channels." Within the U.S. nation-state, having a productive and ordered life "is what it means to have a life at all."[30] Rethinking time, and acknowledging alternative ways of approaching time, can thus be a useful tool in chipping away at normativity, and at the seeming inevitability of the socioeconomic system. Following the telos is an economic imperative, one that the Gayborhood residents are for the most part reluctant to do.

At the same time, the benefits of participating in the system are real and material, and many in the Gayborhood do wish to have more access to them. Retirement savings are scarce, finances are unstable, and jobs either dead-end or short-term. The economy has abandoned this space, largely because of its relation to time: the topography of the hollows is slow. Those with financial resources thus evacuated the hollows because speed was not possible here. It took time to get anywhere, and plants refused to grow as fast as in the fertilized greenhouses on the plateaus. What had been before the advent of car culture the most desirable location in the county because of its agricultural possibilities became poor, backward, a place to escape.

Conclusion

This essay has provided starting points for conceptualizing how queer time functions in rural locales. It is not a conclusive theory of rural queer time, but rather an invitation to think further about the subject. Focusing on the rural makes for a closer attention to the material aspects of time. Not because the rural is somehow more material than the urban, or "closer to nature"—the whole earth is material—but because the materiality of human life is harder to ignore in an environment that includes more interactions with the more-than-human. Time in the Gayborhood is structured by daylight rhythms, long distances, and an abandonment of rural Appalachia by the U.S. state and economy. Taking seriously the lives of rural queer communities enables us to build a stronger and more flexible theory of the intersection of queerness and temporality.

NOTES

1 "Hollow" (or "holler") is a term used in Appalachia to designate a small, narrow valley. The term not only connotes a specific geographical feature, but also serves as a cultural marker for rural Appalachian life.

2 "Bucky's" is a pseudonym, as are all names of people and Gayborhood locations used in this chapter.

3 If we define normative as that which adheres to Western linear scientific thinking, magic, with its disregard for scientific cause and effect and its intermingling of past, present, and future, falls far from the norm.

4 Tennessee was a central locus in the back-to-the-land movement of the 1960s and 1970s, with numerous communes, most famous among them the Farm, which is still in existence.

5 Official statistics are lacking, but my research points to about a dozen queer land projects in North America, all founded after Bucky's.

6 Halberstam, *In a Queer Time and Place*.

7 Edelman, *No Future*, 3.

8 Ibid., 4.

9 According to Gayle Rubin, the urban bias in LGBTQ studies stretches back to the mid-twentieth century, when a series of studies about gay communities were conducted in Chicago. Rubin, "Studying Sexual Subcultures."

10 Muñoz, *Cruising Utopia*, 1.

11 Ibid.

12 Ibid., 25.

13 Freeman, *Time Binds*, 3.

14 Ibid.

15 Camporesi, *The Magic Harvest*, 35.

16 A conch is a large seashell that can be blown like a trumpet, creating a far-ranging sound.

17 Herring, *Another Country*, 16.

18 A chore wheel is a chart for rotating housework tasks used in many collective living arrangements.

19 Hennen, *Faeries, Bears, and Leathermen*, 61.

20 U.S. Census Bureau, 2002, DeKalb County QuickFacts, http://quickfacts.census.gov/qfd/states/47/47041.html.

21 Halberstam, *In a Queer Time and Place*, 25.

22 Qball Productions, http://www.qballproductions.com/ (accessed November 27, 2009).

23 Grover, *North Enough*, 31.

24 T. Spree Vance, interview with T. Fleischman and author, Tennessee, August 2010.

25 TennCare, http://www.state.tn.us/tenncare/news-about.html (accessed September 3, 2010).

26 Gold, "Markets and Public Programs," 650.

27 T. Spree Vance, interview with author, Tennessee, August 2010.

28 Freeman, *Time Binds*, 3.

29 Ibid., 4.

30 Ibid., 4–5.

BIBLIOGRAPHY

Abel, Elizabeth. *Signs of the Times: The Visual Politics of Jim Crow*. Berkeley: University of California Press, 2010. http://www.ucpress.edu/book.?isbn=9780520261839.

Adams, Jane. *The Transformation of Rural Life: Southern Illinois, 1890–1990*. Chapel Hill: University of North Carolina Press, 1994.

Adobe and Mint Judith. "Adobeland." In *Lesbian Land*, edited by Joyce Cheney, 24–29. Minneapolis, MN: Word Weaver, 1985.

Adorno, Theodore W., and Max Horkheimer. Dialectic of Enlightenment. Translated by John Cumming. New York: Continuum, 1994.

Agamben, Giogio. *Homo Sacer: Sovereign Power and Bare Life*. Palo Alto, CA: Stanford University Press, 1998.

Ahmed, Sara. *The Cultural Politics of Emotion*. Edinburgh: Edinburgh University Press, 2004.

———. *Queer Phenomenology: Orientations, Objects, Others*. Durham, NC: Duke University Press, 2006.

Aitkin, Stuart C., and Christopher Lee Lukinbeal. "Disassociated Masculinities and Geographies of the Road." In *The Road Movie Book*, edited by Steven Cohan and Ina Rae Hark, 349–70. London: Routledge, 1997.

Aizura, Aren. "Of Borders and Homes: The Imaginary Community of (Trans)sexual Citizenship." *Inter-Asia Cultural Studies* 7, no. 2 (2006): 289–309.

Alger, Horatio, Jr. *The Young Miner; or Tom Nelson in California*. Philadelphia: John C. Winston, 1879.

———. *The Young Explorer; or Among the Sierras*. Philadelphia: Porter & Coates, 1880.

———. *Ben's Nugget; or A Boy's Search for Fortune*. Philadelphia: John C. Winston, 1882.

———. *Joe's Luck; Or, A Boy's Adventures in California*. New York: A. L. Burt, 1887.

———. *Tom Thatcher's Fortune*. New York: A. L. Burt, 1888.

———. "Writing Stories for Boys—IV." *The Writer*, March 1896.

———. *Strive and Succeed: Julius or the Street Boy Out West and the Store Boy or the Fortunes of Ben Barclay: Two Novels*. New York: Holt, Reinhart and Winston, 1967.

———. *Dean Dunham; or The Waterford Mystery*. Leyden, MA: Aeonian Press, 1975.

———. *Ragged Dick and Struggling Upward*. New York: Penguin Books, 1986.

Allen, Danielle. *Talking with Strangers: Anxieties of Citizenship since Brown v. Board of Education*. Chicago: University of Chicago Press, 2004.

Altman, Dennis. *Homosexual: Oppression and Liberation*. London: Allen Lane, 1971.

———. *Global Sex*. Chicago: University of Chicago Press, 2001.

Anderson, Benedict. *Imagined Communities: Reflections on the Origin and Spread of Nationalism*. London and New York: Verso, 1993.

Anderson, Clifford. "The Metamorphosis of American Agrarian Idealism in the 1920's and 1930's." *Agricultural History* 35, no. 4 (October 1961).

Anderson, Mark. *Black and Indigenous: Garifuna Activism and Consumer Culture in Honduras*. Minneapolis: University of Minnesota Press, 2009.

Anderson, Sherwood. *Poor White*. New York: Modern Library, 1926.

——. *Poor White*. New York: New Directions, 1993.

Andrews, Thomas G. *Killing for Coal: America's Deadliest Labor War*. Cambridge, MA: Harvard University Press, 2008.

Annes, Alexis, and Meredith Redlin. "Coming Out and Coming Back: Rural Gay Migration and the City." *Journal of Rural Studies* 28, (2012): 56–68.

Anzaldúa, Gloria. *Borderlands/La Frontera: The New Mestiza*. San Francisco: Aunt Lute Books, 1987.

Armstrong Percy, William, III. "William Alexander Percy (1885–1942): His Homosexuality and Why It Matters." In *Carryin' On in the Lesbian and Gay South*, edited by John Howard, 75–92. New York: New York University Press, 1997.

Asen, Robert. "Discourse Theory of Citizenship." *Quarterly Journal of Speech* 90 (2004).

Attallah, Paul. "Music Television." In *Watching All the Music: Rock Video and Beyond*, edited by Gareth Sansom, 19–40. Montreal: McGill University Working Papers in Communication, 1987.

Aubin, Christina. "Beltane–Holiday Details and History." *WitchVox*. http://www.witchvox.com/va/dt_va.html?a=usma&c=holidays&id=2765.

Badgett, M. V. Lee. *Money, Myths, and Change: The Economic Lives of Lesbians and Gay Men*. Chicago: University of Chicago Press, 2001.

Baker, O. E. "Rural-Urban Migration and the National Welfare." *Annals of the Association of American Geographers* 23 (June 1933): 92.

Barad, Karen M. *Meeting the Universe Halfway: Quantum Physics and the Entanglement of Matter and Meaning*. Durham, NC: Duke University Press, 2007.

Barry, Dan. "Sewers, Curfews, and a Ban on Gay Bias." *New York Times*, January 28, 2013.

Barthes, Roland. "The Rhetoric of the Image." In *Image-Music-Text*, translated by Stephen Heath. New York: Hill and Wang, 1977.

——. *The Rustle of Language*. Translated by Richard Howard. New York: Hill and Wang, 1986.

——. *Mythologies*. Translated by Annette Leavers. New York: The Noonday Press, 1989.

Bartlett, Neil. "Forgery." In *Camp—Queer Aesthetics and the Performing Subject: A Reader*, edited by Fabio Cleto, 179–84. Ann Arbor: University of Michigan Press, 2002.

Baum, Frank Lyman. *The Wonderful Wizard of Oz*. Toronto: Sterling, 2005.

——. *The Marvelous Land of Oz*. New York: Biblio Bazaar, 2007.

Baxter, Kent. *The Modern Age: Turn-of-the-Century American Culture and the Invention of Adolescence.* Tuscaloosa: University of Alabama Press, 2008.

Bederman, Gail. *Manliness and Civilization: A Cultural History of Gender and Race in the United States, 1880–1917.* Chicago: University of Chicago Press, 1995.

Bell, David. "Anti-Idyll: Rural Horror." In *Contested Countryside Cultures: Otherness, Marginalisation, and Rurality,* edited by Paul Cloke and Jo Little, 94–108. London: Routledge, 1997.

———. "Eroticizing the Rural." In *De-Centering Sexualities: Politics and Representations beyond the Metropolis,* edited by Richard Phillips, David Shuttleton, and Diane Watt, 83–101. New York: Routledge, 2000.

———. "Farm Boys and Wild Men: Rurality, Masculinity and Homosexuality." *Rural Sociology* 65, no. 4 (2000): 547–61.

———. "Homosexuals in the Heartland: Male Same-Sex Desire in the Rural United States." In *Country Visions: Knowing the Rural World,* edited by Paul Cloke, 178–94. New York: Pearson, 2003.

———. "Cowboy Love." In *Country Boys: Masculinity and Rural Life,* edited by Hugh Campbell, Michael M. Bell, and Margaret Finney, 163–80. University Park: Pennsylvania State University Press, 2006.

Bell, David, and Jon Binnie. "Authenticating Queer Space: Citizenship, Urbanism and Governance." *Urban Studies* 41, no. 9 (2004): 1807–20.

Bell, David, and Ruth Holliday. "Naked as Nature Intended." *Body & Society* 6, no. 3 (November 2000): 127–40.

Bell, David, and Gill Valentine. "Queer Country: Rural Lesbian and Gay Lives." *Journal of Rural Studies* 11, no. 2 (1995): 113–22.

Benjamin, Walter. "Theses on the Philosophy of History." In *Illuminations,* edited by Hannah Arendt, 253–56. London: Pimlico Press, 1999.

Bennett, Jeffrey A. *Banning Queer Blood: Rhetorics of Citizenship, Contagion, and Resistance.* Tuscaloosa: University of Alabama Press, 2009.

Berlant, Lauren. *The Queen of America Goes to Washington City: Essays on Sex and Citizenship.* Durham: Duke University Press, 1997.

———. *The Female Complaint: The Unfinished Business of Sentimentality in American Culture.* Durham: Duke University Press, 2008.

———. *Cruel Optimism.* Durham: Duke University Press, 2011.

Berlant, Lauren, ed. *Intimacy.* Chicago: University of Chicago Press, 2000.

Berman, Marshall. *All That Is Solid Melts into Air: The Experience of Modernity.* New York: Simon and Schuster, 1982.

Bernstein, Mary, and Verta Taylor. *The Marrying Kind?.* Minneapolis: University of Minnesota Press, 2013.

Berthoff, Warner. *The Ferment of Realism: American Literature, 1884–1919.* New York: Free Press, 1965.

Berube, Allan. *Coming Out Under Fire: The History of Gay Men and Women in World War II.* Chapel Hill: University of North Carolina Press, 2010.

Betsky, Aaron. *Queer Space: Architecture and Same-Sex Desire*. New York: William Morrow, 1997.

Bhabha, Homi K. *The Location of Culture*. New York: Routledge, 2007.

Boag, Peter. *Same-Sex Affairs: Constructing and Controlling Homosexuality in the Pacific Northwest*. Berkeley: University of California Press, 2003.

Boellstorff, Tom. *The Gay Archipelago: Sexuality and Nation in Indonesia*. Princeton, NJ: Princeton University Press, 2005.

———. *A Coincidence of Desires: Anthropology, Queer Studies, Indonesia*. Durham, NC: Duke University Press, 2007

———. "Queer Studies in the House of Anthropology." *Annual Review of Anthropology* 36, no. 2 (2007): 17–35.

Bourdieu, Pierre. "Cultural Reproduction and Social Reproduction." In *Knowledge, Education and Cultural Change*, edited by Richard K. Brown, 71–112. London: Tavistock, 1973.

———. *Distinction: A Social Critique of the Judgment of Taste*. Translated by Richard Nice. Cambridge, MA: Harvard University Press, 1984.

Boyd, Nan Amilla. *Wide Open Town: A Queer History of San Francisco to 1865*. Berkeley: University of California Press, 2003.

Boy George, with Spencer Bright. *Take It like a Man: The Autobiography of Boy George*. New York: Harper Collins Publishers, 1995.

Brace, Charles Loring. *The Best Method of Disposing of Our Pauper and Vagrant Children*. New York: Wynkoop, Hallenback & Thomas, 1859.

———. *The Dangerous Classes of New York and Twenty Years' Work among Them*. Montclair, NJ: Patterson Smith, 1967.

Bradwin, Edmund. *The Bunkhouse Man: A Study of Work and Pay in the Camps of Canada, 1903–1914*. New York: Columbia University Press, 1928.

Brady, Mary Pat. *Extinct Lands, Temporal Geographies: Chicana Literature and the Urgency of Space*. Durham, NC: Duke University Press, 2002.

Brooks, Van Wyck, and Claire Sprague. *Van Wyck Brooks, the Early Years: A Selection from His Works, 1908–1925*, rev. ed. Boston: Northeastern University Press, 1993.

Brown, David, and Kai Schafft. *Rural People & Communities in the 21st Century: Resilience & Transformation* Malden, MA: Polity Press, 2011.

Brown, Michael. *Closet Space: Geographies of Metaphor from the Body to the Globe*. London: Routledge, 2000.

Brown, Wendy. *States of Injury: Power and Freedom in Late Modernity*. Princeton, NJ: Princeton University Press, 1995.

———. *Edgework: Critical Essays on Politics and Knowledge*. Princeton, NJ: Princeton University Press, 2004.

———. *Regulating Aversion: Tolerance in the Age of Identity and Empire*. Princeton, NJ: Princeton University Press, 2005.

Brownell, Susan. *The 1904 Anthropology Days and Olympic Games: Sport, Race, and American Imperialism*. Lincoln: University of Nebraska Press, 2008.

Brown, Beverly, Tina Wright, and Dragon Fire. "Lesbians on Land without Land." In *Lesbian Land*, edited by Joyce Cheney, 169–73. Minneapolis, MN: Word Weaver, 1985.

Bruni, Frank. "On Gay Marriage, Principle over Politics." *New York Times*, August 20, 2012, sec. Opinion. http://www.nytimes.com/2012/08/21/opinion/bruni-principle-over-politics.html.

Bryson, Norman. "Todd Haynes's 'Poison' and Queer in Cinema." *Invisible Culture: An Electronic Journal for Visual Studies*, February 23, 2005, 16.

Bunge, Nancy L. "The Ambiguous Endings of Sherwood Anderson's Novels." In *Sherwood Anderson: Centennial Studies*, edited by Hilbert H. Campbell and Charles E. Modlin, 249–63. Troy, NY: Whitston Publishing, 1976.

Burack, Cynthia. *Sin, Sex, and Democracy: Antigay Rhetoric and the Christian Right*. Albany: State University of New York Press, 2008.

Burger, John. *One Handed Histories: The Eroto-Politics of Gay Male Video Pornography*. New York: Harrington Park Press, 1995.

Burgett, Bruce. "Between Speculation and Population: The Problem of 'Sex' in Our Long Eighteenth Century." *Early American Literature* 37, no. 1 (2002): 119–53.

Burke, Kenneth. *A Rhetoric of Motives*. Berkeley: University of California Press, 1969.

Butler, Judith. "Imitation and Gender Subordination." In *Inside/Out: Lesbian Theories, Gay Theories*, edited by Diana Fuss, 13–31. New York: Routledge, 1991.

———. *Gender Trouble: Feminism and the Subversion of Identity*. New York: Routledge, 1999.

———. *Precarious Lives: The Powers of Mourning and Violence*. London: Verso, 2004.

Calhoun, Craig. "Imagining Solidarity: Cosmopolitanism, Constitutional Patriotism, and the Public Sphere." *Public Culture* 14, no. 1 (2002): 147–71.

Califia, Pat. *Public Sex: The Culture of Radical Sex*. Pittsburgh: Cleis Press, 1994.

Camporesi, Piero. *The Magic Harvest: Food, Folklore and Society*. Malden, MA: Blackwell Publishers, 1998.

Canaday, Margot. *The Straight State: Sexuality and Citizenship in Twentieth-Century America*. Princeton, NJ: Princeton University Press, 2009.

Carpenter, Daniel. *The Forging of Bureaucratic Autonomy: Reputations, Networks, and Policy Innovations in Executive Agencies, 1862–1928*. Princeton, NJ: Princeton University Press, 2000.

Casey, Janet Galligani. *A New Heartland: Women, Modernity, and the Agrarian Ideal in America*. New York: Oxford University Press, 2009.

Casey, Mark. "De-Dyking Queer Space(s): Heterosexual Female Visibility in Gay and Lesbian Spaces." *Sexualities* 7 (2004): 446–61.

CBC News. "Truro in Gay Flag Flap," August 3, 2007. http://www. cbc.ca/ canada/nova-scotia/ story/2007/08/03/truro-gay.html.

Chauncey, George. *Gay New York: Gender, Urban Culture and the Making of the Gay Male World, 1890–1940*. New York: Basic Books, 1994.

Chavez, Leo R. "The Power of the Imagined Community: The Settlement of Undocumented Mexicans and Central Americans in the United States." In *Academic Read-*

ing and Writing in the Disciplines, edited by J. Giltrow, 216–28. Canada: Broadview Press, 2002.

Cheney, Joyce, ed. *Lesbian Land*. Minneapolis, MN: Word Weavers, 1985.

Children's Aid Society. *The Crusade for Children: A Review of Child Life in New York during 75 Years, 1853–1928*. New York: Children's Aid Society, 1928.

The Children's Aid Society of New York: Its History, Plan, and Results. New York: Wynkoop & Hallenbeck, 1893.

Ching, Barbara, and Gerald W. Creed, eds. *Knowing Your Place: Rural Identity and Cultural Identity*. New York: Routledge, 1997.Chorney, Harold. *City of Dreams: Social Theory and the Urban Experience*. Scarborough, Ontario: Nelson, 1990.

Chuan, Lee Kham. "Exploring the Discursive Construct of Open Non-Monogamy Relationships as Understood by Same-Sex Romantic Partners." M.A. thesis, University of East London, 2010.

Chudacoff, Howard P. *The Age of the Bachelor: Creating an American Subculture*. Princeton, NJ: Princeton University Press, 1999.

Cisneros, Sandra. *Woman Hollering Creek: And Other Stories*. New York: Random House, 1991.

Cloke, Paul, ed. *Country Visions: Knowing the Rural World*. New York: Pearson, 2003.

Cloke, Paul, and Jo Little. "Introduction: Other Countrysides?" In *Contested Countryside Cultures: Otherness, Marginalisation, and Rurality*, edited by Paul Cloke and Jo Little, 1–17. London: Routledge, 1997.

Clymer, Jeffory A. "Modeling, Diagramming, and Early Twentieth-Century Histories of Invention and Entrepreneurship: Henry Ford, Sherwood Anderson, Samuel Insull." *Journal of American Studies* 36, no. 3 (2002).

Coates, Norma. "(R)evolution Now? Rock and the Political Potential of Gender." In *Sexing the Groove: Popular Music and Gender*, edited by Sheila Whiteley, 50–64. New York and London: Routledge, 1997.

Cobb, Michael. *God Hates Fags: The Rhetoric of Religious Violence*. New York: New York University Press, 2006.

Cody, Paul J., and Peter L. Welch. "Rural Gay Men in Northern New England." *Journal of Homosexuality* 33, no. 1 (1997): 51–67.

Cohan, Steven. *Incongruous Entertainment: Camp, Cultural Value, and the MGM Musical*. Durham, NC: Duke University Press, 2005.

Cohn, Susan E., and Jonathan D. Klein. "The Geography of AIDS: Patterns of Urban and Rural Migration." *Southern Medical Journal* 87, no. 6 (1994): 599–606.

Coleman, Kevin P. "A Camera in the Garden of Eden." *Journal of Latin American Cultural Studies: Travesia* 20, no. 1 (2011): 63–96. doi:10.1080/13569325.2011.562634.

———. "A Camera in the Garden of Eden: Fabricating the Banana Republic." Ph.D. diss., Indiana University, 2012.

Comentale, Edward P. "'The Possibilities of Hard-Won Land': Midwestern Modernism and the Novel." In *A Companion to the Modern American Novel, 1900–1950*, edited by John T. Matthews, 240–65. Malden, MA: Wiley-Blackwell, 2009.

Comer, Douglas C. *Ritual Ground: Bent's Old Fort, World Formation, and the Annexation of the Southwest.* Berkeley: University of California Press, 1996.

Connor, Ralph. *The Man from Glengarry.* Toronto: McClelland & Steward, 1993.

Conrad, Ryan, ed. *Against Equality: Queer Critiques of Gay Marriage.* Lewiston, ME: Against Equality Publishing Collective, 2010.

Cook, David A. *Lost Illusions: American Cinema in the Shadow of Watergate and Vietnam.* Berkeley: University of California Press, 2000.

Cook, Harry H. *Like Breeds Like.* Ontario, CA: Research Department, Sans Aloi's Jersey Farm, 1931.

Cook, Jeffrey. *The Architecture of Bruce Goff.* New York: Harper & Row, 1978.

Countryman, Matthew. *Up South: Civil Rights and Black Power in Philadelphia.* Philadelphia: University of Pennsylvania Press, 2005.

Crawford, James Logan. *The Crawford House of Steamboat Springs.* Steamboat Springs, CO: N.p., 2009.

Crimp, Douglas. "Randy Shilts's Miserable Failure." In *A Queer World: The Center or Lesbian and Gay Studies Reader,* edited by Martin Duberman, 641–48. New York: New York University Press, 1997.

Cronon, William. *Nature's Metropolis: Chicago and the Great West.* New York: W. W. Norton, 1991.

Cvetkovich, Ann. *An Archive of Feelings: Trauma, Sexuality, and Lesbian Public Cultures.* Durham, NC: Duke University Press, 2003.

Davis, Clark. *Company Men: White-Collar Life and Corporate Culture in Los Angeles, 1892–1941.* Baltimore: Johns Hopkins University Press, 2000.

Davis, Kathy. "Intersectionality as Buzzword: A Sociology of Science Perspective on What Makes a Feminist Theory Successful." *Feminist Theory* 9, no. 1 (April 2008): 67–85.

Dean, Tim. *Unlimited Intimacy: Reflections on the Subculture of Barebacking.* Chicago: University of Chicago Press, 2009.

De Certeau, Michel. *The Practice of Everyday Life.* Berkeley: University of California Press, 1984.

Delany, Samuel. *Times Square Red, Times Square Blue.* New York: New York University Press, 1999.

De Long, David G. *Bruce Goff: Toward Absolute Architecture.* Cambridge, MA: MIT Press, 1988.

DeLuca, Kevin Michael. "Unruly Arguments: The Body Rhetoric of Earth First!, Act Up, and Queer Nation." *Argumentation and Advocacy* 36, no. 1 (1999): 9–21.

Deleuze, Gilles, and Felix Guattari. *A Thousand Plateaus: Capitalism and Schizophrenia.* Translated by Brian Massumi. Minneapolis: University of Minnesota Press, 1987.

Deleuze, Gilles, and Brian Massumi. *Kafka: Toward a Minor Literature.* Translated by Dana Polan. Minneapolis: University of Minnesota Press, 1986.

D'Emilio, John. "Gay Politics and Community in San Francisco since World War II." In *Hidden from History: Reclaiming the Gay and Lesbian Past,* edited by M. Vicinus, G. Chauncey and M. Duberman, 456–73. New York: Meridian Books, 1989.

———. "Capitalism and Gay Identity." In *The Lesbian and Gay Studies Reader*, edited by Henry Abelove, Michèle Aina Barale, and David Halperin, 467–76. New York: Routledge, 1993.

Demos, John, and Virginia Demos. "Adolescence in a Historical Perspective." *Journal of Marriage and the Family* 31, no. 4 (1969): 632–38.

Dollimore, Johnathan. "Post/Modern: On the Gay Sensibility, or the Pervert's Revenge on Authenticity." In *Camp—Queer Aesthetics and the Performing Subject: A Reader*, edited by Fabio Cleto, 221–36. Ann Arbor: University of Michigan Press, 2002.

Downing, Lisa. "Beyond Safety: Erotic Asphyxiation and the Limits of S/M Discourse." In *Safe, Sane and Consensual: Contemporary Perspectives on Sadomasochism*, edited by Darren Langridge and Meg Barker, 119–32. Basingstoke, UK: Palgrave Macmillan, 2007.

Doyle, Laura, and Laura A. Winkiel. *Geomodernisms: Race, Modernism, Modernity*. Bloomington: Indiana University Press, 2005.

Duberman, Martin. "'Writhing Bedfellows' in Antebellum South Carolina: Historical Interpretation and the Politics of Evidence." In *Carryin' On in the Lesbian and Gay South*, edited by John Howard, 15–33. New York: New York University Press, 1997.

duCille, Ann. "The Occult of True Black Womanhood: Critical Demeanor and Black Feminist Studies." *Signs* 19, no. 3 (1994): 591–629.

Dunn, Thomas R. "Remembering Matthew Shepard: Violence, Identity, and Queer Counterpublic Memories." *Rhetoric & Public Affairs* 13, no. 4 (2010): 611–52.

Dyer, Richard. "Stereotyping." In *Gays and Film*, edited by Richard Dyer, 27–39. London: British Film Institute, 1977.

———. "In Defense of Disco." *Out in Culture: Gay, Lesbian, and Queer Essays on Popular Culture*, edited by Corey K. Creekmur and Alexander Doty, 407–15.Durham, NC: Duke University Press, 1995.

———. *Stars*. London: British Film Institute, 1998.

Dynes, Wayne. "Foucault's Social Construction." *Dyneslines*, September 30, 2004. http://www2.hu-berlin.de/sexology/BIB/DynesFoucault.htm.

Easton, Dossie, and Janet W. Hardy. *The Ethical Slut: A Guide to Infinite Sexual Possibilities*. San Francisco: Greenery Press, 1997.

Eaves, LaToya E. "Space, Place, and Identity in Conversation: Queer Black Women Living in the Rural U.S. South." In *Sexuality, Rurality, and Geography*, edited by Andrew Gorman-Murray, Barbara Pini, and Lia Bryant, 111–25. Lanham, MD: Lexington Books, 2013.

Edelman, Lee. *Homographesis: Essays in Gay Literary and Cultural Theory*. New York: Routledge, 1994.

———. *No Future: Queer Theory and the Death Drive*. Durham, NC: Duke University Press, 2004.

Edmonds, Michael. *Out of the Northwoods: The Many Live of Paul Bunyan*. Wisconsin Historical Society Press, 2009.

Eichhorn, Kate. "Archiving the Movement: The Riot Grrrl Collection at Fales Library and Special Collections." In *Make Your Own History: Documenting Feminist and*

Queer Activism in the 21ˢᵗ Century, edited by Lyz Bly and Kelly Wooten, 23–37. Los Angeles: Litwin Books, 2012.

Elliot, Joy. "Researching Healthy and Sustainable Development in Nova Scotia." *Rural Communities Impacting Policy*, 2005. http://www.ruralnovascotia.ca/documents / comm.%20devlp/CD%20final%20report05.pdf.

Ellis, David H., and Catherine H. Ellis. *Steamboat Springs*. Chicago: Arcadia Publishing, 2009.

Emerson, Robert M., Rachel I. Fretz, and Linda L. Shaw. *Writing Ethnographic Fieldnotes*, 2nd ed. Chicago: University of Chicago Press, 1995.

Eng, David L., and David Kazanjian. Preface. In *Loss: The Politics of Mourning*, edited by David L. Eng and David Kazanjian. Berkeley: University of California Press, 2003.

Engel, Stephen M. *The Unfinished Revolution: Social Movement Theory and the Gay and Lesbian Movement*. Cambridge, UK: Cambridge University Press, 2001.

Enniss, Stephen C. "Alienation and Affirmation: The Divided Self in Sherwood Anderson's 'Poor White.'" *South Atlantic Review* 55, no. 2 (1990).

Ensminger, M. E. *Beef Cattle Husbandry*. Danville, IL: Interstate Printers and Publishers, 1951.

Escobar, Arturo. *Encountering Development: The Making and Unmaking of the Third World*. Princeton, NJ: Princeton University Press, 1994.

Etcheson, Nicole. *The Emerging Midwest: Upland Southerners and the Political Culture of the Old Northwest, 1787–1861*. Bloomington: Indiana University Press, 1996.

Euraque, Darío A. "En Busca de Froylán Turcios." In *Paraninfo* 23, 177–97. Tegucigalpa, Honduras: Instituto de Ciencias del Hombre, Rafael Heliodoro Valle, 2003.

Farland, Maria. "Modernist Versions of Pastoral: Poetic Inspiration, Scientific Expertise, and the 'Degenerate' Farmer." *American Literary History* 19, no. 4 (2007): 905–36.

Farrow, Kenyon. "Making Change: A House of Our Own." *City Limits*, September 26, 2010.

Federal Bureau of Investigation. *Hate Crime Statistics 1998*. Washington, DC, 1998. http://www.fbi.gov/about-us/cjis/ucr/hate-crime/1998.

Fellows, Will, ed. *Farm Boys: Lives of Gay Men from the Rural Midwest*. Madison: University of Wisconsin Press, 1996.

Ferguson, Roderick A. *Aberrations in Black: Toward a Queer of Color Critique*. Minneapolis: University of Minnesota Press, 2003.

Fiedler, Leslie. *Love and Death in the American Novel*. New York: Criterion Books, 1960.

Finegold, Kenneth, and Theda Skocpol. *State and Party in America's New Deal*. Chicago: University of Chicago Press, 1999.

Fink, Deborah. *Agrarian Women: Wives and Mothers in Rural Nebraska, 1880–1940*. Chapel Hill: University of North Carolina Press, 1992.

Fitzpatrick, Alfred. *The University in Overalls: A Plea for Part Time Study*. Toronto: Thompson Educational Publishing, 1999.

Flowers, Paul, Claire Marriott, and Graham Hart. "The Bars, the Bogs, and the Bushes: Impact of Locale on Sexual Cultures." *Culture, Health, Sexuality* 2, no. 1 (2000): 69–86.

Foucault, Michel. *The Archaeology of Knowledge*. New York: Pantheon Books, 1972.

———. *Discipline and Punish: The Birth of the Prison*. New York: Random House, 1977.

———. *The History of Sexuality*, vol. 1. New York: Vintage, 1990.

———. *Security, Territory, Population: Lectures at the Collège de France, 1977–1978*. New York: Picador, 2008.

———. *The Birth of Biopolitics: Lectures at the Collège de France, 1978–1979*. New York: Picador, 2008.

———. *History of Madness*. New York: Routledge, 2009.

Fraser, Nancy. "Rethinking the Public Sphere: A Contribution to the Critique of Actually Existing Democracy." In *Habermas and the Public Sphere*, edited by Craig Calhoun, 109–42. Cambridge, MA: MIT Press, 1993.

Freeman, Elizabeth. *Time Binds: Queer Temporalities, Queer Histories*. Durham, NC: Duke University Press, 2010.

Freud, Sigmund. *Totem and Taboo: Some Points of Agreement between the Mental Lives of Savages and Neurotics*. London: Routledge, 1951.

Fuss, Diana. "Introduction." In *Inside/Out: Lesbian Theories, Gay Theories*, edited by Diana Fuss. New York: Routledge, 1991.

———. "Freud's Fallen Women: Identification, Desire, and a Case of Homosexuality in a Woman." In *Fear of a Queer Planet: Queer Politics and Social Theory*, edited by Michael Warner, 42–65. Minneapolis: University of Minnesota Press, 1993.

Gassan, Richard. "The Birth of American Tourism: New York, the Hudson Valley, and American Culture, 1790–1835." Ph.D. diss., University of Massachusetts, Amherst, 2002.

Gelfant, Blanche Housman. "A Novel of Becoming." In *Sherwood Anderson: A Collection of Critical Essays*, edited by Walter B. Rideout, 59–64. Englewood Cliffs, NJ: Prentice Hall, 1974.

Giddens, Anthony. *The Consequences of Modernity*. Stanford, CA: Stanford University Press, 1990.

Gil, José. *Metamorphosis of the Body*. Minneapolis: University of Minnesota Press, 1998.

Gilfoyle, Timothy J. *City of Eros: New York City, Prostitution, and the Commercialization of Sex, 1790–1920*. New York: W. W. Norton, 1992.

Gill, Anton. *Mad About the Boy: The Life and Times of Boy George and Culture Club*. New York: Holt, Reinhart and Winston, 1984.

Gill, John. *Queer Noises: Male and Female Homosexuality in Twentieth-Century Music*. Minneapolis: University of Minnesota Press, 1995.

Gilmore, Ruth Wilson. *Golden Gulag: Prisons, Surplus, Crisis, and Opposition in Globalizing California*. Berkeley: University of California Press, 2007.

Gladstone, Jim. "Jackson, Wyoming." *Passport Magazine*, April 2009. http://www.passportmagazine.com/destinations/Jackson_Wyoming.php?singlepage=yes.

Gold, Marsha. "Markets and Public Programs: Insights from Oregon and Tennessee." *Journal of Health Politics, Policy, and Law* 22, no. 2 (1997): 633–66.

Goodwin, Andrew. *Dancing in the Distraction Factory: Music Television and Popular Culture*. Minneapolis: University of Minnesota Press, 1992.

Gould, Deborah. *Moving Politics: Emotion and ACT UP's Fight against AIDS*. Chicago: University of Chicago Press, 2009.

Government of Nova Scotia. "Economic and Rural Development: Broadband for Rural Nova Scotia," 2009. http://www.gov.ns.ca/econ/broadband/updates/.

Gramsci, Antonio. *Prison Notebooks: Selections*. New York: International Publishers, 1971.

Gray, Mary. "From Websites to Wal-Mart: Youth, Identity Work, and the Queering of Boundary Publics in Small Town, USA." *American Studies* 48, no. 2 (2007): 49–59.

———. "Engaging Vulnerable Subjects: Queer Social Science Research at the Twilight of the Public University." Plenary presentation delivered at the Tenth Annual Queer Studies Conference, Los Angeles, CA, October 10–11, 2008.

———. *Out in the Country: Youth, Media, and Queer Visibility*. New York: New York University Press, 2009.

Gray, Susan E. *The Yankee West: Community Life on the Michigan Frontier*. Chapel Hill: University of North Carolina Press, 1996.

Green, James N. "'Who Is the Macho Who Wants to Kill Me?' Male Homosexuality, Revolutionary Masculinity, and the Brazilian Armed Struggle of the 1960s and 1970s." *Hispanic American Historical Review* 92, no. 3 (2012): 437–69.

Green, Nicola. "Disrupting the Field: Virtual Reality Technologies and 'Multisited' Ethnographic Methods." *American Behavioral Scientist* 43, no. 3 (1999): 409–21.

Greene, Beverly. "African American Lesbian and Bisexual Women". *Journal of Social Issues* 56, no. 2 (2000): 239–49.

Gregg, Sara. *Managing the Mountains: Land Use Planning, the New Deal, and the Creation of a Federal Landscape in Appalachia*. New Haven, CT: Yale University Press, 2010.

Greven, Andreas, Gerhard Keller, and Gerald Warnecke. "Introduction." In *Entropy*, edited by Andreas Greven, Gerhard Keller, and Gerald Warnecke. Princeton, NJ: Princeton University Press, 2003.

Grosz, Elizabeth. "Bodies—Cities." In *Sexuality & Space*, edited by Beatriz Colomina, 241–51.Princeton: Princeton Architectural Press, 1992.

———. *Space, Time, and Perversion: Essays on the Politics of Bodies*. New York: Routledge, 1995.

Grover, Jan Zita. *North Enough: AIDS and Other Clear-Cuts*. Saint Paul, MN: Graywolf Press, 1997.

Halberstam, Judith [now know as J. Jack]. "The Brandon Teena Archive." In *Queer Studies: An Interdiciplinary Reader*, edited by Robert J. Corber and Stephen Valocchi, 159–69. Malden, MA: Wiley-Blackwell, 2003.

———. *In a Queer Time and Place: Transgender Bodies, Subcultural Lives*. New York: New York University Press, 2005.

Hall, G. Stanley. *Adolescence*. New York: D. Appleton and Company, 1904.

Halperin, David. *Saint Foucault: Towards a Gay Hagiography*. New York: Oxford University Press, 1995.

———. *How to Do the History of Homosexuality*. Chicago: University of Chicago Press, 2002.

Halperin, David M., and Valerie Traub, eds. *Gay Shame*. Chicago: University Of Chicago Press, 2009.

Halperin, Rhoda H. *Cultural Economies Past and Present*. Austin: University of Texas Press, 1994.

Halttunen, Karen. *Confidence Men and Painted Women: A Study of Middle-Class Culture in America, 1830–1870*. New Haven, CT: Yale University Press, 1982.

Hamilton, Shane. *Trucking Country: The Road to America's Wal-Mart Economy*. Princeton, NJ: Princeton University Press, 2008.

Hampsten, Elizabeth. *Read This Only to Yourself: The Private Writings of Midwestern Women, 1880–1910*. Bloomington: Indiana University Press, 1982.

Hancock, Ange-Marie. "When Multiplication Doesn't Equal Quick Addition: Examining Intersectionality as a Research Paradigm." *Perspectives on Politics* 5, no. 1 (March 2007): 63–75.

Hanson, Adelia N., and Joseph A. Hanson. *A History of the Oklahoma State University College of Arts and Sciences*. Centennial History Series 22. Stillwater: Oklahoma State University, 1992.

Hanson, Natasha. *The Maritimer Way? Mobility Patterns of a Small Maritime City*. Ph.D. diss., Dalhousie University, Canada, 2013. Hargrave, James. *The Hargrave Correspondence, 1821–1843*. Toronto: The Champlain Society, 1938.

Hariman, Robert, and John Louis Lucaites. "Public Identity and Collective Memory in U.S. Iconic Photography: The Image of 'Accidental Napalm.'" *Critical Studies in Media Communication* 20, no. 1 (2003): 35–66.

———. *No Caption Needed: Iconic Photographs, Public Culture, and Liberal Democracy*. Chicago: University of Chicago Press, 2008.

———. "Visual Tropes and Late-Modern Emotion in U.S. Public Culture." *Poroi* 5, no. 2 (2008): 47–93.

Harley, Mei Lin. "Strengthening Rural Nova Scotia in the Knowledge-Based Economy." *Canadian Federation of Independent Business*, 2001. http://www.fcei.ca/legis/novascot/ pdf/5137.pdf.

Harold, Christine, and Kevin Michael DeLuca. "Behold the Corpse: Violent Images and the Case of Emmett Till." *Rhetoric and Public Affairs* 8, no. 2 (2005): 263–86.

Harris, Carmen V. "States' Rights, Federal Bureaucrats, and Segregated 4-H Camps in the United States, 1927–1969." *Journal of African American History* 93 (Summer 2008): 362–88.

Hawkins, Stan. "The Pet Shop Boys: Musicology, Masculinity and Banality." In *Sexing the Groove: Popular Music and Gender*, edited by Sheila Whiteley, 118–33. New York: Routledge, 1997.

Haynes, John. "Revolt of the Timber Beast: IWW Lumber Strike in Minnesota." *Minnesota History*, Spring 1971.

Heap, Chad. *Slumming: Sexual and Racial Encounters in American Nightlife, 1885–1940*. Chicago: University of Chicago Press, 2009.

Hegeman, Susan. *Patterns for America: Modernism and the Concept of Culture*. Princeton, NJ: Princeton University Press, 1999.

Hedler, Glenn. *Public Sentiments: Structures of Feeling in Nineteenth-Century American Literature*. Chapel Hill: University of North Carolina Press, 2001.

Hennen, Peter. *Faeries, Bears, and Leathermen: Men in Community Queering the Masculine*. Chicago: University of Chicago Press, 2008.

Hennessy, Rosemary. *Profit and Pleasure: Sexual Identities in Late Capitalism*. New York: Routledge, 2000.

Herring, Scott. *Queering the Underworld: Slumming, Literature, and the Undoing of Lesbian and Gay History*. Chicago: University of Chicago Press, 2007.

———. *Another Country: Queer Anti-Urbanism*. New York: New York University Press, 2010.

Hill Collins, Patricia. *Black Sexual Politics: African Americans, Gender, and the New Racism*. New York: Routledge, 2005.

Hoffert, Melanie. *Prairie Silence*. Boston: Beacon Press, 2013.

Hogue, Beverly J. "From Mulberries to Machines: Planting the Simulated Garden." *Interdisciplinary Studies in Literature and Environment* 15, no. 1 (2008): 101–10

Holden, Stephen. "The Pop Life: Out of the Mainstream." *New York Times*, July 17, 1991.

Holloway, Pippa. *Sexual Politics and Social Control in Virginia, 1920–1945*. Chapel Hill: University of North Carolina Press, 2006.

Holt, Marilyn Irvin. *Linoleum, Better Babies, and the Modern Farm Woman, 1890–1930*. Albuquerque: University of New Mexico Press, 1995.

Homosexuals in Unexpected Places? A Special Issue. American Studies 48, no. 2 (2007).

hooks, bell. "Eating the Other: Desire and Resistance." In *Media and Cultural Studies: KeyWorks*, edited by Meenakshi Gigi Durham and Douglas M. Kellner, 424–38. Malden, MA: Blackwell Publishing, 2001.

Howard, John. *Men Like That: A Southern Queer History*. Chicago: University of Chicago Press, 1999.

———. "Queer Marriages of Convenience." Presentation delivered at the American Studies Association Annual Conference, Atlanta, GA, November 2004.

———. "Of Closets and Other Rural Voids." *GLQ: A Journal of Lesbian and Gay Studies*, Brokeback Mountain Dossier, 13, no. 1 (2007): 100–2.

———. "Homosexuals in Unexpected Places?: A Comment." *American Studies* 48, no. 2 (Summer 2007): 61–68.

———. "Me and Mrs. Jones: Screening Working-Class Trans-Formations of Southern Family Values." In *Creating and Consuming the U.S. South*, edited by Martyn Bone, Brian Ward, and William A. Link. Gainsville: University Press of Florida, 2015.

Howe, Irving. *Sherwood Anderson*. New York: Frederick Ungar, 1977.

Hutcheon, Linda. *The Politics of Postmodernism*. London: Routledge, 2003.

Isin, Engin F. *Being Political: Genealogies of Citizenship*. Minneapolis: University Of Minnesota Press, 2002.

Jacob, Sue Ellen, Wesley Thomas, and Sabine Lang. "Introduction." In *Two-Spirit People: Native American Gender Identity, Sexuality and Spirituality*, edited by Sue Ellen Jacob, Wesley Thomas, and Sabine Lang. Chicago: University of Chicago Press, 1997.

Jameson, Fredric. *Postmodernism: Or, The Cultural Logic of Late Capitalism*. Durham, NC: Duke University Press, 1991.

Jaynes, Edwin T. "Concentration of Distributions at Entropy Maxima." In *E. T. Jaynes: Papers on Probability, Statistics and Statistical Physics*, edited by Roger D. Rosenkrantz, 315–36. Dordrecht, The Netherlands: Kluwer Academic Publishers, 1979.

———. "Where Do We Stand on Maximum Entropy?" In *The Maximum Entropy Formalism*, edited by Raphael D. Levine and Myron Tribus, 15–118. Cambridge, MA: MIT Press, 1979.

Johnson, Alex. "Getting Out." *Earth Island Journal* 26, no. 3 (Autumn 2011): 64.

Johnson, Colin R. "Columbia's Orient: Gender, Geography, and the Invention of Sexuality in Rural America." Ph.D. diss., University of Michigan, 2003.

———. "Homosexuals in Unexpected Places: An Introduction." *American Studies* 48, no. 2 (Summer 2007): 5–8.

———. "Camp Life: The Queer History of 'Manhood' in the Civilian Conservation Corps, 1933–1938," *American Studies* 48, no. 2 (2007): 19–36.

———. *Just Queer Folks: Gender and Sexuality in Rural America*. Philadelphia: Temple University Press, 2013.

Johnson, David K. *The Lavender Scare: The Cold War Persecution of Gays and Lesbians in the Federal Government*. Chicago: University of Chicago Press, 2004.

Johnson, E. Patrick. "The Scene in Wyoming: For Matthew Shepard." *Callaloo* 23, no. 1 (2000): 122–24.

———. *Sweet Tea: Black Gay Men of the South*. Chapel Hill: University of North Carolina Press, 2008.

Johnson, Kay L. "Creativity and the Organic Architecture of Bruce Goff." In *Bruce Goff: A Creative Mind*, edited by Scott W. Perkins. Norman: University of Oklahoma and Price Tower Arts Center, 2010.

Johnson, Susan Lee. *Roaring Camp: The Social World of the California Gold Rush*. New York: W. W. Norton, 2000.

Johnston, Lynda, and Robyn Longhurst, eds. *Space, Place, and Sex: Geographies of Sexualities*. New York: Rowman & Littlefield, 2010.

Jones, John Paul Keith Woodward, and Sallie Marston, "Situating Flatness." *Transactions of the Institute of British Geographers* 32 (Spring 2007): 264–76.

Joseph, Miranda. *Against the Romance of Community*. Minneapolis: University of Minnesota Press, 2002.

Kaplan, Amy. *The Social Construction of American Realism*. Chicago: University of Chicago Press, 1988.

Karmeshu. "Uncertainty, Entropy and Maximum Entropy Principle: An Overview." In *Entropy Measures, Maximum Entropy Principle and Emerging Applications.* Berlin: Springer-Verlag, 2003.

Kasson, John F. *Houdini, Tarzan, and the Perfect Man: The White Male Body and the Challenge of Modernity in America.* New York: Hill and Wang, 2001.

Katz, Jonathan Ned. *Love Stories: Sex between Men before Homosexuality.* Chicago: University of Chicago Press, 2001.

Katz, Sandor Ellix. *Wild Fermentation: The Flavor, Nutrition, and Craft of Live-Culture Foods.* White River Junction, VT: Chelsea Green Publishing, 2003.

Kazyak, Emily. "Disrupting Cultural Selves: Constructing Gay and Lesbian Identities in Rural Locales." *Qualitative Sociology* 34, no. 4 (2011): 561–81.

———. "Midwest or Lesbian: Gender, Rurality, and Sexuality." *Gender and Society* 26, no. 6 (2012): 825–48.

Kennedy, Elizabeth Lapovsky, and Madeline D. Davis. *Boots of Leather, Slippers of Gold: The History of a Lesbian Community.* New York: Routledge, 1993.

Kennedy, Hubert C. *Karl Ulrichs: The Life and Works of Karl Heinrich Ulrichs, Pioneer of the Modern Gay Movement.* Boston: Alyson Publications, 1988.

Kett, Joseph F. *Rites of Passage: Adolescence in America, 1790 to the Present.* New York: Basic Books, 1977.

Kevles, Daniel. *In the Name of Eugenics: Genetics and the Uses of Human Heredity.* Berkeley: University of California Press, 1986.

Kidd, Kenneth B. *Making American Boys: Boyology and the Feral Tale.* Minneapolis: University of Minnesota Press, 2004.

Kilmer, Richard. "Farm Boys." In *Farm Boys: Lives of Gay Men from the Rural Midwest,* edited by Will Fellows, 78–179. Madison: University of Wisconsin Press, 2001.

Kimmel, Michael S. *Manhood in America: A Cultural History.* New York: Free Press, 1997.

Kincaid, James R. "Producing Erotic Children." In *Curiouser: On the Queerness of Children,* edited by Steven Bruhm and Natasha Hurley, 3–16. Minneapolis: University of Minnesota Press, 2004.

Kline, Wendy. *Building a Better Race: Gender, Sexuality, and Eugenics from the Turn of the Century to the Baby Boom.* Berkeley: University of California Press, 2005.

Kumar, Krishan. *Utopianism.* Buckingham, UK: Open University Press, 1991.

Lacan, Jacques. *Four Fundamental Concepts of Psycho-Analysis.* Edited by Jacques-Alian Miller and Alan Sheridan. New York: Norton, 1978.

Lappé, Frances Moore, and Joseph Collins. *Food First: Beyond the Myth of Scarcity.* New York: Ballantine Books, 1978.

Latour, Bruno. *We Have Never Been Modern.* Cambridge, MA: Harvard University Press, 1993.

Leach, Belinda. "Producing Globalization: Gender, Agency, and the Transformation of Rural Communities of Work." In *Social Transformation in Rural Canada: Community, Cultures, and Collective Action,* edited by John R. Parkins and Maureen G. Reed, 131–47. Toronto, ON: University of British Columbia Press, 2012.

Lee, Ang. *Brokeback Mountain*. DVD. Focus Features, USA, 2005.

Lee, David. *Lumber Kings and Shantymen: Logging, Lumber and Timber in the Ottawa Valley*. Toronto: Natural Heritage/Natural History, 1978.

Lefebvre, Henri. *The Production of Space*. Translated by Donald Nicholson-Smith. Malden, MA: Blackwell Publishing, 1992.

Legal-Miller, Althea. "'The Unmentionable Ugliness of the Jailhouse': Sexualized Violence, the Black Freedom Movement, and the Leesburg Stockade Imprisonment of 1963." Ph.D. diss., King's College, London, 2011.

Leong, Karen J. "'A Distinct and Antagonistic Race': Constructions of Chinese Manhood in the Exclusionist Debates, 1869–1878." In *Across the Great Divide: Cultures of Manhood in the American West*, edited by Matthew Basso, Lauren McCall, and Dee Garceau, 131–48. New York: Routledge, 2001.

Leung, Helen Hok-Sze. *Undercurrents: Queer Culture and Postcolonial Hong Kong*, Vancouver, BC: University of British Columbia Press, 2008.

Levy, Ariel. "Lesbian Nation: When Gay Women Took to the Road." *New Yorker*, March 2, 2009.

Levy, David W. "The Hunt for Red Professors: The Loyalty Oath Crisis of 1951." *Sooner Magazine*, Summer 1995.

Lewin, Ellen, and William L. Leap. *Out in Public: Reinventing Lesbian/Gay Anthropology in a Globalizing World*. New York: Wiley-Blackwell, 2009.

Lewis, Jon. *Hollywood vs. Hardcore: How the Struggle over Censorship Saved the Modern Film Industry*. New York: New York University Press, 2000.

Lewis, Lisa A. *Gender Politics and MTV: Voicing the Difference*. Philadelphia: Temple University Press, 1990.

Lewis, R. W. B. *The American Adam: Innocence, Tragedy, and Tradition in the Nineteenth Century*. Chicago: University of Chicago Press, 1955.

Liao, Hanwen, and Adrian Pitts. "A Brief Historical Review of Olympic Urbanization." *International Journal of the History of Sport* 23, no. 7 (2006): 1232–52.

"Life Magazine and LOOK Magazine Popularize Photojournalism in the 1930s," n.d. http://www.things-and-other-stuff.com/magazines/life-magazine.html.

Little, Jo, and Michael Leyshon. "Embodied Rural Geographies: Developing Research Agendas." *Progress in Human Geography* 27, no. 3 (2003): 257–72.

Littleton, Taylor, and Maltby Sykes. *Advancing American Art: Painting, Politics, and Cultural Confrontation at Mid-Century*. Tuscaloosa: University of Alabama Press, 1999.

Locke, Lawrence F., Waneen Wyrick Spirduso, and Stephen Silverman. *Proposals that Work: A Guide for Planning Dissertations and Grant Proposals*. 5th ed. London: Sage Publications, 2007.

Loffreda, Beth. *Losing Matt Shepard: Life and Politics in the Aftermath of Anti-Gay Murder*. New York: Columbia University Press, 2000.

Lohr, Steve. "The Internet as an Influence on Urbanization." *New York Times*, September 16, 1996. http://www.nytimes.com/1996/09/16/business/the-internet-as-an-influence-on-urbanization.html.

London, James Henke. "Oscar! Oscar! Great Britain Goes Wilde for the 'Fourth-Gender' Smiths." *Rolling Stone*, June 7, 1985.

Love, Heather. *Feeling Backward: Loss and Politics of Queer History*. Cambridge, MA: Harvard University Press, 2007.

Lovett, Laura. *Conceiving the Future: Family, Reproduction, and the Family in the United States, 1898–1938*. Chapel Hill: University of North Carolina Press, 2007.

Lovett, Robert Morss. "Mr. Sherwood Anderson's America." In *Critical Essays on Sherwood Anderson*, edited by David D. Anderson, 35–37. Boston: G. K. Hall, 1981.

Lynd, Robert S., and Helen Merrell Lynd. *Middletown: A Study in Contemporary American Culture*. New York: Harvest/HBJ, 1957.

MacDonald, J. E. *Shantymen and Sodbusters: An Account of Logging and Settlement in Kirkwood Township, 1869–1928*. Sault Sainte Marie, ONT: Sault Star Commercial Printing Department, 1966.

MacKay, Donald. *The Lumberjacks*. Toronto: Natural Heritage/Natural History, 1978.

MacKell, Jan. *Brothels, Bordellos, and Bad Girls: Prostitution in Colorado, 1860–1930*. Albuquerque: University of New Mexico Press, 2007.

Mahan, Krissy. "Rockin' the Flannel Shirt." In *It Gets Better: Coming Out, Overcoming Bullying, and Creating a Life Worth Living*, edited by Dan Savage and Terry Miller, 71–73. New York: Dutton, 2011.

Manalansan, Martin. *Global Divas: Filipino Gay Men in the Diaspora*. Durham, NC: Duke University Press, 2003.

Marcus, George E. "Ethnography in/of the World System: The Emergence of Multi-Sited Ethnography." *Annual Review of Anthropology* 24, no. 1 (1995): 95–117.

Marin, Louis. *Utopics: Spatial Play*. Highlands, NJ: Humanities Press, 1984.

Marston, Sallie A, John Paul Jones, and Keith Woodward. "Human Geography without Scale." *Transactions of the Institute of British Geographers* 30, no. 4 (2005): 416–32.

Martin, David E., and Roger W. H. Gynn. *The Olympic Marathon: The History and Drama of Sport's Most Challenging Event*. Champaign, IL: Human Kinetics Press, 2000.

Martin, Jay. *Harvests of Change: American Literature, 1865–1914*. Englewood Cliffs, NJ: Prentice Hall, 1967.

Marx, Leo. *The Machine in the Garden: Technology and the Pastoral Ideal in America*. New York: Oxford University Press, 1964.

Mason, Carol. *Oklahomo: Lessons in Unqueering America*. Albany: State University of New York Press, forthcoming.

Massad, Joseph. *Desiring Arabs*. Chicago: University of Chicago Press, 2007.

Massey, Doreen. *Space, Place, and Gender*. Minneapolis: University of Minnesota Press, 1994.

———. *For Space*. London: SAGE, 2005.

Massumi, Brian. *A User's Guide to Capitalism and Schizophrenia: Deviations from Deleuze and Guattari*. Cambridge, MA: MIT Press, 1992.

Maud's Land Residents. "Maud's Land." In *Lesbian Land*, edited by Joyce Cheney, 87–95. Minneapolis, MN: Word Weaver, 1985.

McCall, Leslie. "The Complexity of Intersectionality." *Signs: Journal of Women in Culture and Society* 30, no. 3 (2005): 1771–1800.

McCann, Marcus. "Pride Toronto, Toronto Police Cocktail Party Turns Ugly." *Xtra.ca*, June 29, 2010.

McCarthy, Linda. "Poppies in a Wheat Field: Exploring the Lives of Rural Lesbians." *Journal of Homosexuality* 39, no. 1 (April 2000): 75–94.

McDermott, William. "Rebirth of the Barefoot Boy and Girl." *Rotarian* 51 (November 1937).

McGinnis, Anthony. *Counting Coup and Cutting Horses: Intertribal Warfare on the Northern Plains, 1738–1889*. New York: Johnson Books, 1990.

McGregor, John. *Historical and Descriptive Sketches of the Maritime Colonies of British North America*. London, 1828.

McGuire, Danielle. *At the Dark End of the Street: Black Women, Rape, and Resistance: A New History of the Civil Rights Movement from Rosa Parks to the Rise of Black Power*. New York: Knopf, 2010.

McKay, Richard. "Imagining 'Patient Zero': Sexuality, Blame, and the Origins of the North American AIDS Epidemic." Ph.D. diss., Oxford University, 2011.

McKittrick, Katherine. *Demonic Grounds: Black Women and the Cartographies of Struggle*. Minneapolis: University of Minnesota Press, 2006.

McLean, Stuart A. "Opposition to the California Gold Rush: The Sentimental Argument—1849–1853." In *American Renaissance and American West: Proceedings of the Second University of Wyoming American Studies Conference*, edited by Christopher S. Durer, Herbert R. Dietrich, Henry J. Laskowsky, and James W. Welke, 87–94. Laramie: University of Wyoming Press, 1982.

McRuer, Robert. *Crip Theory: Cultural Signs of Queerness and Disability*. New York: New York University Press, 2006.

Mercer, Kobena. *Welcome to the Jungle: New Positions in Black Cultural Studies*. New York: Routledge, 1994.

———. "Reading Racial Fetishism: The Photographs of Robert Mapplethorpe." In *Visual Culture: The Reader*, edited by Jessica Evans and Stuart Hall, 435–47. New York: Sage, 1999.

Merrill, Marcellus Samuel, and David Merrill Primus. *Steamboat Springs: Memories of a Young Colorado Pioneer*. Lake City, CO: Western Reflections, 2008.

Metcalfe, Robin, and Stephen Bruhm, eds. *Queer Looking, Queer Acting: Lesbian and Gay Vernacular*. Halifax, NS: Dufferin Press, 1997.

Miller, D. A. "Anal Rope." In *Inside/Out: Lesbian Theories, Gay Theories*, edited by Diana Fuss, 119–42. New York: Routledge, 1991.

Miller, Jim. "Britain Rocks America—Again." *Newsweek*, January 23, 1984.

Miller, Neil. *Out of the Past: Gay and Lesbian History from 1869 to Present*. New York: Vintage Books, 1995.

Miller, Peter, and Nikolas Rose. *Governing the Present: Administering Economic, Social, and Personal Life*. Princeton, NJ: Princeton University Press, 2006.

Miller, Tony. *The Well-Tempered Self: Citizenship, Culture, and the Postmodern Subject.* Baltimore: John Hopkins University Press, 1993.

Minkowitz, Donna. "Love and Hate in Laramie." *Nation*, June 24, 1999. http://www. thenation.com/doc/19990712/minkowitz.

Moodie, T. Dunbar. "Migrancy and Male Sexuality on the South African Gold Mines." In *Hidden from History: Reclaiming the Gay and Lesbian Past*, edited by Martin Duberman, Martha Vicinus, and George Chauncey, 228–56. New York: Dutton, 1989.

Moon, Michael. "'The Gentle Boy from the Dangerous Classes': Pederasty, Domesticity, and Capitalism in Horatio Alger." *Representations*, no. 19 (Summer 1987): 87–110.

Moore, John. *The Cheyenne*. New York: Blackwell Publishing, 1996.

Moore, Mignon. *Invisible Families: Gay Identities, Relationships, and Motherhood among Black Women*. Berkeley: University of California Press, 2011.

Moran, Jeffrey P. *Teaching Sex: The Shaping of Adolescence in the 20th Century*. Cambridge, MA: Harvard University Press, 2000.

Morgensen, Scott. "Back and Forth to the Land: Negotiating Rural and Urban Sexuality among the Radical Faeries." In *Out in Public: Reinventing Lesbian/Gay Anthropology in a Globalizing World*, edited by Ellen Lewin and William L. Leap, 143–63. New York: Wiley-Blackwell, 2009.

Morris, Gary. "Keep on Truckin': An Interview with Joe Gage." *Bright Lights Film Journal*, no. 42 (November 2003). http://www.brightlightsfilm.com/42/gage.htm.

Moss, Kirby. *The Color of Class: Poor Whites and the Paradox of Privilege*. Philadelphia: University of Pennsylvania Press, 2003.

Mouffe, Chantal. "Democracy, Power, and the 'Political.'" In *Democracy and Difference: Contesting the Boundaries of the Political*, edited by Seyla Benhabib. Princeton, NJ: Princeton University Press, 1996.

Muller, Amber. "Virtual Communities and Translation into Physical Reality in the 'It Gets Better' Project." *Journal of Media Practice* 12, no. 3 (December 2011): 269–77.

Muñoz, José Esteban. *Disidentifications: Queers of Color and the Performance of Politics*. Minneapolis: University of Minnesota Press, 1999.

———. *Cruising Utopia: The Then and There of Queer Futurity*. New York: New York University Press, 2009.

Muñoz, Manuel. *The Faith Healer of Olive Avenue*. Chapel Hill, NC: Algonquin Books, 2007.

Murphy, Lucy Eldersveld. "Journeywoman Milliner: Emily Austin, Migration, and Women's Work in the Nineteenth-Century Midwest." In *Midwestern Women: Work, Community, and Leadership at the Crossroads*, edited by Murphy, Lucy Eldersveld, and Wendy Hamand Venet, 38–60. Bloomington: Indiana University Press, 1997.

Nancy, Jean-Luc. *The Inoperative Community*, edited by Peter Connor. Minneapolis: University of Minnesota Press, 1991.

Nesvig, Martin. "The Complicated Terrain of Latin American Homosexuality." *Hispanic American Historical Review* 81, nos. 3–4 (2001): 689–729.

Neth, Mary. *Preserving the Family Farm: Women, Community, and the Foundations of Agribusiness in the Midwest, 1900–1940*. Baltimore: John Hopkins University Press, 1995.

Neumann, John von. *Mathematical Foundations of Quantum Mechanics*. Princeton, NJ: Princeton University Press, 1955.

Norton, Judy. "Transchildren and the Discipline of Children's Literature." *Lion and the Unicorn* 23 (1999): 415–36.

"Nova Scotia." *Encyclopedia of Canadian Provinces*, 2004. http://www.nationsencyclopedia. com/canada/Alberta-to-Nova-Scotia.html.

Novak, William. "The Myth of the 'Weak' American State." *American Historical Review* 112 (June 2008): 752–72.

O'Connor, Stephen. *Orphan Trains: The Story of Charles Loring Brace and the Children He Saved and Failed*. Boston: Houghton Mifflin, 2001.

Olson, Jimmy. "Kansas City Trucking Co." *Advocate*, January 12, 1977.

Osborne, Karen Lee, and William Spurlin, eds. *Reclaiming the Heartland: Lesbian and Gay Voices from the Midwest*. Minneapolis: University of Minnesota Press, 1996.

Oswald, Ramona. "Who Am I in Relation to Them? Gay, Lesbian, and Queer People Leave the City to Attend Rural Family Weddings." *Journal of Family Issues* 23, no. 3 (2002): 323–48.

Ott, Brian L., and Eric Aoki. "The Politics of Negotiating Public Tragedy: Media Framing of the Matthew Shepard Murder." *Rhetoric and Public Affairs* 5, no. 3 (2002): 483–505.

Ownby, Ted. *Subduing Satan: Religion, Recreation, and Manhood in the Rural South, 1865–1920*. Chapel Hill: University of North Carolina Press, 1990.

Panzarino, Concetta. "Beechtree." In *Lesbian Land*, edited by Joyce Cheney, 41–45. Minneapolis, MN: Word Weaver, 1985.

Parkins, John, and Maureen Reed. "Introduction: Towards a Transformative Understanding of Rural Social Change." In *Social Transformation in Rural Canada: Community, Cultures, and Collective Action*, edited by John R. Parkins and Maureen G. Reed. Toronto, ON: University of British Columbia Press, 2012.

Parrington, Vernon Louis. *Main Currents in American Thought: An Interpretation of American Literature from the Beginnings to 1920, Volume Three, 1860–1920: The Beginnings of Critical Realism in America*. New York: Harcourt, Brace, 1990.

Patterson, Romaine. *The Whole World Was Watching: Living in the Light of Matthew Shepard*. New York: Advocate Books, 2005.

Petz, Denes. "Entropy, von Neumann and the von Neumann Entropy." In *John von Neumann and the Foundations of Quantum Physics*, 2001. http://arxiv.org/ absmath-ph/0102013.

Phelan, Peggy. *Unmarked: The Politics of Performance*. New York: Routledge, 1993.

Phelan, Shane. *Sexual Strangers: Gays, Lesbians, and Dilemmas of Citizenship*. Philadelphia: Temple University Press, 2001.

Phillips, Richard. "Imagined Geographies and Sexual Politics." In *De-Centering Sexualities: Politics and Representations beyond the Metropolis*, edited by Richard Phillips, David Shuttleton, and Diane Watt, 102–24. New York: Routledge, 2000.

Phillips, Richard, David Shuttleton, and Diane Watt, eds. *De-Centering Sexualities: Politics and Representations beyond the Metropolis.* New York: Routledge, 2000.

Phillips, Sarah. *This Land, This Nation: Conservation, Rural America, and the New Deal.* New York: Cambridge University Press, 2007.

Pihach, Michael. "On the Set of Degrassi: Sneak Peek at Trans Character's Upcoming Episode." *Xtra.ca*, August 2010.

Pollan, Michael. *Botany of Desire: A Plant's-Eye View of the World.* New York: Random House, 2002.

Power, Richard Lyle. *Planting Corn Belt Culture: The Impress of the Upland Southerner and Yankee in the Old Northwest.* Indianapolis: Indiana Historical Society, 1953.

Price, Joe. "Introduction: Adventures in Architecture." In *Bruce Goff: A Creative Mind*, edited by Scott W. Perkins, Norman: University of Oklahoma Press, 2010.

"Pride Toronto 2010: All of Our Coverage in One Place." *Xtra.ca*, n.d.

Prosser, Jay. *Second Skins: The Body Narratives of Transsexuality.* New York: Columbia University Press, 1998.

Proulx, Annie. "Brokeback Mountain." In *Close Range: Wyoming Stories.* New York: Scribers, 2000.

Puar, Jasbir. *Terrorist Assemblages: Homonationalism in Queer Times.* Durham, NC: Duke University Press, 2007.

Pugh, Tison. "'Are We Cannibals, Let Me Ask? Or Are We Faithful Friends?': Food, Interspecies Cannibalism, and the Limits of Utopia in L. Frank Baum's Oz Books." *Lion and the Unicorn* 32, no. 3 (2008): 324–43.

———. "'There Lived in the Land of Oz Two Queerly Made Men': Queer Utopianism and Antisocial Eroticism in L. Frank Baum's Oz Series." *Marvels & Tales* 22, no. 2 (2008): 217–39.

Pulido, Laura. *Environmentalism and Economic Justice: Two Chicano Struggles in the Southwest.* Tucson: University of Arizona Press, 1996.

Putnam, Lara. *The Company They Kept: Migrants and the Politics of Gender in Caribbean Costa Rica, 1870–1960.* Chapel Hill: University of North Carolina Press, 2002.

Quinn, D. Michael. *Same-Sex Dynamics among Nineteenth-Century Americans: A Mormon Example.* Urbana: University of Illinois Press, 1996.

Raimondo, Meredith. "'Corralling the Virus': Migratory Sexualities and the 'Spread of AIDS' in the U.S. Media." *Environment & Planning D: Society & Space* 21, no. 3 (2003): 389–408.

Reding, Nick. *Methland the Death and Life of an American Small Town.* Princeton, NJ: Bloomsbury USA, 2009.

Reed, Christopher Robert. *"All the World Is Here!" The Black Presence at White City.* Bloomington: Indiana University Press, 2000.

Retter, Yolanda, Anne-Marie Bouthillette, and Gordon Brent Ingram, eds. *Queers in Space: Communities, Public Places, Sites of Resistance.* Seattle, WA: Bay Press, 1997.

Rideout, Walter B. *Sherwood Anderson: A Writer in America*, 2 vols. Madison: University of Wisconsin Press, 2006–2007.

Rifkin, Adrian. "Sexual Anaphora: A Reverie of Kinds . . ." *Parallax* 14, no. 2 (2008): 42–52.

Rifkin, Mark. *Manifesting America: The Imperial Construction of U.S. National Space.* New York: Oxford University Press, 2009.

Riordon, Michael. *Out Our Way: Gay and Lesbian Life in Rural Canada.* Toronto: Between the Lines, 1996.

Rivera-Severa, Ramón. Review of *José, Can You See?: Latinos On and Off Broadway* by Alberto Sandoval-Sánchez. *TDR: The Drama Review* 45, no. 4 (2001): 167–71.

Roberts, Brian. *American Alchemy: The California Gold Rush and Middle-Class Culture.* Chapel Hill: University of North Carolina Press, 2000.

Rocío Tábora. *Masculinidad y violencia en la cultura política Hondureña.* Tegucigalpa: Centro de Documentación de Honduras, 1995.

Rodríguez, Richard. *Next of Kin: The Family in Chicano/a Cultural Politics.* Durham, NC: Duke University Press, 2009.

Rome, Dennis. *Black Demons: The Media's Depiction of the African American Male Criminal Stereotype.* Westport, CT: Praeger, 2004.

Romero, Lora. "When Something Goes Queer: Familiarity, Formalism, and Minority Intellectuals in the 1980s." *Yale Journal of Criticism: Interpretation in the Humanities* 6 (Winter 1993): 121–42.

Rosenberg, Gabriel. *The 4-H Harvest: Sexuality and the State in Rural America.* Philadelphia: University of Pennsylvania Press, 2015.

Roseneil, Sasha. "The Heterosexual/Homosexual Binary." In *Handbook of Gay and Lesbian Studies,* edited by Diane Richardson and Steven Seidman, 27–43. London: Sage, 2002.

Ross, Andrew. "Uses of Camp." In *Camp—Queer Aesthetics and the Performing Subject: A Reader,* edited by Fabio Cleto, 308–29. Ann Arbor: University of Michigan Press, 2002.

Rotundo, Anthony. *American Manhood: Transformations in Masculinity from the Revolution to the Modern Era.* New York: Basic Books, 1994.

Rubin, Gayle. "Studying Sexual Subcultures: Excavating the Ethnography of Gay Communities in Urban America." In *Out in Theory,* edited by Ellen Lewin and William L. Leap, 17–67. Champaign: University of Illinois Press, 2002.

Rubin, Gayle. "Thinking Sex: Notes for a Radical Theory of the Politics of Sexuality." In *Pleasure and Danger: Exploring Female Sexuality,* edited by Carole Vance, 267–319. Boston: Routledge, 1984.

Ruddy, Jenn. "Edmonton Police Service's Queer Liaison Committee Is Out of Touch." *Xtra.ca,* May 2, 2010.

Rupp, Leila. *A Desired Past: A Short History of Same-Sex Love in America.* Chicago: University of Chicago Press, 1999.

———. "Toward a Global History of Same-Sex Sexuality." *Journal of the History of Sexuality* 10, no. 2 (April 2001): 287–302.

———. *Sapphistries: A Global History of Love between Women.* New York: New York University Press, 2009.

Rural Report: Demographics. Rural Communities Impacting Policy Report, October 2003. http://www.ruralnovascotia.ca/RCIP/Demographics/Demographics. htm#PopulationOfCountyByAge.

Rushbrook, Dereka. "Cities, Queer Space, and the Cosmopolitan Tourist." *GLQ: A Journal of Lesbian and Gay Studies* 8, no. 1 (2002): 183–206.

Russell, James E. *Heredity in Dairy Cattle: Lessons in Breeding and Herd Development for 4H and FFA Dairy Clubs and Other Beginners*. Peterborough, NH: American Guernsey Cattle Club, 1944.

Russo, Vito. "All About Camp." In *Long Road to Freedom: The Advocate History of the Gay and Lesbian Movement*, edited by Mark Thompson, 113–14. New York: St. Martin's Press, 1994.

Rydell, Robert. *World of Fairs: The Century of Progress Expositions*. Chicago: University of Chicago Press, 1993.

Rydström, Jens. *Sinners and Citizens: Bestiality and Homosexuality in Sweden, 1880–1950*. Chicago: University of Chicago Press, 2003.

Said, Edward. *Orientalism*. New York: Vintage, 1979.

Sanders, Elizabeth. *The Roots of Reform: Farmers, Workers, and the American State*. Chicago: University of Chicago Press, 1999.

Sandweiss, Martha. *Print the Legend: Photography and the American West*. New Haven, CT: Yale University Press, 2004.

Saul, Leon J. "Freud's Death Instinct and the Second Law of Thermodynamics." *International Journal of Psycho-Analysis* 39, no. 5 (October 1958): 323–25.

Saussure, Ferdinand de. *Course in General Linguistics*. Peru, IL: Open Court Publishing, 1973.

Savage, Dan. Introduction. In *It Gets Better: Coming Out, Overcoming Bullying, and Creating a Life Worth Living*, edited by Dan Savage and Terry Miller. New York: Dutton, 2011.

Scarry, Elaine. *The Body in Pain: The Making and Unmaking of the World*. Oxford: Oxford University Press, 1985.

Schaefer, Eric. "Gauging a Revolution: 16mm Film and the Rise of the Pornographic Feature." In *Porn Studies*, edited by Linda Williams, 370–400. Durham, NC: Duke University Press, 2004.

Scharff, Virginia J. *Seeing Nature through Gender*. Cambridge, MA: Harvard University Press, 2008.

Scharnhorst, Gary. "'Ways that Are Dark': Appropriations of Bret Harte's 'Plain Language from Truthful James.'" *Nineteenth-Century Literature* 51, no. 3 (December 1996): 377–99.

Scharnhorst, Gary, and Jack Bales. *The Lost Life of Horatio Alger, Jr*. Bloomington: Indiana University Press, 1985.

Schrecker, Ellen. *No Ivory Tower: McCarthyism and the Universities*. New York: Oxford University Press, 1986.

Schudson, Michael. *The Good Citizen: A History of American Civic Life*. Cambridge, MA: Harvard University Press, 1998.

Schueller, Malini Johar. "Analogy and (White) Feminist Theory: Thinking Race and the Color of the Cyborg Body." *Signs: Journal of Women in Culture and Society* 31, no. 3 (2005): 64–91.

Scott, James C. *Seeing like a State: How Certain Schemes to Improve the Human Condition Have Failed*. New York: Vail-Ballou Press, 1998.

Sears, Clare. "All that Glitters: Trans-Ing California's Gold Rush Migrations." *GLQ: A Journal of Lesbian and Gay Studies* 14, nos. 2–3 (2008): 383–402.

Sedgwick, Eve Kosofsky. *Between Men: English Literature and the Male Homosocial Desire*. New York: Columbia University Press, 1985.

———. *Epistemology of the Closet*. Berkeley: University of California Press, 1990.

———. *Tendencies*. Durham, NC: Duke University Press, 1993.

Seidman, Steven. *Beyond the Closet: The Transformation of Gay and Lesbian Life*. New York: Routledge, 2004.

Sergeant, John, and Stephen Mooring, eds. *Bruce Goff: The Michelangelo of Kitsch*." Special issue, *Architectural Design*, 48, no. 10 (1978).

Seshadri-Crooks, Kalpana. *Desiring Whiteness: A Lacanian Analysis of Race*. London: Routledge, 2000.

Shah, Nayan. *Contagious Divides: Epidemics and Race in San Francisco's Chinatown*. Berkeley: University of California Press, 2001.

Shannon, Claude E. "A Mathematical Theory of Communication." *Bell System Technical Journal* 27, no. 3 (1948): 379–423.

Shopes, Linda. "Oral History, Human Subjects, and Institutional Review Boards." *Oral History Association*. http://www.oralhistory.org/do-oral-history/oral-history-and-irb-review/.

Shover, John. *First Majority-Last Minority: The Transformation of Rural Life in America*. DeKalb: Northern Illinois University Press, 1976.

Shuttleton, David. "The Queer Politics of the Gay Pastoral." In *De-Centering Sexualities: Politics and Representations beyond the Metropolis*, edited by Richard Phillips, David Shuttleton, and Diane Watt, 125–46. New York: Routledge, 2000.

Siebenand, Paul. "The Beginnings of Gay Cinema in Los Angeles: The Industry and the Audience." Ph.D. diss., University of Southern California, 1975.

Silverstein, Charles, and Edmund White. *The Joy of Gay Sex: An Intimate Guide for Gay Men to the Pleasures of a Gay Lifestyle*. New York: Crown, 1977.

Simmel, George. *The Sociology of Georg Simmel*. Edited and translated by Kurt Wolff. Glencoe, IL: The Free Press, 1950.

Simons, Patricia. "Homosociality and Erotics in Italian Renaissance Portraiture." In *Portraiture: Facing the Subject*, edited by Joanna Wodall, 29–51. Manchester, UK: Manchester University Press, 1997.

Smith, Donna Jo. "Queering the South: Constructions of Southern/Queer Identity." In *Carryin' On in the Lesbian and Gay South*, edited by John Howard, 370–85. New York: New York University Press, 1997.

Smith, Henry Nash. *Virgin Land: The American West as Symbol and Myth*. Cambridge, MA: Harvard University Press, 1950.

Smith, James D., and Ronald J. Mancoske, eds. *Rural Gays and Lesbians: Building on the Strengths of Communities.* New York: Harrington Park Press, 1997.

Snitow, Ann, Christine Stansell, and Sharon Thompson, eds. *Powers of Desire.* New York: Monthly Review Press, 1983.

Sobal, Jeffery. "Sample Extensiveness in Qualitative Nutrition Education Research." *Journal of Nutrition Education* 33, no. 4 (2001): 184–92.

Soja, Edward W. *Thirdspace: Journeys to Los Angeles and Other Real-and-Imagined Places.* Oxford, UK: Basil Blackwell, 1996.

Somerville, Siobhan. *Queering the Color Line: Race and the Invention of Homosexuality.* Durham, NC: Duke University Press, 2000.

Soto, Sandra K. *Reading Chican@ like a Queer: The De-Mastery of Desire.* Austen: University of Texas Press, 2009.

Spade, Dean. "The Identity Victim." *Georgetown Journal of Gender and the Law* 7 (2006): 255–85.

———. "Trans Law and Politics on a Neoliberal Landscape." *Temple Political & Civil Rights Law Review* 18 (2009): 353–73.

———. "Tramp, V., and N." *The Oxford English Dictionary.* Oxford, UK: Oxford University Press, 2010.

Spade, Dean, and Rickke Mananzala. "The Nonprofit Industrial Complex and Trans Resistance." *Sexuality Research & Social Policy* 5, no. 1 (2008): 53–71.

Spencer, Benjamin T. "Sherwood Anderson: American Mythopoeist." *American Literature* 41, no. 1 (1969): 1–18.

Spring, Justin. *Secret Historian: The Life and Times of Samuel Steward, Professor, Tattoo Artist, and Sexual Renegade.* New York: Farrar, Straus, and Giroux, 2010.

Stansell, Christine. *City of Women: Sex and Class in New York, 1789–1860.* Urbana: University of Illinois Press, 1987.

Statistics Canada. *Population Urban and Rural, by Province and Territory,* 2001. http://www.statcan.gc.ca/tables-tableaux/sum-som/l01/cst01/demo62a-eng.htm.

Straw, Will. "The Contexts of Music Video: Popular Music and Postmodernism in the 1980s." In *Watching All the Music: Rock Video and Beyond,* edited by Gareth Sansom, 41–55. Montreal: McGill University Working Papers in Communication, 1987.

Stringer, Julian. "Exposing Intimacy in 'Russ Myers,' 'Motorpyscho!' And 'Faster Pussycat! Kill! Kill!.'" In *The Road Movie Book,* edited by Steven Cohan and Ina Rae Hark, 165–78. London: Routledge, 1997.

Strott, Richard. *Jolly Fellows: Male Milieus in Nineteenth-Century America.* Baltimore: Johns Hopkins University Press, 2009.

"Sumaria Instruida contra Onesiforo Escobar Lazo." *El Progreso, D. L.,* December1941.

Sweetman, Paul. "Shop Window Dummies? Fashion, the Body, and Emergent Socialities." In *Body Dressing,* edited by Joanne Entwistle and Elizabeth Wilson, 59–77. Oxford, UK: Berg, 2000.

Syrett, Nicholas L. "The Boys of Beaver Meadow: A Homosexual Community at 1920s Dartmouth College." *American Studies* 48, no. 2 (Summer 2007): 9–18.

———. *The Company He Keeps: A History of White College Fraternities*. Chapel Hill: University of North Carolina Press, 2009.

Tamashiro, Dustin. "Coming Out." In *GLBTQ: An Encyclopedia of Gay, Lesbian, Bisexual, Transgender, and Queer Culture*, edited by Claude J. Summers. Chicago: glbtq, 2004. www.glbtq.com/social-sciences/coming_out_ssh.html.

Taylor, Verta, Elizabeth Kaminksy, and Kimberly Dugan. "From the Bowery to the Castro: Communities, Identities and Movements." In *Handbook of Gay and Lesbian Studies*, edited by Diane Richardson and Steven Seidman, 99–114. London: Sage, 2002.

Thompson, Ashley B., and Melissa M. Sloan. "Race as Region, Region as Race: How Black and White Southerners Understand Their Regional Identities." *Southern Cultures* 18, no. 4 (2012): 72–95.

Thompson, Eric. "Urban Cosmopolitan Chauvinism and the Politics of Rural Identity. In *Cleavage, Connection and Conflict in Rural, Urban and Contemporary Asia*, edited by Tim Bunnell, D. Parthasarathy, and Eric C. Thompson, 168–69. New York: Springer, 2012.

Thompson, Mark, ed. *Long Road to Freedom: The Advocate History of the Gay and Lesbian Movement*. New York: St. Martin's Press, 1994.

Thomsen, Carly. "The Politics of Narrative, Narrative as Politic: Rethinking Reproductive Justice Frameworks through the South Dakota Abortion Story." *Feminist Formations* 27, no. 2 (2015): 1–26.

Tichi, Cecelia. *Shifting Gears: Technology, Literature, Culture in Modernist America*. Chapel Hill: University of North Carolina Press, 1987.

Tiemeyer, Phil. "'Male Stewardesses': Male Flight Attendants as a Queer Miscarriage of Justice." *Genders* 45 (2007). http://www.genders.org/g45/g45_tiemeyer.html.

Ting, Jennifer. "Bachelor Society: Deviant Heterosexuality and Asian American Historiography." In *Privileging Positions: The Sites of Asian American Studies*, edited by Gary Y. Okihiro, Marilyn Alquizola, Dorothy Fujita Rony, and K. Scott Wong, 271–79. Pullman: Washington State University Press, 1995.

Tinkcom, Matthew. *Camp and the Question of Value: Cinema, Capital, and the Alibis of Queer Work*. Durham, NC: Duke University Press, 2002.

Tompkins, Jane. *West of Everything: The Inner Life of Westerns*. New York: Oxford University Press, 1992.

Tongson, Karen. "The Light that Never Goes Out: Butch Intimacies and Sub-Urban Sociabilities in 'Lesser Lost Angeles.'" In *A Companion to Lesbian, Gay, Bisexual, Transgender, and Queer Studies*, edited by George Haggerty and Molly McGarry, 355–76. Malden, MA: Blackwell, 2007.

———. *Relocations: Queer Suburban Imaginaries*. New York: New York University Press, 2011.

Tonkiss, Fran. *Space, the City and Social Theory: Social Relations and Urban Forms*. Cambridge, UK: Polity Press, 2005.

Trachtenberg, Alan. *The Incorporation of America: Culture and Society in the Gilded Age*. New York: Hill and Wang, 2007.

Tsai, Shih-Shan Henry. *The Chinese Experience in America*. Bloomington: Indiana University Press, 1986.

Tseëlon, Efrat. "From Fashion to Masquerade: Toward an Ungendered." In *Body Dressing*, edited by Joanne Entwistle and Elizabeth Wilson, 103–17. Oxford, UK: Berg, 2000.

Turner, Frederick Jackson. "The Significance of the Frontier in American History." In *The Frontier in American History*. New York: Henry Holt, 1920.

Valentine, Gillian, ed. *From Nowhere to Everywhere: Lesbian Geographies*. New York: Routledge, 2000.

———. "Queer Bodies and the Production of Space." In *Handbook of Gay and Lesbian Studies*, edited by Diane Richardson and Steven Seidman, 145–60. London: Sage, 2002.

Valentine, Gillian, and Tracey Skelton. "Finding Oneself, Losing Oneself: The Lesbian and Gay 'Scene' as a Paradoxical Space." *International Journal of Urban and Regional Research* 27, no. 4 (2003): 849–66.

Van Doren, Carl. *Contemporary American Novelists, 1900–1920*. New York: MacMillan, 1923.

Van Lieshout, Maurice. "Leather Nights in the Woods: Homosexual Encounters in a Dutch Highway Rest Area." *Journal of Homosexuality* 29, no. 1 (1995): 19–39.

Verghese, Abraham, Steven L. Berk, and Felix Sarubbi. "Urbs in Rure: Human Immunodeficiency Virus Infection in Rural Tennessee." *Journal of Infectious Diseases* 160, no. 6 (1989): 1051–55.

Viramontes, Helena María. *The Moths and Other Stories*. Houston: Arte Publico Press, 1985.

Viveiros de Castro, Eduardo. "Perspectivism and Mulitnaturalism in Indigenous America." In *The Land Within: Indigenous Territory and Perception of the Environment*, edited by Alexandre Surralles and Pedro Garcia Hierro, 36–74. Copenhagen: IWGIA Press, 2005.

Wakeford, Nina. "New Technologies and 'Cyber-Queer' Research." In *Handbook of Gay and Lesbian Studies*, edited by Diane Richardson and Steven Seidman, 115–44. London: Sage, 2002.

Walters, Suzanna Danuta. *All the Rage: The Story of Gay Invisibility in America*. Chicago: University of Chicago Press, 2001.

Warner, Michael. *Fear of a Queer Planet: Queer Politics and Social Theory*. Minneapolis: University Of Minnesota Press, 1993.

———. *The Trouble with Normal: Sex, Politics, and the Ethics of Queer Life*. New York: Free Press, 1999.

———. *The Trouble with Normal: Sex, Politics, and the Ethics of Queer Life*. Cambridge: Harvard University Press, 2000.

———. *Publics and Counterpublics*. New York: Zone Books, 2002.

Warner, Michael, and Lauran Berlant. "Sex in Public." In *The Cultural Studies Reader*, edited by Simon During, 547–66. New York: Routledge, 1999.

Warwick, Alexandra, and Dani Cavallaro. *Fashioning the Frame: Boundaries, Dress and the Body*. Oxford, UK: Berg, 1998.

Waters, Darin J. "Life beneath the Veneer: The Black Community in Asheville, North Carolina, from 1793 to 1900." Ph.D. diss., University of North Carolina at Chapel Hill. Ann Arbor: ProQuest/UMI (Publication No. 3526162), 2012.

Waters, Henry Jackson. *Animal Husbandry*. New York: Ginn and Company, 1925.

Waugh, Thomas. *Hard to Imagine: Gay Male Eroticism in Photography and Film from Their Beginnings to Stonewall*. New York: Columbia University Press, 1996.

———. *Out/Lines: Underground Graphics from Before Stonewall*. Vancouver: Arsenal Pulp Press, 2002.

"Wayves Magazine," 2009. www.wayves.ca.

Welch, Philip B. *Goff on Goff: Conversations and Lectures*. Norman: University of Oklahoma Press, 1996.

West, Isaac. *Transforming Citizenships: Transgender Articulations of the Law*. New York: New York University Press, 2013.

Weston, Kath. "Lesbian/Gay Studies in the House of Anthropology." *Annual Review of Anthropology* 22 (1993): 339–67.

———. *Long Slow Burn: Sexuality and Social Science*. New York: Routledge, 1998.

———. "Get Thee to a Big City: Sexual Imaginary and the Great Gay Migration to a Big City." In *Long, Slow Burn: Sexuality and Social Science*. New York: Routledge, 1998.

———. *Families We Choose: Lesbians, Gays, Kinship*. New York: Columbia University Press, 2001.

———. "Fieldwork in Lesbian and Gay Communities." In *Feminist Perspectives on Social Research*, edited by Sharlene Nagy Hesse-Biber and Michelle Yaiser, 199–205. New York: Oxford University Press, 2004.

White, Edmund. *States of Desire: Travels in Gay America*. New York: Dutton, 1980.

White, Mark. "'Steadily to the Ideal': The Paintings of Bruce Goff." In *Bruce Goff: A Creative Mind*, edited by Scott W. Perkins. Norman: University of Oklahoma and Price Tower Arts Center, 2010.

White, Richard. *"It's Your Misfortune and None of My Own": A New History of the American West*. Tulsa: University of Oklahoma Press, 1993.

Whiteley, Sheila. *Women and Popular Music: Sexuality, Identity and Subjectivity*. New York: Routledge, 2000.

Whitney, Leon. *The Basis of Breeding*. New Haven, CT: Earle C. Fowler, 1928.

Willams, Linda. *Hard Core: Power, Pleasure, and the "Frenzy of the Visible."* Berkeley: University of California Press, 1989.

Williams, Raymond. *The Country and the City*. New York: Oxford University Press, 1975.

———. *Marxism and Literature*. Oxford, UK: Oxford University Press, 1977.

Wilson, Angelica. "Getting Your Kicks on Route 66! Stories of Gay and Lesbian Life in Rural America." In *De-Centering Sexualities: Politics and Representations beyond the Metropolis*, edited by Richard Phillips, David Shuttleton, and Diane Watt, 195–212. New York: Routledge, 2000.

Wilson, Brian C. *Yankees in Michigan*. East Lansing: Michigan State University Press, 2008.

Winters, Thomas. *Making Men, Making Class: The YMCA and Working Men, 1870–1920*. Chicago: University of Chicago Press, 2002.

Wong, K. Scott. "Cultural Defenders and Brokers: Chinese Responses to the Anti-Chinese Movement." In *Claiming America: Constructing Chinese American Identities during the Exclusion Era*, edited by K. Scott Wong and Sucheng Chan, 3–40. Philadelphia: Temple University Press, 1998.

Wood, Robin. *Hollywood from Vietnam to Regan . . . and Beyond*. New York: Columbia University Press, 1986.

Woods, Clyde. *Development Arrested: The Blues and Plantation Power in the Mississippi Delta*. New York: Verso, 1998.

Woodward, Keith, John Paul Jones, and Sallie Marston. "Of Eagles and Flies: Orientations toward the Site." *Area* 42 (Summer 2010): 271–80.

———. "The Politics of Autonomous Space." *Progress in Human Geography* 36 (Spring 2012): 204–24.

Worster, Donald. *Rivers of Empire: Water, Aridity and the Growth of the American West*. New York: Oxford University Press, 1992.

Wright, Gerard. "Gay Grief in Cowboy Country." *Guardian*, March 27, 1999. http://www.guardian.co.uk/books/1999/mar/27/books.guardianreview7?INTCMP=SRCH

Yacovone, Donald. "Abolitionists and the Language of Fraternal Love." Groups." In *Meanings for Manhood*, edited by Mark C. Carnes and Clyde Griffen, 85–95. Chicago: University of Chicago Press, 1990.

Young, Donna. "Maritime Gothic Sensibility: An Ethnography of Memory." Ph.D. diss., University of Toronto, 2006.

Zipes, Jack. "The Wizard of Oz as American Myth: A Critical Study of Six Versions of the Story, 1900–2007." In *Fairy Tale as Myth, Myth as Fairy Tale*, edited by Alissa Burger, 119–38. Lexington: University Press of Kentucky, 1994.

Žižek, Slavoj. *The Plague of Fantasies*. New York: Verso, 1997.

Zuckerman, Michael. "The Nursery Tales of Horatio Alger." *American Quarterly* 24, no. 2 (1972): 191–209.

ABOUT THE CONTRIBUTORS

Kelly Baker is a Ph.D. candidate in the Department of Anthropology at the University of Western Ontario. She holds an M.A. in Anthropology from Dalhousie University, Nova Scotia, where her research focused on the constructions of identity and experiences of community among GLBT individuals living in rural Canada.

Geoffrey W. Bateman is Assistant Professor in the Peace and Justice Studies Program and Director of Women's and Gender Studies at Regis University. His publications include *Don't Ask, Don't Tell: Debating the Gay Ban in the Military* (2003), as well as articles on queer rhetorics and service-learning; the ethics of community-based literacy work; and gender, homelessness, and film.

Mary Pat Brady is Associate Professor of English at Cornell University. She is the author of *Extinct Lands, Temporal Geographies: Chicana Literature and the Urgency of Space* (2002), and is an associate editor of the sixth edition of the *Heath Anthology of American Literature* (2008–2009). She is currently working on a project that examines the relationship between neoliberalism and Latina/o literatures and cultures.

E. Cram is Visiting Assistant Professor in the Department of Performance and Communication Arts at St. Lawrence University. Cram received a Ph.D. in 2015 from the Department of Communication and Culture at Indiana University, specializing in rhetoric and public culture, gender studies, and cultural studies. Their dissertation reconstructs the linkages among queer feeling, environments, and regions as they intersect with memories of place and violence. Cram has been published in the *Quarterly Journal of Speech* and *Philosophy & Rhetoric*. They are currently writing a book manuscript, *Violent Inheritance and Queer Generation: Landscape Memory and Movement in the American West.*

379

Lucas Crawford is Ruth Wynn Woodward Lecturer in Gender Studies at Simon Fraser University in Vancouver. His poetry and scholarship addresses transgender, architecture, food, fat, affect, rurality, and design. He has published widely, and his work is forthcoming in *Transgender Studies Quarterly*, *English Studies in Canada*, *Rattle*, *Rampike*, *Room*, and in several book collections.

LaToya E. Eaves is a doctoral student in the Department of Global and Sociocultural Studies at Florida International University. In 2013, Eaves was selected as an inaugural in-residence fellow with the Women's, Gender, and Sexuality Studies program at the University of Connecticut. Her research considers the interactions of queer black women's identity and queer women's community formation in the rural American South.

Brian J. Gilley is Director of the First Nations Educational and Cultural Center and Professor of Anthropology at Indiana University. He is the author of *A Longhouse Fragmented: Ohio Iroquis Autonomy in the Nineteenth Century* (2014) and *Becoming Two-Spirit* (2006), and a co-editor, with S. Morgenson, Q. Driscoll, and C. Finley, of *Queer Indigenous Studies* (2011).

Mary L. Gray is Associate Professor in the Media School, Affiliate Faculty of Gender Studies, and Adjunct in American Studies and Anthropology at Indiana University. She is also Senior Researcher at Microsoft Research, New England. She is the author of *In Your Face: Stories from the Lives of Queer Youth* (1999) and *Out in the Country: Youth, Media, and Queer Visibility in Rural America* (2009).

Mark Hain received his Ph.D. from the Department of Communication and Culture at Indiana University. His dissertation examined audience response to the actress Theda Bara from the 1910s to the present. He has been published in the *Quarterly Review of Film and Video* and the anthology *Early Cinema and the "National."*

Robin Henry is Associate Professor in the Department of History at Wichita State University and the author of *Criminalizing Sex, Defining Sexuality: Sexual Regulation and Masculinity in the American West, 1850–1927* (2015).

Peter Hobbs is a Ph.D. candidate in the Faculty of Environmental Studies at York University, Toronto.

John Howard is Professor of American Studies at King's College, London. He is the author of *Men Like That* (1999) and *Concentration Camps on the Home Front* (2008).

Colin R. Johnson is Associate Professor of Gender Studies and Adjunct Assistant Professor of History, American Studies, and Human Biology at Indiana University. He is the author of *Just Queer Folks: Gender and Sexuality in Rural America* (2013).

Andy Oler received a Ph.D. in English from Indiana University in 2012. His dissertation situates early twentieth-century Midwestern novelists' treatments of masculine gender identities amidst the convergence of the region's modernizing socioeconomic system and nostalgically conceived notions of ruralized people, spaces, and communities.

Ryan Powell is Assistant Professor of Film Studies in the Media School at Indiana University. He has published on rurality and radical gay discourse in the 1970 revisionist Western *Song of the Loon in Little Joe* (2010) and on the cinema of James Bidgood in *Rare Birds of Paradise: Costume as Cinematic Spectacle* (2014). He is currently completing a monograph titled *Coming Together: The Cinematic Invention of Gay Life: 1968–1979*.

Gabriel N. Rosenberg is Assistant Professor in the Program in Women's Studies at Duke University and the author of *The 4-H Harvest: Sexuality and the State in Rural America (2015)*.

Katherine Schweighofer is Visiting Assistant Professor in the Department of Women and Gender Studies at Dickinson College. Her research analyzes the impact of rural radical lesbian feminist collectives during the 1970s and 1980s, with a focus on the intersections of geography, identity, and sexuality.

Stina Soderling is a Ph.D. candidate in the Department of Women's and Gender Studies at Rutgers University. Her research focuses on rural queer space/time, genealogies of (anti)capitalism, and fermentation theory.

Carly Thomsen is a Postdoctoral Fellow at Rice University's Center for the Study of Women, Gender, and Sexuality. Her work is published or forthcoming in *Hypatia: A Journal of Feminist Philosophy*, *Feminist Studies*, *Feminist Formations*, *Atlantis: Critical Studies in Gender, Culture, and Social Justice*, and *The Oxford Handbook of Feminist Theory*.

INDEX